AF681755

# Derrida and Negative Theology

# Derrida and Negative Theology

Edited by

*Harold Coward and Toby Foshay*

With a Conclusion by

*Jacques Derrida*

*State University of New York Press*

Chapter 2, "Of an Apocalyptic Tone Newly Adopted in Philosophy," by Jacques Derrida, originally appeared in volume 23 of *Semeia* (Atlanta: Scholars Press, 1982).

Chapter 3, "How to Avoid Speaking: Denials," by Jacques Derrida, is reprinted from *Languages of the Unsayable: The Play of Negativity in Literature and Literary Theory*, edited by Sanford Budick and Wolfgang Iser (New York: Columbia University Press, 1989).

Published by
State University of New York Press, Albany

© 1992 State University of New York

All rights reserved

Printed in the United States of America

No part of this book may be used or reproduced
in any manner whatsoever without written permission
except in the case of brief quotations embodied in
critical articles and reviews.

For information, address State University of New York
Press, State University Plaza, Albany, N.Y. 12246

Production by Dana Foote
Marketing by Bernadette LaManna

Library of Congress Cataloging in Publication Data

Derrida and negative theology/edited by Harold Coward and Toby Foshay.
p. cm.
Includes bibliographical references and index.
ISBN 0-7914-0963-5 (hard : alk. paper), — ISBN 0-7914-0964-3 (pbk. : alk. paper)
1. Derrida, Jacques—Religion. 2. Deconstruction. 3. Theology—Methodology. 4. God—Knowableness. I. Coward, Harold G. II. Foshay, Toby A.
BT83.3.D47 1992 91-9956
231'.042—dc20 CIP

10 9 8 7 6 5 4 3 2

# Contents

Acknowledgments [ix]

Contributors [xi]

ONE Introduction: Denegation and Resentment [1]
Toby Foshay

TWO Of an Apocalyptic Tone Newly Adopted in Philosophy [25]
Jacques Derrida

THREE How to Avoid Speaking: Denials [73]
Jacques Derrida

FOUR On Not Solving Riddles Alone [143]
Michel Despland

FIVE nO nOt nO [167]
Mark C. Taylor

SIX A Hindu Response to Derrida's View of Negative Theology [199]
Harold Coward

SEVEN The Deconstruction of Buddhism [227]
David Loy

EIGHT Conclusion: Divine Reservations [255]
Morny Joy

NINE Post-Scriptum: Aporias, Ways and Voices [283]
Jacques Derrida

Index [325]

The ability to portray ourselves in terms of those things which are antithetical to our own experience is what allows us not just a mathematical measure of the world in which we live (though without the negative we would not go far in mathematics) but also a philosophical measure of ourselves; it allows us a frame within which to define those things which we regard as positive acts. That frame can represent many things. It can represent restraint. It can represent a shelter from all those antithetical directions pursued by the world outside ourselves—directions which may have consistency and validity elsewhere but from which our experience seeks protection. That frame can represent a most arbitrary tariff against those purely artificial but totally necessary systems which we construct in order to govern ourselves—our social selves, our moral selves, our artistic selves, if you will. The implication of the negative in our lives reduces by comparison every other concept that man has toyed with in the history of thought. It is the concept which seeks to make us better—to provide us with structures within which our thought can function—while at the same time it concedes our frailty, the need that we have for this barricade behind which the uncertainty, the fragility, the tentativeness of our systems can look for logic.

—Glen Gould,
*Advice to a Graduation*

# Acknowledgments

Established in 1976, the Calgary Institute for the Humanities has as its aim the fostering of advanced study and research in all areas of the humanities. Apart from supporting work in the traditional "arts" disciplines such as philosophy, history, ancient and modern languages, and literatures, it also promotes research into the philosophical and historical aspects of the sciences, social sciences, fine arts, and the various "professional" disciplines.

The Institute's program in support of advanced study attempts to provide scholars with time to carry out their work. In addition, the Institute sponsors formal and informal gatherings among people who share common interests, in order to promote intellectual dialogue and discussion. Recently, the Institute has moved to foster the application of humanistic knowledge to contemporary social problems.

The project *Derrida and Negative Theology* brought together scholars from literature, philosophy, and religious studies to reflect on two of Jacques Derrida's recent writings on negative theology. Our aim was to engage Derrida on this topic from both Eastern and Western perspectives. Although negative theology has attracted Derrida's attention from his early writings to the present, this book is a first attempt to open a detailed exploration of the topic in his writing. As such it offers a new dimension to the growing body of reflection on the thought of Jacques Derrida.

We wish to record our gratitude to the Social Sciences and Humanities Research Council of Canada for a grant that enabled the research required for this book to be completed. The support of the Department of Religious Studies of the University of Calgary is also acknowledged. Without the careful attention to detail of Gerry Dyer, the Institute Administrator, and Cindy Atkinson, the Institute Secretary, this project would not have been successful.

Harold Coward
Director
The Calgary Institute for the Humanities

# Contributors

HAROLD COWARD is Professor of Religious Studies at the University of Calgary and Director of the Calgary Institute for the Humanities, University of Calgary. He received his Ph.D. in Religious Studies from McMaster University. Among his publications are *Sphota Theory of Language*, Delhi: Motilal Banarsidass, 1980; *Jung and Eastern Thought*, Albany, N.Y.: State University of New York, 1985; *Pluralism: Challenge to World Religions*, Maryknoll, N.Y.: Orbis Books, 1985; *Sacred Word and Sacred Text: Scripture in World Religions*, Maryknoll, N.Y.: Orbis Books, 1988; *The Philosophy of the Grammarians*, Princeton: Princeton University Press, 1991; and *Derrida and Indian Philosophy*, Albany, N.Y.: State University of New York, 1990.

JACQUES DERRIDA is Professor at the Ecole des Hautes Études en Sciences Sociales, Paris, and holds visiting professorships at the University of California, Irvine, and at Cornell University. His books *The Truth in Painting*, *The Post Card*, *Spurs: Nietzsche's Styles/Eperons: Les Styles de Nietzsche*, *Positions*, *Dissemination*, and *Margins of Philosophy* are published by the University of Chicago Press, Chicago.

MICHEL DESPLAND is Professor of Religion at Concordia University. He received his Th.D. from Harvard University. His publications include: *La Religion en Occident: Evolution des idées et du véci*, Paris, 1979; *The Education of Desire: Plato and the Philosophy of Religion*, Toronto, Ont., University of Toronto Press, 1985; *Christianisme: Dossier corps*, Paris, 1987.

MORNY JOY is Assistant Professor of Religious Studies at the University of Calgary. She received her Ph.D. in Philosophy of Religion from McGill University. Her publications include "Entry on 'Imagination,'" in *Encyclopedia of Religion*, New York: Macmillan, 1987; "Derrida and Ricoeur: A Case of Mistaken Identity and Difference," *Journal of Religion*, 68(4),

1988; "Rhetoric and Hermeneutics," *Philosophy Today*, 32(4), 1988.

DAVID LOY is Professor in English and Philosophy at the new International Division of Bunkyo University in Japan. He received his Ph.D. in Philosophy from the National University of Singapore. Among his publications are "The Cloture of Deconstruction: A Mahayana Critique of Derrida," *International Philosophical Quarterly*, 1987; *Nonduality: A Study in Comparative Philosophy*, New Haven: Yale University Press, 1988; "The Nonduality of Life and Death: A Buddhist View of Repression," *Philosophy East and West*, 1990; "A Zen Cloud? Comparing Zen Koan Practice with *The Cloud of Unknowing*," *Buddhist-Christian Studies* 9, 1989; "The Path of No Path: Sankara and Dogen on the Paradox of Practice," *Philosophy East and West*, 1988, and *Pointing at the Moon*, published by Young Buddhist Association of Malaysia, 1985.

TOBY FOSHAY is Assistant Professor of English at the University of Victoria. He received his Ph.D. in English from Dalhousie University. Among his publications are *The Politics of the Intellect: Wyndham Lewis and the Avant-Garde* (forthcoming, McGill-Queen's University Press); editor, Wyndham Lewis, *Rude Assignment: An Intellectual Autobiography*, Black Sparrow Press, 1984; "Wyndham Lewis: Between Nietzsche and Derrida," *English Studies in Canada* 16, 1990.

MARK C. TAYLOR is Professor of Religion and Director of the Center for the Humanties and Social Sciences, Williams College. Among his publications are *Kierkegaard's Pseudonymous Authorship: A Study of Time and the Self*, Princeton: Princeton University Press, 1975; *Religion and the Human Image*, with Carl Raschke and James Kirk, Englewood Cliffs, N.J.: Prentice-Hall, 1976; *Journeys to Selfhood: Hegel and Kierkegaard*, Berkeley: University of California Press, 1980; *Unfinished: Essays in Honor of Ray L. Hart*, editor and contributor, Chico, CA: Scholars Press, 1981; *Deconstructing Theology*, New York: Crossroad and Scholars Press, 1982; *Erring: A Postmodern A/Theology*, Chicago: University of Chicago Press, 1984; *Deconstruction In Context: Literature and Philosophy*, Chicago: University of Chicago Press, 1986, *Altarity*, Chicago: University of Chicago Press, 1987; *Tears*, State University of New York Press, 1989.

# ONE

# *Introduction: Denegation and Resentment*

Toby Foshay

It should be no surprise that we here address the question of the role of negation and of negative theology in contemporary thought. Why should there not be an increasing captivation with negation in a modern epoch characterized as it is by its difference with a classical age in which the energy of synthesis and perception of unity was so necessary to forming its consciousness of self and world? Isn't it inevitable (or, as Derrida would emphasize, "ineluctable"[1]) that modernity's understandable concern with difference, discontinuity, and the novelty of an evolving, unfolding, unfinished (and unfinishable) experience should issue in a progressive sensitivity to and wariness of all positive terms, predications, equations, adequations? Formerly trapped within a statically hierarchial vision of the world and having won a costly freedom from a transcendentally determined world structure, our autonomy is most characteristically expressed in its capacity to exceed all centrally defined and anticipatable limits and boundaries. Naturally, we could say, negation in all its forms would haunt modern attempts at (self-)definition. Nor do we want our longing to exceed and to overcome prescribed limits to be itself anticipated and used to ambush our sense of the world as new and unfolding. We do not want to be contained by our own predictable impulse to transgression, and so we seek a negation that subverts the dialectic of ancient and modern. So we could say that—rather than measuring deconstruction as negative theology—we are rather attempting to gauge the way in and the degree to which the modern in its negativity is prefigured by the classical tradition in its own characteristic search for autonomy, to better appreciate the genealogy and/or disjunction of our era. So, again, naturally, apophaticism should inversely repeat the structure of being, should mirror, reflect, imitate it. The Orient works with a different relation of transcendental/immanent—a less absolutely dual one, in some cases a nondual one—but then neither has the ancient/modern dialectic arisen as much from its history as from that of the Occident. The question of ancient and modern, East and West, is the same and yet different: Are we the same or different, but, perhaps more to the point, what is the ethos of this question?

And so it seems, we might venture to say, altogether appropriate that a thinker such as Jacques Derrida should early, from the essay "Différance" forward, have to mark off the thought of differance and the trace from negative theology. In his recent essay "How to Avoid Speaking: Denials," he finally takes up the threads of his implicit relation to negative theology, acknowledging the "more or less tenable analogy" and "family resemblance" between negative theology and "every discourse that seems to return in a regular and insistent manner to this rhetoric of negative determination." He mimes this discourse thus:

> This, which is called *X* (for example, text, writing, the trace, differance, the hymen, the supplement, the pharmakon, the parergon, etc.) "is" neither this nor that, neither sensible nor intelligible, neither positive nor negative, neither inside nor outside, neither superior nor inferior, neither active nor passive, neither present nor absent, not even neutral, not even subject to a dialectic with a third moment, without any possible sublation ("Aufhebung"). Despite appearances, then, this X is neither a concept nor even a name; it does lend itself to a series of names, but calls for

> another syntax, and exceeds even the order and the structure of predicative discourse. It "is" not and does not say what "is." It is written completely otherwise.[2]

Yet, despite this, Derrida again refuses this "analogy" and "family resemblance" between negative theology and the discourse of deconstruction, but this time in some detail, since the attempt to assimilate deconstruction to negative theology has been insistent in the twenty years intervening between the two essays, beginning with the discussion following the first oral presentation of the essay "Différance."[3] The attempt of Derrida's critics to turn the analogy of negative theology and deconstruction into an equation and the family resemblance into a filiation is itself conducted from two opposing fronts. On the one hand, there are those who accuse Derrida of being a "mere" negative theologian, simply negating and turning on its head the ontotheological tradition, and thus as contained within the dialectical play of the logocentricity which he purports to deconstruct. On the other hand are negative theologians themselves, such as Jean-Luc Marion, cited by Derrida, who challenge Derrida's analysis of the God of apophatic theology as a hyperessentiality, which, as a "beyond being," can only be grasped in its relation to classical cataphatic ontotheology. In other words, as is to be expected, the challenge to Derrida reflects the ambiguous role that negative theology plays within the Western tradition. Is it a correlative moment of affirmative theology that an enlightened philosophy rightly suspects as a mere strategic elusion of the inherent finitude of categories? Or does negative theology exceed the predicative and constative determinations of logic in a performative enactment of a *via negativa* that intends not merely to think but to *realize* a relation to a divinity not only greater than which cannot be conceived but that exceeds the furthest reach of our conceptions, and that can be named and conceived only in that it is necessarily the very origin of articulation?

If deconstruction *is* a negative theology, then, Derrida acknowledges his critics as saying, it is either (1) merely a rhetoric of negation, and, as a rhetoric that is itself opposed to the rhetoric of negative theology, a radical skepticism or a nihilism, or (2) it is an apophatic theology that, by implication, in refusing or failing to recognize itself as such, confirms the inescapability of divine economy. Indeed, it would be seen to confirm it in a striking and unprecedented way for nontheists and theists alike. This view takes the form of a reversible accusation, which runs, in Derrida's précis:

> Once the apophatic discourse is analyzed in its logical-grammatical form, it is not merely sterile, repetitive, obscurantist, mechanical, it perhaps leads us to consider the becoming theological of all discourse. From the moment a proposition takes a negative form, the negativity that manifests itself need only be pushed to the limit, and it at least resembles an apophatic theology. . . . God's name would then be the hyperbolic effect of that negativity or all negativity that is consistent in its discourse. . . . If there is a work of negativity in discourse it will produce divinity.[4]

But, as Derrida points out, this argument could simply be inverted by a theist or an idealist "in order to say that divinity is not produced but productive," arriving at a kind of "proof of God by His effects, or more precisely . . . by effects without cause, by the *without cause*,"[5] the result being that "those who would like to consider 'deconstruction' a symptom of modern nihilism could indeed, if they wished, recognize in it the last testimony—not to say the martyrdom—of faith in the present *fin de siècle*."

Derrida does not precisely refute the legitimacy of this challenge. As he says: "This reading could always be possible. Who could prohibit it? In the name of what?" But he implies that such a prohibition is obviated by his writings, however "brief, elliptical, and dilatory"[6] his references to negative theology since the essay "Différance." This most interesting of real and potential challenges to deconstruction as a negative theology is turned aside, Derrida says, by "two stages" of his writing. The first stage is his argument that negative theology is a discourse of the hyperessential and, as such, is merely a "wager" of ontotheological comprehension. The second is more complex, an exploration of the obligation generated or inherent in his comments on negative theology that he should at some point treat the matter more fully.

It is with this second "stage" that Derrida takes his departure in "How to Avoid Speaking," taking up his often-stated "fascination" with negative theology:[7] "As I have always been fascinated by the supposed movements of negative theology . . ., I objected in vain to the assimilation of the thinking of the trace or of differance to some negative theology, and my response amounted to a promise: one day I would have to stop deferring, one day I would have to try to explain myself directly on this subject, and at last speak of 'negative theology' *itself*."[8] Here is the problematic that shapes "How to Avoid Speaking." To speak of negative theology "itself" is clearly a contradiction in terms. To attempt to do so would be to buy into the restricted economy of ontological and theological cataphasis, even in following the apophatic "wager" of a "beyond being" that exceeds every predicative determination. The very departure of the discourse of the trace and of differance, in its attempt to think "otherwise than being, or beyond essence," in Levinas's terms,[9] would be potentially contained precisely by the relation between the discourse of essence and the negative attributions of hyperessentiality and hypercategorial knowing as "unknowing." How to speak of a transgressive negative theology otherwise than in the language that negative theology was itself dedicated to exceeding? Hasn't negative theology in this sense precisely anticipated every discourse respecting it? "Is one not compelled to speak of negative theology according to the modes of negative theology, in a way that is at once impotent, exhausting, and inexhaustible? Is there ever anything other than a 'negative theology' of 'negative theology'?"[10]

"How to Avoid Speaking" begins in a narrative of Derrida's own attempts to think the obligation and promise inherent in his terse comments marking off the thought of differance from the discourse of negative theology. Therefore, he says: "If I speak of the promise, I will not be able to keep any metalinguistic distance in regard to it. Discourse on the promise is already a promise: in the promise. I will thus not speak of this or that promise, but that which . . . inscribes us by its trace in language—before language. . . . The promise of which I shall speak will have always escaped this demand of presence."[11] And so he relates the circumstances in which he is forced to submit a title in advance of the essay:

> I thus improvised this title on the telephone. Letting it be dictated to me by I do not know what uncon-

> scious order—in a situation of absolute urgency—I thus translated my desire to defer still further. This "fight or flight" reaction reproduces itself on the occasion of every lecture.[12]

The "promise" that Derrida makes in giving a title for the yet-to-be-written essay instantiates the "promise" implicit in his fascination for negative theology. It is a promise that cannot be fulfilled *as such*, insofar as any attempt to speak of negative theology *itself* will inevitably be subsumed within the discourse of negative theology. So that the "fight or flight" reaction of which he speaks in this instance is not one that merely repeats itself with every lecture on no matter what subject, but is rather (and in addition) of the very type of the position of the "subject" within a discourse that in its phonological and grammatological expressions both (1) affirms and denies the subject's presence, its position in time and space as a topic (*topos*), and (2) neither affirms nor denies such identity. And this is the dilemma that becomes most explicit precisely in Derrida's promise to position himself in relation to a discourse that positions itself as a nonplace, "beyond being," attempting to exceed the very language of its expression. How to avoid speaking of that (negative theology) that, through speaking, itself already avoids speaking?

In Derrida's narrative, the agent of his title, of his promise of a discourse on apophatic thought (i.e., that will "avoid speaking" of the topic), is an "unconscious order" that the "I" of the narrative "does not know." What is this unknown unconscious order that commands him, this unknown, known as an unconscious—i.e., as that which is not conscious of, does not know, itself? And what is the "I," the narrator, the persona, the "Derrida" who names and knows of it as an unknown, and as an unconscious, an unknowable "as such," a presence impossibly absent to itself, and an absence that nevertheless presents, orders, and commands attention to this undecidable paradox of its desire to represent itself in language only as some "thing" that cannot and must not be determined as—i.e., *merely* as—language? Derrida's narrative probes the abyssal apophasis of the speaking "subject." And here we can recall the rhetorical trope of apophasis, which as "a kind of irony, whereby we deny that we say or doe that which we especially say or doe" (OED, quoting J. Smith) is itself troped and inverted by Derrida so that we who employ the trope are enabled to do so only because discourse so orders constructs, and "subjects" us, we know not how, unconsciously, in a kind of inverse apophatics, a *dénégation*, as Derrida designates it.

We cannot but agree with Mark Taylor's recommendation that *dénégation* be left untranslated, taken over in its complex double negation from the French in preference to the monivocal "denial" of the published translation. To quote Taylor: "*Verneinung* [of which *dénégation* is the French translation] is an affirmation that is a negation and a negation that is an affirmation." This formulation captures the undecidable oscillation that Derrida figures between the narratorial "I" and its "unconscious." As Taylor goes on to explain: "To de-negate is to un-negate. . . . More precisely, denegation is an un-negation that affirms rather than negates negation." And so denegation, as the inversion of the relation of the subject in and to language, is the subversion, too, of the dialectical negation of negation by which it might render sublime its self-relation and so come into undifferentiated possession of the revelation, of a necessarily (because to-be-revealed) "secret" knowledge.[13] It is in terms of a motif of the "secret" that Derrida explicates denegation:

> There is a secret of the denial and a denial of the secret. The secret, *as secret*, separates and already institutes a negativity; it is a negation that denies itself. It de-negates itself. This denegation does not happen to it by accident; *it is essential and originary*. [my emphasis][14]

Derrida declares his desire to understand denegation "prior even to its Freudian context." Thus, when he speaks of denegation as "essential and originary," he evokes the problematic relation of the subject of discourse to an "unconscious order" that determines and already "institutes" a negativity in its desire to avoid betraying its secret resources. And lest there be any doubt as to the relation between the unconscious order previously evoked by Derrida and the *topos* of the secret, the following should be noted:

> I refer first of all to the secret shared *within itself*, its partition "proper," which divides the essence of a secret that cannot even appear to one alone except in starting to be lost, to divulge itself, hence to dissimulate itself as secret, in *showing* itself: dissimulating its dissimulation.[15]

Derrida's desire to go behind, or rather to anticipate the "metaphysical presuppositions which sustain the psychoanalytical theorems"[16] enhances our appreciation of the narrative form adopted by him in leading into the problematic of apophasis as denegation.

But, as we might expect, it is not as if "denegation," even in its pre-Freudian, that is "essential and originary," form, in which it "gives no chance to dialectic," could itself establish what it suggests and marks, as if the notion itself were "essential and originary." How, between narrative and explication, do we hear Derrida's thinking-through of denegation here? As Heidegger would remind and caution us:

> We do not hear it rightly [the language of thinkers], because we take that language to be mere expression, setting forth philosophers' views. But the thinker's language says what is. To hear it is in no case easy. Hearing it presupposes that we meet a certain requirement, and we do so only on rare occasions. We must acknowledge and respect it. To acknowledge and respect consists in letting every thinker's thought come to us as something in each case unique, never to be repeated, inexhaustible—and being shaken to the depths by what is unthought in a thinker's thought is not a lack inherent in his thought. What is *un*-thought is such in each case only as an un-*thought*.[17]

We are cautioned, but we are not much further ahead, when we read that it is precisely with Heidegger's unthought that Derrida, in his recent essay "Désistance," associates denegation.

> And what about "denegation?" Especially when it is a matter . . . of a vast movement by Heidegger, . . . in a thought concerned with thinking, over and above an onto-theology without which the very concept of denegation could not have been formed, the *unthought*

> itself. Concerned with thinking not just this or that unthought, but the structure, the possibility, and the necessity of the unthought in general, its quasi-negativity (the *un*-thought is an un-*thought*, he reminds us).[18]

So it should not be surprising that Derrida might think denegation, the "quasi-negativity" of which could not even be formulated without the propriety of ontotheology, which is also to say, without its negative theological shadow—it should not be surprising that Derrida does not explicate denegation *as such*, in its "essential and originary" function, in the essay "How to Avoid Speaking: Denegations" itself. It is in the more recent essay, "Désistance," that he continues his thinking out of denegation, and he does so not through the term *dénégation* but through the term *désistance*, a neologism generated in his discussion of the work of Philippe Lacoue-Labarthe, to the selection of English translations of whose essays "Désistance" serves as the Introduction.

Derrida avoids saying very much about denegation in "How to Avoid Speaking," deferring the discussion to the later essay, and pursuing it under a different term (desistance), one moreover that is not "proper" in either French or English, and does not, in this neologistic form, even appear in Lacoue-Labarthe's text on which he is reflecting,[19] which is also to say that the thought of denegation is displaced—that is, it takes place only in the context of Derrida's reading of the work of Lacoue-Labarthe, and specifically of texts in which the latter is himself thinking through particular issues in Heidegger's reading of Nietzsche and Plato. Desistance for Derrida addresses the constitution of subjectivity within a double movement of negation (as occurs with such terms as the *unavoidable*, the *ineluctable*, and the *undeniable*), a denegation in which the "supplementary redoubling of negation is not necessarily reducible to the work of dialectic or to an unconscious denegation. Lacoue-Labarthe will help us, perhaps, in stepping back from a Hegelian, Marxist, or Freudian interpretation of such a possibility."[20] So Derrida looks to Lacoue-Labarthe in his attempt to "understand [denegation] prior even to its elaboration in a Freudian context," or a Hegelian one. To "step back from" such contexts is to desist, to "stand away." As a name for the structure of subjectivity, desistance, Derrida says, "does not let itself be determined reflexively. . . . But if the 'desistance' of the subject does not first signify a 'self-desistance,' we should not come to some conclusion thereby about the passivity of this subject. Or about its activity. Desistance is better for marking the middle voice." But subjectivity does not *consist* in desistance. "No," Derrida says, "that is just the point—what is involved here is the impossibility of *consisting*, a singular impossibility: something entirely different from a lack of consistency. Something more in the way of a '(de)constitution.'"[21]

It is such a "(de)constitution," a deconfiguration of subjectivity, that appears in Derrida's narrative in "How to Avoid Speaking." Derrida's title, his *topos* in relation to negative theology, he relates, is "dictated to me by I do not know what unconscious order."[22] The speaking subject of Derrida's narrative is constituted neither actively nor passively (he "lets" it be dictated to him). It is neither constituted nor deconstituted, but *(de)*constituted. And it is so, as Heidegger reminds us, not as a "lack inherent in his thought." As Lacoue-Labarthe specifies, (de)constitution designates a "loss of the subject [that] is imperceptible, . . . and not because it is equivalent to a secret failing or a hidden lack, but because it is strictly indissoluble from, and doubles, the process of constitution or appropriation."[23] The subject is both constituted and deconstituted in the configuration of self. And further, Lacoue-Labarthe says:

> The theoretical consequence . . . : the figure is never *one*. . . . There is no "proper image" with which to identify totally, no essence of the imaginary. . . . The subject "desists" because it must always confront *at least* two figures (or one figure that is *at least* double).[24]

This is what Derrida (re)presents to us in the form of a narrative preamble to his discussion of "negative theology *itself*."[25] The figures of the narrator and of the "unconscious order" that dictates to him the promise to speak on the avoidance of speaking, that speaks on negative theology as denegation, are neither one nor two, both one and two. His narration at once presents and performs a denegation as a "desistance," a standing away from negative theology that subsists in the middle voice, both constituting and deconstituting the topic, (re)presenting the subject of such a discourse as (de)constituted in its very attempt to confront its relation to negative theology, so that the *topos* of negative theology is itself (de)constituted. It cannot be placed or figured without being split within itself between the issues of theology and of subjectivity (following of course upon its own dialectical configuration). We seem to have what Derrida perceives in the work of Lacoue-Labarthe, a "supplementary torsion" of deconstruction, a supplementary moment in deconstruction in the form of a (de)constitution, or what Lacoue-Labarthe sees as a "(de)construction, something more positive than critical, something, as it were, *not very negative*."[26]

It is in relation to such a reading of "How to Avoid Speaking: Denegations" that we can turn to Kevin Hart's recent book, *The Trespass of the Sign: Deconstruction, Theology, and Philosophy*, and to his valuable contributions to the question of negative theology and deconstruction. Hart draws on a commentary on Pseudo-Dionysius by John Jones, in which the latter elucidates two independent movements of negative theology, one metaphysical and the other mystical. Quoting Jones:

> On the one hand, negative theology functions within affirmative theology or, more specifically, metaphysics to express the preeminence of the divine cause. Here, if you will, the negations are 'super affirmations.' On the other hand negative theology provides for mystical unity with the divinity. Here negative (mystical) theology denies all that is and all reference to beings and, by my interpretation, ultimately denies all affirmative theology and hence, all metaphysics.[27]

Hart accepts the distinction as a clarification, but disagrees that what Jones calls negative (mystical) theology achieves an exit from metaphysics, since, as Hart observes, "the *denial* of metaphysics is itself a metaphysical gesture,"[28] precisely the point that Derrida makes respecting hyperessentiality. Hart describes the relation between the metaphysical and mystical forms of negative theology as *supplemental,* and as the relation between a restricted and a general economy. On the subtle hierarchical play between the two negative theologies, Hart observes:

> Negative theology plays a role within the phenomenon of positive theology but it also shows that positive theology is situated with regards to a radical negative theology which precedes it. *In short, negative theology performs the deconstruction of positive theology.*[29]

Hart explicates this claim with respect to Derrida's emphasis on hyperessentiality in Dionysius:

> The prefix *'hyper'* has a negative rather than a positive force. To say that God is *hyperousious* is to deny that God is a being of any kind, even the highest or original being. As Jones remarks, Pseudo-Dionysius denies that God is a being and denies that God is being (*on*). . . . Given this Derrida is wrong to say that negative theology reserves a supreme being beyond the categories of being. Just as 'sign' must be crossed out in the deconstruction of metaphysics, so too must 'God' in the deconstruction of positive theology.[30]

So Hart aligns himself with Jean-Luc Marion, who, as Derrida notes in "How to Avoid Speaking,"[31] employs the word *Dieu* under erasure in his book *Dieu sans être.*

Liddell and Scott cite as one of the nuances of *hyper* the sense of beyond as a "transgression" or "violation" of what is exceeded, appearing to support Hart's claim of a negative connotation to the notion of hyperessentiality. At any rate, Hart's argument for a relation of supplementarity between the metaphysical and mystical moments of negative theology, of a deconstruction of metaphysical by mystical theology, is clarifying and helpful. Hart's book was in press when "Comment ne pas parler: dénégations" first appeared, so that text does not figure in his deliberations, but his argument adds to our appreciation of Derrida's itinerary in this essay. The complex and tangential approach to avoidance of negative theology in "How to Avoid Speaking" is dictated by the careful delineation of a prior condition of negation in a denegation, an un-negation that subsists in the very structure of discourse and of the constitution of consciousness in discourse.

As instantiated in Derrida's narrative of his complex response to the proposed topic of negative theology, prior to any negative determination within discourse there is a denegation of the perspective of consciousness in its very discursive formation, that works, in Lacoue-Labarthe's helpful formulation, a (de)constitution of subjectivity. Prior to addressing the secret place of a divinity beyond being, the subject is addressed by a secret abyss in its constitution. As Lacoue-Labarthe observes, "The subject 'desists' because it must confront *at least* two figures (or one figure that is *at least* double)."[32]

Prior to negative theology is, so to speak, an apophatic psychagogy. As Derrida comments in "How to Avoid Speaking," "it would be necessary to reelaborate a problematic of consciousness, that thing that, more and more, one avoids discussing as if one knew what it is and as if its riddle were solved. But is any problem more novel today than that of consciousness?"[33] The deconstruction of negative theology by mystical theology that Hart points to is preempted (and preemptied) by "something more positive than critical, something, as it were, *not very negative*"[34] a (de)construction of the subject of negative theological, as of every, discourse.

Immediately following his narrative of the circumstances under which his title was generated, Derrida acknowledges: "Under this title 'how to avoid speaking,' it is necessary to speak of the secret."[35] Regarding secrecy he observes:

> According to [a] somewhat naive philosophy of the animal world, one may nevertheless observe that animals are incapable of keeping or even having a secret, because they cannot *represent as such*, as an *object* before consciousness, something that they would then forbid themselves from showing. One would thus link the secret to the objective representation (*Vorstellung*) that is placed before consciousness and that is expressible in a form of words. The essence of such a secret would remain rigorously alien to every other nonmanifestation; and, notably, unlike that of which the animal is capable.[36]

This is a delineation of something approaching a "material" basis for a characterization of human consciousness. "According to this hypothesis," Derrida says, "it would be necessary to reconsider all the boundaries between consciousness and the unconscious, as between man and animal and an enormous system of oppositions."[37] Nonetheless, Derrida declares that the "negativity of the secret and the secret of denegation"[38] is "essential and originary,"[39] is, in other words, in the order of a *founding difference* of human consciousness as *representation*.

Eric Gans, in his 1981 essay on Derrida and René Girard, "Differences," anticipates this question when he suggests that "difference 'always already' exists, in a form that Derrida refuses to recognize, and that Girard recognizes but then forgets. The original difference is precisely that of life itself, which from its own problematic origin has distinguished structurally, if not conceptually, between the organism and its appetitive objects."[40] Gans roots the difference and deferral that structures systems of representation in this material reality, explaining human as distinct from animal representation as a system of socialization motivated by the avoidance of conflict. Human systems of representation, he reasons, are structured around absence and difference because they are founded on a gesture of renunciation of appetitive desire, as an avoidance of the conflict to which it inevitably gives rise.

> Culture is truly *différance* because it *re-presents* this primal difference [between the organism and its appetitive objects]. The attractive object will indeed be appropriated; but for this appropriation to proceed in an orderly fashion—for an order to be founded according to which the peaceful attribution of the object can indeed be made—immediate, instinctive appropriation must be renounced. That is why the first cultural act, the act of representation, must originate in an *aborted* act of appropriation. It is when the fear of conflict leads man to *designate* this object rather than to grasp at it that the deferral of conflict by the differentiation of the object can be adequate to its task.[41]

That the founding act of specifically human culture is a gesture of renunciation of instinctual and appetitive desire lends to human culture, Gans says, its structure of simultaneous presence and absence, the presence of the community and of the individual to themselves and the absence through deferral of the instinctual content of desires:

> The position I propose . . . is that the difference of man is one of form, not content, and that the birth of this form derives from the felt need to defer the immediacy of this (appetitive) content. It is this deferral that produces presence in the uniquely human sense—the presence of the community to itself and of each member to the others. The world of traditional culture as expressed in privileged discourse—within which category I include both religion *and* philosophy—has envisioned this presence as itself an immediate reality, guaranteed either by a transcendent divinity, the self-presence of the thinking self, or a more or less well-defined combination of both. It is this hypostasized presence that is the primary target of Derrida's deconstruction which reintroduces into it the anthropological reality of deferral. But Derrida . . . sees deferral and absence as incompatible.[42]

The act of representation, in that it arises in "an *aborted* act of appropriation," constructs an *imaginative* desire that compensates for the inaccessibility of the real object of appetite. For Gans explains in his *The End of Culture:*

> The origin of desire is directly linked to that of the imaginary. The imaginary prolongation of the designative gesture toward the object constitutes the original experience of desire. This prolongation takes place on the imaginary scene of representation, which it exploits to create an impossible image. For the object is *necessarily* inaccessible, and it is precisely this that permits each individual to imagine himself as alone acceding to it. The imagination thus originates as essentially paradoxical.[43]

The paradoxical and imaginary structure of desire become problematic, says Gans, not in early, ritual culture with its reciprocal and communal vehicles for the sublimation of desire, but in later hierarchical and nonreciprocal cultures where some have the means to satisfy desire while others inevitably go without. "Instead of . . . desir[ing] in vain a central position in the community," says Gans, "the victim of nonreciprocity comes to desire as well the ousting of the actual holder of this position. . . . The social inferior's desire, whether or not it gives rise to a praxis, constitutes a source of impotent frustration."[44]

It is this "impotent frustration" that Nietzsche characterized as *ressentiment,* which he saw as the impetus behind Judeo-Christian morality as a revolutionary cultural movement. Gans argues that the very same phenomenon gave rise to Greek art forms as much as to Judeo-Christian morality,[45] but the two traditions, Judeo-Christian and Hellenic, adopt different modes of mediation of resentment. Judeo-Christianity is a moralism that, while it may lead to "hypocritical denunciations of those whose real accomplishments one envies,"[46] as Nietzsche accuses, at its best it seeks to effect real social and political change: "The real recentering carried out by the Judeo-Christian tradition is more strenuous than the aesthetic recentering of the Greeks, for it must overcome the resistance of the real order of things, whereas the aesthetic operation offers rather a means of adapting to this order."[47] Greek secular culture transforms and transcends resentment in its works of art:

> In contrast with abstract morality, which poses as a norm the reciprocity that has become an ethical impossibility, art renounces normativity in order to realize this reciprocity in the purely imaginary relationship between the spectator and a fictional universe. Within this relationship, resentment is demystified and abolished. The artist . . . acts as the regnant divinity of the fictional universe, the spectator's temporary subordination to whom is untroubled by resentment because it is purely transcendental, lacking in any element of worldly rivalry.[48]

Unlike in ritual culture like the Judeo-Christian, where the otherness of the desired image, "reinforce[s] the solidarity of the community, all of whose members are equal in being unable to possess it,"[49] in Greek secular culture, "esthetic otherness must now guarantee the imaginary existence of a fictive universe wherein the inaccessibility of the object is the same for all."[50] Thus, Greek esthetic culture achieves a negative transcendence of resentment, in which the "spectator can imagine himself, secure in his awareness that the desiring imagination of his fellow spectators is no less unrealizable than his own."[51]

In Greek culture, Gans includes the theoretical, that is philosophy and science, with the esthetic in this negative transcendence of resentment. As he observes, resentment "is a negative revelation; it constitutes the Self by the centrality if lacks, but of itself conceives no transfigured image of centrality to which it might legitimately aspire." Such a negative transcendence is not, he emphasizes, a "ritually induced catharsis," but "a transformation of the old structure of significance that requires a lucid awareness of the futility of the utopian desires that this structure has—always already—aroused in us." Nor is Gans blind to the implication of his own analysis in the mechanism that he attempts to elucidate:

> For if what is resented is the significant other, and if one's choice of subject is significant by definition, then there is no way to avoid resentment toward whatever one speaks about, to the extent, at least, that it concerns the human subject. . . . But the point is precisely that resentment in itself is not a source of falsification, but a means of discovery—the only means, indeed, by which we as readers are called upon to put into question the founding oppositions by means of which texts signify. For all such oppositions are versions of the fundamental one between the significant and the nonsignificant.[52]

Gans's analysis of resentment provides a perspective from which to observe Derrida's strategy of avoidance of negative theology in "How to Avoid Speaking." Derrida's commentary on the secret gives rise to his reflections on what characterizes human, as distinct from animal, consciousness. This secret representation of the object before consciousness is seen by him as the basis for its designation in language. But this secret representation within ourselves, is "first of all . . . the secret shared *within itself*, its partition 'proper,' which divides the essence of a secret that cannot even appear to one alone except in starting to be lost." It "separates and already institutes a negativity,"[53] Derrida says, and for Gans it founds representation as a fiction, as an imaginative desire that compensates for a renunciation of appetitive desire that avoids conflict, an aborted act of appropriation. As Lacoue-Labarthe sees it, the subject is (de)constituted in representation, because there is no " 'proper image' with which to identify totally, no essence of the imaginary."[54] The subject "desists" in its secret (de)constitution, for, as Derrida says, "the secret amounts to a negation that denies itself. It de-negates itself."[55] And so Derrida need not avoid the revelation:

> There is no secret *as such:* I deny it. And this is what I confide in secret to whomever allies himself to me. This is the secret of the alliance. If the theo-logical necessarily insinuates itself there, this does not mean that the secret itself is theo-logical.[56]

As Gans helps us to appreciate, the secret is itself not moral and theological, because the secret subsists in and with the philosophical subject, rather than the theological soul. As Raoul Mortley concludes in his two-volume study of negative theology, with the exception of Pseudo-Dionysius, "there is almost no formal *via negativa* in the Christian thought of antiquity" he says. And he explains:

> The absence of the *via negativa* in ancient Christian thought may be explained by the fact that the nature of God is scarcely an issue in Christianity. It is the character of Greek thought, from its Presocratic origins, that ontological questions predominate; the traditional Greek question is: "What is X?" If one reads the teachings of Jesus as reported in the Gospels, one notes an absolute lack of interest in the question "What is God?" . . . It is with the progressive Hellenization of Christianity that questions about the essence of reality come to the fore, and the nature of God becomes an issue.[57]

Thus, insofar as negative theology is an ontological, rather than a characteristically theological, movement of thought, its concern is not the righteous supplanting of a worldly order by the realization of a divine one, as with the Church, but the noetic transcendence of the resentment aroused by a material order that will not yield to a secret desire, except in the equivocal realm of the imagination, the realm not of the soul but of the desiring subject that knows its denegation, its desistance from its own appropriation, its (de)constitution, in imaginal transcendence of a resentment aroused by the powerlessness of its relation to any actual or potential Transcendent.

In the Orient, the history is more consistent because of a lesser tendency to anthropomorphize and personalize the Transcendent, a more universally ontological than theomorphic ethos. Because Hinduism thinks in terms of a positively subsisting self, however contingent and readily subsumable Atman is within Brahman and vice versa, the more comfortable it is with the thematizing and essentializing tendencies of language. Because Buddhism not only refuses anthropomorphizing but resists essentializing the relation of samsara and nirvana, no-self and sunyata, we find in its tradition the most thoroughgoing philosophical and praxial apophaticisms in either the East or the West. However, since the realm of the historical is either bracketed or thought ontologically in the East, language is either sublimated and transcendentalized, as seems to be the tendency in Hinduism, or conceived as *upaya*, skillful means, as in Buddhism. But the realm of history is the realm of the performative rather than the constative, and it is here that language—along with every action and passion—challenges us as praxis.

In our approach to the question of "Derrida and Negative Theology," two texts are chosen on which to focus: "Of an Apocalyptic Tone Newly Adopted in Philosophy" and "How to Avoid Speaking: Denials." These texts are reprinted here, with Derrida's kind permission. The principal chapters in the book are the four by Mark C. Taylor, Michel Despland, Harold Coward, and David Loy. The order of presentation is intended to promote East/West and classical/modern associations. Taylor's and Despland's essays are on Western apophatic ontotheology, with Taylor writing from a deconstructionist, and Despland from a Platonist, orientation. Coward's and Loy's papers are on apophaticism in Hinduism and Buddhism in relation to deconstruction.

As we have learned to expect from his seminal work in the area of deconstruction and religious thought, in "nO nOt nO" Mark Taylor offers an important probing of negation and affirmation in "Of an Apocalyptic Tone" and "How to Avoid Speaking." The four principal sections of his essay—"[L]et[t]re[s]," "Titles," "Recuperation," and "Avoidances," explore the moments of a nondialectical negation, an apophatic atheology in Derrida, ranging at times beyond the two principal texts, and drawing on Freud, Bataille, and particularly Blanchot. Taylor frames his essay with considerations as to what it actually implies to gather and write "in the name of" Derrida, and particularly in the name of a function of negativity and of "negative theology" in his writing. Taylor's rich and whimsical grasp of the ambiguity of the enterprise harbors and engenders a differentiated analysis of Derrida's strategic and laminate handling of negation and of theology throughout his work. That these questions open, Derrida admits in "How to Avoid Speaking," onto the matter of "autobiography" and what it would mean for him to write one, Taylor is particularly sensitive to. What is affirmed and denied, and who affirms and denies, under the signature of Derrida?

In Michel Despland's "On Not Solving Riddles Alone," we find a living Platonism fully capable of responding in stride to Derrida's challenge to classicism, of seeing it as participant in the Socratic tradition and as integral with an attempt to recapture the fuller dialogical intentions of antique philosophy. But Despland's focus is on theology and on what Platonist and Neoplatonist apophaticisms, in the light of Derrida, have to teach us about (re)gaining a theology responsive to lived (and spoken and written) experience. He contends that "the promise of negative theologies comes from . . . their disruption of the rolling waves of ordinary theological rhetoric, alerts us to the matter of virtuosity in textual procedures and to the rapport with the reader that is being cultivated by any teacher." He suggests that logocentrism is a phallocentric and monologic perversion of reason, rather than the authentic expression of *logos*, and that "the distinction between positive and negative theology can be replaced by the broader distinction between didactic (or scholastic) theology, and literarily crafted theology" (as in Kierkegaard). Despland concludes with four points for or invitations to theologians, suggested by his reading of Derrida, that bear on the subtle relations of theologies to their own and other traditions and to the cultures from which they are (in some ways) inseparable.

Harold Coward's "A Hindu Response to Derrida's View of Negative Theology" explores apophatic movements in the thought of the Advaitan Śaṇkara and the Grammarian Bhartrhari. While the transcendent noumenal is realized in Sankara by means of the negation of every phenomenon, including all language and the very conception of distinct negative and affirmative moments, in Bhartrhari language itself has phenomenal and noumenal dimensions, the latter manifesting the very kernel or seed of ultimate reality as Brahman. Advaita constitutes a classical heuristic *via negativa* (as distinct from a cognitive negative theology), but the Grammarian philosophy affirms an inescapability of language that Coward relates to Derridean textuality, seeing, as a correlative, a demystifying and therapeutic dimension to deconstruction.

It is significant that the distinction between negative theology and *via negativa*, between cognitive and heuristic apophaticisms, though subtly informing both Taylor's and Despland's essays, emerges most explicitly in David Loy's "The Deconstruction of Buddhism." While unfolding the thoroughgoing deconstructive movement of Indian Buddhist Mādhyamikan thought as exemplified in Nāgārjuna, Loy acknowledges Sanskrit's Indo-European tendency to essentialize and dichotomize, to philosophize even in its antiphilosophical advocacy of language as *upaya*, skillful means, over cognitive approaches to language, self, and world. This tendency is countered in the Chinese (Ch'an) and Japanese (Zen) Buddhist emphasis on meditative practice and the experiential character of the nondifference between samsara and nirvana. Loy concludes with a challenging view of the relation between deconstructive textual *praxes*—whether Derridean or Mādhyamikan—and the character of meditative *praxis* in Buddhism.

## Notes

1. Jacques Derrida, "Desistance," Introduction to Philippe Lacoue-Labarthe, *Typography: Mimesis, Philosophy, Politics*, ed. Christopher Fynsk (Cambridge: Harvard University Press, 1989), pp. 1–6.

2. Jacques Derrida, "How to Avoid Speaking: Denials," in *Languages of the Unsayable: The Play of Negativity in Literature and Literary Theory*, ed. Sanford Budick and Wolfgang Iser (New York: Columbia University Press, 1989), p. 4.

3. See Derrida, "The Original Discussion of 'Différance,' " in *Derrida and Différance*, ed. David Wood and Robert Bernasconi (Evanston, Ill.: Northwestern University Press, 1988), p. 84.

4. Derrida, "How to Avoid Speaking," p. 6.

5. Ibid., p. 6.

6. Ibid., p. 7.

7. See Derrida, "The Original Discussion of 'Différance,'" p. 85, and Derrida's "Letter to John Leavey," *Semeia* 23 (1982), p. 61.

8. Derrida, "How to Avoid Speaking," p. 12.

9. Ibid., p. 64 n. 3.

10. Ibid., p. 13.

11. Ibid., pp. 14–15.

12. Ibid., p. 16.

13. On the enigmatic material and tropic character of initiation into the secret, see Derrida's meditation on poetic singularity, circumcision, and the password in "Shibboleth," in *Midrash and Literature*, ed. Geoffrey Hartman and Sanford Budick (New Haven: Yale University Press, 1986), pp. 307–47.

14. Derrida, "How to Avoid Speaking," p. 25.

15. Ibid., p. 25.

16. Ibid., p. 25.

17. Quoted in Lacoue-Labarthe, *Typography*, pp. 60–61 n. 22.

18. Derrida, "Desistance," p. 11.

19. Ibid., pp. 1–5.

20. Ibid., p. 4.

21. Ibid., p. 5.

22. Derrida, "How to Avoid Speaking," p. 16.

23. Lacoue-Labarthe, *Typography*, p. 174.

24. Ibid., p. 175.

25. Derrida, "How to Avoid Speaking," p. 12.

26. Lacoue-Labarthe, *Typography*, p. 123.

27. Quoted in Kevin Hart, *The Trespass of the Sign: Deconstruction, Theology, and Philosophy* (Cambridge: Cambridge University Press, 1989), p. 200.

28. Ibid., p. 201.

29. Ibid., pp. 201–202; my emphasis.

30. Ibid., p. 202.

31. Derrida, "How to Avoid Speaking," p. 64 n. 3.

32. Lacoue-Labarthe, *Typography*, p. 175.

33. Derrida, "How to Avoid Speaking," p. 17.

34. Lacoue-Labarthe, *Typography*, p. 123.

35. Derrida, "How to Avoid Speaking," p. 16.

36. Ibid., p. 17.

37. Ibid., p. 17.

38. Ibid., p. 18.

39. Ibid., p. 25.

40. Eric Gans, "Differences," *MLN* 96 (1981), pp. 803–4.

41. Ibid., p. 804.

42. Ibid., pp. 804–5.

43. Eric Gans, *The End of Culture: Toward a Generative Anthropology* (Berkeley and London: University of California Press, 1985), p. 27.

44. Ibid., p. 173.

45. Ibid., p. 179–300; and Eric Gans, "The Culture of Resentment," *Philosophy and Literature* 8 (1984), pp. 55–66.

46. Gans, *The End of Culture*, p. 173.

47. Gans, "The Culture of Resentment," p. 62.

48. Gans, *The End of Culture*, p. 174.

49. Ibid., p. 174.

50. Ibid., p. 174–75.

51. Ibid., p. 175.

52. Gans, "The Culture of Resentment," p. 64.

53. Derrida, "How to Avoid Speaking," p. 25.

54. Lacoue-Labarthe, *Typography*, p. 175.

55. Derrida, "How to Avoid Speaking," p. 25.

56. Ibid., p. 26.

57. Raoul Mortley, *From Word to Silence*, vol. 2 (Bonn and Frankfurt-on-Main: Hanstein, 1986), pp. 274–75.

TWO

# *Of an Apocalyptic Tone Newly Adopted in Philosophy*[1]

Jacques Derrida

Translated by John P. Leavey, Jr.

I shall speak then of/in an apocalyptic tone in philosophy.

The Seventy have bequeathed us a translation of *gala.* It is called the Apocalypse.

In Greek, *apokalupsis* would translate words derived from the Hebrew verb *gala.* I am referring here, without drawing any authority from them, to some indications of André Chouraqui to which I shall return. But I must forewarn you right now: the (hi)stories or enigmas of translation I hear spoken of, that I intend to speak about, and that I shall get myself entangled in for reasons more serious than my incompetence, they are, I believe, without solution or exit.

That will be my theme. More than a theme, a task (*Aufgabe des Übersetzers,* Benjamin's just assignation) I shall not discharge.

The other day Jean Ricardou asked me, we were talking then about translation, to say a little more about what I had sketched out on a grace given beyond work, thanks to [*grâce au*] work, but without it. I was talking then of a *gift* "given there" (*"il y a," es gibt*), but above all given there without having, *in the final account,* to be merited in responsibility. One must translate and one must not translate. I am thinking of the *double bind* of YHWH when, with the name of his choice, with his own name one could say, Babel, he gives *to translate and not to translate.* And no one, forever, since then, eludes the double postulation.

Well, to Jean Ricardou I shall reply as follows and do so in the form of an elliptical thanks for what I am given here, given to think or simply given, beyond the thinkable, that is to say—that would be to say in German—beyond all memory and some thanks, given by our hosts at Cerisy, by Philippe Lacoue-Labarthe and by Jean-Luc Nancy, by all you with so much work and grace, so much grace in your work: translation-proof, grace would perhaps come when the writing of the other absolves you, from time to time, from the infinite *double bind* and first of all, such is a gift's condition, absolves itself, unbinds itself from this double bind, unburdens or clears itself, it, the language [*langue*] of writing, this given trace that always comes from the other, even if it is no one. To clear oneself of the gift, of the given gift, of giving itself, is the grace I now know you have and in any case that I wish for you. This grace is always improbable; it is never proved. But must we not believe it happens? That was perhaps, yesterday, belief itself. Another way of saying: for what you have given me during these ten days I not only thank you, I pardon you. But who can authorize him or herself to pardon? Let's say that I ask pardon for you, of you yourselves for you yourselves.

*Apokaluptō* no doubt was a good word [*bon mot*] for *gala. Apokaluptō,* I disclose, I uncover, I unveil, I reveal the thing that can be a part of the body, the head or the eyes, a secret part, the sex or whatever might be hidden, a secret, the thing to be dissimulated, a thing that is neither shown nor said, signified perhaps but that cannot or *must* not first be delivered up to self-evidence. *Apokekalummenoi logoi* are indecent remarks. So it is a matter of the secret and the *pudenda.*

The Greek tongue shows itself hospitable here to the Hebrew *gala.* As André Chouraqui recalls in his short "Liminaire pour l'Apocalypse" of John (of which he recently offered a new translation),[2] the word *gala* recurs more than one hundred times in the Hebrew Bible and seems in effect to say *apokalupsis*, disclosure, uncovering, unveiling, the veil lifted from about the thing: first of all, if we can say this, man's or woman's sex, but also their eyes or ears. Chouraqui specifies:

> Someone's ear is uncovered in lifting up the hair or the veil that covers it in order to whisper a secret into it, a word [*parole*] as hidden as a person's genitals. YHWH can be the agent of this disclosure, this uncovering. The arm or the glory of YHWH can also be uncovered to man's gaze or ear. So nowhere does the word *apocalypse* [concludes the translator referring here as well to the Greek as to the Hebrew] have the sense it finally takes on in French and other tongues: fearsome catastrophe. Thus the Apocalypse is essentially a contemplation (*hazôn*) [and in fact Chouraqui translates what we are accustomed to call the Apocalypse of John by *Contemplation of Yohanân*] or an inspiration [*neboua*] at the sight, the uncovering or disclosure of YHWH and, here, of Yéshoua' the Messiah. [*Un pacte neuf* 157]

Perhaps it would be necessary, and I thought for a moment of doing this, to collect [*lever*] or bring out [*relever*] all the senses pressing around this Hebrew *gala*, vis-à-vis the columns and colossi of Greece, vis-à-vis the galactic under all the *voies lactées*, the *milky ways* whose constellation had not long ago fascinated me. Curiously, there again we would have found significations like those of stone [*pierre*], of stone rolls, of cylinder, of parchment rolls and books, of rolls that envelop or furnish, but above all (and this is what I retain for the moment) the idea of laying bare [*mise à nu*], of specifically apocalyptic unveiling, of the disclosure that lets be seen what till then remained enveloped, withdrawn, held back, reserved, for example, the body when the clothes are removed or the glans when the foreskin is removed in circumcision. And what seems the most remarkable in all the biblical examples I was able to find and must forgo exposing here is that the gesture of denuding or of affording sight [*donner à voir*]—the *apocalyptic* movement—is more serious here, sometimes more culpable and more dangerous than what follows and what it can give rise to, for example, copulation. Thus when, in Genesis 9:21, Noah gets drunk and uncovers himself in his tent, Ham sees his father's genitals, and his two brothers to whom he reports this come to cover Noah again but turn away from him in order not to see his sex. Even there the unveiling is not the most culpable moment of a copulation. But when YHWH, speaking to Moses, declares a certain number of sexual prohibitions, the fault does indeed seem to consist essentially in the unveiling that affords seeing. Thus, in Leviticus 20:11, 17:

> The man who lies with his father's wife
> has uncovered his father's sex.
> Both are put to death. . . .
>
> The man who takes his sister,
> his father's daughter or his mother's daughter,
> he sees her sex,
> she sees his sex:
> it is incest.[3]

But the terrifying and sacred gravity of this apocalyptic uncovering is not any the less, of course, in the case of the arm of YHWH, of his glory, or of ears open to his revelation. And the disclosure opens not only to vision or contemplation, affords not only seeing but also hearing/understanding.

For the moment I forgo interpreting all the accords between *gala* and the *apocalyptic*, the Hebrew and the Greek. These accords are numerous and powerful; they support—even if they do not exclude dissonances, deviations, or betrayals—the great concert of translations.

In order to let them resound all alone, I have chosen to speak to you rather of/in an apocalyptic tone newly adopted in philosophy. No doubt I wanted thus to mime in citation but also to transform into a genre, and then parody, deport, deform the well-known title of a perhaps less well-known pamphlet of Kant, *Von einem neuerdings erhobenen vornehmen Ton in der Philosophie* (1796). The established French translation: *D'un ton grand seigneur adopté naguère en philosophie.* The English translation: "On a Newly Raised Superior Tone in Philosophy."[4] What happens to a title when made to undergo this treatment, when it begins thus to resemble the category of a genre, here a genre that comes down to mocking those who give themselves a genre?

In making this choice, I also hoped to go meet those who, in one of the seminars of these ten days, have precisely organized their work by privileging the reference to a certain Kantian caesura in the time of philosophy.

But I also let myself be seduced by another thing. The attention to tone, which is not just style, seems rather rare to me. Tone has been little studied for itself, if we suppose that is possible or has ever been done. A tone's distinctive signs are difficult to isolate, if they even exist in complete purity, which I doubt, above all in a written discourse. By what is a tone marked, a change or a rupture of tone? And how do you recognize a tonal difference within the same corpus? What traits are to be trusted for analyzing this, what signposting [*signalisation*] neither stylistic, nor rhetorical, nor evidently thematic or semantic? The extreme difficulty of this question, indeed of this task, becomes more accentuated in the case of philosophy. Isn't the dream or the ideal of philosophical discourse, of philosophical address [*allocution*], and of the writing supposed to represent that address, isn't it to make tonal difference inaudible, and with it a whole desire, affect, or scene that works (over) the concept in contraband? Through what is called neutrality of tone, philosophical discourse must also guarantee the neutrality or at least the imperturbable serenity that should accompany the relation to the true and the universal. Consequently, will it be possible to listen to or detect the tone of a philosopher, or rather (this precision is important) the so-called or would-be philosopher?

And if someone promised us to do this, wouldn't s/he be engaging to pick out all the traits that in a corpus are not yet or no longer philosophical, all the regrettable deviations in relation to the atonal norm of philosophical address?

In fact, if Kant did have the audacity, very singular in history, to concern himself systematically with a certain tone in philosophy, we must immediately nuance the praise we would like to give him for this. First, it is not certain that he is bent on or succeeds in analyzing the pure phenomenon of a tonality, as we are going to verify. Next, less does he analyze a tone in philosophy than denounce a *manner* of giving oneself airs; now it is a manner or a mannerism that, precisely, does not seem to him to be a very good tone [*de très bon ton:* also, in very good taste] in philosophy and so marks already a deviation in relation to the norm of philosophical discourse. More seriously, he attacks a tone that announces something like *the death of philosophy.*

The expression is Kant's and appears twice in this twenty-page lampoon; each time, this death is associated with the idea of a supernatural revelation, of a vision provoking a mystic exaltation or at least a visionary's pose. The first time it is a question of a "supernatural communication" or a "mystical illumination" (*übernatürliche Mitteilung [mystische Erleuchtung]*) that promises a substitute or a supplement, a surrogate of a knowable object, "which is then the death of all philosophy (*der Tod aller Philosophie*)" [*Ton* 398]. And right near the end, Kant warns against the danger of an "exalting vision (*schwärmerische Vision*), which is the death of all philosophy" (once more *"der Tod aller Philosophie"*) [*Ton* 405].

Kant's comments are also marked with the tone he gives himself, with the effects he searches for, with his polemical or satiric verve. This is a social critique, and its premises have a properly political character. But if he derides a tone that announces the death of all philosophy, the tone in itself is not what is being mocked. Besides, the tone itself, what is it? Is it something other than a distinction, a tonal difference that no longer refers except by figure to a social code, to group or caste mores, to class behaviors, by a great number of relays that no longer have anything to do with the pitch [*la hauteur*] of the voice or of the timbre? Although, as I suggested a moment ago, the tonal difference does not pass for the essentially philosophical, the fact that there is tone, tonal marking, is not by itself alone, for Kant, what announces the death of all philosophy. It is a certain tone, a certain inflection socially coded to say such and such a determinate thing. The tonal loftiness [*la hauteur*] he overwhelms with his sarcasm remains a metaphoric loftiness. These people speak in a lofty pitch [or loudly]; these loudspeakers raise the voice, but this is only said by figure and by reference to social signs. Kant never disregards [*fait abstraction de*] the content. Nevertheless—this fact is far from insignificant—the first time a philosopher comes to speak of the tone of other self-styled philosophers, when he comes to inaugurate this theme and names it in his very title, it is in order to be frightened or indignant faced with the death of philosophy. He brings to judgment those who, by the tone they take and the air they give themselves when saying certain things, place philosophy in danger of death and tell philosophy or philosophers the imminence of their end. The imminence matters no less than the end. The end is near, they seem to say, which does not exclude that it may have already taken place, a little as in John's Apocalypse the imminence of the end or of the last judgment does not exclude a certain "'"you are dead. / Stay awake!"'" [3:1–2], whose dictation follows close on the allusion to a "'second death'" that will never overtake the victor.

Kant is sure that those who speak in this tone expect some benefit from it, and that is what will first interest me.

What benefit? What bonus of seduction or intimidation? What social or political advantage? Do they want to cause fear? Do they want to give pleasure? To whom and how? Do they want to terrify? To blackmail? [*Faire chanter?*] To lure into an outmatching in enjoyment? Is this contradictory? In view of what interests, *to what ends* do they wish to come with these heated proclamations on the end to come or the end already accomplished? I wanted to speak to you today a little about this: in/of a certain tone and of what comes [*arrive*] to philosophy as its death, of the relation between this tone, this death, and the apparently calculated benefit of this eschatological mystagogy. The eschatological tells the *eskhaton*, the end, or rather the extreme, the limit, the term, the last, what comes *in extremis* to close a history, a genealogy, or very simply a countable series.

*Mystagogues*, that is Kant's word and specific charge. Before coming to my topic [*propos*], I shall draw out some paradigmatic traits in Kant's indictment, paradigmatic and contraparadigmatic traits, for I am perhaps, in repeating what he does, going to come round to doing the contrary—or preferably something else.

The mystagogues make a scene, that is what interests Kant. But at what moment do the mystagogues come on the scene and sometimes go into a trance? At what moment do they begin to play the mysterious?

The instant philosophy, more precisely the name philosophy, lost its first signification, "*seine erste Bedeutung*." And this primitive signification—Kant does not doubt this for a single instant—is "scientific wisdom of life," literally a wisdom of life regulating itself according to a knowledge or a science (*wissenschaftlichen Lebensweisheit*) [*Ton* 389]. The mystagogues get hold of the name philosophy the instant it loses its signification or its original reference, that name from then on empty or usurped, that pseudonym or that cryptonym, which is first a homonym. And that does not fail to occur in a regular, recurrent way, ever since the sense was lost: this is not the first time. To be sure, Kant is more closely interested in some recent examples of this mystagogic and psychagogic imposture, but he supposes at the outset that the usurpation is recurrent and obeys a law. There has been and will always be philosophical mystification, speculation on the end and the ends of philosophy. This depends on an event that Kant himself does not date and that he seems to situate right up against the origin, namely, that the name philosophy can circulate without its original *reference*, in other words without its *Bedeutung* and without guarantee of its value. While still remaining in the Kantian axiomatic, as it were, we can already infer from this that no harm would have happened [*arrivé*], no mystagogic speculation would have been credible or efficient, nothing or no one would have detoned [*détonné*] in philosophy without this errance of the name far from the thing, and if the relation of the name philosophy to its originary sense had been insured against every accident.

So some slackness was indeed necessary in this relation of sign to thing in order to contrive the space for a rerouting of sense or the grip for a perversion. Too slack a reference, then, there where it should be tighter, more exact, more rigorous. Here I hand you an association that will perhaps seem verbal, but since the lack of rigor or tension in the verbalization is already our concern, it occurs to me that *tonos*, tone, first signified the tight ligament, cord, rope when it is woven or braided, cable, strap, briefly the privileged figure of everything subject to strict-ure. *Tonion* is the ligament as band and surgical bandage. In short, the same tension runs across tonic difference (that which under the word *strict-ure* forms both the theme and the instrument, the cord of *Glas*)[5] and tonal difference, the deviation, the changes or mutation of tones (Hölderlin's *Wechsel der Töne* constituting one of the most obsessive motifs of *The Post Card*).[6] From this value of tension, or of elasticity (for example in a ballistic machine), we pass to the idea of tonic accent, of rhythm, of mode (Dorian, Phrygian, etc.). The tone's pitch is tied to tension; it has a bond to the bond, to the bond's more or less tight tension. This is not sufficient for determining the sense of the word *tone* when it is a matter of the voice. Even less when, through a great number of figures and tropical displacements, the tone of a discourse or of a piece in writing is analyzed in terms of content, manners of speaking, connotations, rhetorical staging, and pose taken, in semantic, in pragmatic, scenographic terms, and so on; in short, rarely or not at all, in tuning in to the pitch of a voice or to a quality of timbre. I close this parenthesis.

So the bond fastening the name philosophy to its signification really had to be slackened for the philosophical title to be regularly available as a simple ornament, adornment, decoration, costume, or ceremonial dress (*Ausschmückung*), a signifier usurped and treated as intellectual travesty, as intellectual transvestism by those Kant nonetheless calls thinkers, and thinkers self-styled uncommon.

These people place themselves out of the common, but they have this in common: they say they are in immediate and intuitive relation with a mystery. And they wish to attract, seduce, lead toward the mystery and by the mystery. *Mystagogein* is indeed this: to lead, initiate into the mystery; that is the mystagogue's or the initiatory priest's function. This *agogic* function of the leader of men, of *duce*, of *Führer*, of *leader* places him above the crowd he manipulates through the intermediary of a small number of followers gathered into a sect with a crypted language, a band, a clique or a small party with its ritualized practices. The mystagogues claim to possess as if in private the privilege of a mysterious *secret* (*Geheimnis* is the word that recurs most often). The revelation or unveiling of the secret is reserved to them; they jealously protect it. Jealousy is a major trait here. They never transmit the secret to others in everyday language, only by initiation or inspiration. The mystagogue is *philosophus per initiationem* or *per inspirationem*. Kant envisages a whole differential list and a historical typology of these mystagogues, but he recognizes in all of them one common trait: they never fail to take themselves for lords (*sich für* Vornehme *halten*), elite beings, distinguished subjects, superior and apart in society. Whence a series of value oppositions I am content to indicate very quickly: they scoff at [*prennent de haut*] work, the concept, schooling; to what is given they believe they have access effortlessly, gracefully, intuitively or through genius, outside of school. They are partisans of intellectual intuition, and the whole Kantian systematic could be recognized, though I shall not do so here, in this lampoon [*libelle*]. The hierarchized opposition of gift to work, of intuition to concept, of genius's mode to scholar's mode (*geniemäßig/schulmäßig*) [*Ton* 390] is homologous to the opposition between aristocracy and democracy, eventually between demagogic oligarchy and authentic rational democracy. Masters and slaves: the overlord reaches with a leap and through feeling what is immediately given him; the people work, elaborate, conceive.

And there we approach the more acute problem of tone. Kant does not find fault with true aristocrats, with persons truly "vornehme," with authentic distinction, only with those who give or take themselves for distinguished beings, with the grand air of those pretentious people who elevate their voice, with those who raise the tone in philosophy. Kant does not incriminate the lofty pitch of the overlordly tone when it is just, natural or legitimate. He takes aim at the rise in tone when an upstart [*parvenu*] authorizes himself to do so by giving himself airs and by sporting usurped signs of social membership. So the satire aims at the mimicry and not the tone itself. For a tone can be mimicked, feigned, faked. I shall go so far as to say *synthesized.*

But what does the fiction of the tone presuppose? How far can that fiction go? Here I am going to force and accelerate a bit the interpretation beyond commentary. A tone can be taken, and taken from the other. To change voice or mimick the intonation of the other, one must be able to confuse or induce a confusion between two voices, two voices of the other and, necessarily, of the other in oneself. How is one to discriminate the voices of the other in oneself? Instead of engaging myself directly in this immense problem, I return to the Kantian text and to a figure that seems to belong to the current rhetoric and to so-called used up [*usées*] metaphors. The question concerns the distinction between the voice of reason and the voice of the oracle. (Perhaps here I shall echo, without being sure I am responding to, the questioning, the injunction, or the request Jean-Luc Nancy addressed to me the other day.)

Kant is lenient with highly placed persons who devote themselves to philosophy, even if they do so badly, who multiply the faults against the School and believe they reach the peaks of metaphysics. They have a certain merit; they have condescended to mingle with the others and to philosophize "in the same shoes of civic equality" (bourgeois, *bürgerlichen* equality) [*Ton* 394]. On the other hand, philosophers by profession are unpardonable when they play the overlord and take on grand airs. Their crime is properly political; it is a matter for [*relève de*] a kind of police. Farther on Kant will speak of "the police in the realm of sciences (*die Polizei im Reiche der Wissenschaften*)" [*Ton* 404]. The police will have to stay vigilant to suppress—symbolically—not only the individuals who improperly adorn themselves with the title of philosopher, who take hold of and bedeck themselves [*s'emparent et se parent*] with the overlordly tone in philosophy, but also those who flock around them; for that haughtiness [*morgue*] with which one settles on the peaks of metaphysics, that wordy arrogance is contagious; it gives rise to aggregations, congregations, and chapels. This dream of a knowledge police could be related to the plan for a university tribunal presented in *The Conflict of Faculties.*[7] The tribunal was intended to arbitrate the conflicts between the provisionally lower faculty (the faculty of philosophy) and the higher faculties, so called because they represent the power whose official instrument they are (theology, law, and medicine). This tribunal is also a parliament of knowledge. And philosophy, which has the right to inspect everything touching on the truth of theoretical (constative) propositions but no power to give orders, occupies in the parliament the bench on the left and in the conflicts concerning practical reason has the authority only to treat formal questions. The other questions, the most serious for existence, are a matter for the higher faculties, singularly theology. In the indictment before us, philosophers by profession are not pardoned when they take on a tone, overlordly because, in raising thus the tone, they hoist themselves above their colleagues or comrades (*Zunftgenossen*) [*Ton* 394], and wrong them in their inalienable right to freedom and equality regarding everything touching on reason alone. And they do this precisely—here's what

I was wanting to come to—by perverting the voice of reason, by mixing the two voices of the other in us, the voice of reason and the voice of the oracle. Those people believe work to be useless in philosophy: it would suffice to "listen to . . . the oracle within oneself (*nur das Orakel in sich selbst anhören*)" [*Ton* 390]. These are Kant's first words.

Since this voice speaks to them in private, through what is properly their idiomatic feeling, their desire or their pleasure, they make it say what they want. On the other hand, you do not make the voice of reason say just anything. These are the lampoon's last words: the voice of an oracle (*die Stimme eines Orakels*) always lends itself to all kinds of interpretations (*Auslegungen*) [*Ton* 405]. The priest-mystagogues are also interpreters; the element of their agogic power is the hermeneutic or hermetic seduction (and here one thinks of what Warburton said about the political power in ancient Egypt of the scribes and of the priests as decipherers of hieroglyphs).[8] The overlordly tone dominates and is dominated by the oracular voice that covers over the voice of reason, rather parasitizes it, causes it to derail or become delirious. To raise the tone, in this case, is to make it jump, is to make the inner voice delirious, the inner voice that is the voice of the other in us. The word delirium appears once in Latin, in citing the verse of a monk of the Middle Ages ("*Quaerit delirus, quod non respondet Homerus*" [*Ton* 393]), and one other time in the French translation (here I find it a little forced but interesting) for a word that interests me even more, *Verstimmung*.

Guillermit translates "*Verstimmung der Köpfe zur Schwärmerei*" [*Ton* 398] as "*délire de têtes qui s'exaltent*" [*D'un ton* 99] 'delirium in the heads of those who exalt themselves,' and he is right. The overlordly tone is authorized by a *salto mortale* (which is also Kant's expression [*Ton* 398]), a leap from concepts to the unthinkable or the irrepresentable, an obscure anticipation of the mysterious secret come from beyond. This leap toward the imminence of a vision without concept, this impatience turned toward the most crypted secret sets free a poetico-metaphorical overabundance. To that extent this overabundance has indeed an apocalyptic affinity, but Kant never speaks the word for reasons we shall glimpse in a moment. *Verstimmen*, which Guillermit translates not without reason by *délirer*, to be delirious, is first of all to put out of tune [*désaccorder*], when speaking of a stringed instrument [*instrument à cordes*] and, or again, for example, a voice. This is currently said of a piano. Less strictly this signifies derange, put out of order, jumble. One is delirious when one is deranged in the head. *Verstimmung* can come to spoil a *Stimmung:* pathos, or the humor that then becomes testy. The *Verstimmung* we are speaking about here is indeed a social disorder and a derangement, an out-of-tune-ness [*désaccordement*] of strings and voices in the head. The tone leaps and rises when the voice of the oracle, uncovering your ear, jumbling, covering, or parasitizing the voice of reason equally speaking in each and using the same language with everyone, takes you aside, speaks to you in a private code, and whispers secrets to you. The voice of reason, Kant says, "*die Stimme der Vernunft,*" speaks to each without equivocation (*deutlich*) and gives access to scientific knowledge. But it is essentially for giving orders and prescribing. For if we had the time to reconstitute the whole internal and properly Kantian necessity of this address, we would have to go as far as the extreme finesse of the objection made to the mystagogues. Not only do they confuse the voice of the oracle with that of reason. They do not distinguish either between pure speculative reason and pure practical reason; they believe they *know* what is solely *thinkable* and reach through feeling alone the universal laws of practical reason. So there is a voice of practical reason; it describes nothing; it says nothing describable; it dictates, prescribes, orders. Kant also names it in Latin: "*dictamen rationis*" [*Ton* 402]. Although it gives rise to autonomy, the law it dictates is as little flexible, as little subject to free interpretation as if it came from the completely other in me. It is a "brazen voice" [*Ton* 402 (modified)], Kant says. It resounds in every man, for every man has in him the idea of duty. And it resounds rather loud in him; it strikes rather percussively and repercussively; it even thunders in him, for man trembles (*zittert*) to hear this brazen voice that, from the height of its majesty, orders him to sacrifice his drives, to resist seductions, to forgo his desires. And the voice promises me nothing in return; it assures me no compensation. It is sublime in this; it orders, mandates, demands, commands without giving anything in exchange; it thunders in me to the point of making me tremble; it thus provokes the greatest questions and the greatest astonishment (*Erstaunen*) [*Ton* 402]. That is the *true* mystery. Kant also calls it *Geheimnis* [*Ton* 403], but it is no longer the mystery of the mystagogues. It is the mystery at once domestic, intimate, and transcendent, the *Geheimnis* of practical reason, the sublimity of moral law and moral voice. The mystagogues fail to recognize that *Geheimnis;* they confuse it with a mystery of vision and contact, whereas the moral law never gives itself to be seen or touched. In this sense, the *Geheimnis* of moral law is more in tune with the essence of the voice that hears/understands itself but neither touches nor sees itself, thus seeming to hide itself from every external intuition. But in its very transcendence the moral voice is nearer, and thus more autoaffective, more autonomous. The moral law then is more auditory, more audible than the mystagogic oracle still contaminated by feeling, illumination, or intuitive vision, contact and mystical tact ("*ein . . . mystischer Takt,*" Kant says [*Ton* 398]). The overlordly tone detones because it is foreign to the essence of the voice.

Why did I feel inclined, at this moment of my reading of an overlordly tone, to add this piece to the dossier (if I can say that) of *The Post Card?* Or again to file it in what is called *dossier* therein, between the word and the thing, the word *dossier* packed with all the *dos* [back, *do,* etc.] whose note and syllable punctuate the "Envois" on each page, at Socrates's back and on the back of the postcard, with all the words in *do* and with the back [*dossier*] of the chair, of the partition between Plato and Socrates when the latter seems to write what the former dictates? Not only on account of the mixing or changing of tones (*Wechsel der Töne*) that would form in this book at once a theme and a manner. Nor on account of the word and the thing "apocalypse" that regularly recur there, with the numerological obsession and the insistence of the number 7 that also gives rhythm to John's Apocalypse. The signer of the "Envois" mocks what he calls "my post card apocalypse," our "small, library apocalypse" (*The Post Card* 13, 11). Nor is this the satire of academic philosophy. No, at this point of my reading of "an overlordly tone," what I did feel inclined to add to *The Post Card*'s dossier is the difficulty Plato gives to Kant, the devilish job Kant gives himself with Plato, the untiring rhetoric for distinguishing between the good Plato and the bad Plato, the true and the false, his authentic writings and his more or less reliable or apocryphal ones.

That is to say, his Letters. Kant wants at once to accuse and excuse Plato of this continuous catastrophe that has corrupted philosophy, the strict relation between the name and the thing "philosophy," which ends up in this detoning *Verstimmung.* He wants to accuse *and* excuse him of delirium in philosophy, one would say in the same movement of a double postulation. *Double bind* again of filiation: Plato is the father of the delirium, of all exaltation in philosophy (*der Vater aller Schwärmerei* mit der Philosophie), but without it having been his fault (*ohne seine Schuld*). So we must divide Plato; we must distinguish between the Academic and the presumed author of the Letters, the teacher and the sender [*envoyeur*].

> Plato the *academic* was, therefore, although it was not his fault (for he used his intellectual intuitions only backward, to *explain* the possibility of synthetic knowledge *a priori,* not forward, to *widen* this knowledge through such intuition into Ideas readable [*lesbare*] in the divine intellect [the innocent Plato is Kant's father, as well as the postcard[9] of a self-portrait by Kant; the innocent Plato is not the father of delirium]), the father of all exaltation in *philosophy.* But I would not at all want to confuse Plato the *letter-writer* (*Plato den* Briefsteller) (newly translated into German) with Plato the academic. [*Ton* 398]

Kant's pamphlet, which came out in the *Berliner Monatsschrift,* is dead set against a certain Schlosser who had just translated the Letters of Plato, in a work entitled *Plato's Letters on the Syracuse Revolution, With an Introduction and Some Remarks* (1795). Kant seems to denounce Schlosser *directly* when he appeals to Plato and certain of his so-called esoteric doctrines; but *indirectly,* we know he wants to get at Jacobi. And what is intolerable in this letter-writer Plato is aristocratic esotericism—Kant cites that Letter recommending that secrets not be divulged to the crowd—a cryptophilia combined with a mystical interpretation of mathematics. The great stake between Plato and Kant is, of course, the philosophical interpretation of mathematics. Plato, enchanted by geometric figures, as Pythagoras was by numbers [*nombres*], would have done nothing but have a presentiment of the problematic of the *a priori* synthesis and too quickly would have taken refuge in a mysticism of geometry, as Pythagoras in the mysticism of numbers. And this mathematizing mysticism, this idolatry of figures and numbers [*chiffres*] always goes hand in hand with the phenomena of sect, cryptopolitics, indeed superstitious theophany that Kant opposes to rational theology. Numerology, mystic illumination, theophanic vision—all that indeed belongs to the apocalyptic world. And here I note in passing that, in the vast and overabundant corpus of the apocalyptic "genre," from the Persian and Zoroastrian heritage up to the very numerous Jewish and Christian apocalypses, the experts often inscribe this or that text of Plato, especially the myth of Er in the *Republic.* This apocalyptic corpus has been collected, identified, and studied as such only in the nineteenth century. Kant never names the Apocalypse in this text, but he does make, three years earlier, a brief allusion to it, between parentheses, in *Religion Within the Limits of Reason Alone*—which is one of the most indispensable contextual surroundings for understanding the essay "On a Newly Raised Superior Tone. . . ." In this parenthesis, the Apocalypse is invoked in order to designate the punishment of the guilty ones at the end of the world as the end of history (Book Three, Division Two, "Historical Account of the Gradual Establishment of the Sovereignty of the Good Principle on Earth";[10] also cf. *The Conflict of Faculties* 113).

This cryptopolitics is also a cryptopoetics, a poetic perversion of philosophy.

And it is again a matter of the veil and of castration.

Eight years ago, right here in fact, I had spoken of veil and castration, of interpreters, of hermeneutics and hermetics. *I have forgotten my umbrella* is a statement at once hermetic and totally open, as secret and superficial as the postcard apocalypse it announces and protects against.[11] And elsewhere, in *Glas* [187, 256] and in "Economimesis,"[12] I had indicated the intrigue of a certain veil of Isis around which Kant and Hegel had more than once busied themselves. I am going to expose myself to taking (and tying) up again with the threads of this intrigue and with the treatment of castration, faced with Isis.

On the veil of Isis and on castration Kant says nothing that visibly refers them to one another within the same demonstrative argument. I observe only a kind of tropical continuity, but the tropical transfer(ence), the metaphorical and the analogical, is exactly our problem.

The mystagogues of modernity, according to Kant, do not simply tell us what they see, touch, or feel. They *have a presentiment of,* they anticipate, they approach, they smell out, they are the men of imminence and the trace. For example, they say they have a presentiment of the sun and cite Plato. They say that every philosophy of men can point to or designate the dawn, but that one can have only a presentiment of the sun. Kant is ironical about this presentiment of the sun; he multiplies his sarcastic remarks. These new Platonists give us through sentiment or presentiment (*Gefühl, Ahnung*) only a theatrical sun (*Theatersonne*), a chandelier in sum [*un lustre en somme*]. And then these people abuse metaphors, figurative expressions (*bildliche Ausdrücke*) [*Ton* 399], in order to sensitize us, to make us presensitive to this presentiment.

Here is an example of this—Kant cites his adversaries: "'to approach so near the goddess wisdom that one can perceive the *rustle* of her garment'" [*Ton* 399] (its rustling [*Rauschen*], rather than its light touch [*frôlement*] as the French translation says [*D'un ton* 101]). Or again: "'since he cannot lift up the veil of Isis, he can nevertheless make it so thin (*so dünne*) that one can *have a presentiment of* the goddess under this veil (*unter ihm*)'" [*Ton* 399 (modified)]. To lift up the veil of Isis here is *aufheben* (*"da er den Schleier der Isis nicht aufheben kann"*), and one can still dream between the *gala* of this *Aufhebung* and that apocalyptic unveiling.

Kant fires off his dart [*son trait*]: thin to what point, he asks; that we are not told. Probably not thin enough, still too thick, so that one can do what one wants with the ghost (*Gespenst*) behind its veil or sheet. For otherwise, if the veil was absolutely thin, and transparent, this would be a vision, a seeing (*Sehen*), and, Kant notes in quite mercilessly taking aim, that must be avoided (*vermieden*). Above all we must not see; we must have only a presentiment under the veil. Then our mystagogues play on the ghost and the veil; they replace the evidences and proofs with "'analogies,'" "'probabilities'" (*"Analogieen, Wahrscheinlichkeiten"*) [*Ton* 399]. T hese are their words. Kant cites them and calls us to witness: you see, they are not true philosophers; they resort to poetic schemas. All that [*ça*] is so much literature. We know this scene well today, and it is, among other things, to this repetition that I would like to draw your attention. Not to take sides or come to a decision—I shall do no such thing—between metaphor and concept, literary mystagogy and true philosophy, but for a start to recognize the old solidarity of these antagonists or protagonists.

Consider now that Kant first proposes the word or the image of castration, or more rigorously of "'emasculating (*Entmannung*)'" [*Ton* 399], as one example of those "'analogies'" or "'probabilities'" that this "new mystical-Platonic language" [*Ton* 398] abuses to manipulative ends. He first takes them from a sentence of that Schlosser who just translated and introduced Plato's Letters. Nietzsche might have made something of this name Schlosser, as he did of Schleiermacher, the first "maker of" hermeneutic "veils." Schlosser is the locksmith, the man who makes or keeps the keys, true or false, but also the official in charge of locking up, the one who closes and knows all about closure, expert as he is in speaking of it, in producing it, or in getting the better of it. This Schlosser then had spoken, by figure, of "'emasculating . . . reason (*Entmannung der . . . Vernunft*),'" and he had accused "'metaphysical sublimation (*metaphysische Sublimation*)'" of this emasculation. An inadmissible analogy in Kant's eyes, abusive because it takes the place of proof by coming to the place where the demonstration leaves a "lack (*Mangel*)," but also scandalous because in truth those who adorn themselves with this new tone in philosophy are they who emasculate and make a corpse of reason. "For the purpose of argumentation," he says, "since there is a lack of rigorous proofs, the following are offered as arguments: 'analogies, probabilities' (which were discussed above), thus 'the danger of emasculating [the French translation [*D'un ton* 101] says "castration" for "emasculating"] a faculty of reason that has become so high-strung by metaphysical sublimation that it can hardly maintain itself in the struggle with vice. . . .'" And Kant immediately turns the argument inside out, I would say like a glove: ". . . whereas," he says, "it is in precisely these principles *a priori* that practical reason rightly feels its otherwise never intimated strength, and it is, on the other hand, in falsely attributed empirical properties (which are, for precisely this reason, unfit for universal legislation) that reason is emasculated and paralyzed (*entmannt und gelähmt*)" [*Ton* 399–400 (modified)] ("castrated and paralyzed" in *D'un ton* [104]).

If castration is a metaphor or a simulacrum—and so it must be, it seems, since it concerns the phallus, not the penis or the clitoris—then the metaphorical stake is clear between the two opposing parties sketched out [*campés*] by a Kant who is no less a party in this. The stake for this *Kampfplatz* of metaphysics is the castration of reason. Which of the two parties facing each other most surely castrates reason? Or more seriously: which of the two unmans, *entmannt,* this descendant of *logos* that is *ratio?* Each of the two, we just heard them without the least equivocation, would accuse the other of castrating the *logos* and of defalcating its phallus. And into this debate, phallogocentric on both sides, therefore throughout, we could put Freud on the scene as a third robber procuring the key (true or false), "sexual theory," namely, that for this stage of reason in which there is only male reason, only a masculine *or* castrated organ or canon of reason, everything proceeds in this just as for that stage of infantile genital organization in which there is definitely a masculine but no feminine. Perhaps he would speak of a *phallic stage* of reason. "The antithesis here," Freud says at the end of "The Infantile Genital Organization," "is between having a male genital and being castrated."[13] No sexual difference [*Pas de différence*] as opposition, but only the masculine! This strange logic (reason since Freud, Lacan would say) could be followed quite far into the details of the text, above all in the moments when the veil of Isis unleashes what Freud calls *Bemächtigungstrieb,* the drive for mastery. Kant, for example, accuses the mystagogic metaphysicians of behaving like "strong men (*Kraftmännern*)" who lately preach with enthusiasm a wisdom that costs them nothing, since they claim they have caught this goddess by the end of her robe and thus have made themselves her masters and lords; they would have "mastered (*bemächtigt*)" her [401n (modified)], and so on.

The castration or not of *logos* as *ratio* is a central form of this debate around metaphysics. It is also a fight around the poetic (between poetry and philosophy), around the death or the future of philosophy. The stake is the same. Kant does not doubt this: the new preachers need to pervert philosophy into poetry in order to give themselves grand airs, to occupy through simulacrum and mimicry the place of the great, to usurp thus an essentially symbolic power.

Schlosser, the locksmith, we could say, right here, the man of the lordly castle, not only abuses poetic metaphors. He accuses his century of being prosaic, and he dares to write to Plato, addresses him, invokes him, apostrophizes him, calls him to witness: "'*Armer Plato*, poor Plato, if you did not have the seal of Antiquity about you . . . who would still want to read you in this *prosaic* age in which the highest wisdom is to see nothing but what lies at our feet and to assume nothing but what we can grasp with our hands?'" Locked in combat with Schlosser, who thrashes the new sons of the earth, Kant plays Aristotle against Plato: "But this conclusion unfortunately does not follow; it proves too much. For *Aristotle*, an extremely prosaic philosopher, certainly has the seal (*Siegel*) of antiquity about him, and according to the principle stated above, he has a claim to being read!—At bottom, all philosophy is indeed prosaic; and the suggestion that we should now start to philosophize poetically (*wiederum poetisch zu philosophiren*) would be just as welcome as the suggestion that a businessman (*Kaufmann*) should in the future no longer write his account books in prose but in verse" [*Ton* 406n].

But the strategy on both sides is more twisted still. The mystagogues, the analogists, and the anagogists, they too play the Aristotle card. And at that moment of play it is a matter of the ends and the end of philosophy. The wake [*La veillée*] over the death or the end of philosophy, the vigil [*la veille*] by the corpse of philosophy is not just an ancient (hi)story because it would date back to Kant. For it was already said that if philosophy were finished, that was not a deferred action [*un aprés-coup*] of the Kantian limitation or of the bounds [*termes*] placed on the empire of metaphysics, but already "two thousand years ago." Already two thousand years ago we finished with philosophy, said a disciple of Schlosser, a real count, this one, Count Leopold Stolberg, because "'the Stagirite has conquered so much for science that he has left behind little of importance for his followers to espy'" [*Ton* 394n].

Kant's rejoinder is that of a decided progressive; he believes in philosophy's finally open and unveiled future. It is also the response of an egalitarian democrat: you want to put an end to philosophy through obscurantism (*durch Obscuriren*) [*Ton* 394n], and you are disguised monarchists; you want all to be equal among themselves, but with the exception of one single individual, all are nothing. Sometimes the individual is Plato, sometimes Aristotle, but in truth through this monarchism you play the philosophers and elevate yourselves by proclaiming the end of philosophy in an overlordly tone.

Naturally, even when he fights like this, Kant declares that he does not like war. As in *The Conflict of Faculties* (in which he distinguished moreover between natural warfare and the conflict arbitrated by a law), he ends by proposing to the castrating adversary a kind of concordat, a deal, a peace treaty, or a contract, in short the solution of a conflict that is not an antinomy. As you have perhaps foreseen, this contract is more important to me than the whole combinatory strategy, the play, and the exchange of places. What can deeply bind the two opposing parties and procure for them a neutral ground of reconciliation for speaking together again in a fitting tone? In other words, what do they together exclude as the inadmissible itself? What is the *inadmissible?*

Kant speaks of modernity, and of the mystagogues of his time, but you will have quickly perceived in passing, without my even having to designate explicitly, name, or draw out all the threads, how many transpositions we could indulge in on the side of *our* so-called modernity. I will not say that today everyone would recognize him or herself on this or that side, purely and simply. But I am sure it could be demonstrated that today every slightly organized discourse is found or claims to be found on both sides, alternately or simultaneously, even if this emplacement exhausts nothing, does not go round the turn or the contour [*ne fait pas le tour ou le contour*] of the place and the discourse held. And this inadequation, always limited itself, no doubt indicates the densest difficulty. Each of us is the mystagogue *and* the *Aufklärer* of an other. I leave to you to try some of these transpositions; we could return to them in the discussion.

What, then, is the contract? What condition does Kant lay down for those who, like himself, declare their concern to speak the truth, to *reveal* without emasculating the *logos?* For they agree on this together, this is the place of consensus where they can meet and come together, their synagogue. Kant first asks them to get rid of the veiled goddess before which they both tend to kneel. He asks them no longer to personify the moral law or the voice that incarnates it. No longer, he says to the mystagogues, should we personify the law that speaks in us, above all not in the "esthetic," sensible, and beautiful form of this veiled Isis. Such will be the condition for understanding/hearing the moral law itself, the unconditioned, and for understanding/hearing ourselves and getting along [*pour nous entendre*]. In other words, and this is a trenchant motif for thought of the law or of the ethical today, Kant calls for placing the law above and beyond, not the person, but personification and the body, above and beyond as it were the sensible voice that speaks in us, the singular voice that speaks to us in private, the voice that could be said in his language to be "pathological" in opposition to the voice of reason. The law above the body, above this body found here to be represented by a veiled goddess. Even if you do not want to grant some *signifiance* or "significance" to the fact that what the concordat excludes is precisely the body of a veiled Isis, the universal principle of feminity, murderess of Osiris all of whose pieces she later recovers except for the phallus. Even if you also think that that is a personification too analogical or metaphorical, grant me at least this: the truce proposed between the two declared defenders of a non-emasculated *logos* supposes some exclusion. It supposes some *inadmissible.* There is an excluded middle and that will be enough for me.

Enough for me in view of what? Before pursuing this question, I shall read the proposition of peace or alliance addressed by Kant to his adversaries of the day, but perhaps to his accomplices of all times:

> But what is the good of all this conflict between two parties that at bottom share one and the same intention: to make people wise and virtuous? It is much noise about nothing, disunity out of a misunderstanding in which no reconciliation but only a reciprocal

> clarification is needed in order to conclude a treaty that makes future concord even more heartfelt.
>
> The veiled goddess for whom we of both parties bend our knees is the moral law in us, in its inviolable majesty. We do indeed perceive her voice and also understand very well her command. But when we are listening, we are in doubt whether it comes from man, from the perfected power of his own reason, or whether it comes from an other, whose nature is unknown to us and speaks to man through this, his own reason. At bottom we would perhaps do better to rise above and thus spare ourselves research into this matter; since such research is only speculative and since what obliges us (objectively) to act remains always the same, one may place one or the other principle down as a foundation. But the didactic procedure of bringing the moral law within us into clear concepts according to a logical methodology is the only authentically *philosophical* one, whereas the procedure whereby the law is personified and reason's moral bidding is made into a veiled Isis (even if we attribute to her no other properties than those that were discovered according to the method above), is an *aesthetic* mode of representing (*eine* ästhetische *Vorstellungsart*) precisely the same object; one can doubtless use this mode of representation backward, after the first procedure has already purified the principles, in order to enliven those ideas by a sensible, albeit only analogical, presentation (*Darstellung*), and yet one always runs the danger of falling into an exalting vision [*schwärmerische Vision*], which is the death of all philosophy. [*Ton* 405]

Among the numerous traits characterizing an apocalyptic type of writing [*écrit*], let us provisionally isolate prediction and eschatological preaching [*prédication*], the fact of telling, foretelling, or preaching the end, the extreme limit, the imminence of the last. Can one not say then that all the parties to such a concordat are the subjects of eschatological discourses? No doubt, other contexts taken into account, this situation is older than the Copernican revolution; the numerous prototypes of apocalyptic discourses would suffice to attest to this, as would so many others in the meantime. But if Kant denounces those who proclaim that philosophy has been at an end for two thousand years, he has himself, in marking a limit, indeed the end of a certain type of metaphysics, freed another wave of eschatological discourses in philosophy. His progressivism, his belief in the future of a certain philosophy, indeed of another metaphysics, is not contradictory to this proclamation of ends and of the end.

And I shall now start again from this fact: from then on and with multiple and profound differences, indeed mutations, being taken into account, the West has been dominated by a powerful program that was also an untransgressible contract among discourses of the end. The themes of the end of history and the death of philosophy represent [*figurent*] only the most comprehensive, massive, and gathered forms of this. To be sure there are obvious differences between Hegelian eschatology, that Marxist eschatology people have too quickly wanted to forget these last years in France (and perhaps this was another eschatology *of Marxism*, its eschatology and its death knell [*glas*]), Nietzschean eschatology (between the last man, the higher man, and the overman), and so many other more recent varieties. But aren't these differences measured as deviations in relation to the fundamental tonality of this *Stimmung* audible across so many thematic variations? Haven't all the differences [*différends*] taken the form of a going-one better in eschatological eloquence, each newcomer, more lucid than the other, more vigilant and more prodigal too, coming to add more to it: I tell you this in truth; this is not only the end of this here but also and first of that there, the end of history, the end of the class struggle, the end of philosophy, the death of God, the end of religions, the end of Christianity and morals (that [*ça*], that was the most serious naïveté), the end of the subject, the end of man, the end of the West, the end of Oedipus, the end of the earth, *Apocalypse Now*, I tell you, in the cataclysm, the fire, the blood, the fundamental earthquake, the napalm descending from the sky by helicopters, like prostitutes, and also the end of literature, the end of painting, art as a thing of the past, the end of psychoanalysis, the end of the university, the end of phallocentrism and phallogocentrism, and I don't know what else? And whoever would come to refine, to say the finally final [*le fin du fin*], namely the end of the end [*la fin de la fin*], the end of ends, that the end has always already begun, that we must still distinguish between closure and end, that person would, whether wanting to or not, participate in the concert. For it is also the end of metalanguage on the subject of eschatological language. With the result that we can wonder if eschatology is a tone, or even the voice itself.

Isn't the voice always that of the last man? Voice or language [*langue*] itself, song or accent in language itself? Hölderlin closes his second version of *Patmos*, the poem bearing as its title the name of the apocalyptic island, that of John, by invoking the poem of the German tongue ("*Dem folgt deutscher Gesang*" ["This end German song pursues"]). Heidegger often cites the first lines of this poem:

> Nah ist
> Und schwer zu fassen der Gott.
> Wo aber Gefahr ist, wächst
> Das Rettende auch.
>
> (Near and
> Hard to grasp is the God.
> But where danger is,
> Deliverance also grows.)[14]

And if Heidegger thinks the *Überwindung* of metaphysics or of ontotheology as that of the eschatology inseparable from it, he does so in the name of another eschatology. Several times he says of thought, here distinct from philosophy, that it is essentially "eschatological." That is his word.

Isn't the voice of language, I was asking, always that of the last man? Forgoing reading with you Blanchot's *Last Man*,[15] I recall, since I spoke of the voice and of Oedipus, this fragment from the *Philosophenbuch*. Nietzsche, under the title "Oedipus" and in an absolute soliloquy, has the last philosopher, who is also the last man, speak with himself. He speaks *with* his voice; he converses with himself [*s'entretient*] and maintains [*entretient*] what life remains for him with the phantom of his voice; and he calls (on) himself, he is called Oedipus:

> "I call myself the last philosopher, because I am the last man. No one speaks with me but myself, and my voice comes to me like the voice of a dying man! Let me associate for but one hour more with you, dear voice, with you, the last trace of the memory of all

> human happiness. With you I escape loneliness through self-delusion and lie myself into multiplicity and love. For my heart resists the belief that love is dead. It cannot bear the shudder of the loneliest loneliness, and so it forces me to speak as if I were two. . . ."

"'As if I were two'": for the moment he thus sends himself this message by acting *as if* he could still really address it to himself; this impossible destination signs the death of the last man, in and outside him. He knows him beyond the *as if:*

> "And yet, I still hear you, dear voice! *Something* else dies, something other than me, the last man in this universe. The last sigh, *your* sigh, dies with me. The drawn-out 'alas! alas!' sighed for me, Oedipus, the last miserable man."[16]

Then if eschatology surprises us at the first word, at the first as at the last, always at the last but one, what are we to say? What are we to do? The response to this question is perhaps impossible, because it never lets itself be expected. For the question is that of the response, and of a call promising or responding before the question.

Clarity is necessary, Philippe Lacoue-Labarthe said yesterday. Yes. But there is light, and there are lights, daylight, and also the madness of the day [*la folie du jour*]. "The end is beginning," we read in *The Madness of the Day.*[17] Without even referring to apocalypses of the Zoroastrian type (there were more than one of them), we know that every apocalyptic eschatology is promised in the name of light, of the visionary and vision, and of a light of light, of a light brighter than all the lights it makes possible. John's apocalypse, which dominates the whole of the Western apocalyptic, is lit by the light of El, of Elohim:

> yes, the glory of Elohim illuminates it.
> . . .
> the kings of the earth bring their glory into it.
>
> Its gates are never closed for the day:
> no, there is no night there.
> They bring the glory. . . .
>
> (21:23-26)

Night is no more,
they do not need lamplight
nor sunlight:
Adônaï Elohim illuminates them,
  and they rule to the ages of ages.

(22:5)

There is light, and there are lights, the lights of reason or of *logos*, that are not, for all that, some other thing. And it is in the name of an *Aufklärung* that Kant, for example, undertakes to demystify the overlordly tone. In the light of today we cannot not have become the heirs of these *Lumières*. We cannot and we must not—this is a law and a destiny—forgo the *Aufklärung*, in other words, what imposes itself as the enigmatic desire for vigilance, for the lucid vigil, for elucidation, for critique and truth, but for a truth that at the same time keeps within itself some apocalyptic desire, this time as desire for clarity and revelation, in order to demystify or, if you prefer, to deconstruct apocalyptic discourse itself and with it everything that speculates on vision, the imminence of the end, theophany, parousia, the last judgment. Then each time we intractably ask ourselves where they want to come to, and to what ends, those who declare the end of this or that, of man or the subject, of consciousness, of history, of the West or of literature, and according to the latest news, of progress itself, the idea of which has never been in such bad health to the right and the left? What effects do these noble, gentile [*gentils*] prophets or eloquent visionaries want to produce? In view of what immediate or adjourned benefit? What do they do, what do we do in saying this? To seduce or subjugate whom, intimidate or make whom come [*jouir*]? These effects and these benefits can be related to an individual or collective, conscious or unconscious speculation. They can be analyzed in terms of libidinal or political mastery, with all the differantial relays and thus all the economic paradoxes that overdetermine the idea of power or mastery and sometimes drag them into the abyss. Lucid analysis of these interests or of these calculations should mobilize a very great number and a great diversity of interpretative apparatus available today. It must and can do this, for our epoch would be rather superarmed in this regard. And a deconstruction, if it does not stop there, nonetheless never goes without some secondary work on the system that joins this superarmament to itself, that articulates, as is said, psychoanalysis to Marxism or to some Nietzscheanism; to the resources of linguistics, rhetoric, or pragmatics; to the theory of *speech acts;* to Heideggerian thought on the history of metaphysics, the essence of science or of technology. Such a demystification must give in [*se plier*] to the finest diversity of apocalyptic ruses. The interest or the calculation of these ruses can be so dissimulated under the desire for light, well hidden (*eukalyptus*, as is said of the tree whose calycine limb remains closed after flowering), well hidden under the avowed desire for revelation. And one dissimulation can hide another. The most serious thing, for then it is endless, the most fascinating thing, depends on this: the subject of eschatological discourse can have an interest in forgoing its own interest, can forgo everything in order to place yet its death on your shoulders and make you inherit in advance its corpse, that is, its soul, the subject hoping thus to arrive at its ends through the end, to seduce you on the spot by promising you to guard your guard in his absence.

I am not sure that there is just *one* fundamental *scene, one* great paradigm according to which, except for some deviations, all the eschatological strategies would regulate themselves. It would still be a philosophical, onto-eschato-teleological interpretation to say: the apocalyptic strategy is fundamentally one, its diversity is only a diversity of procedures [*procédés*], masks, appearances, or simulacra.

This caution being taken, let us yield for a short time to the temptation of a fiction and imagine this fundamental scene. Let us imagine that there is *one* apocalyptic tone, a unity of the apocalyptic tone, and that *the* apocalyptic tone is not the effect of a generalized derailment, of a *Verstimmung* multiplying the voices and making the tones shift [*sauter*], opening each word to the haunting memory [*hantise*] of the other in an unmasterable polytonality, with grafts, intrusions, interferences [*parasitages*]. Generalized *Verstimmung* is the possibility for the other tone, or the tone of another, to come at no matter what moment to interrupt a familiar music. (Just as I suppose this is readily produced in analysis, but also elsewhere, when suddenly a tone come from one knows not where renders speechless, if this can be said, the tone that tranquilly seemed to determine (*bestimmen*) the voice and thus insure the unity of destination, the self-identity of some addressee [*destinataire*] or sender [*destinateur*]. *Verstimmung*, if that is henceforth what we call the derailment, the sudden change [*saute*] of tone, as one would say *la saute d'humeur* 'the sudden change of mood,' is the disorder or the delirium of destination (*Bestimmung*), but also the possibility of all emission. The unity of tone, if there were any, would certainly be the assurance of destination, but also death, another apocalypse.) So let us imagine that there is *one* apocalyptic tone and *one* fundamental scene. Then whoever takes on the apocalyptic tone comes to tell you or itself something. But what? I say "whoever takes," "whosoever takes," in order not to say "he who" or "she who," "those men who" or "those women who," and I do indeed say tone, which one must be able to distinguish from all articulated discursive content. What tone means (to say) is not perforce what the discourse says, and either can always contradict, deny, make drift or derail the other.

Whoever takes on the apocalyptic tone comes to signify to, if not tell, you something. What? The truth, of course, and to signify to you that it reveals the truth to you; tone is revelatory of some unveiling in process. Unveiling or truth, apophantics of the imminence of the end, of whatever comes down, finally, to the end of the world. Not only truth as the revealed truth of a secret on the end or of the secret of the end. Truth itself is the end, the destination, and that truth unveils itself is the advent of the end. Truth is the end and the instance of the last judgment. The structure of truth here would be apocalyptic. And that is why there would not be any truth of the apocalypse that is not the truth of truth.

Then whoever takes on the apocalyptic tone will be asked: with a view to what and to what ends? In order to lead where, right now or soon?

The end is beginning, signifies the apocalyptic tone. But to what ends does the tone signify this? The apocalyptic tone naturally wants to attract, to get to come, to arrive at this, to seduce in order to lead to this, in other words, to the place where the first vibration of the tone is heard, which is called, as will be one's want, subject, person, sex, desire (I think rather of a pure differential vibration, without support, insupportable). The end is soon, it is imminent, signifies the tone. I see it, I know it, I tell you, now you know, come. We're all going to die, we're going to disappear, and this death sentence [*cet arrêt de mort*] cannot fail to judge us, we're going to die, you and I, the others too, the goyim, the gentiles, and all the others, all those who don't share this secret with us, but they don't know it. It's as if they're already dead. We're alone in the world, I'm the only one able to reveal to you the truth or the destination, I tell you it, I give it to you, come, let us be for a moment, we who don't yet know who we are, a moment before the end the sole survivors, the only ones to stay awake, it will be so much better. We'll be a sect, we'll form a species, a sex or gender, a race (*Geschlecht*) all by ourselves, we'll give ourselves a name. (That is just a bit the Babel scene, of which we can speak again, but there is also a Babel in John's Apocalypse that would lead us to think, not on the side of the confusion of tongues or tones, but of prostitution, if we suppose such distinctions can be made. Babel the great is the mother of whores: "'Come. I shall show you the judgment / of the great whore . . .'" (17:1).) They sleep, we stay awake.

This discourse, or rather this tone I translate into discourse, this tone of the vigil at the moment of the end, which is also that of the funeral watch, of the *Wake*, it always cites or echoes [*répercute*] in a certain way John's Apocalypse or at least the fundamental scene that already programs the Johannine writing. Thus, for example:

> "'I know your works:
> you are renowned for living,
> but you are dead.
>
> Stay awake! [*Esto vigilans*, says the Latin translation.]
> Strengthen what remains, so near dying. . . .
>
> . . .
> If you do not stay awake,
> I shall come like a thief:
> you will not know at what hour I shall come upon you.'"
> (3:1–3)

I shall come: the coming is always to come. The *Adôn*, named as the aleph and the tav, the alpha and the omega, is the one who has been, who is, and who comes, not who shall be, but who comes, which is the present of a to-come [*à-venir*]. *I am coming* means: I am going to come, I am to-come in the imminence of an "I am going to come," "I am in the process of coming," "I am on the point of going to come." "Who comes" (*ho erkhomenos*) is translated here in Latin by *venturus est* [1:8].

Jesus is the one who says, "Stay awake!" But it would be necessary, perhaps beyond or before a narratology, to unfold a detailed analysis of the narrative voice in the Apocalypse. I use the expression "narrative voice" in order to distinguish it, as Blanchot does, from the narrating voice, that of the identifiable subject, of the narrator or determinable sender in a narrative, a *récit*. In addition, I believe that all the "come" s resounding in the *récits* or *non-récits* of Blanchot also resound, harmonize with a certain "come" (*erkhou, veni*) of the Johannine Apocalypse. Jesus is the one who says, """Stay awake. . . . I shall come upon you."" But John is the one speaking, citing Jesus, or rather writing, appearing to transcribe what he says in recounting that he cites Jesus the moment Jesus dictates to him to write—which he does presently and which we read—to the seven communities, to the seven churches of Asia. Jesus is cited as the one who dictates without himself writing and says, "'write, *grapson*.'" But even before John writes, saying presently that he writes, he hears as a dictation the great voice of Jesus—

> I, Yohanân. . . .
> I am in the island called Patmos,
> because of the word of Elohim and the testimony
> of Yéshoua'.
> I am in the breath (*en pneumati, in spiritu*), on the day
> of the Adôn.
> I hear behind me a great voice,
> like that of a shofar. It says:
> "What you see, write it into a volume,
> send it to the seven communities. . . ."
>
> [1:9–11]

Write and send, dictates the voice come from behind, behind John's back, like a shofar, *grapson eis biblion kai pempson, scribe in libro: et mitte septem ecclesiis. I see* and *I hear,* in the present tense in Chouraqui's translation, are in the past in the Greek and the Latin, which does not simplify the premises of an analysis.[18] Now even before this narrative scene citing a dictation or literally a present inspiration, there was a preamble without narrative, or in any case narrating, voice, a kind of title or name tag [*médaille*] come from one knows not where and binding the apocalyptic disclosure to the sending, the dispatch [*envoi*]. These lines are properly the apocalypse as sending of the apocalypse, the apocalypse that sends itself:

> Disclosure of Yéshoua' the messiah
> (*Apokalupsis Jēsou Khristou*):
> Elohim gives it to him
> to show to his servants
> what will happen soon.
>
> He signifies it by sending it through his messenger
> (*esēmanen aposteilas dia tou angelou autou, significavit mittens per angelum suum*)
> to his servant Yohanân.
>
> [1:1–2]

So John is the one who already receives mail [*courrier*] through the further intermediary of a bearer who is an angel, a pure messenger. And John transmits a message already transmitted, testifies to a testimony that will again be that of another testimony, that of Jesus; so many sendings, *envois*, so many voices, and this puts many people on the line.

> He signifies it by sending it through his messenger
> to his servant Yohanân.
>
> He reports the testimony of the word of Elohim
> and the testimony of Yéshoua' the messiah,
> all he has seen.
>
> Joys of the reader, of the hearer
> of the words of the inspiration
> of those who keep what is written:
> yes, the time approaches, *o gar kairos engus, tempus enim prope est.*
>
> [1:2–3]

If, in a very insufficient and scarcely even preliminary way, I draw your attention to the narrative sending [*envoi*], the interlacing of voices and *envois* in the dictated or addressed writing, I do so because, in the hypothesis or the program of an intractable demystification of the apocalyptic tone, in the style of the *Lumières* or of an *Aufklärung* of the twentieth century, and if one wanted to unmask the ruses, traps, trickeries, seductions, machines of war and pleasure, in short, all the interests of the apocalyptic tone today, it would be necessary to begin by respecting this differential multiplication [*démultiplication*] of voices and tones that perhaps divides them beyond a distinct and calculable plurality. One does not know (for it is no longer of the order of knowing) to whom the apocalyptic sending returns; it leaps [*saute*] from one place of emission to the other (and a place is always determined *starting from* the presumed emission); it goes from one destination, one name, and one tone to the other; it always refers [*renvoie*] to the name and to the tone of the other that is there but as having been there and before yet coming, no longer being or not yet there in the present of the *récit*.

And there is no certainty that man is the exchange [*le central*] of these telephone lines or the terminal of this endless computer. No longer is one very sure who loans its voice and its tone to the other in the Apocalypse; no longer is one very sure who addresses what to whom. But by a catastrophic reversal here more necessary than ever, one can just as well think this: as soon as one no longer knows who speaks or who writes, the text becomes apocalyptic. And if the *envois* always refer [*renvoient*] to other *envois* without decidable destination, the destination remaining to come, then isn't this completely angelic structure, that of the Johannine apocalypse, isn't it also the structure of every scene of writing in general? This is one of the suggestions I wanted to submit for your discussion: wouldn't the apocalyptic be a transcendental condition of all discourse, of all experience even, of every mark or every trace? And the genre of writings called "apocalyptic" in the strict sense, then, would be only an example, an *exemplary* revelation of this transcendental structure. In that case, if the apocalypse reveals, it is first of all the revelation of the apocalypse, the self-presentation of the apocalyptic structure of language, of writing, of the experience of presence, in other words, of the text or of the mark in general: *that is, of the divisible* envoi *for which there is no self-presentation nor assured destination.*

But let's leave this, there is an apocalyptic *pli* [fold, envelope, letter, habit, message] here. Not only a *pli* as *envoi*, a *pli* inducing a tonal change [*changement*] and an immediate tonal duplicity in every apocalyptic voice. Not only a fold in the signifier "apocalyptic" that designates at times the content of the *récit* or of what is announced, namely, the end-of-the-world catastrophes and cataclysms, the upheavals, the thunderbolts and earthquakes, the fire, the blood, the mountain of fire and the sea of blood, the afflictions, the smoke, the sulphur, the burning, the multiplicity of tongues and kings, the beast, the sorcerers, Satan, the great whore of the Apocalypse, and so on; and at other times, it designates the announcement itself and no longer what is announced, the discourse revealing the to-come or even the end of the world rather than what it says, the truth of the revelation rather than the revealed truth.

But I am thinking of another *pli* we are also in, in the light of today: everything that can now inspire a de-mystifying desire regarding the apocalyptic tone, namely, a desire for light, for lucid vigilance, for the elucidating vigil, for truth—all that is already found on the way, and I shall say in apocalyptic transfer(ence), it is already a citation or a recitation of John or of what already programmed John's *envois*, when, for example, he writes, for a messenger, under the dictate of the great voice come from behind his back and extended like a shofar, like a ram's horn:

> To the messenger of the community in Ephesus, write:
> "He says this,
> he who seizes the seven stars in his right hand,
> he who walks amid the seven gold lamps.
>
> 'I know your works, your toil,
> your endurance:
> you cannot endure the wicked.
>
> You have tested those who call themselves envoys and
> are not (*tous legontas eautous apostolous kai ouk eisin, qui se dicunt apostolos esse, et non sunt*),
> you find them liars.
>
> . . .
> But I have this against you:
> your first love, you have left it.'"
>
> (2:1–2, 4)

And the *envois* multiply, then the seven messengers come, up to the seventh, after which

> The temple of Elohim opens to the sky.
> The coffer of his pact appears in his temple.
> There come lightning flashes, voices, thunders,
> an earthquake, great hail.
>
> A great sign (*sēmeion mega*) appears in the sky:
> a woman enveloped in sun,
> the moon under her feet,
> and on her head a crown of twelve stars.
>
> (11:19–12:1)

So we, *Aufklärer* of modern times, we continue to denounce the impostor apostles, the "so-called envoys" not sent [*envoyés*] by anyone, the liars and unfaithful ones, the turgidity and the pomposity of all those charged with a historic mission of whom nothing has been requested and who have been charged with nothing. Shall we thus continue in the best apocalyptic tradition to denounce false apocalypses?

Since the habit [*pli*] has already been acquired, I am not going to multiply the examples; the end approaches, but the apocalypse is long-lived. The question remains and comes back: what can be the limits of a demystification?

No doubt one can think—I do—that this demystification must be led as far as possible, and the task is not modest. It is interminable, because no one can exhaust the overdeterminations and the indeterminations of the apocalyptic strategems. And above all because the ethico-political motif or motivation of these strategems is never reducible to some simple. I recall thus that their rhetoric, for example, is not only destined to mislead the people rather than the powerful in order to arrive at retrograde, backward-looking, conservative ends. Nothing is less conservative than the apocalyptic genre. And as it is an apocalyptic, apocryphal, masked, coded *genre*, it can use the detour to mislead another vigilance, that of censorship. We know that apocalyptic writings increased the moment State censorship was very strong in the Roman Empire, and precisely to catch the censorship unawares. Now this possibility can be extended to all censorships, and not only to the political, and in politics to the official. Even if we remained with political censorship and were alert enough to know that it is practiced not only starting from specialized State lairs [*officines*], but everywhere, like a thousand-eyed Argus, in a majority, in an opposition, in a virtual majority, with respect to everything that does not let itself be centered [*cadrer*] by the logic of the current political discourse and of the conceptual oppositions legitimated by the contract between the legitimate adversaries, well then we would perhaps think that apocalyptic discourse can also get round censorship thanks to its genre and its cryptic ruses. By its very tone, the mixing of voices, genres, and codes, apocalyptic discourse can also, in dislocating [*détraquant*] destinations, dismantle the dominant contract or concordat. It is a challenge to the established receivability [*la recevabilité*] of messages and to the policing of destination, in short to the postal police or the monopoly of posts. Conversely, we could even say that every discord or every tonal disorder, everything that detones and becomes inadmissible [*irrecevable*] in general collocution, everything that is no longer identifiable starting from established codes, from both sides of a front, will necessarily pass for mystagogic, obscurantistic, and apocalyptic. It will be made to pass for such.

If we now inquire about another limit of demystification, a limit (perhaps) more essential that would (perhaps) distinguish a deconstruction from a simple progressive demystification in the style of the Enlightenment, I would be tempted by another bearing [*démarche*]. For finally, to demystify the seductive or agogic maneuver is fine and necessary, but must we not first ask ourselves with a view to what, to what end it [*ça*] seduces, uses trickery, misleads, maneuvers? About this other bearing, I am going to say a very quick word, in order to conclude and try to respond, if possible, to a request. Several times I have been asked (and that is why I shall allow myself a brief galatic ostentation of certain of my writings) why (with a view to what, to what ends, and so on) I had or had *taken on* an apocalyptic tone and put forward apocalyptic themes. That is how they have often been qualified, sometimes with suspicion, and above all, I have noticed, in the United States where people are always more sensitive to phenomena of prophetism, messianism, eschatology, and apocalypse-here-now. That I have multiplied the distinctions between closure and end, that I was aware of speaking of discourses *on* the end rather than announcing the end, that

I intended to analyze a genre rather than practice it, and even when I would practice it, to do so with that ironic genre clause I tried to show never belonged to the genre itself; nevertheless, for the reasons I gave a few minutes ago, all language on apocalypse is also apocalyptic and cannot be excluded from its object. Then I also asked myself why, to what ends, with a view to what, the Apocalypse itself, I mean the historic writings thus named and first the one signed by John of Patmos, had little by little settled in, above all for the last six or seven years, as a theme, a concern, a fascination, an explicit reference, and the horizon for me of work or a task, although I know these rich and secret texts very badly. This was first the case in *Glas*, whose columns are constantly shaken by apocalyptic shocks or laughs on the subject of apocalypse and which in a certain moment (196) mixes the remains of genres and of John, the John of the Gospel, of the Apocalypse, and of Genet. We see there: "The Gospel and the Apocalypse, violently selected, fragmented, redistributed, with blanks, shifts of accent, lines skipped or moved out of place, as if they reached us over a broken-down teletype, a wiretap [*table d'écoute*] in an overloaded telephone exchange." And a long sequence jumbling the citations comes to an end thus:

> "And I, John, I have heard and seen all these things." As his name indicates: the apocalyptic, in other words, capital unveiling, in truth lays bare self-hunger. *Funeral Rites*, you recall, on the same page: "Jean was taken away from me. . . . Jean needed a compensation. . . . the . . . revelation of my friendship for Jean. . . . I was hungry for Jean." That [*Ça*] is called a colossal compensation. The absolute phantasm as an absolute self-having [*s'avoir absolu*] in its most mournful glory: to engulf (one)self in order to be close-by-(one)self, to make (one)self a mouthful [*bouchée*], to be(come) (in a word, band (erect)) one's own proper bit [*mors*]. [198]

That was finally, as I said a few minutes ago, the case with *The Post Card*, where the allusions increase to the Apocalypse and to its arithmosophy, where everything speculates on figures and notably seven, the "written 7," the angels, "my angel," messengers and postmen [*facteurs*], prediction, the announcement of the news, the holocaustic "burning," and all the phenomena of *Verstimmung,* of change of tone, of mixing genres, of *destinerrance,* if I can say that, or of *clandestination,* so many signs of more or less bastard apocalyptic filiation. But it is not this thematic or tonal network that I wanted, in concluding, to stress. For want of time, I shall limit myself to the word, if it is a word, and to the motif "Come" that occupies other texts written in the meantime, in particular "Pas,"[19] "Living On,"[20] and "At This Very Moment in This Work Here I Am,"[21] three texts dedicated, we can say, to Blanchot and to Levinas. I was not immediately aware of the citational resonance of this "Come," or at least that its citation (for the drama of its citationality was what mattered to me at the outset, its repetitive structure and what, even in a tone, must be able to be repeated, thus mimicked, indeed "synthesized") was also a reference to John's Apocalypse. I was not thinking of this when I wrote "Pas," but I did know it at the time of the other two texts. And I noted it. "Come," *erkhou, veni, viens,* this appeal resounds in the heart of the vision, in the "I see" following Christ's dictation (starting from chapter 4) when it is said:

> I see in the right hand of him who is sitting on the throne
> a volume written on the inside and out,
> sealed with seals: seven.
>
> I see a messenger, strong.
> He cries in a great voice:
> "Who is worthy to open the volume,
> and break its seals?"
>
> No one can,
> in heaven, on earth, or under the earth,
> open the volume or look at it.
>
> [5:1–3]

And each time the Lamb opens one of the seven seals, one of the four living says, "'Come,'" and it is the continuation of the Horsemen of the Apocalypse. (In the "Envois" of *The Post Card,* one or the other often says: they will believe that we are two, or that I am alone, or that we are three, or that we are four; and it is not certain that they are wrong; but everything happens as if the hypothesis could not go beyond four; in any case that is the fiction.) Farther on, I mean in John's Apocalypse, in chapter 17, one of the seven messengers with the seven cups says, "'Come. I shall show you the judgment / of the great whore . . .'" [17:1]. It is a question of Babel. And in 21, "'Come! I shall show you / the bride, the wife of the Lamb . . .'" [21:9]. And above all at the end of ends, "Come" launches into or echoes itself in an exchange of calls and responses that is precisely no longer an exchange. The voices, the places, the routes of "Come" traverse the partition [*paroi*] of a song, a volume of citational and recitative echoes, as if it [*ça*] began by responding. And in this traversal or this transfer(ence), the voices find their spacing, the space of their movement, but they nullify it with one stroke [*d'un trait*]; they no longer give it time.

There is a kind of general narrator there: at the moment of the signature, he will call himself the witness (*marturōn, testimonium*). There is the angelic messenger there whose *envoi* he reports. There is John there who begins to speak again and says that presently he is prostrating himself before the messenger who speaks to him:

> He tells me:
> "Do not seal the words of the inspiration of this volume:
> yes, the time is near."
>
> [22:10]

*Double bind* of an order John could only disobey in order to obey. Then Jesus speaks again, naturally in this mode reported live [*ce mode rapporté en direct*] that Plato called mimetic or apocryphal, and the play of quotation marks in the translation poses all the problems you can imagine. Each time we know that so-and-so speaks because he introduces himself: I, so-and-so; but he does this in the text written by the witness or the general narrator who is always a party to it. Here it is, and it is the end:

> "I, Yéshoua', I have sent my messenger
> to testify this to you about the communities.
> I am the scion and the seed of Dawid,
> the shining star of the morning."
>
> [22:16]

Close quote. The text of the witness resumes:

> The breath and the bride (*numphē, sponsa,* the promised)
> say [together]: "Come."
> Let the hearer say: "Come."
> Let the thirsty come,
> let the volunteer take the water of life, freely.
> I myself testify to every hearer
> of the words of the inspiration of this volume:
> if anyone adds to them,
> Elohim will add to him the afflictions described in this volume.
> If anyone takes away from the words
> of the volume of this inspiration,
> Elohim will take away his share of the tree of life,
> outside the city of the sanctuary described in this volume.
>
> The witness to these things says: "Yes, I come quickly."
> Amen.
> Come, Adôn Yéshoua'.
> Dilection of the Adôn Yéshoua' to all . . .
>
> [22:17–20]

The event of this "Come" precedes and calls the event. It would be that starting from which there is any event, the coming, the to-come of the event that cannot be thought under the given category of event. "Come" appeared to me to appeal to the "place" (but here the word *place* becomes too enigmatic), let us say to the place, the time, and to the advent of what in the apocalyptic in general no longer lets itself be contained simply by philosophy, metaphysics, onto-eschato-theology, and by all the readings they have proposed of the apocalyptic. I cannot reconstitute what I have attempted in this respect in a milieu of resonances, responses, citations referred, referring to texts of Blanchot, Levinas, Heidegger, or others such as one could hazard to do today with the latest book of Marguerite Duras, *The Seated Man in the Passage.*[22] What I had then tried to expose to an analysis that would be, among other things, a spectrography of tone and of change of tone could not by definition keep itself at the disposal or to the measure of philosophical, pedagogical, or teaching demonstration. First of all, because "Come," opening the scene, could not become an object, a theme, a representation, or indeed a citation in the current sense, and subsumable under a category, even were it that of coming or event. For the same reason, that bends itself difficultly to the rhetoric required by the present scene. Nonetheless I am trying to extract from this, at the risk of essentially deforming it, the demonstrative function in terms of philosophical discourse.

Accelerating the movement, I shall then say this. Come from the other already as a response, and a citation without past present, "Come" tolerates no metalinguistic citation, even when it is, "Come" itself, a narrative [*un récit*], already, a recitative and a song whose singularity remains at once absolute and absolutely divisible. "Come" no more lets itself be arraigned [*arraisonner*] by an onto-theo-eschatology than by a logic of the event, however new they may be and whatever politics they announce. In this *affirmative* tone, "Come" marks in itself, in oneself, neither a desire nor an order, neither a prayer nor a request [*demande*]. More precisely, the grammatical, linguistic, or semantic categories from which the "Come" would thus be determined are traversed by the "Come." This "Come," I do not know what *it is*, not because I yield to obscurantism, but because the question "what is" belongs to a space (ontology, and from it the knowledge of grammar, linguistics, semantics, and so on) opened by a "come" come from the other. Between all the "come" s, the difference is not grammatical, linguistic, semantic, pragmatic—and which permits saying: it's an imperative, it's a jussive modality, it's a performative of such and such a type, and so on—the difference is tonal. And I do not know whether a tonal difference finally lends itself to all these questions. Try to say "come"—it can be said in every tone, and you'll see, you'll hear, the other will hear first—perhaps or not. It is the gesture in speaking [*parole*], that gesture that does not let itself be recovered [*reprendre*] by the analysis—linguistic, semantic, or rhetorical—of speaking.

Come [*Viens*] beyond being—that, engaging perhaps in the place in which *Ereignis* (no longer can this be translated by event) and *Enteignis* unfold the movement of propriation, comes from beyond being and calls beyond being. If "Come" does not try to lead, if it no doubt is an-agogic, it can always be led back higher than itself, anagogically, toward conductive violence, toward authoritarian "duction." This risk is ineluctable; it threatens the tone as its double. And even in the confession of seduction: in saying in a certain tone, "I am in the act of seducing you," I do not suspend, I can even increase, the seductive power. Perhaps Heidegger would not have liked this apparently personal conjugation or declension of coming. But such conjugation and declension are not personal, subjective, or egological. "Come" cannot come from a voice or at least not from a tone signifying "I" or "self," a so-and-so (male or female) in my "determination," my *Bestimmung:* vocation to the destination *myself.* "Come" does not address itself to an identity determinable in advance. It is a drift [*une dérive*] underivable from the identity of a determination. "Come" is *only* derivable, absolutely derivable, but only from the other, from nothing that may be an origin or a verifiable, decidable, presentable, appropriable identity, from nothing not already derivable and arrivable without *rive* [bank, shore].

Perhaps you will be tempted to call this disaster, catastrophe, apocalypse. Now here, precisely, is announced—as promise or threat—an apocalypse without apocalypse, an apocalypse without vision, without truth, without revelation, *envois* (for the "come" is plural in itself, in oneself), addresses without message and without destination, without sender or decidable addressee, without last judgment, without any other eschatology than the tone of the "Come," its very differance, an apocalypse beyond good and evil. "Come" does not announce this or that apocalypse: already it resounds with a certain tone; it is in itself the apocalypse of apocalypse; *Come* is apocalyptic.

Our *apocalypse now:* there would be no more chance, save chance itself, for a thought of good and evil whose announcement would come to *gather* itself in order to be with itself in a revelatory speaking; (no) more chance, unless a chance, the unique, chance itself, for a collection of truth, a *legein* of *alētheia* that would no longer be a legendary unveiling; and (no) more chance even for such a gathering of gift, *envoi,* destiny (*Schicken, Geschick*), for the destination of a "come" whose promise at least would be assured of its own proper event.

But then what is someone doing who says to you: I tell you this, I have come to tell you this, there is not, there has never been, there will not be apocalypse, "the apocalypse is disappointing"? There is the apocalypse *without* apocalypse.

The word *sans, without,* I pronounce here in the so necessary syntax of Blanchot, who often says *X without X.* The *without* marks an internal and external catastrophe of the apocalypse, an overturning of sense that does not merge with the catastrophe announced or described in the apocalyptic writings without however being foreign to them. Here the catastrophe would perhaps be *of* the apocalypse itself, its fold [*pli*] and its end, a closure without end, an end without end.

But what reading, what history of reading, what philology, what hermeneutic competence authorizes one to say that this very thing, this catastrophe *of* the apocalypse, is not the catastrophe described, in its movement and its very course [*trajet*], in its outline [*tracé*], by *this* or *that* apocalyptic writing? For example, the one from Patmos that would then be doomed to going out of itself in this aleatory errance?

And what if this outside of apocalypse were *inside* the apocalypse? What if it were the apocalypse itself, what precisely breaks in [*fait effraction*] in the "Come"? What is "inside" and what is "outside" a text, of *this* text, both inside and outside these volumes of which we do not know whether they are open or closed?

Of this volume written, you remember, "on the inside and out," it is said at the very end: do not seal this; "'Do not seal the words of the inspiration of this volume. . . .'"

Do not seal, that is to say, do not close, but also do not sign.

The end approaches, now it's too late to tell the truth about the apocalypse. But what are you doing, all of you will still insist, to what ends do you want to come when you come to tell us, here now, let's go, come, the apocalypse, it's finished, I tell you this, that's what's happening.

## Notes

All notes except those marked *JD* are those of the translator.

1. Earlier versions of this translation appeared in the journals *Semeia* and *The Oxford Literary Review.* The text in *Semeia* is a translation of the lecture given the last full day of the conference at Cerisy-la-Salle, France, on the work of Jacques Derrida, or rather, starting from his work: "'Les fins de l'homme' (A partir du travail de

Jacques Derrida)," and published in the proceedings of the conference, *Les fins de l'homme* (Paris: Galilée, 1981). The one in *The Oxford Literary Review* is a translation of the revised version published under separate cover by Editions Galilée, 1983. The present text is a "final" revision of the version in *The Oxford Literary Review* and incorporates Peter Fenves's translation of the Kant text (see note 4 below) and other translations of Derrida and Blanchot now available.

Convened from 23 July to 2 August 1980, the conference where Derrida's lecture was first delivered consisted of lectures, discussions, and seminars on Derrida's effects within diverse perspectives and disciplines. The format of the ten-day gathering explains the references in the text to the organizers, seminars, and some participants: Philippe Lacoue-Labarthe, Jean-Luc Nancy, and Jean Ricardou, as well as to questions left open for discussion following the presentation.

Derrida refers in this text to the translations of André Chouraqui of the Apocalypse of John and other biblical texts. I have translated the biblical texts cited from the French of Chouraqui. I have also consulted *The Four Gospels and the Revelation*, trans. Richmond Lattimore (New York: Farrar, 1962, 1979), for the translations of the Apocalypse. For the Greek text I have used the U. B. S. Greek New Testament, 2nd edition; for the Latin, Wordsworth's and White's edition of *Novum Testamentum Latine* according to the edition of St. Jerome.

I would like to thank Geoff Bennington for his scrupulous reading of and his suggestions and corrections for improvement of the version that appeared in *The Oxford Literary Review*. And once again I am indebted to Jacques Derrida for his gracious help and patience.

2. *JD:* Translation from the Greek, of course, but with some conditions I must specify here, at once because they will be in question in the course of the discussion and because what is at stake could be named the *appropriation* of apocalypse: that is also the theme of this exposition. In sum, Chouraqui's very singular attempt consists, for John's Apocalypse as well as for the New Testament generally, in reconstituting a new Hebrew original, under the Greek text at our disposal, and *in acting as if* he were translating that *phantom* original text about which he supposes that, linguistically and culturally, it had already had to let itself be translated (if that can be said in a largely metaphorical sense) in the so-called original Greek version. "The translation I publish, nourished by the contribution of the traditional versions, has the calling to search under the Greek text for its historical context and its Semitic substratum. Such a course [*démarche*] is possible to-

day . . ." (*Un pacte neuf: Lettres, Contemplation de Yohanân,* trans. André Chouraqui [Paris: Desclée de Brouwer, 1977]: 9). According to Chouraqui, it passes through an "Aramaic or Hebrew retroversion" of the Greek text taken for a "filter." So the historic translations of the New Testament into Aramaic or Hebrew will have played here an indispensable but only a mediating role.

> [E]ven if the text is expressed in Greek and, for what is from Jesus, if it is based on an Aramaic or a Hebrew (Mishnaic, rabbinic, or Qumranic) whose traces have disappeared, the thought of the Evangelists and the Apostles has as ultimate terms of references the word of YHWH, that is, for all of them, the Bible. It is the Bible that is recovered in analyzing the Greek text, even if one must preliminarily pass through an Aramaic filter or through that of the translation of the Seventy. . . .
>
> . . . Starting from the Greek text, knowing the techniques of the translations from the Hebrew into Greek, and the Hebrew resonances of the Koine, I have tried with each word, with each verse, to touch the Semitic ground in order then to return to the Greek that it was necessary to recover, enriched by a new substance, before passing to the French. [*Un pacte neuf* 11–12]

Such is the project; it gives as its reference a *double authority* and invokes in turn the "quasi-unanimity of the exegetes" or "the great ecumenical current," the "ecumenism of sources" [*Un pacte neuf* 11, 15, 16]. For multiple reasons I shall not discuss directly the authority of these authorities. But when the matter concerns language, text, event, and destination, etc., the questions I shall propose today could not have been unfolded if the foundation of such authorities had to be kept under cover in the unquestionable. A secondary consequence of this precaution: it is not as to an *authorized* translation that I shall often refer to that of André Chouraqui.

3. *La Bible: Il crie . . .*, trans. André Chouraqui (Paris: Desclée de Brouwer, 1974).

4. Immanuel Kant, *Von einem neuerdings erhobenen vornehmen Ton in der Philosophie,* in vol. 8 of *Gesammelte Schriften,* ed. Royal Prussian Academy of Sciences (Berlin: Gruyter, 1923): 387–406—hereafter *Ton; D'un ton grand seigneur adopté naguère en philosophie,* in *Première introduction à la Critique de la faculté de juger . . .*, trans. L. Guillermit (Paris: Vrin, 1975): 87–109—hereafter *D'un ton;* "On a Newly Raised Superior Tone in Philosophy," trans. Peter Fenves, in *On the Rise of Tone in Philosophy: Kant and Derrida,* ed. Peter

Fenves (Baltimore: Johns Hopkins University Press, 1992). Since the English translation indicates the Academy edition's pagination, I give those page numbers exclusively for the German and English references to Kant's text.

5. Jacques Derrida, *Glas*, trans. John P. Leavey, Jr., and Richard Rand (Lincoln: University of Nebraska Press, 1986).

6. Jacques Derrida, *The Post Card: From Socrates to Freud and Beyond*, trans. Alan Bass (Chicago: University of Chicago Press, 1987).

7. Immanuel Kant, *The Conflict of the Faculties*, trans. Mary J. Gregor (New York: Abaris, 1979).

8. See Jacques Derrida, "Scribble (writing-power)," trans. Cary Plotkin, *Yale French Studies* 58 (1979): 116–47.

9. *JD:* I am thinking of that bust of Kant "in the Greek style" (Emanuel Bardou, 1798) reproduced on a postcard in a Berlin museum.

10. Immanuel Kant, *Religion Within the Limits of Reason Alone*, tr. Theodore M. Greene and Hoyt H. Hudson (New York: Harper Torchbooks, 1960): 125; vol. 6 of *Gesammelte Schriften*, ed. Prussian Royal Academy of Sciences (Berlin: Reimer, 1914): 134.

11. See Jacques Derrida, *Spurs: Nietzsche's Styles / Eperons: Les styles de Nietzsche*, trans. Barbara Harlow (Chicago: University of Chicago Press, 1979).

12. Jacques Derrida, "Economimesis," trans. Richard Klein, *Diacritics* 11:2 (Summer 1981): 3–25.

13. Sigmund Freud, "The Infantile Genital Organization: An Interpolation Into the Theory of Sexuality (1923)," in vol. 19 of *The Standard Edition of the Complete Psychological Works of Sigmund Freud*, trans. ed. James Strachey (London: Hogarth Press and the Institute of Psycho-Analysis, 1961): 145.

14. Friedrich Hölderlin and Eduard Mörike, *Selected Poems*, trans. Christopher Middleton (Chicago: University of Chicago Press, 1972): 74–75, 88–89 (modified).

15. Maurice Blanchot, *The Last Man*, trans. Lydia Davis (New York: Columbia University Press, 1987).

16. Friedrich Nietzsche, *Philosophy and Truth: Selections from Nietzsche's Notebooks of the Early 1870's*, trans. Daniel Breazeale (New Jersey: Humanities Press, 1979): 33–34 (#87); *Nachgelassene*

*Fragmente: Sommer 1872 bis Ende 1874*, 3:4 of *Nietzsche Werke: Kritische Gesamtausgabe*, ed. Giorgio Colli and Mazzino Montinari (Berlin: Gruyter, 1978): 48–49.

17. Maurice Blanchot, *The Madness of the Day*, trans. Lydia Davis (Barrytown, NY: Station Hill, 1981): 10, 24.

18. *JD:* The stake here, this goes without saying, can be very grave, above all in an eschatological or apocalyptic text. Chouraqui has clearly assumed his responsibility as translator; here one can only leave it to him:

> The most constant liberty I have taken with the Greek text concerns the verb tenses. Already Joüon had noted this: "The attention given to the Aramaic substratum is particularly useful for avoiding too mechanical a translation of the Greek tenses."
>
> The Greek verb conceives time above all as a function of a past, a present, and a future; the Hebrew or the Aramaic, on the contrary, instead of specifying the time of an action, describes its state under two modes: the finished and the unfinished. As Pedersen has seen so well, the Hebrew verb is essentially *intemporal*, that is, *omnitemporal*.
>
> I have tried, between two notions of time irreducible to each other, to resort most often to the present, which in contemporary French usage is a very supple, very ample, very evocative tense, whether in its normal use or in the form of the historic present or the prophetic present. ("Une nouvelle traduction du Nouveau Testament," Preface to *Un pacte neuf* 13)

19. Jacques Derrida, "Pas," in *Parages* (Paris: Galilée, 1986): 19–116.

20. Jacques Derrida, "Living On," trans. James Hulbert, in *Deconstruction and Criticism* (New York: Seabury, 1979): 75–176; "Survivre," in *Parages:* 117–218.

21. Jacques Derrida, "At This Very Moment in This Work Here I Am," trans. Ruben Berezdivin, in *Re-Reading Levinas*, ed. Robert Bernasconi and Simon Critchley (Bloomington: Indiana University Press, 1991): 11–48.

22. Marguerite Duras, *The Seated Man in the Passage*, trans. Mary Lydon, in *Contemporary Literature* 24:2 (1983): 268–75.

THREE

# *How to Avoid Speaking: Denials*

Jacques Derrida

Translated by Ken Frieden

## *I*

Even before starting to prepare this lecture, I knew that I wished to speak of the "trace" in its relationship to what one calls, sometimes erroneously, "negative theology." More precisely, I knew that I would have to do this in Jerusalem. But what does such an obligation mean here? When I say that I knew that I would have to do it even before the first word of this lecture, I already name a singular anteriority of the obligation—is an obligation before the first word possible?—which would be difficult to situate and which, perhaps, will be my theme today.

Under the very loose heading of "negative theology," as you know, one often designates a certain form of language, with its *mise en scène*, its rhetorical, grammatical, and logical modes, its demonstrative procedures—in short a textual practice attested or rather situated "in history," although it does sometimes exceed the predicates that constitute this or that concept of history. Is there *one* negative theology, *the* negative theology? In any case, the unity of its legacy (*archive*)

---

*Editors' note:* The French version of this essay, "Comment ne pas parler: Dénégations," has appeared in Jacques Derrida, *Psyché: Inventions de l'autre* (Paris: Galilée, 1987), pp. 535–95.

is difficult to delimit. One might try to organize it around certain attempts that are considered exemplary or explicit, such as the *Divine Names* of Dionysius the Areopagite (Pseudo-Dionysius). But as we shall see, for essential reasons one is never certain of being able to attribute to anyone a project of negative theology as such.[1] Before Dionysius, one may search within a certain Platonic or Neoplatonic tradition; after him up to modernity in Wittgenstein and many others. In a less rigorous or less informed manner, then, "negative theology" has come to designate a certain typical attitude toward language, and within it, in the act of definition or attribution, an attitude toward semantic or conceptual determination. Suppose, by a provisional hypothesis, that negative theology consists of considering that every predicative language is inadequate to the essence, in truth to the hyperessentiality (the being beyond Being) of God; consequently, only a negative ("apophatic") attribution can claim to approach God, and to prepare us for a silent intuition of God. By a more or less tenable analogy, one would thus recognize some traits, the family resemblance of negative theology, in every discourse that seems to return in a regular and insistent manner to this rhetoric of negative determination, endlessly multiplying the defenses and the apophatic warnings: this, which is called *X* (for example, text, writing, the trace, differance, the hymen, the supplement, the pharmakon, the parergon, etc.) "is" neither this nor that, neither sensible nor intelligible, neither positive nor negative, neither inside nor outside, neither superior nor inferior, neither active nor passive, neither present nor absent, not even neutral, not even subject to a dialectic with a third moment, without any possible sublation ("Aufhebung"). Despite appearances, then, this *X* is neither a concept nor even a name; it does *lend itself* to a series of names, but calls for another syntax, and exceeds even the order and the structure of predicative discourse. It "is" not and does not say what "is." It is written completely otherwise.

I have deliberately chosen examples that are close and, one might think, familiar to me. For two reasons. On the one hand, very early I was accused of—rather than congratulated for—resifting the procedures of negative theology in a scenario that one thinks one knows well. One would like to consider these procedures a simple rhetoric, even a rhetoric of failure—or worse, a rhetoric that renounces knowledge, conceptual determination, and analysis: for those who have nothing to say or don't want to know anything, it is always easy to mimic the technique of negative theology. Indeed, this necessarily does include an apparatus of methodological rules. In a moment I will try to show how negative theology at least claims not to be assimilable to a technique that is subject to simulation or parody, to mechanical repetition. It would escape from this by means of the *prayer* that precedes apophatic utterances, and by the address to the other, to you, in a moment that is not only the preamble or the methodological threshold of the experience. Naturally, the prayer, invocation, and apostrophe can also be mimicked, and even give way, as if despite themselves, to repetitive technique. In conclusion, I will come back to this risk which, fortunately *and* unfortunately, is also a piece of luck. But if the risk is inevitable, the accusation it incurs need not be limited to the apophatic moment of negative theology. It may be extended to all language, and even to all manifestation in general. This risk is inscribed in the structure of the mark.

There is also an automatic, ritualistic, and "doxic" exercise of the suspicion brought against everything that resembles negative theology. It has interested me for a long time. Its matrix includes at least three types of objections:

a) You prefer to negate; you affirm nothing; you are fundamentally a nihilist, or even an obscurantist; neither knowledge nor even theology will progress in this way. Not to mention atheism, of which one has been able to say in an equally trivial fashion that it is the truth of negative theology.

b) You abuse a simple technique; it suffices to repeat: "X is no more this, than that," "X seems to exceed all discourse or predication," and so on. This comes back to speaking for nothing. You speak only for the sake of speaking, in order to experience speech. Or, more seriously, you speak thus with an eye to writing, since what you write then does not even merit being said. This second critique already appears more interesting and more lucid than the first: to speak for the sake of speaking, to experience what happens to speech through speech *itself*, in the trace of a sort of quasi-tautology, is not entirely to speak in vain and to say nothing. It is perhaps to experience a possibility of speech which the objector himself must presuppose at the moment when he addresses his criticism. To speak for *nothing* is not: not to speak. Above all, it is not to speak to no one.

c) This criticism does not, then, threaten the essential possibility of the address or the apostrophe. It encompasses still a third possibility, less evident but no doubt more interesting. Here the suspicion takes a form that can reverse the process of the accusation: once the apophatic discourse is analyzed in its logical-grammatical form, if it is not merely sterile, repetitive, obscurantist, mechanical, it perhaps leads us to consider the becoming-theological of all discourse. From the moment a proposition takes a negative form, the negativity that manifests itself need only be pushed to the limit, and it at least resembles an apophatic theology. Every time I say: X is neither this nor that, neither the contrary of this nor of that, neither the simple neutralization of this nor of that with which it *has nothing in common,* being absolutely heterogeneous to or incommensurable with them, I would start to speak of God, under this name or another. God's name would then be the hyperbolic effect of that negativity or all negativity that is consistent in its discourse. God's name would suit everything that may not be broached, approached, or designated, except in an indirect and negative manner. Every negative sentence would already be haunted by God or by the name of God, the distinction between God and God's name opening up the very space of this enigma. If there is a work of negativity in discourse and predication, it will produce divinity. It would then suffice to change a sign (or rather to show, something easy and classical enough, that this inversion has *always already* taken place, that it is the essential movement of thought) in order to say that divinity is not produced but productive. Infinitely productive, Hegel would say, for example. God would be not merely the end, but the origin of this work of the negative. Not only would atheism not be the truth of negative theology; rather, God would be the truth of all negativity. One would thus arrive at a kind of proof of God—not a proof of the *existence* of God, but a proof of God *by His effects,* or more precisely a proof of what one calls God, or of the name of God, by effects without cause, by the *without cause.* The import of this word *without* (*sans*) will concern us in a moment. In the absolutely singular logic of this proof, "God" would name *that without which* one would not know how to account for any negativity: grammatical or logical negation, illness, evil, and finally neurosis which, far from permitting psychoanalysis to reduce religion to a symptom, would obligate it to recognize in the symptom the negative manifestation to God. Without saying that there must be at least as much "reality" in the cause as in the effect, and that the "existence" of God has no need of any proof other than the religious symptomatics, one would see on the contrary—in the negation or suspension of the predicate, even of the thesis of "existence"—the first mark of respect for a divine cause which does not even need to "be." And those who would like to consider "deconstruction" a symptom of modern or postmodern nihilism could indeed, if they wished, recognize in it the last testimony—not to say the martyrdom—of faith in the present *fin de siècle.* This reading will always be possible. Who could prohibit it? In the name of what? But what has happened, so that what is thus permitted is never necessary as such? In order that it be thus, what must the writing of this deconstruction be, writing according to this deconstruction?

That is a first reason. But I chose examples that are close to me for a second reason. I also wanted to say a few words about a quite long-standing wish: to broach—directly and in itself—the web of questions that one formulates prematurely under the heading of "negative theology." Until now, confronted by the question or by the objection, my response has always been brief, elliptical, and dilatory.[2] Yet it seems to me already articulated in two stages.

1. No, what I write is not "negative theology." First of all, *in the measure* to which this belongs to the predicative or judicative space of discourse, to its strictly propositional form, and privileges not only the indestructible unity of the word but also the authority of the name—such axioms as a "deconstruction" must start by reconsidering (which I have tried to do since the first part of *Of Grammatology*). Next, in the measure to which "negative theology" seems to reserve, beyond all positive predication, beyond all negation, even beyond Being, some hyperessentiality, a being beyond Being. This is the word that Dionysius so often uses in the *Divine Names: hyperousios, -ôs, hyperousiotes.* God as being beyond Being or also God as *without* Being.[3] This seems to exceed the alternative of a theism or an atheism which would only

set itself against what one calls, sometimes ingenuously, the existence of God. Without being able to return to the syntax and semantics of the word *without* (*sans*) which I have tried to analyze elsewhere, I limit myself here to the first stage of this response. No, I would hesitate to inscribe what I put forward under the familiar heading of negative theology, precisely because of that ontological wager of hyperessentiality that one finds at work both in Dionysius and in Meister Eckhart, for example, when he writes:

> Each thing works in its being [Ein ieglich dinc würket in wesene]; nothing can work above its being [über sîn wesen]. Fire can only work in wood. God works above Being [Got würket über wesene], in space, in which He can move. He works in non-being [er würket in unwesene]. Before there was Being, God worked [ê denne wesen wære, dô worhte got]; and He brought about being when there was no Being. Unrefined masters say that God is a pure Being [ein lûter wesen]; He is as high above Being as the highest angel is above a fly. I would be speaking as wrongly in calling God a being as I would in calling the sun pale or black. God is neither this nor that [Got enist weder diz noch daz]. A master says: if anyone thinks that he has known God, even if he did know something, he did not know God. But when I said that God is not being and that He is above Being [über wesen], I have not denied Him being [ich im niht wesen abegesprochen] but, rather, I have exalted Being in Him [ich hân ez in im gehœhet].[4]

In the movement of the same paragraph, a quotation from St. Augustine recalls the simultaneously negative and hyperaffirmative meaning of *without* (*sans*): "St. Augustine says: God is wise without wisdom [wîse âne wîsheit], good without goodness [guot âne güete], powerful without power [gewaltic âne gewalt]." *Without* does not merely dissociate the singular attribution from the essential generality: wisdom as *being*-wise in general, goodness as *being*-good in general, power as *being*-powerful in general. It does not only avoid the abstraction tied to every common noun and to the being implied in every essential generality. In the same word and in the same syntax it transmutes into affirmation its purely phenomenal negativity, which ordinary language, riveted to finitude, gives us to understand in a word such as *without*, or in other analogous words. It deconstructs grammatical anthropomorphism.

To dwell a bit longer on the first stage of my response, I thought I had to forbid myself to write in the register of "negative theology," because I was aware of this movement toward hyperessentiality, beyond Being. What *differance*, the *trace*, and so on "mean"—which hence *does not mean anything*—is "before" the concept, the name, the word, "something" that would be nothing, that no longer arises from Being, from presence or from the presence of the present, nor even from absence, and even less from some hyperessentiality. Yet the onto-theological reappropriation always remains possible—and doubtless *inevitable* insofar as one speaks, precisely, in the element of logic and of onto-theological grammar. One can always say: hyperessentiality is precisely that, a supreme Being who remains incommensurate to the being of all that is, which *is* nothing, neither present nor absent, and so on. If the movement of this reappropriation appears in fact irrepressible, its ultimate failure is no less necessary. But I concede that this question remains at the heart of a thinking of differance or of the writing of writing. It remains a question, and this is why I return to it again. Following the same "logic," and I continue with the first stage of this response, my uneasiness was nevertheless also directed toward the promise of that presence given to intuition or vision. The promise of such a presence often accompanies the apophatic voyage. It is doubtless the vision of a dark light, no doubt an intuition of "more than luminous [hyperphoton] darkness,"[5] but still it is the immediacy of a presence. Leading to union with God. After the indispensable moment of prayer (of which I will speak again later), Dionysius thus exhorts Timothy to *mystika theamata:*

> This is my prayer. And you, dear Timothy, exercise yourself earnestly in mystical contemplations, abandon all sensation and all intellectual activities, all that is sensed and intelligible, all non-being and all being [panta ouk onta kai onta]; thus you will un-

> knowingly [agnôstos] be elevated, as far as possible, to the unity of that beyond Being and knowledge [tou hyper pasan ousian kai gnôsin]. By the irrepressible and absolving ecstasis [extasei] of yourself and of all, absolved from all, and going away from all, you will be purely raised up to the rays of the divine darkness beyond Being [pros ten hyperousion tou theiou]. (*MT*, ch. 1:998b–1000a)

This mystic union, this act of *un*knowing, is also "a genuine vision and a genuine knowledge [to ontôs idein kai gnôsai]" (*MT*, ch. 2:1025b). It knows unknowing itself in its truth, a truth that is not an adequation but an unveiling. Celebrating "what is beyond Being in a hyperessential mode [ton hyperousion hyperousiôs hymnesai]," this union aims to "know unveiled [aperikaluptôs; in an open, unhidden manner] this unknowing [agnosian] which conceals in every being the knowledge which one can have of this Being" (*MT*, ch. 2:1025bc). The revelation is invoked by an elevation: toward that contact or vision, that pure intuition of the ineffable, that silent union with that which remains inaccessible to speech. This ascent corresponds to a rarefaction of signs, figures, symbols—and also of fictions, as well as of myths or poetry. Dionysius treats this *economy* of signs as such. The *Symbolic Theology* is more voluble and more voluminous than the *Mystical Theology*. For it treats "metonymies of the sensible which stand for the divine [ai apo tôn aisthetôn epi ta theia metonumiai]" (*MT*, ch. 3:1033a); it describes the signification of forms (*morphai*) and figures (*skhemata*) in God; it measures its discourse against "symbols" which "demand more words than the rest, so that the *Symbolic Theology* was necessarily much more voluminous than the *Theological Sketches* and than the *Divine Names*." With the elevation beyond the sensible, one gains in "conciseness," "because what is *intelligible* presents itself in a more and more synoptic manner" (*MT*, ch. 3:1033b). But there is also something beyond this economical conciseness. By the passage beyond the intelligible itself, the *apophatikai theologai* aim toward absolute rarefaction, toward silent union with the ineffable:

> Now, however, that we are to enter the darkness beyond intellect, you will not find a brief [brakhylogian] discourse but a complete absence of discourse [alogian]

> and intelligibility [anoesian]. In affirmative theology the *logos* descends from what is above down to the last, and increases according to the measure of the descent toward an analogical multitude. But here, as we ascend from the highest to what lies beyond, the *logos* is drawn inward according to the measure of the ascent. After all ascent it will be wholly without sound and wholly united to the unspeakable [aphthegktô]. (*MT*, ch. 3:1033bc)

This economy is paradoxical. In principle, the apophatic movement of discourse would have to negatively retraverse all the stages of symbolic theology and positive predication. It would thus be coextensive with it, confined to the same quantity of discourse. In itself interminable, the apophatic movement cannot contain within itself the principle of its interruption. It can only indefinitely defer the encounter with its own limit.

Alien, heterogeneous, in any case irreducible to the intuitive *telos*—to the experience of the ineffable and of the mute vision which seems to orient all of this apophatics, including the prayer and the encomium which prepare its way—the thinking of differance would thus have little affinity, for an analogous reason, with the current interpretation of certain well-known statements of the early Wittgenstein. I recall these words often quoted from the *Tractatus*, for example, "6.522—The inexpressible, indeed, exists [Es gibt allerdings Unaussprechliches]. It *shows itself;* it is the mystical," And "7.—Concerning that about which one cannot speak, one must remain silent."

The nature of this "one must" (*"il faut"*) is significant here: it inscribes the injunction to silence into the order or the promise of a "one must speak," "one must—not avoid speaking"; or rather, "it is necessary (*il faut*) that there be a trace." No, "it is necessary that there *have been* a trace," a sentence that one must simultaneously turn toward a past *and* toward a future that are as yet unpresentable. It is (now) necessary that there *have been* a trace (in an unremembered past; because of this amnesia, the "necessity" of the trace is necessary). But also, it is necessary (from now on, it will be necessary; the "it is necessary" always also points toward the future) that in the future there will have been a trace.

But we should not be too hasty. In a moment it will be necessary to differentiate between these modalities of the "it is necessary."

2. Turning to what was often the second stage of my improvised responses: the general name of "negative theology" may conceal the confusions it causes and sometimes gives rise to simplistic interpretations. Perhaps there is within it, hidden, restless, diverse, and itself heterogeneous, a voluminous and nebulous multiplicity of potentials to which the single expression "negative theology" yet remains inadequate. In order to engage oneself seriously in this debate, I have often responded, it would be necessary to clarify this designation by considering quite dissimilar corpuses, scenes, proceedings, and languages. As I have always been fascinated by the supposed movements of negative theology (which, no doubt, are themselves never foreign to the experience of fascination in general), I objected in vain to the assimilation of the thinking of the trace or of differance to some negative theology, and my response amounted to a promise: one day I would have to stop deferring, one day I would have to try to explain myself directly on this subject, and at last speak of "negative theology" *itself*, assuming that some such thing exists.

Has the day come?

In other words, how is it possible to avoid speaking about negative theology? How can one resolve this question, and decide between its *two* meanings? 1. How is it possible to avoid speaking of it henceforth? This appears impossible. How could I remain silent on this subject? 2. How, if one speaks of it, to avoid speaking of it? How not to speak of it? How is it necessary not to speak of it? How to avoid speaking of it without rhyme or reason? What precautions must be taken to avoid errors, that is, inadequate, insufficient, simplistic assertions?

I return to my opening words. I knew, then, what I would *have to* do. I had implicitly promised that I would, one day, speak directly of negative theology. Even before speaking, I knew that I was committed to doing it. Such a situation leaves room for at least two possible interpretations. 1. Even before speech, in any case before a discursive event as such, there is necessarily a commitment or a promise. This event presupposes the open space of the promise. 2. This commitment, this word that has been given, already belongs to the time of the *parole* by which I "keep my word," or *"tiens parole,"* as one says in French. In fact, at the moment of promising to speak one day of negative theology, I already started to do it. But this is only an as yet confused hint of the structure that I would like to analyze later.

Having already promised, *as if in spite of myself,* I did not know *how* I would keep this promise. How to speak suitably of negative theology? Is there a negative theology? A single one? A regulative model for the others? Can one adapt a discourse to it? Is there some discourse that measures up to it? Is one not compelled to speak of negative theology according to the modes of negative theology, in a way that is at once impotent, exhausting, and inexhaustible? Is there ever anything other than a "negative theology" of "negative theology"?

Above all, I did not know when and where I would do it. Next year in Jerusalem! I told myself, in order to defer, perhaps indefinitely, the fulfillment of this promise. But also to let myself know—and I did indeed receive this message—that on the day when I would in fact go to Jerusalem it would no longer be possible to delay. It would be necessary to do it.

Will I do it? Am I in Jerusalem? This is a question to which one will never respond in the present tense, only in the future or in the past.[6]

Why insist on this postponement? Because it appears to me neither avoidable nor insignificant. One can never decide whether deferring, as such, brings about precisely that which it defers and alters (*diffère*). It is not certain that I am keeping my promise today; nor is it certain that in further delaying I have not, nevertheless, already kept it.

In other words, am I in Jerusalem or elsewhere, very far from the Holy City? Under what conditions does one find oneself in Jerusalem? Is it enough to be there physically, as one says, and to live in places that carry this name, as I am now doing? What is it to live in Jerusalem? This is not easy to decide. Allow me to cite Meister Eckhart again. Like that of Dionysius, his work sometimes resembles an endless meditation on the sense and symbolism of the Holy City: a logic, a rhetoric, a topology, and a tropology of Jerusalem. Here is an example among many others:

> Yesterday I sat in a place where I said something [dâ sprach ich ein wort] that sounds incredible—I said

> that Jerusalem is as near to my soul as the place where I am now [mîner sele als nâhe als diu stat, dâ ich nû stân]. In truth, that which is a thousand miles beyond Jerusalem is as near to my soul as my own body; I am as sure of this as of being a man.[7]

I will speak of a promise, then, but also within the promise. The experience of negative theology perhaps holds to a promise, that of the other, which I must keep because it commits me to speak where negativity ought to absolutely rarefy discourse. Indeed, why should I speak *with an eye* to explaining, teaching, leading—on the paths of a psychagogy or of a pedagogy—toward silence, toward union with the ineffable, mute vision? Why can't I avoid speaking, unless it is because a promise has committed me even before I begin the briefest speech? If I therefore speak of the promise, I will not be able to keep any metalinguistic distance in regard to it. Discourse on the promise is already a promise: in the promise. I will thus not speak of this or that promise, but of that which, as necessary as it is impossible, inscribes us by its trace in language—before language. From the moment I open my mouth, I have already promised; or rather, and sooner, the promise has seized the *I* which promises to speak to the other, to say something, at the extreme limit to affirm or to confirm by speech at least this: that it is necessary to be silent; and to be silent concerning that about which one cannot speak. One could have known as much beforehand. This promise is older than I am. Here is something that appears impossible, the theoreticians of speech acts would say: like every genuine performative, a promise must be made in the present, in the first person (in the singular or in the plural). It must be made by one who is capable of saying *I* or *we*, here and now, for example in Jerusalem, "the place where I am now" and where I can therefore be held responsible for this speech act.

The promise of which I shall speak will have always escaped this demand of presence. It is older than I am or than we are. In fact, it renders possible every present discourse on presence. Even if I decide to be silent, even if I decide to promise nothing, not to commit myself to saying something that would confirm once again the destination *of* speech, and the destination *toward* speech, this silence yet remains a modality of speech: a memory of promise and a promise of memory.

I knew, then, that I could not avoid speaking of negative theology. But how and under what heading would I do it? One day, at Yale, I received a telephone message:[8] it was necessary for me to give a title on the spot. In a few minutes I had to improvise, which I first did in my language: "Comment ne pas dire . . .?" The use of the French word *dire* permits a certain suspension. "Comment ne pas dire?" can mean, in a manner that is both transitive and intransitive, how to be silent, how not to speak in general, how to avoid speaking? But it can also mean: how, in speaking, not to say this or that, in this or that manner? In other words: how, in saying and speaking, to avoid this or that discursive, logical, rhetorical mode? How to avoid an inexact, erroneous, aberrant, improper form? How to avoid such a predicate, and even predication itself? For example: how to avoid a negative form, or how not to be negative? Finally, how to say something? Which comes back to the apparently inverse question: How to say, how to speak? Between the two interpretations of "Comment ne pas dire . . .?" the meaning of the uneasiness thus seems to turn again: from the "how to be silent?" (how to avoid speaking at all?) one passes—in a completely necessary and as if intrinsic fashion—to the question, which can always become the heading for an injunction: how not to speak, and which speech to avoid, in order to speak *well?* "How to avoid speaking" thus means, at once or successively: How must one not speak? How is it necessary to speak? (This is) how it is necessary not to speak. And so on. The "how" always conceals a "why," and the "it is necessary" (*"il faut"*) bears the multiple meanings of "should," "ought," and "must."

I thus improvised this title on the telephone. Letting it be dictated to me by I do not know what unconscious order—in a situation of absolute urgency—I thus also translated my desire to defer still further. This "fight or flight" reaction reproduces itself on the occasion of every lecture: how to avoid speaking, and yet from the outset to commit oneself by giving a title even before writing one's text? But also, in the economy of the same gesture: how to speak, how to do this *as is necessary, comme il faut,* assuming the responsibility for a promise? Not only for the arch-originary promise which establishes us *a priori* as people who are responsible for speech, but for this promise: to give a lecture on "absence and negation," on the *not* ("how not to," "ought not," "should not," "must not," etc.), on the "how" and the "why" (of the) *not*, the negation and the denial, and so on, and thus to commit oneself to giving a title *in advance*. Every title has the import of a promise; a title given in advance is the promise of a promise.

It was thus necessary for me to respond, but I assumed responsibility only while deferring it. Before or rather within a double bind: "how to avoid speaking" since I have already started to speak and have always already started to promise to speak? That I have already started to speak, or rather that at least the trace of a speech will have preceded this very speech, one cannot deny. Translate: *one can only deny it*. There can only be denial of this which is undeniable. What, then, do we make of negations and of denials? What do we make of them before God, that is the question, if there is one. Because the posing of every question is perhaps secondary; it perhaps follows as a first, reactive response, the undeniable *provocation*, the unavoidable denial of the undeniable provocation.

To avoid speaking, to delay the moment when one will have to say something and perhaps acknowledge, surrender, impart a secret, one amplifies the digressions. I will here attempt a brief digression on the secret itself. Under this title, "how to avoid speaking," it is necessary to speak of the secret. In certain situations, one asks oneself "how to avoid speaking," either because one has promised not to speak and to keep a secret, or because one has an interest, sometimes vital, in keeping silent even if put to the rack. This situation again presupposes the possibility of speaking. Some would say, perhaps imprudently, that only man is capable of speaking, because only he can *not* show what he could show. Of course, an animal may inhibit a movement, can abstain from an incautious gesture, for example in a defensive or offensive predatory strategy, such as in the delimitation of sexual territory or in a mating ritual. One might say, then, that animals can *not* respond to the inquisition or requisition of a stimulus or of a complex of stimuli. According to this somewhat naive philosophy of the animal world, one may nevertheless observe that animals are incapable of keeping or even having a secret, because they cannot *represent as such*, as an *object* before consciousness, something that they would then forbid themselves from showing. One would thus link the secret to the objective representation (*Vorstellung*) that is placed before consciousness and that is expressible in the form of words. The essence of such a secret would remain rigorously alien to every other nonmanifestation; and, notably, unlike that of which the animal is capable. The manifestation or nonmanifestation of *this* secret, in short its possibility, would never be on the order of the symptom. An animal can neither choose to keep silent, nor keep a secret.

I will not take up this immense problem here. To deal with it, it would be necessary to account for numerous mediations, and then to question in particular the possibility of a preverbal or simply nonverbal secret—linked, for example, to gestures or to mimicry, and even to other codes and more generally to the unconscious. It would be necessary to study the structures of denial before and outside of the possibility of judgment and of predicative language. Above all, it would be necessary to reelaborate a problematic of consciousness, that thing that, more and more, one avoids discussing as if one knew what it is and as if its riddle were solved. But is any problem more novel today than that of consciousness? Here one would be tempted to designate, if not to define, consciousness as that place in which is retained the singular power not to *say* what one knows, to keep a secret in the form of representation. A conscious being is a being capable of lying, of not presenting in speech that of which it yet has an articulated representation: a being that can avoid speaking. But in order to be able to lie, a second and already mediated possibility, it is first and more essentially necessary to be able to keep for (and say to) oneself what one already knows. To keep something to oneself is the most incredible and thought-provoking power. But this keeping-for-oneself—this dissimulation for which it is already necessary to be multiple and to differ from oneself—also presupposes the space of a promised speech, that is to say, a trace to which the affirmation is not symmetrical. How to ascertain absolute dissimulation? Does one ever have at one's disposal either sufficient criteria or an apodictic certainty that allows one to say: the secret has been kept, the dissimulation has taken place, one has avoided speaking? Not to mention the secret that is wrested by physical or mental torture, uncontrolled manifestations that are direct or symbolic, somatic or figurative, may leave in reserve a possible betrayal or avowal. Not because everything manifests itself. Simply, the nonmanifestation is never assured. According to this hypothesis, it would be necessary to reconsider all the boundaries between consciousness and the unconscious, as between man and animal and an enormous system of oppositions.

But I will avoid speaking of the secret as such. These brief allusions to the negativity of the secret and to the secret of denegation seemed necessary to me in order to situate another problem. I will only touch upon it. "Negative theologies" and everything that resembles a form of esoteric sociality have always been infortuitously associated with phenomena of secret society, as if access to the most rigorous apophatic discourse demanded the sharing of a "secret"—that is, of an ability to keep silent that would always be something more than a simple logical or rhetorical technique that is easily imitated and has a withheld content—and of a place or of a wealth that it would be necessary to conceal from the many. It is as if divulgence imperiled a revelation promised to apophasis, to this deciphering which, to make the thing appear uncovered (*aperikalyptôs*), must first find it hidden. A recurrence and a rule-governed analogy: today, for example, those who still denounce "deconstruction"—with its thinking of differance or the writing of writing—as a bastardized resurgence of negative theology are also those who readily suspect those they call the "deconstructionists" of forming a sect, a brotherhood, an esoteric corporation, or more vulgarly, a clique, a gang, or (I quote) a "mafia." Since a law of recurrence operates here, up to a certain point the logic of suspicion may be formalized. Those who lead the instruction or the trial say or tell themselves, successively or alternatively:

> 1. Those people, adepts of negative theology or of deconstruction (the difference matters little to the accusers), must indeed have a secret. They hide something since they say nothing, speak in a negative manner, respond "no, it's not that, it's not so simple" to all questions, and say that what they are speaking about is neither this, nor that, nor a third term, nei-

ther a concept nor a name, in short *is* not, and thus is nothing.

2. But since this secret obviously cannot be determined and is nothing, as these people themselves recognize, they have no secret. They pretend to have one in order to organize themselves around a social power founded on the magic of a speech that is suited to speaking in order to say nothing. These obscurantists are terrorists who remind one of the Sophists. A Plato would be of use in combating them. They possess a real power, which may be situated inside or outside the Academy: they contrive to blur even this boundary. Their alleged secret belongs to sham, mystification, or at best to a politics of grammar. Because for them there is only writing and language, nothing beyond, even if they claim to "deconstruct logo–centrism" and even start there.

3. If you know how to question them, they will finish by admitting: "The secret is that there is no secret, but there are at least two ways of thinking or proving this proposition," and so on. Experts in the art of evasion, they know better how to negate or deny than how to say anything. They always agree to avoid speaking while speaking a lot and "splitting hairs." Some of them appear "Greek," others "Christian"; they have recourse to many languages at once, and one knows some who resemble Talmudists. They are perverse enough to make their esotericism popular and "fashionable." Thus ends a familiar indictment.

One finds hints of this esotericism in the Platonism, and Neoplatonism, which themselves remain so present at the heart of Dionysius' negative theology. But in the works of Dionysius himself, and in another way in those of Meister Eckhart, one may say that no mystery is made of the necessity of the secret—to be kept, preserved, shared. It is necessary to stand or step aside, to find the *place* proper to the experience of the secret. This detour through the secret will lead, in a moment, to the question of the *place* that will henceforth orient my talk. Following the prayer that opens his *Mystical Theology*, Dionysius frequently names the secret of the divinity beyond Being, the "secrets" (*cryphio-mystiques*) of the "more than luminous darkness of silence." The "secret" of this revelation gives access to the unknowing beyond knowledge. Dionysius exhorts Timothy to divulge the secret neither to those who know, think they know, or think they can know by the path of knowledge, nor *a fortiori* to the ignorant and profane. Avoid speaking, he advises him in short. It is thus necessary to separate oneself twice: from those who know—one could say here, from the philosophers or the experts in ontology—and from the profane, who employ predicative language as naive idolaters. One is not far from the innuendo that ontology itself is a subtle or perverse idolatry, which one will understand, in an analogous and different way, through the voice of Levinas or of Jean-Luc Marion.

The paragraph I will read has a surfeit of interest in defining a beyond that exceeds the opposition between affirmation and negation. In truth, as Dionysius expressly says, it exceeds *position* (*thesis*) itself, and not merely curtailment, subtraction (*aphairesis*). At the same time, it exceeds privation. The *without* of which I spoke a moment ago marks neither a privation, a lack, nor an absence. As for the *beyond* (*hyper*) of that which is beyond Being (*hyperousios*), it has the double and ambiguous meaning or what is above in a hierarchy, thus both beyond and more. God (is) beyond Being but as such is more (being) than Being: *no more being* and *being more than Being:* being more. The French expression *plus d'être* (more being, no more being) formulates this equivocation in a fairly economical manner. Here is the call to an initiatory secret, and the warning:

> Disclose this not to the *uninitiated* [tôn amuetôn]: not to those, I say, who are entangled in beings [tois ousin], imagine nothing to be hyperessentially [hyperousiôs] beyond beings, and claim to know by the knowledge in them "Him who has made the dark his hiding place" [Ps. 18:12]. If the divine mystical initiations are beyond these, what about those yet more profane, who characterize the cause which lies beyond all [hyperkeimenen aitian] by the last among beings, and deny it to be preeminent to their ungodly phantasies and diverse formations [polyeidôn

> morphomatôn] of it? For while to it, as cause of all one must posit and affirm all the positions of beings, as beyond be-ing, beyond all, one must more properly deny all of these. Think not that affirmations and denials are opposed but rather that, long before, the cause transcends all privation [tas stereseis], since it *situates* itself beyond all affirmative and negative position [hyper pasan kai aphairesin kai thesin]. (*MT*, ch. 1:1000ab; my italics)

It *situates* itself, then. It situates itself *beyond* all position. What is thus this place? Between the place and the place of the secret, between the secret place and the topography of the social link which must protect the nondivulgence, there must be a certain homology. This must govern some (secret) relation between the topology of what stands beyond Being, without being—without Being, and the topology, the initiatory politopology which at once organizes the mystical community and makes possible the address to the other, this quasi-pedagogical and mystagogical speech, which Dionysius singularly directs to Timothy (*pros Timotheon:* the dedication of the *Mystical Theology*).

In this hierarchy,[9] where does the speaker stand, and where the one who listens and receives? Where does the one stand who speaks while *receiving* from the Cause which is also the Cause of this community? Where do Dionysius and Timothy stand, both they and all those who potentially read the text addressed by one of them to the other? Where do they stand in relationship to God, the Cause? God resides in a place, Dionysius says, but He is not this place. To gain access to this place is not yet to contemplate God. Even Moses must retreat. He receives this order from a place that is not a place, even if one of the names of God can sometimes designate place itself. Like all the initiated, he must purify himself, step aside from the impure, separate himself from the many, join "the elite of the priests." But access to this divine place does not yet deliver him to passage toward the mystical Darkness where profane vision ceases and where it is necessary to be silent. It is finally *permitted* and *prescribed* to be silent while closing one's eyes:

> It [the good and universal Cause] lies hyperessentially beyond all, it is truly and undisguisedly manifested

> only to those who step beyond all that is pure and impure, scale every ascent of the holy summits, relinquish every divine light, celestial sounds and *logoi*, and enter into the divine darkness. . . . It is not to be taken lightly that the divine Moses was *ordered first to purify himself*, and again *to be separated* from those who were not pure; after every purification he hears the many sounded trumpets, he sees the many pure lights which flash forth and the greatly flowing rays. Then he is *separated* from the many and, with *those who are sacred and select* [tôn ekkritôn iereôn], he overtakes the summits of the divine ascents. Yet with these he does not come to be with God Himself; *he does not see God—for God is unseen* [atheatos gar]—*but the place* [topon] *where God is*. This signifies to me that the most divine and highest *of what is seen and intelligible* are hypothetical logoi of what is subordinate to that beyond-having all. Through these is shown forth the presence [parousia] of that which walks upon the intelligible summits of His most holy *places* [tôn agiôtatôn autou topôn].
>
> And then Moses abandons those who see and what is seen and enters into the really mystical darkness of unknowing [tes agnôsias]; in this he shuts out every knowing apprehension and comes to be in the wholly imperceptible and invisible, be-ing entirely of that beyond all—of nothing, neither himself nor another, united most excellently by the completely unknowing inactivity of every knowledge, and knowing beyond intellect by knowing nothing. (*MT*, ch. 1:1000cd; my italics)

I will take up three motifs from this passage.

1. To separate oneself, to step aside, to withdraw with an elite, from the start this topolitology of the secret obeys an order. Moses "was ordered first to purify himself, and again to be separated from those who were not pure." This order cannot be distinguished from a promise. It is the promise itself. The knowledge of the High Priest—who intercedes, so to speak, between God and the holy institution—is the knowledge of the promise. Dionysius makes this more precise, in the *Ecclesiastical Hierarchy*, on the subject of the prayer for

the dead. *Epaggelia* signifies both the commandment and the promise: "Knowing that the divine promises will infallibly realize themselves [tas apseudeis epaggelias], he teaches all the assistant priests that the gifts for which he supplicates by virtue of a holy institution [Kata thesmon ieron] will be abundantly granted to those who lead a perfect life in God."[10] Earlier, it was said that "the grand priest knows well the promises contained in the infallible Scriptures" (*ibid.*, p. 561d).

2. In this topolitology of the secret, the figures or *places* of rhetoric are also political stratagems. The "sacred symbols," the compositions (*synthemata*), the signs and figures of the sacred discourse, the "enigmas," and the "typical symbols" are invented as "shields" against the many. All of the anthropomorphic emotions which one attributes to God, the sorrows, the angers, the repentances, the curses, all negative moments—and even the "sophistries" (*sophismata*) which He uses in the Scripture "to evade His promises"—are nothing but "sacred allegories [iera synthemata] which one has had the audacity to use to represent God, projecting outward and multiplying the visible appearances of the mystery, dividing the unique and indivisible, figuring in multiple forms what has neither form nor figure [kai typôtika, kai polymorpha tôn amorphôtôn kai atypôtôn], so that one who could see the beauty hidden in the interior [of these allegories] would find them entirely mystical, consistent with God and full of a great theological light" (Letter 9:1105b et seq.). Without the divine promise which is also an injuction, the power of these *synthemata* would be merely conventional rhetoric, poetry, fine arts, perhaps literature. It would suffice to doubt this promise or transgress this injunction in order to see an opening—and also a closing upon itself—of the field of rhetoricity or even of literariness, the lawless law of fiction.

Since the promise is also an order, the allegorical veil becomes a political shield, the solid barrier of a social division; or, if you prefer, a *shibboleth*. One invents it to protect against access to a knowledge which remains in *itself* inaccessible, untransmissible, unteachable. We will see that what is unteachable is nevertheless taught in another mode. This nonmatheme can and must become a matheme. Here I have recourse to the use Lacan makes of this word in a domain that is doubtless not without relationship to the present context. One must not think, Dionysius specifies, that the rhetorical compositions are fully sufficient unto themselves in their simple phenomenality. They are instruments, technical mediations, weapons, at least defensive weapons, "shields [probeblesthai] which secure this inaccessible ['intransmissible,' ms.] science, which the many must not contemplate, so that the most sacred mysteries should not readily offer themselves to the profane, and so that they should not unveil themselves except to the true friends of sanctity, because only they know how to disentangle sacred symbols from all puerile imagination" (Letter 9:1105c).

There is another political and pedagogical consequence, another institutional trait: the theologian must practice not a double language, but the double inscription of his knowledge. Here Dionysius evokes a double tradition, a double mode of transmission (*ditten paradosin*); on the one hand unspeakable, secret, prohibited, reserved, inaccessible (*aporreton*) or mystical (*mystiken*), "symbolic and initiatory"; on the other hand, philosophic, demonstrative (*apodeiktiken*), capable of being shown. The critical question evidently becomes: How do these two modes relate to each other? What is the law of their reciprocal translation or of their hierarchy? What would be its institutional or political figure? Dionysius recognizes that these two modes "intersect." The "inexpressible" (*arreton*) is woven together or intersects (*sympeplektai*) "the expressible" (*tô retô*).

To what mode does this discourse belong, then, both that of Dionysius and that which I hold about him? Must it not necessarily keep to the place, which cannot be an indivisible point, where the two modes cross—such that, properly speaking, the crossing itself, or the *symploke*, belongs to neither of the two modes and doubtless even precedes their distribution? At the intersection of the secret and of the nonsecret, what is the secret?

At the crossing point of these two languages, each of which *bears* the silence of the other, a secret must and must not allow itself to be divulged. It can and it cannot do this. One must not divulge, but it is also necessary to make known or rather allow to be known this "it is necessary," "one must not," or "it is necessary not to."

*How not to divulge a secret?* How to avoid saying or speaking? Contradictory and unstable meanings give such a question its endless oscillation: what to do in order that the secret remain secret? How to make it known, in order that the secret of the secret—as such—not remain secret? How to avoid this divulgence itself? These light disturbances underlie the same sentence. At one and the same time stable and unstable, this sentence allows itself to be carried by the movements which here I call *denial* (*dénégation*), a word that I would like to understand prior even to its elaboration in the Freudian context. (This is perhaps not easy and assumes at least two preconditions: that the chosen examples extend beyond both the predicative structure and the onto-theological or metaphysical presuppositions which sustain the psychoanalytic theorems.)

There is a secret of denial and a denial of the secret. The secret as such, *as secret,* separates and already institutes a negativity; it is a negation that denies itself. It de-negates itself. This denegation does not happen to it by accident; it is essential and originary. And in the *as such* of the secret that denies itself because it appears to itself in order to be what it is, this de-negation gives no chance to dialectic. The enigma of which I am speaking here—in a manner that is too eliptical, too "concise," Dionysius would say, and also too verbose—is the *sharing of the secret.* Not only the sharing of the secret with the other, my partner in a sect or in a secret society, my accomplice, my witness, my ally. I refer first of all to the secret shared *within itself,* its partition "proper," which divides the essence of a secret that cannot even appear to one alone except in starting to be lost, to divulge itself, hence to dissimulate itself, as secret, in showing itself: dissimulating its dissimulation. There is no secret *as such;* I deny it. And this is what I confide in secret to whomever allies himself to me. This is the secret of the alliance. If the theo-logical necessarily insinuates itself there, this does not mean that the secret itself is theo-logical. But does something like the secret *itself,* properly speaking, ever exist? The name of God (I do not say God, but how to avoid saying God here, from the moment when I say the name of God?) can only be *said* in the modality of this secret denial: above all I do not want to say that.

3. My third remark also concerns the place. The *Mystical Theology* thus distinguishes between access to the contemplation of God and access to the place where God resides. Contrary to what certain acts of designation may allow one

to think, God is not simply His place; He is not even in His most holy places. He is not and He does not take place ("il n'est pas et il n'a pas lieu"), or rather He is and takes place, but without Being and without place, without being His place. What is the place, what takes place or gives place to thought, henceforth, in this word? We will have to follow this thread in order to ask ourselves what an event can be—*ce qui a lieu* or that which *takes place*—in this atopics of God. I say *atopics*, hardly even playing: *atopos* is the senseless, the absurd, the extravagant, the mad. Dionysius often speaks of God's madness. When he cites Scripture ("God's madness is wiser than human wisdom"), he evokes "the theologians' practice of turning back and denying all positive terms in order to apply them to God under their negative aspect" (*DN*, ch. 7:865b). For the moment a single clarification: if God's place, which is not God, does not communicate with the divine hyperessence, this is not only because it remains either perceptible or visible. This is also the case inasmuch as it is an intelligible place. Whatever may be the ambiguity of the passage and the difficulty of knowing whether "the place where God resides"—and which is not God—does or does not belong to the order of the sensible, the conclusion seems unambiguous: "The presence" (*parousia*) of God situates itself "upon the intelligible summits of His most holy places [tais noetai akrotesi tôn agiôtatôn autou topôn]" (*MT*, ch. 1:1000d).

## *II*

We are still on the threshold.

How to avoid speaking? ("Comment ne pas parler?") Why direct this question now toward the question of the place? Wasn't it already there? And isn't to lead always to give oneself over from one place to another? A question about the place does not stand outside place; it properly *concerns* the place.

In the *three stages* that now await us, I have thought it necessary to privilege the experience of the place. But already the word *experience* appears risky. The relation to the place about which I shall speak will perhaps no longer have the form of experience—if this still assumes the encounter with or crossing over a presence.

Why this privilege of the place? Its justifications will appear along the way, I hope. Nevertheless, here are some preliminary and schematic hints.

Since such is the *topos* of our colloquium in Jerusalem, poetry, literature, literary criticism, poetics, hermeneutics, and rhetoric will be at stake: everything that can articulate speech or writing, in the current sense, together with what I call here a trace. Each time, problems are inevitable: *on the one hand*, the immense problem of figurative spatialization (both *in* speech or writing in the current sense and in the space *between* the current sense and the other, of which the current sense is only a figure); and, *on the other hand*, that of meaning and reference, and *finally*, that of the event insofar as it takes place.

As we have already glimpsed, figuration and the so-called places (*topoi*) of rhetoric constitute the very concern of apophatic procedures. As for meaning and reference, here is another reminder—in truth, the recall of the other, the call of the other as *recall*. At the moment when the question "how to avoid speaking?" is raised and articulates itself in all its modalities—whether in rhetorical or logical forms of saying, or in the simple fact of speaking—it is already, so to speak, *too late*. There is no longer any question of not speaking. Even if one speaks and says nothing, even if an apophatic discourse deprives itself of meaning or of an object, it takes place. That which committed or rendered it possible *has taken place*. The possible absence of a referent still beckons, if not toward the thing of which one speaks (such is God, who is nothing because He takes place, *without place, beyond Being*), at least toward the other (other than Being) who calls or to whom this speech is addressed—even if it speaks only in order to speak, or to say nothing. This call of the other, having always already preceded the speech to which it has never been present a first time, announces itself in advance as a *recall*. Such a reference to the other will always have taken place. Prior to every proposition and even before all discourse in general—whether a promise, prayer, praise, celebration. The most negative discourse, even beyond all nihilisms and negative dialectics, preserves a trace of the other. A trace of an event older than it *or* of a "taking-place" to come, both of them: here there is neither an alternative nor a contradiction.

Translated into the *Christian* apophatics of Dionysius (although other translations of the same necessity are possible), this signifies that the power of speaking and of speaking *well of* God already proceeds from God. This is the case even if to do this it is necessary to avoid speaking in one manner or another, or even if, in order to speak *rightly* or *truly,* it is necessary to avoid speaking entirely. This power is a gift and an effect of God. The Cause is a kind of absolute reference for it, but from the outset both an order and a promise. The Cause, the gift of the gift, the order and the promise are the same, that same to which or rather to Whom the responsibility for who speaks and "speaks well" responds. At the end of the *Divine Names,* the very possibility of speaking of the divine names and of speaking of them in a correct manner returns to God, "to That One who is the Cause of all good, to Him who has first given us the gift to speak and, then, to speak well [kai to legein kai to eu legein]" (*DN,* ch. 13:981c). Following the implicit rule from this utterance, one may say that it is always possible to call on God, to call this assumed origin of all speech by the name of God, its required cause. The exigence of its Cause, the responsibility before what is responsible for it, demands what is demanded. It is for speech, or for the best silence, a request, a demand, or a desire, if you wish, for what one equally well calls meaning, the referent, truth. This is what God's name always names, before or beyond other names: the trace of the singular event that will have rendered speech possible even before it turns itself back toward—in order to respond to—this first or last reference. This is why apophatic discourse must also open with a prayer that recognizes, assigns, or ensures its destination: the Other as Referent of a *legein* which is none other than its Cause.

This always presupposed event, this singular having-taken-place, is also for every reading, every interpretation, every poetics, every literary criticism, what one currently calls the œuvre: at least the "already-there" (*déjà-là*) of a phrase, the trace of a phrase of which the singularity would have to remain irreducible and its reference indispensable in a given idiom. A trace has taken place. Even if the idiomatic quality must necessarily lose itself or allow itself to be contaminated by the repetition which confers on it a code and an intelligibility, even if it *occurs only to efface itself,* if it arises only in effacing itself, the effacement will have taken place, even if its place is only in the ashes. *Il y a là cendre.*

What I have just alluded to seems to concern only the finite experience of finite works. But since the structure of the trace is *in general* the very possibility of an experience of finitude, I dare to say that the distinction between a finite and an infinite cause of the trace appears secondary here. It is itself an effect of trace or differance, which does not mean that the trace or differance (of which I have tried to show elsewhere that it is finite, insofar as it is infinite)[11] have a cause or an origin.

Thus, at the moment when the question "How to avoid speaking?" arises, it is already too late. There was no longer any question of not speaking. Language has started without us, in us and before us. This is what theology calls God, and it is necessary, it will have been necessary, to speak. This "it is necessary" (*il faut*) is *both* the trace of undeniable necessity—which is another way of saying that one cannot avoid denying it, one can only deny it—*and* of a past injunction. Always already past, hence without a past present. Indeed, it must have been possible to speak in order to allow the question "How to avoid speaking?" to arise. Having come from the past, language before language, a past that was never present and yet remains unforgettable—this "it is necessary" thus seems to beckon toward the event of an order or of a promise that does not belong to what one currently calls history, the discourse of history or the history of discourse. Order or promise, this injunction commits (me), in a rigorously asymmetrical manner, even before I have been able to say *I*, to sign such a *provocation* in order to reappropriate it for myself and restore the symmetry. That in no way mitigates my responsibility; on the contrary. There would be no responsibility without this *prior coming* (*prévenance*) of the trace, or if autonomy were first or absolute. Autonomy itself would not be possible, nor would respect for the law (sole "cause" of this respect) in the strictly Kantian meaning of these words. In order to elude this responsibility, to deny it and try to efface it through an absolute regression, it is still or already necessary for me to endorse or countersign it. When Jeremiah curses the day he was born,[12] he must yet—or already—*affirm*. Or rather, he must confirm, in a movement that is no more positive than negative, according to the words of Dionysius, because it does not belong to position (*thesis*) or to deposition (privation, subtraction, negation).

Why these steps? Why should I now proceed in three stages? I am certainly not bent on acquitting myself of some dialectical obligation. Despite appearances, here we are involved in a thinking that is essentially alien to dialectic, even if Christian negative theologies owe much to Platonic or Neoplatonic dialectic; and even if it is difficult to read Hegel without taking account of an apophatic tradition that was not foreign to him (at least by the mediation of Bruno, hence of Nicholas of Cusa and of Meister Eckhart, etc.).

The three "stages" or the three "signs" that I will now link together, as in a fable, do not form the moments or signs of a history. They will not disclose the order of a teleology. They rather concern deconstructive questions on the subject of such a teleology.

Three stages or three places in any case to avoid speaking of a question that I will be unable to treat; to deny it in some way, or to speak of it without speaking of it, in a negative mode: what do I understand by negative theology and its phantoms in a tradition of thought that is neither Greek nor Christian? In other words, what of Jewish and Islamic thought in this regard?[13] By example, and in everything that I will say, a certain void, the place of an internal desert, will perhaps allow this question to resonate. The three paradigms that I will too quickly have to situate (for a paradigm is often an architectural model) will surround a resonant space of which nothing, almost nothing, will ever be said.

## *A*

The first paradigm will be *Greek*.

I quickly mention its names, whether proper or not: Plato and the Neoplatonisms, the *epekeina tes ousias* of the *Republic*, and the *khora* of the *Timaeus*. In the *Republic*, the movement that leads *epekeina tes ousias*, beyond Being (or beyond beingness—a serious question of translation on which I cannot dwell here), no doubt inaugurates an immense tradition. One may follow its pathways, detours, and overdeterminations until arriving at what in a moment will be the second paradigm, the Christian apophases, and those of Dionysius in particular. Much has been written about this affiliation and its limits; this will not concern me here. In the short time that I have at my disposal, since there can be no question of allowing myself a minute study, or even of summarizing what I am attempting elsewhere—now, in seminars or texts in preparation—I will content myself with a few schematic traits. I choose them from our present standpoint, that of the question "How to avoid speaking?" such as I have started to define it: a question of the place as place of writing, of inscription, of the trace. For lack of time, I will have to lighten my talk, employing neither long quotations nor "secondary" literature. But this will not, we shall see, render the hypothesis of a "naked" text any less problematic.

In the Platonic text and in the tradition it marks, it seems to me that one must distinguish between *two* movements or *two* tropics of negativity. These two structures are radically heterogeneous.

1. One of them finds both its principle and its exemplification in the *Republic* (509b et seq.). The idea of the Good (*idea tou agathou*) has its place beyond Being or essence. Thus the Good is not, nor is its place. But this not-being is not a non-being; one may say that it transcends presence or essence, *epekeina tes ousias*, beyond the beingness of Being. From what is beyond the presence of all that is, the Good gives birth to Being or to the essence of what is, to *einai* and *ten ousian*, but without itself being. Whence comes the homology between the Good and the sun, between the intelligible sun and the sensible sun. The former gives to beings their visibility, their genesis (growth and nutrition). But it is not in becoming; it is not visible and it does not belong to the order of what proceeds from it, either in regard to knowledge or in regard to Being.

Unable to get involved in the readings that this immense text demands and has already provoked, I will observe two points that concern me in this context.

*On the one hand*, whatever may be the discontinuity marked by this beyond (*epekeina*) in relation to Being, in relation to the Being of beings or beingness (nevertheless, three distinct hypotheses), this singular limit does not give place to simply neutral or negative determinations, but to a *hyperbolism* of that, beyond which the Good gives rise to thinking, to knowing, and to Being. Negativity serves the *hyper* movement that produces, attracts, or guides it. The

Good is not, of course, in the sense that it is not Being or beings, and on this subject every ontological grammar must take on a negative form. But this negative form is not neutral. It does not oscillate between the *ni ceci—ni cela* (the neither/nor). It first of all obeys a logic of the *sur,* of the *hyper,* over and beyond, which heralds all the hyper-essentialisms of Christian apophases and all the debates that develop around them (for example, the criticism of Dionysius by Saint Thomas, who reproaches him for having placed *Bonum* before or above *Ens* or *Esse* in the hierarchy of divine names). This maintains a sufficiently homogeneous, homologous, or analogous relationship between Being and (what is) beyond Being, in order that what exceeds the border may be compared to Being; albeit through the figure of hyperbole; but most of all, in order that what is or is known may *owe* its being and its being-known to this Good. This analogical continuity allows for the translation, and for the comparison of the Good to the intelligible sun, and of the latter to the perceptible sun. The excess of this Good which (is) *hyperekhon,* its transcendence, situates it at the origin of Being and of knowledge. It permits one to *take account,* to speak both of what is and of what the Good is. Knowable things draw from the Good not only the property of being known, but also Being (*einai*) and existence or essence (*ousia*), even if the Good does not belong to essence ("ouk ousias ontos tou agathou") but to something that by far surpasses (*hyperekhontos*) Being in dignity, antiquity (*presbeia*), and power ("all'eti epekeina tes ousias presbeia kai dynamei hyperekhontos"; *Republic,* 509b). The excellence is not so alien to Being or to light that the excess itself cannot be described in the terms of what it exceeds. A bit earlier, an allusion to a third species (*triton genos*) seems to disorient the discourse, because this is neither the visible nor sight or vision; it is precisely light (507e), itself produced by the sun, and son of the Good ("ton tou agathou ekgonon") which the Good has engendered in its own likeness ("on tagathon agennesen analogon"). This analogy between the perceptible and intelligible sun will yet permit one to have confidence in the resemblance between the Good (*epekeina tes ousias*) and that to which it gives birth, Being and knowledge. Negative discourse on that which stands beyond Being, and apparently no longer tolerates ontological predicates, does not interrupt this analogical continuity. In truth, it assumes it; it even allows itself to be guided by it. Ontology remains possible and necessary. One might discern the effects of this analogical continuity in the rhetoric, grammar, and logic of all the discourses on the Good and on what is beyond Being.

*On the other hand,* soon after the passage on what (is) *epekeina tes ousias* and *hyperekhon,* Glaucon addresses himself or pretends to address himself to God, to the god of the sun, Apollo: "Oh Apollo, what divine hyperbole [daimonias hyperboles: what daemonic or supernatural excess]!" We should not assign too much weight to this invocation or address to God at the moment when one speaks of that which exceeds Being. It seems to be made lightly, in a somewhat humorous manner (*geloiôs*), as if to punctuate the scene with a breathing. I emphasize it for reasons that will become clear in a moment, when the necessity for every discourse on apophatic theology to begin with an address to God will become something completely other than a theatrical rhetoric: it will have the seriousness of a prayer.

Why have I just pointed out the allusion to the "third species" destined to play a role of analogical mediation, that of light between vision and the visible? Because in the *Sophist* (243b), this schema of the *third* also concerns Being. Of all the paired oppositions, one may say that each term *is.* The being (*einai*) of this *is* figures as a third that is beyond the two others ("triton para ta duo ekeina"). It is indispensable to the interweaving (*symploke*) or to the dialectical intersection of the forms or of the ideas in a *logos* capable of receiving the other. After having raised the question of nonbeing, which is in itself unthinkable (*adianoeton*), ineffable (*arreton*), unpronounceable (*aphtegkton*), foreign to discourse and to reason (*alogon;* 238c), one arrives at the presentation of dialectic itself. Passing through the parricide and the murder of Parmenides, this dialectic receives the thinking of nonbeing as *other* and not as absolute nothingness or simple opposite of Being (256b, 259c). This confirms that there cannot be an absolutely negative discourse: a *logos* necessarily speaks about something; it cannot avoid speaking of something; it is impossible for it to refer to nothing ("logon anag–kaion, otanper è, tinos einai logon, mè dè tinos adunaton"; 262e).

2. I will distinguish the tropics of negativity, which I have just outlined in such a schematic manner, from another tropics in Plato's works; it is another manner of treating

what is beyond (*epekeina*) the border, the third species, and the place. This place is here called *khora;* I am, of course, alluding to the *Timaeus.* When I say that this is found "in Plato's works," I leave aside, for lack of time, the question of whether or not it has its place at the interior of the Platonic text, and what "at the interior of" means here. These are questions that I will treat at length elsewhere in a future publication. From this work in progress,[14] I will permit myself to set off a few elements that are indispensable to the formulation of a hypothesis that relates to the present context.

*Khora* also constitutes a third species (*triton genos; Timaeus* 48e, 49a, 52a). This place is not the intelligible paradigm with which the demiurge inspires itself. Nor does it belong to the order of copies or sensible mimemes that it impresses in the *khora.* It is difficult to speak of this absolutely necessary place, this place "in which" the mimemes of the eternal beings originate by impressing themselves (*typothenta*) there, and it is difficult to speak of the impression (*ekmageion*) for all the types and all the schemas. It is difficult to adjust to it a true or firm *logos.* One glimpses it only in an "oneiric" manner and one can only describe it by a "bastard reasoning" (*logismô tini nothô*). This spatial interval neither dies nor is born (52b). Nevertheless, its "eternity" is not that of the intelligible paradigms. At the moment, so to speak, when the demiurge organizes the cosmos by cutting, introducing, and impressing the images of the paradigms "into" the *khora,* the latter must already have been *there,* as the "there" itself, beyond time or in any case beyond becoming, in a beyond time without common measure with the eternity of the ideas and the becoming of sensible things. How does Plato deal with this disproportion and heterogeneity? There are, it seems to me, *two concurrent languages* in these pages of the *Timaeus.*

To be sure, one of these languages multiplies the negations, the warnings, the evasions, the detours, the tropes, but *with a view to* reappropriating the thinking of the *khora* for ontology and for Platonic dialectic in its most dominant schemas. If the *khora*—place, spacing, receptacle (*hypodokhè*)—is neither sensible nor intelligible, it seems to *participate* in the intelligible in an enigmatic way (51a). Since it "receives all," it makes possible the formation of the cosmos. As it is neither this nor that (neither intelligible nor sensible), one may speak as *if* it were a joint participant in both. *Neither/nor* easily becomes *both . . . and*, both this and that. Whence the rhetoric of the passage, the multiplication of figures which one traditionally interprets as metaphors: gold, mother, nurse, sieve, receptacle, impression, and so on. Aristotle provided the matrix for many of the readings of the *Timaeus* and, since his *Physics* (bk. 4), one has always interpreted this passage on the *khora* as being *at the interior* of philosophy, in a consistently anachronistic way, as if it prefigured, on the one hand, the philosophies of space as *extensio* (Descartes) or as pure sensible form (Kant); or on the other hand, the materialist philosophies of the substratum or of substance which stands, like the *hypodokhè*, *beneath* the qualities or the phenomena. These readings, the wealth and complexity of which I can only touch upon here, are still possible, and up to a certain point justifiable. As for their anachronistic character, it seems to me not only evident but structurally inevitable. The *khora* is the atemporality (*l'anachronie*) itself of the spacing; it (a)temporalizes (*anachronise*), it calls forth atemporality, provokes it immutably from the pretemporal *already* that gives place to every inscription. But this is another story with which we cannot get involved here.

The other language and the other interpretive decision interest me more, without ceasing to be atemporal or anachronistic in their way. The synchronicity of a reading has no chance here and no doubt would lack exactly that to which it claimed to adjust itself. This other gesture would inscribe an irreducible spacing interior to (but hence also exterior to, once the interior is placed outside) Platonism, that is, interior to ontology, to dialectic, and perhaps to philosophy in general. Under the name of *khora*, the place belongs neither to the sensible nor to the intelligible, neither to becoming, nor to non-being (the *khora* is never described as a void), nor to Being: according to Plato, the quantity or the quality of Being are measured against its intelligibility. All the aporias, which Plato makes no effort to hide, would signify that *there is* something that is neither a being nor a nothingness; something that no dialectic, participatory schema, or analogy would allow one to rearticulate together with any philosopheme whatsoever, neither "in" Plato's works nor in the history that Platonism inaugurates and dominates. The *neither/nor* may no longer be reconverted into *both . . . and*. Hence the so-called "metaphors" are not only inadequate, in that they borrow figures from the sensible forms inscribed in the *khora*, without pertinence for designating the *khora* itself. They are no longer metaphors. Like all rhetoric which makes of it a systematic web, the concept of metaphor issues from this Platonic metaphysics, from the distinction between the sensible and the intelligible, and from the dialectic and analogicism that one inherits with it. When the interpreters of Plato discuss these metaphors, whatever may be the complexity of their debates and analyses, we never see them suspicious of the concept of metaphor itself.[15]

But to say that Plato does not use metaphor or sensible figures to designate the place does not imply that he speaks appropriately of the proper and properly intelligible meaning of *khora*. The import of receptivity or of receptacle which, one may say, forms the elementary nonvariable of this word's determination, seems to me to transcend the opposition between figurative and proper meaning. The spacing of *khora* introduces a dissociation or a difference in the proper meaning that it renders possible, thereby compelling tropic detours which are no longer rhetorical figures. The typography and the tropics to which the *khora* gives place, *without giving anything*, are explicitly marked in the *Timaeus* (50bc). Hence Plato says this in his way: it is necessary to avoid speaking of *khora* as of "something" that is or is not, that could be present or absent, intelligible, sensible, or both at once, active or passive, the Good (*epekeina tes ousias*) or the Evil, God or man, the living or the nonliving. Every theomorphic or anthropomorphic schema would thus also have to be avoided. If the *khora* receives everything, it does not do this in the manner of a medium or of a container, not even in that of a receptacle, because the receptacle is yet a figure inscribed in it. This is neither an intelligible extension, in the Cartesian sense, a receptive subject, in the Kantian sense of *intuitus derivativus*, nor a pure sensible space, as a form of receptivity. Radically nonhuman and atheological, one cannot even say that it gives place or that *there is* the *khora*. The *es gibt*, thus translated, too vividly announces or recalls the dispensation of God, of man, or even that of the Being of which certain texts by Heidegger speak (*es gibt Sein*). *Khora* is not even *that* (*ça*), the *es* or *id* of giving, before all subjectivity. It does not give place as one would give something, whatever it may be; it neither creates nor produces anything, not even an event insofar as it takes place. It gives no order and makes no promise. It is radically ahistorical, because nothing happens through it and nothing happens to it. Plato insists on its necessary indifference; to receive all and allow itself to be marked or affected by what is inscribed in it, the *khora* must remain without form and without proper determination. But if it is amorphous (*amorphon; Timaeus*, 50d), this signifies neither lack nor privation. *Khora* is nothing positive or negative. It is impassive, but it is neither passive nor active.

How to speak of it? How to avoid speaking of it? In this context, the singularity that interests me is that the impossibility of speaking of it and of giving it a proper name, far from reducing it to silence, yet dictates an obligation, by its very impossibility: *it is necessary* to speak of it and there is a rule for that. Which? If one wishes to respect the absolute singularity of the *khora* (there is only one *khora*, even if it can be pure multiplicity of places), *it is necessary always to refer to it in the same manner.* Not to give it the same name, as one French translation suggests, but to call it, address oneself to it in the same manner ("tauton auten aei prosreteon"; 49b). This is not a question of proper name, but rather of appellation, a manner of addressing oneself. *Proserô:* I address myself to, I address speech to someone, and sometimes: I adore—divinity; *prosrema* is speech addressed to someone; *prosresis* is the salutation that calls. One respects the absolute uniqueness of the *khora* by always calling it in the same way—and this is not limited to the name; a phrase is necessary. To obey this injunction with neither order nor promise, an injunction that has always already taken place, one must think of that which—beyond all given philosophemes—has nevertheless left a trace in language; for example, the word *khora* already existed in the Greek language, as it is caught up in the web of its usual meanings. Plato did not have another. Together with the word, there are also grammatical, rhetorical, logical, and hence also philosophical possibilities. However insufficient they may be, they are given, already marked by that unheard trace, promised to the trace that has promised nothing. This trace and this promise always inscribe themselves in the body of a language, in its vocabulary and syntax, but one must be able to rediscover the trace, still unique, in other languages, bodies, and negativities.

## *B*

The question now becomes the following: what happens between, *on the one hand,* an "experience" such as this—the experience of the *khora* which is above all not an experience, if one understands by this word a certain relation to presence, whether it is sensible or intelligible or even a relation to the presence of the present in general—and, *on the other hand,* what one calls the *via negativa* in its Christian stage?

The passage through the negativity of discourse on the subject of the *khora* is neither the last word nor a mediation in service of a dialectic, an elevation toward a positive or proper meaning, a Good or a God. This has nothing to do with negative theology; there is reference neither to an event nor to a giving, neither to an order nor to a promise, even if, as I have just underscored, the absence of promise or of order—the barren, radically nonhuman, and atheological character of this "place"—obliges us to speak and to refer to it in a certain and unique manner, as to the wholly-other who is neither transcendent, absolutely distanced, nor immanent and close. Not that we are obliged to speak of it; but if, stirred by an obligation that does not come from it, we think and speak of it, then it is necessary to respect the singularity of this reference. Although it is nothing, this referent appears irreducible and irreducibly other: one cannot invent it. But since it remains alien to the order of presence and absence, it seems that one could only invent it in its very otherness, at the moment of the address.

But this unique address is not a prayer, a celebration, or an encomium. It does not speak to You.

Above all, this "third species" that the *khora* also is does not belong to a *group of three.* "Third species" is here only a *philosophical* way of naming an X that is not included in a group, a family, a triad or a trinity. Even when Plato seems to compare it to a "mother" or to a "nurse," this always virginal *khora* in truth does not couple with the "father" to whom Plato "compares" the paradigms; the *khora* does not *engender* the sensible forms that are inscribed in it and that Plato "compares" to a child (*Timaeus*, 50d).

To ask what *happens* between this type of experience (or the experience of the *typos*) and the Christian apophases is neither necessarily nor exclusively to think of history, of events, of influences. Indeed, the question that arises here concerns the historicity or eventuality (*événementialité*), that is, of significations foreign to the *khora*. Even if one wishes to describe "what happens" in terms of structures and relations, it is no doubt necessary to recognize that what happens between them is, perhaps, precisely the event of the event, the story, the thinking of an essential "having-taken-place," of a revelation, of an order and of a promise, of an anthropo-theologicalization which—despite the extreme rigor of the negative hyperbole—seems to dominate anew, even closer to the *agathon* than to the *khora*. And in Dionysius' works, for example, the trinitarian schema appears absolutely indispensable to ensure the passage through or crossing between discourses on the divine names, between the symbolic and mystical theology. The affirmative theologemes celebrate God as the Good, the intelligible Light, even the Good "beyond all light" (it is a "principle of all light and hence it is too little to call it light"; *DN*, ch. 4:701ab). Even if this Good is called formless (like the *khora*), this time it itself gives form: "But if the Good transcends all being, as is in effect the case, then it is necessary to say that it is the formless that gives form, and that the One who remains in Himself without the essence is the height of the essence, and the reality without supreme life" (*DN*, ch. 4:697a). This Good inspires an entire erotics, but Dionysius warns us: it is necessary to avoid using the word *erôs* without first clarifying the meaning, the intention. It is always necessary to start from the intentional meaning and not from the mere words (*DN*, ch. 4:708bc): "one should not imagine that we oppose Scripture in venerating this word of amorous desire [erôs]. . . . It even seemed to some of our sacred authors that 'amorous love' ['erôs'] is a term more worthy of God than 'charitable love' ['agapè']. For the divine Ignatius wrote: 'It is the object of my amorous love that they crucified'" (*DN*, ch. 4:708c–709b). The holy theologians attribute the same import, the same power of unification and gathering to *erôs* and to *agapè*, which the many poorly understand, which assigns desire to the body, to the division, to the carving up (*ibid.*). In God, desire is at once ecstatic, jealous, and condescending (*DN*, ch. 4:712a et seq.). This erotics leads forward and hence leads back to the Good, circularly, that is, toward what "is situated far beyond both being considered in itself and non-being" (*DN*, ch. 4:716d). As for Evil, "it belongs neither to Being nor to non-Being. Rather, it is more absent and estranged from the Good than non-Being; it is more greatly without being than non-Being" (*ibid*). What is the more of this less in regard to what is already without essence? Evil is even more without essence than the Good. If possible, one should draw the full consequences of this singular axiomatics. For the moment, this is not my concern.

Between the theological movement that speaks and is inspired by the Good beyond Being or by light and the apophatic path that exceeds the Good, there is necessarily a passage, a transfer, a translation. An experience must yet guide the apophasis toward excellence, not allow it to say just anything, and prevent it from manipulating its negations like empty and purely mechanical phrases. This experience is that of prayer. Here prayer is not a preamble, an accessory mode of access. It constitutes an essential moment, it adjusts discursive asceticism, the passage through the desert of discourse, the apparent referential vacuity which will only avoid empty deliria and prattling, by addressing itself from the start to the other, to you. But to you as "hyperessential and more than divine Trinity."

I will distinguish at least two traits in the experiences and in the so manifold determinations of what one calls prayer. I isolate them here even if at the neglect of everything else, in order to clarify my talk. 1. In every prayer there must be an address to the other as other; *for example*—I will say, at the risk of shocking—*God*. The act of addressing oneself to the other as other must, of course, mean praying, that is, asking, supplicating, searching out. No matter what, for the pure prayer demands only that the other hear it, receive it, be present to it, be the other as such, a gift, call, and even cause of prayer. This first trait thus characterizes a discourse (an act of language even if prayer is silent) which, as such, is not predicative, theoretical (theo*logical*), or constative. 2. But I will differentiate it from another trait with which it is most often associated, notably by Dionysius and his interpreters, namely, the encomium or the celebration (*hymnein*). That the association of these two traits is essential for Dionysius does not signify that one trait is identical with the other, nor even in general inseparable from the other. Neither the prayer nor the encomium is, of course, an act of constative predication. Both have a performative dimension, the analysis of which would merit long and difficult expositions, notably as to the origin and validation of these performatives. I will hold to one distinction: prayer in itself, one may say, implies nothing other than the supplicating address to the other, perhaps beyond all supplication and giving, to give the promise of His presence as other, and finally the transcendence of His otherness itself, even without any other determination; the encomium, although it is not a simple attributive speech, nevertheless preserves an irreducible relationship to the attribution. No doubt, as Urs von Balthasar rightly says, "Where God and the divine are concerned, the word ὑμνεῖν almost replaces the word 'to say.' "[16] Almost, in fact, but not entirely; and how can one deny that the encomium qualifies God and *determines* prayer, *determines* the other, Him to whom it addresses itself, refers, invoking Him even as the source of prayer? How can one deny that, in this movement of determination (which is no longer the pure address of the prayer to the other), the appointment of the *trinitary* and hyperessential God distinguishes Dionysius' *Christian* prayer from all other prayer? To reject this doubtless subtle distinction, inadmissible for Dionysius and perhaps for a Christian in general, is to deny the essential quality of prayer to every invocation that is not Christian. As Jean-Luc Marion correctly remarks, the encomium is "neither true nor false, not even contradictory,"[17] although it says something *about* the thearchy, about the Good and the analogy; and if its attributions or namings do not belong to the ordinary signification of truth, but rather to a hypertruth that is ruled by a hyperessentiality, in this it does not merge with the movement of prayer itself, which does not speak *of*, but *to*. Even if this address is immediately determined by the discourse of encomium and if the prayer addresses itself to God by speaking (to Him) of Him, the apostrophe of prayer and the determination of the encomium form a pair, two different structures: "hyperessential and more than divine Trinity, You who preside over the divine wisdom. . . ." In a moment I will quote more extensively from this prayer which opens the *Mystical Theology* and prepares the definition of apophatic theologemes. For "it is necessary to start with prayers" (*eukhès aparkhesthai khreôn; DN*, ch. 3:680d), Dionysius says. Why? No doubt, to attain union with God; but to speak of this *union*, it is still necessary to speak of *places*, of height, of distance and of proximity. Dionysius proposes to his immediate addressee—or to the one to whom he dedicates his work, Timothy—to examine the name of Good, which expresses divinity, *after* having invoked the Trinity, that principle of Good which transcends all goods. It is necessary to pray in order to *approach* it, "most intimately"—that is, to raise oneself toward it—and receive from it the initiation of its gifts:

> It is necessary that we first be lifted up toward it, the source of good, by our prayers, and then, by drawing near to it, that we be initiated into the all-good gifts of what is founded around it. For while it is present to all, not all are present to it. Then, when we invoke it by our most holy prayers with an unpolluted intellect which is suited for the divine union, we shall be present to it. For it is not in a place, so that it would be absent from some beings or have to go from one being to another. Moreover, even the statement that it is "in" all beings falls far too short of its infinity, which is beyond all and encompasses all. (*DN*, ch. 3:680b)

By a series of analogies, Dionysius then explains that, in approaching and elevating ourselves thus, we do not traverse the distance that separates us from a place (since the residence of the Trinity is not localized: it is "everywhere and nowhere"). On the other hand, the Trinity draws us toward it, while it remains immobile, like the height of the sky or the depth of marine bedrock from which we will pull on a rope in order to come to it, and not to draw it toward us:

> before everything and especially before a discourse about God, it is necessary to begin with a prayer—not so that the power present both everywhere and nowhere shall come to us but so that by our divine remembrance and invocations we ourselves shall be guided to it and be united with it. (*ibid.*)

The principle of the Good is beyond Being, but it also transcends the Good (*DN*, ch. 3:680b). God is the Good that transcends the Good and the Being that transcends Being. This "logic" is also that of the "without" which I evoked a moment ago in the quotations from Meister Eckhart, citing Saint Augustine ("God is wise *without* wisdom, good *without* goodness, powerful *without* power") or Saint Bernard ("To love God is a mode *without* a mode"). We could recognize in the negativity without negativity of these utterances—concerning a transcendence which is nothing other (and wholly other) than what it transcends—a principle of multiplication of voices and discourses, of disappropriation and reappropriation of utterances, with the most distant appearing the closest, and vice versa. A predicate can always conceal another predicate, or rather the nakedness of an absence of predicate—as the (sometimes indispensable) veil of a garment can at once dissimulate and reveal the very fact that it dissimulates and renders attractive at the same time. Hence the voice of an utterance can conceal another, which it then appears to quote without quoting it, presenting itself as another form, namely as a quotation of the other. Whence the subtlety, but also the conflicts, the relations of power, even the aporias of a politics of doctrine; I want to say: a politics of initiation or of teaching in general, and of an institutional politics of interpretation. Meister Eckhart, for example (but what an example!) knew something about this. Not to mention the arguments he had to deploy against his inquisitorial judges ("They tax with error everything they don't understand. . . ."), the strategy of his sermons put to work a multiplicity of voices and of veils, which he superimposed or removed like skins or garments, thematizing and himself exploring a pseudo-metaphor until reaching that extreme flaying of which one is never sure that it allows one to see the nakedness of God or to hear the voice of Meister Eckhart himself. *Quasi stella matutina*, which furnishes so many pretexts to the Cologne judges, stages the drama of twenty-four masters (*Liber 24 philosophorum* of pseudo-Hermes Trismegistus) who are reunited to speak of God. Eckhart chooses one of their assertions: "God is necessarily above Being [got etwaz ist, daz von nôt über wesene sîn muoz]."[18] Speaking thus of what one of his masters says, he *comments* in a voice that no longer permits one to decide that it is not his own. And in the same movement, he cites other masters, Christians or pagans, great or subordinate masters (*kleine meister*). One of them seems to say, "God is neither being nor goodness [Got enist niht wesen noch güete]. Goodness clings to being and is not more comprehensive [breiter] than being; for if there were no being, there would be no goodness, and being is purer than goodness. God is not good, nor better, nor best. Whoever were to say that God is good, would do Him as great an injustice as if he called the sun black" (*ibid.*, 1:148). (The Bull of condemnation mentions this passage only in an appendix, without concluding that Eckhart truly taught it.) The theory of archetypes that forms the context of this argument attenuates its provocative character: God does not share any of the modes of Being with other beings (divided into ten categories by these masters), but "He is not thereby deprived of any of them [er entbirt ir ouch keiner]."

But here is what "a pagan master" says: the soul that loves God "takes Him under the garment of goodness [nimet in under dem velle der güete]," but reason or rationality (*vernunfticheit*) raises this garment and grasps God in His nakedness (*in blôz*). Then He is derobed (*entkleidet*), shorn "of goodness, of Being, and of all names" (*ibid.*, 1:152). Eckhart does not contradict the pagan master; nor does he agree with him. He remarks that, unlike the "holy masters," the pagan speaks in accordance with "natural light." Next, in a voice that appears to be his own, he differentiates—I do not dare say that he makes dialectical—the preceding proposition. In the lines that I am preparing to quote, a certain signification of unveiling, of laying bare, of truth as what is beyond the covering garment—appears to orient the entire axiomatics of this apophasis, at the end of ends and after all. Doubtless, here one cannot speak in full rigor of signification and axiomatics, since what orders and rules the apophatic course precisely exceeds the Good or goodness. But there is indeed a rule or a law: it is necessary to go beyond the veil or the garment. Is it arbitrary to still call truth or hyper-truth this unveiling which is perhaps no longer an unveiling of Being? A light, therefore, that is no longer elucidated by Being? I do not believe so. Consider:

> I once said in the school that intellect [vernünfticheit] is nobler than will, and yet both belong to this light.

> Then a master in another school said that will is nobler than intellect, for will takes things as they are in themselves, while the intellect takes things as they are in it. That is true. An eye is nobler in itself than an eye painted on the wall. But I say that intellect is nobler than will. The will apprehends God under the garment [under dem kleide] of goodness. The intellect apprehends God naked, as He is divested of goodness and being [Vernünfticheit nimet got blôz, als er entkleidet ist von güete und von wesene]. Goodness is a garment [kleit] under which God is hidden, and will apprehends God under the garment of goodness. If there were no goodness in God, my will would not want Him. (*ibid.*, 1:152–53)

Light and truth, these are Meister Eckhart's words. *Quasi stella matutina,* that is what it is, and it is also a topology (height and proximity) of our relation to God. Like the adverb *quasi,* we are *beside* the verb that is the truth:

> "As [als] a morning star in the midst of the mist." I refer to the little word "quasi," which means "as" [als]; in school the children call it an adverb [ein bîwort]. This is what I refer to in all my sermons. The most appropriate [eigenlîcheste] things that one can say of God are word and truth [wort und wârheit]. God called Himself a word [ein wort]. St. John said: "In the beginning was the Word," and means that beside the word [wort], man is an adverb [bîwort]. In the same way, the free star [der vrîe sterne] Venus, after which Friday [vrîtac] is named, has many names. . . . Of all the stars, it is always equally near to the sun; it never moves farther from or nearer to it [niemer verrer noch næher], and symbolizes [meinet] a man who wants to be near God always, and present [gegenwertic] to Him, so that nothing can remove him from God, neither happiness, unhappiness, nor any creature. . . . The more the soul is raised [erhaben] above earthly things, the stronger [kreftiger] it is. Even a person who knows nothing but the creatures would never need to think of any sermons, for every creature is full of God and is a book [buoch]. (*ibid.*, 1:154–56)

In its pedagogical necessity and initiatory virtue, the sermon supplements—not so much the Word (*Verbe*), which has no need of it, but—the incapacity of reading in the authentic "book" that we are, as creatures, and the adverbial quality that we must hence be. This supplement of adverbial quality, the sermon, must be accomplished and oriented (as one orients oneself by the morning star) by the prayer or invocation of the trinitary God. This is at once the end and the orientation point of the sermon: "The soul is thus like an 'adverb,' working together with God and finding its beautification in the same self-knowledge that exalts him. That for all time, may the Father, the Verbum, and the Holy Spirit help us to remain adverbs of this Verbum. Amen" (*ibid.*, 1:158).

This is the end of the Sermon; the prayer does not directly address itself, in the form of apostrophe, to God Himself. In contrast, at the opening and from the first words of the *Mystical Theology*, Dionysius addresses himself directly to You, to God, from now on determined as "hyperessential Trinity" in the prayer that prepares the theologemes of the *via negativa:*

> O Trinity beyond being [Trias hyperousiè], beyond divinity [hyperthèe], beyond goodness [hyperagathè], and guide of Christians in divine wisdom [theosophias], direct us to the mystical summits more than unknown and beyond light. There the simple, absolved, and unchanged mysteries of theology lie hidden in the darkness beyond light of the hidden mystical silence, there, in the greatest darkness, that beyond all that is most evident exceedingly illuminates the sightless intellects. There, in the wholly imperceptible and invisible, that beyond all that is most evident fills to overflowing, with the glories beyond all beauty the intellects who know how to close their eyes [tous anommatous noas]. This is my prayer ['Emoi men oun tauta eutkhtô]. And you, dear Timothy, be earnest in the exercise of mystical contemplation. (ch. 1:998a)

What happens here?

*After* having prayed (he writes, we read), he presents his prayer. He quotes it and I have just quoted his quotation. He quotes it in what is properly an *apostrophe* to its addressee,

Timothy. The *Mystical Theology* is dedicated to him; in order to initiate him, it must lead him on the paths toward which Dionysius himself has prayed to God to lead him, or more literally to *direct* him in a straight (*ithunon*) line. A peda*gogy* which is also a mysta*gogy* and a psycha*gogy*: here the gesture of leading or directing the *psyche* of the other passes through apostrophe. The one who asks to be led by God turns for an instant toward another addressee, in order to lead him in turn. He does not simply turn himself away from his first addressee who is in *truth* the first Cause of his prayer and already guides it. It is exactly because he does not turn away from God that he can turn toward Timothy and *pass from one address to the other without changing direction.*

The writing of Dionysius—which we presently believe we are reading or read in view of believing—stands in the space of that *apostrophe* which *turns aside* the discourse in the *same* direction, between the prayer itself, the quotation of the prayer, and the address to the disciple. In other words, it is addressed to the best reader, to the reader who ought to allow himself to be led to become better, to us who presently believe we are reading this text. Not to us as we are, at present, but as we would have to be, in our souls, if we read this text as it ought to be read, aright, in the proper direction, correctly: according to its prayer and its promise. He also prays—that we read correctly, in accordance with his prayer. None of this would be possible without the possibility of quotations (more generally, of repetition), and of an apostrophe that allows one to speak to several people at once. To more than one other. The prayer, the quotation of the prayer, and the apostrophe, from one you to the other, thus weave the *same* text, however heterogeneous they appear. There is a text because of this repetition.[19] Where, then, does this text have its place? Does it have a place, at present? And why can't one separate the prayer, the quotation of prayer, and the address to the reader?

The identity of *this* place, and hence of *this* text, and of *its* reader, comes from the future of what is promised by the promise. The advent of this future has a provenance, the event of the promise. Contrary to what seemed to happen in the "experience" of the place called *khora*, the apophasis is brought into motion—it is *initiated*, in the sense of initiative and initiation—by the event of a revelation which is also a promise. This apophasis belongs to a history; or rather, it opens up a history and an anthropo-theological dimension. The *hyphen* ("trait d'union") unites the "new, adjunct writing with that which God himself dictated" (*DN*, ch. 3:681b); it marks the very place of this adjunction. This place itself is assigned by the event of the promise and the revelation of Scripture. It is the place only after what will have taken place—according to the time and history of this future perfect. The place is an event. Under what conditions is one situated in Jerusalem, we asked a moment ago, and where is the place thus named situated? How can one measure the distance that separates us from or draws us closer to it? Here is the answer of Dionysius, who cites Scripture in the *Ecclesiastical Hierarchy:* "Do not distance yourself from Jerusalem, but await the promise of the Father which you have heard from my mouth, and according to which you will be baptised by the Holy Spirit" (512c). The situation of this speech situates a place: he who transmitted the promise (Jesus, "divine founder of our own hierarchy") speaks of Jerusalem as the place that takes place since the event of the promise. But the place that is thus revealed remains the place of waiting, awaiting the realization of the promise. Then it will take place fully. It will be fully a place.

Hence an event prescribes to us the good and accurate apophasis: how to avoid speaking. This prescription is at once a revelation and a teaching of the Holy Scriptures, the architext before all supplementary "adjunction":

> with regard to the secret Deity beyond Being, *it is necessary to avoid all speech, that is, every incautious thought [ou tolmeteon eipein, oute men ennoesai]*, beyond what the Holy Scriptures divinely reveal to us [para ta theoeidôs emin ek tôn ierôn logiôn ekpephasmena]. For in these sacred texts, the Deity itself manifested that which suited its Goodness. (*DN*, ch. 1:588c; my italics)[20]

This hyperessential goodness is not entirely incommunicable; it can manifest *itself*, but it remains separated by its hyperessentiality. As for those theologians who have "praised" its inaccessibility and penetrated its "secret infinity," they have left no *"trace"* (*ikhnous; ibid.;* my italics).

*A secret manifestation*, then, if some such thing is possible. Even before commanding the extreme negativity of the apophasis, this manifestation is transmitted to us as a "secret gift" by our inspired masters. We thus learn to decipher symbols, we understand how "the love of God for man envelops the intelligible in the sensible, what is beyond Being in being, gives form and fashion to the unformable and the unfashionable, and through a variety of partial symbols, multiplies and figures the unfigurable and marvelous Simplicity" (*DN*, ch. 1:592b). In brief, we learn to read, to decipher the rhetoric without rhetoric of God—and finally to be silent.

Among all these figures for the unfigurable, there stands the figure of the seal. This is not one figure among others; it figures the figuration of the unfigurable itself; and this discourse on the imprint appears to displace the Platonic typography of the *khora*. The latter gave rise to the inscriptions, to *typoi*, for the copies of the paradigms. Here the figure of the seal, which also seals a promise, is valid for the entire text of the creation. It carries over a Platonic argument, one of the two schemas that I have just tried to distinguish, into another order. God at once permits and does not permit participation in Him. The text of creation exists as the typographic inscription of the nonparticipation in participation:

> as the central point of a circle is shared by all the radii, which constitute the circle, and as the multiple imprints [ektypomata] of a single seal [sphragidos] share the original which is entirely immanent and identical in each of the imprints, not fragmenting itself in any manner. But the nonparticipation [amethexia] of the Deity, the universal cause, yet transcends all these figures [paradeigmata]. (*DN*, ch. 2:644ab)

For unlike what happens with the seal, here there is neither contact, community, or synthesis. The subsequent discussion recalls again, while displacing, the necessity for the *khora* to be without form and virginal. Otherwise, it could not suitably lend itself to the writing of the impressions in it:

> One might object that the seal is not complete and identical in all its imprints [en olois tois ekmageiois]. I respond that this is not the fault of the seal which

> transmits itself to each one completely and identically; rather, the otherness of the participants differentiates between the reproductions of the unique, total and identical model [arkhetypias]. (*DN*, ch. 2:644b)

Thus everything will depend on the material or wax (*keros*) which receives the imprints. It must be receptive, soft, flexible, smooth, and virginal, in order that the imprint remain pure, clear, and lasting (*DN*, ch. 2:644b).

If one recalls that the *khora* was also described as a receptacle (*dekhomenon*), one may follow another displacement of this figure, the figure of figures, the place of the other figures. Henceforth the "receptacle" is at once *physical* and *created*. It was neither in Plato's works. Later, Saint Augustine once again assures the mediation, and Meister Eckhart cites him in his sermon *Renouamini spiritu:* "Augustine says that in the superior part of the soul, which is called *mens* or *gemüte*, God created, together with the soul's being, a potential [craft] which the masters call a receptacle [sloz] or screen [schrin] of spiritual forms, or of formal images."[21] The creation of the place, which is also a potential, is the basis for the resemblance of the soul with the Father. But beyond the Trinity, one may say, beyond the multiplicity of images and beyond the created place, the *unmovability without form*—which the *Timaeus* attributed, one may say, to the *khora*—is here found to suit God alone: "when all the images of the soul are pushed aside and it contemplates only the unique One [das einig ein], the naked being of the soul encounters the naked being without form [das blose formlose wesen] of the divine unity, which is the hyperessential Being resting unmoved in itself [ein uberwesende wesen, lidende ligende in ime selben]" (*ibid.*, 3:437–438). This unmovability of the formless is the unique and wondrous source of our movability, of our emotions, of our noblest suffering. Thus we can suffer only God, and nothing other than Him: "Oh! wonder of wonders [wunder uber wunder], what noble suffering lies therein, that the being of the soul can suffer nothing else than the solitary and pure unity of God!" (*ibid.*, 3:438).

Thus named, "God is without name [namloz]," and "no one can either speak of Him or understand Him." Of this "supereminent Being [uber swebende wesen]" which is also a "hyperessential nothingness [ein uber wesende nitheit]" (*ibid.*,

3:441–42), it is necessary to avoid speaking. Eckhart allows St. Augustine to speak: "what man can say that is most beautiful in respect to God is that he knows how to be silent [swigen] on account of the wisdom of the internal [divine] wealth." Eckhart adds: "Because of this, be silent" (*ibid.*, 3:442). Without that you lie and you commit sin. This duty is a duty of love; the apostrophe orders love, but it speaks out of love and implores the aid of God in a prayer: "You must love Him inasmuch as he is a Non-God, a Non-Intellect, a Non-Person, a Non-Image. More than this, inasmuch as He is a pure, clear, limpid One, separated from all duality. And we must eternally sink ourselves in this One, from the Something to the Nothing. May God help us. Amen" (*ibid.*, 3:448).

This is to speak in order to command not to speak, to say what God is not, that he *is* a non-God. How may one hear the copula of being that articulates this singular speech and this order to be silent? Where does it have its place? Where does it take place? It is the place, the place of this writing, this trace (left in Being) of what is not, and the writing of this place. The place is only a place of passage, and more precisely, a threshold. But a threshold, this time, to give access to what is no longer a place. A subordination, a relativization of the place, and an extraordinary consequence; the place is Being. What finds itself reduced to the condition of a threshold is Being itself, Being as a place. Solely a threshold, but a sacred place, the outer sanctuary (*parvis*) of the temple:

> When we apprehend God in Being, we apprehend Him in his *parvis* [vorbürge], for Being is the *parvis* in which He resides [wonet]. Where is He then in His temple, in which he shines in His sanctity [heilic]? Intellect [vernünfticheit: rationality] is the Temple of God.[22]

The soul, which exercises its power in the eye, allows one to see what is not, what is not present; it "works in non-being and follows God who works in non-being." Guided by this *psyche*, the eye thus passes the threshold of Being toward non-being in order to see what does not present itself. Eckhart compares the eye to a sieve. Things must be "passed through the sieve [gebiutelt]." This sieve is not one figure among others; it tells the difference between Being and non-being. It discerns this difference, it allows one to see it, but as the eye itself. There is no text, above all no sermon, no possible predication, without the invention of such a filter.

## C

I thus decided *not to speak* of negativity or of apophatic movements in, for example, the Jewish or Islamic traditions. To leave this immense place empty, and above all that which can connect such a name of God with the name of the Place, to remain thus on the threshold—was this not the most consistent possible apophasis? Concerning that about which one cannot speak, isn't it best to remain silent? I let you answer this question. It is always entrusted to the other.

My first paradigm was Greek and the second Christian, without yet ceasing to be Greek. The last will be neither Greek nor Christian. If I were not afraid of trying your patience I would recall that which, in Heidegger's thinking, could resemble the most questioning legacy, both the most audacious and most liberated repetition of the traditions I have just evoked. Here I will have to limit myself to a few landmarks.

One could read *What Is Metaphysics?* as a treatise on negativity. It establishes the basis for negative discourse and negation in the experience of the Nothing which itself "nothings" ("das Nichts selbst nichtet"). The experience of anguish puts us in relation to a negating (*Nichtung*) which is neither annihilation (*Vernichtung*), nor a negation or a denial (*Verneinung*). It reveals to us the strangeness (*Befremdlichkeit*) of what is (being, *das Seiende*) as the wholly other (*das schlechthin Andere*). It thus opens up the possibility of the question of Being for *Dasein*, the structure of which is characterized precisely by what Heidegger calls transcendence. This transcendence, *Vom Wesen des Grundes* will say, is "properly expressed" (*eigens ausgesprochen*) by the Platonic expression *epekeina tes ousias*. Unable to involve myself, here, in the interpretation of the *agathon* subsequently proposed by Heidegger, I merely wished to mark this passage beyond Being, or rather beyond beingness, and the reinterpretation of negativity that accompanies it. Heidegger specifies immediately that Plato could not elaborate "the original content of the *epekeina tes ousias* as transcendence of *Dasein* [der ursprüngliche Gehalt des *epekeina* als Transzendenz des Daseins]." He makes an analogous gesture with regard to the *khora:* in the *Einführung in die Metaphysik,* a brief parenthesis suggests that Plato fell short of thinking of the place (*Ort*) which, however, signaled to him. In truth, he only prepared (*vorbereitet*) the Cartesian interpretation of place or space as *extensio* (*Ausdehnung*).[23] Elsewhere I try to show what is problematic and reductive about this perspective. Some seventeen years later, the last page of *Was heisst Denken?* mentions *khora* and *khorismos* anew, without any explicit reference to the *Timaeus.* Plato, who is supposed to have given the most determinative *Deutung* for Western thought, situates the *khorismos*—the interval or the separation, the spacing—between beings (*Seiendes*) and Being (*Sein*). But "e khora heisst der Ort," "the *khora* means the place." For Plato, beings and Being are thus "placed differently [verschieden geortet]." "If Plato takes the *khorismos* into consideration, the difference of place [die verschiedene Ortung] between Being and beings, he thus poses the question of the wholly other place [nach dem ganz anderen Ort] of Being, by comparison with that of beings." That Plato is afterward suspected of having fallen short of this wholly *other* place, and that one must lead the diversity (*Verschiedenheit*) of places back to the difference (*Unterschied*) and the fold of a duplicity (*Zwiefalt*) which must be given in advance, without one ever being able to give it "proper attention"—I can follow this process neither at the end of *Was heisst Denken?* nor elsewhere. I merely underscore this movement toward a *wholly* other place, as place of Being or *place of the wholly other:* in and beyond a Platonic or Neoplatonic tradition. But also in and beyond a Christian tradition of which Heidegger—while submerged in it, as in the Greek tradition—never ceased claiming, whether by denial or not, that it could in no case entertain a philosophy. "A Christian philosophy," he often says, "is a squared circle and a misconception [Missverständnis]."[24] It is necessary to distinguish between, on the one hand, onto-theology or theiology, and, on the other hand, theology.[25] The former concerns the supreme being, the being *par excellence,* ultimate foundation or *causa sui* in its divinity. The latter is a science of faith or of divine speech, such as it manifests itself in revelation (*Offenbarung*). Heidegger again seems to distinguish between manifestation, the possibility of Being to reveal itself (*Offenbarkeit*), and, on the other hand, the revelation (*Offenbarung*) of the God of theology.[26]

Immense problems are screened behind these distinctions. One may follow, through Heidegger's works, the threads that we have already recognized: revelation, the promise, or the gift (*das Geben, die Gabe,* and the *es gibt,* which progressively and profoundly displace the question of Being and its transcendental horizon, time, in *Sein und Zeit*),[27] or yet the *Ereignis* which one sometimes translates, in such a problematic manner, by "event." I will limit myself to the question that my title commands: *How to avoid speaking?* More precisely: How to avoid speaking *of Being?* A question in which I will underscore equally the importance of avoiding and that of Being, as if to grant them equal dignity, a sort of common essentiality, which will not go without consequences. These are the consequences that interest me.

What does the avoidance signify here? In regard to Being or the word "Being," does it always have the mode that we have recognized for it in apophatic theologies? For Heidegger, would these be examples of aberration or of the "squared circle"—namely Christian philosophies or unacknowledged onto-theologies? Does the avoidance belong to the category or to the diagnostic of denial (*Verneinung*), in a sense determined this time by a Freudian problematic ("least of all do I say that")? Or again: with regard to the traditions and texts that I have just evoked, and in particular those of Dionysius and Meister Eckhart,[28] does Heidegger stand in a relationship of avoidance? What abyss would this simple word, *avoidance,* then designate?

(*To say nothing*, once again, of the mysticisms or theologies in the Jewish, Islamic, or other traditions.)

Twice, in two apparently different contexts and senses, Heidegger *explicitly proposed* to avoid (is there denial, in this case?) the word *being*. More exactly, not to *avoid* speaking of Being but to avoid *using* the word *being*. Even more exactly, not to avoid mentioning it—as certain speech-act theorists, who distinguish between mention and use, would say—but to avoid using it. Thus he explicitly proposes, not to avoid speaking of Being, nor in some way to avoid mentioning the word *being*, but to refrain from using it normally, one may say, without placing it in quotation marks or under erasure.

And in both cases, we may suspect, the stakes are serious—even if they seem to hold to the subtle fragility of a terminological, typographical, or more broadly, "pragmatic" artifice. But in both cases, the *place* is at issue, and this is why I privilege them.

1. First, in *Zur Seinsfrage* (1952), precisely in regard to thinking the essence of modern nihilism, Heidegger reminds Ernst Jünger of the necessity for a topology of Being and of the Nothing. He distinguishes this topology from a simple topography, and he has just proposed a reinterpretation of the seal, of the *typos*, of the Platonic and of the modern typography. It is then that Heidegger proposes to write *Being*, the word *being*, under erasure, an erasure in the form of a crossing out (*kreuzweise Durchstreichung*). The word *being* is not avoided; it remains readable. But this readability announces that the word may solely be read, deciphered; it cannot or must not be pronounced, used normally, one might say, as a speech-act of ordinary language. It is necessary to decipher it under a spatialized typography, spaced or spacing, printing over. Even if this does not avoid the strange word *being*, it should at least prevent and warn against, deviate from, while designating, the normal recourse (if such exists) to it. But Heidegger also warns us against the simply *negative* use of this *Durchstreichung*. This erasure does not, then, have *avoidance* as its essential function. No doubt, Being is not a being, and it reduces to its turns, turnings, historical tropes (*Zuwendungen*); one must therefore avoid representing it (*vorzustellen*) as something, an object that stands *opposite* (*gegenüber*) man and then comes toward him. To avoid this objectifying representation (*Vorstellung*), one will thus write the word *being* under erasure. It is henceforth not heard, but is read in a certain manner. In what manner? If this *Durchstreichung* is neither a sign nor merely a negative sign ("kein bloss negatives Zeichen"), this is because it does not efface "Being" beneath conventional and abstract marks. Heidegger understands it as showing (*zeigen*) the four regions (*Gegenden*) of what he here and elsewhere calls the fourfold (*Geviert*): earth and heavens, mortals and the divine. Why does this written cross, according to Heidegger, have nothing of a negative signification? 1. In withdrawing Being from the subject/object relation, it allows Being to be read, both the word and the meaning of Being. 2. Next it "shows" the four-

fold (*Geviert*). 3. But above all it *gathers*. This gathering takes place and has its *place* (*Ort*) in the crossing point of the *Durchkreuzung*.[29] The gathering of the *Geviert*, in a place of crossing ("Versammlung im Ort der Durchkreuzung"), lends itself to writing and reading in an indivisible *topos*, in the simplicity (*die Einfalt*) of the point, of this *Ort* whose name appears so difficult to translate. Heidegger tells us elsewhere that this name "originally signifies" "the point of the sword,"[30] that toward which all converges and assembles. This indivisible point always assures the possibility of the *Versammlung*. It gives place to it; it is always the gathering, *das Versammelnde*. "The place gathers toward itself at the greatest height and extremity [Der Ort versammelt zu sich ins Höchste und Äusserste]."

Nevertheless, in order to think the negative appearance of this erasure, to gain access to the origin of negativity, of negation, of nihilism, and perhaps also of avoidance, it would thus be necessary to think the place of the Nothing. "What is the place of the Nothing [der Ort des Nichts]?" Heidegger has just asked. Now he specifies: the Nothing should also be *written*, that is to say *thought*. Like Being, it should also be written and read under erasure: "Wie das ~~Sein~~, so müsste auch das Nichts geschrieben und d.h. gedacht werden."

2. Elsewhere, in an apparently different context, Heidegger explains the sense in which he would *avoid* speaking of Being, this time without placing it under erasure. More precisely, the sense in which he would avoid *writing* the word *being*. More precisely still (while remaining in the conditional mode, and this counts for much here), the sense in which "the word 'being' [das Wort 'Sein']" should not take place, occur, happen (*vorkommen*) in his text. It is not a matter of "remaining silent," as one would prefer to do, he says elsewhere,[31] when the "thinking of God" (on the subject of God) is in question. No; the point is, rather, not to allow the word *being* to occur, on the subject of God.

The text is presented as a *transcription*. Responding to students at the University of Zürich in 1951, Heidegger recalls that Being and God are not identical, and that he would always avoid thinking God's essence by means of Being. He makes this more precise in a sentence in which I underscore the words *were*, *ought*, and *write*: "If I *were* yet to *write* a theology, as I am sometimes tempted to do, the word 'being' *ought* not to appear there [take place there, occur, figure, or happen there] [Wenn ich noch eine Theologie *screiben würde,* wozu es mich manchmal reizt, dann *dürfte* in ihr das Worth 'Sein' nicht vorkommen]."[32]

How may one analyze the folds of denial in this conditional of writing, in the course of an oral improvisation? Can one recognize the modalities in it without first departing from the foundation and from the thing itself—here, that is, from Being and God? Heidegger speaks in order to say what *would happen if he were to write* one day. But he knows that what he says is already being written. If he were to write a theology, the word *being* would not be under erasure; it wouldn't even appear there. For the moment, speaking and writing on the subject of what he *ought to* or *could* write regarding theology, Heidegger allows the word *being* to appear; he does not use it, but mentions it without erasure when he is indeed speaking of theology, of that which he would be tempted to write. Where does this, then, take place? Does it have place? What would take place?

Heidegger continues, "Faith has no need for the thinking of Being." As he often recalls, Christians ought to allow themselves to be inspired by Luther's lucidity on this subject. Indeed, even if Being is "neither the foundation nor the essence of God [Grund und Wesen von Gott]," the experience of God (*die Erfahrung Gottes*) —that is, the experience of revelation—"occurs in the dimension of Being [in der Dimension des Seins sich ereignet]." This revelation is not that (*Offenbarung*) of which the religions speak, but the possibility of this revelation, the opening for this manifestation, this *Offenbarkeit* of which I spoke earlier and in which an *Offenbarung* can take place and man can encounter God. Although God is not and need not be thought from Being as His essence or foundation, the *dimension of Being* opens up access to the advent, the experience, the encounter with this God who nevertheless is not. The word *dimension*—which is also difference—here gives a measure while giving place. One could sketch a singular chiasmus. The anguished experience of the Nothing discloses Being. Here, the dimension of Being discloses the experience of God, who is not or whose Being is either the essence nor the foundation.

How not to think of this? This dimension of disclosure, this place that gives place without being either essence or foundation—would not this step or passage, this threshold that gives access to God, yet be the "parvis" (*vorbürge*) of which Meister Eckhart spoke? "When we apprehend God in Being, we apprehend Him in His outer sanctuary [*parvis*], for Being is the *parvis* in which He resides." Is this a theiological, an onto-theological, tradition? A theological tradition? Would Heidegger adopt it? Would he disown it? Would he deny it?

I do not intend to respond to these questions, nor even to conclude with them. More modestly, in a more hasty but also more programmatic manner, I return to the enigma of avoidance, of negation, or of denial in a scene of writing. Heidegger *says* (then allows to be written in his name) that if he *were to write* a theology, he would avoid the word *being;* he would avoid writing it and this word would not figure in his text; or rather should not be present in it. What does he mean? That the word would figure in it yet under erasure, appearing there without appearing, quoted but not used? No; it should not figure in it at all. Heidegger well knows that this is not possible, and perhaps it is for this profound reason that he did not write this theology. But didn't he write it? And in it did he avoid writing the word *being?* In fact, since Being is not (a being) and in truth is nothing (that is), what difference is there between writing *Being,* this Being which is not, and writing *God,* this God of whom Heidegger also says that He is not? Indeed, Heidegger does not merely say that God is not a being; he specifies that He "has nothing to do here with Being [Mit dem Sein, ist hier nichts anzusichten]." But since he recognizes that God announces Himself to experience in the "dimension of Being," what difference is there between writing a theology and writing on Being, of Being, as Heidegger never ceases doing? Most of all, when he writes the word *being* under and in the place (*Ort*) of the cancellation in the form of a cross? Hasn't Heidegger written what he says he would have liked to write, a theology *without* the word *being*? But didn't he also write what he says should not be written, what he should not have written, namely a theology that is opened, dominated, and invaded by the word *being*?

With and without the word *being,* he wrote a theology with and without God. He did what he said it would be necessary to avoid doing. He said, wrote, and allowed to be written exactly what he said he wanted to avoid. He was not there without leaving a trace of all these folds. He was not there without allowing a trace to appear, a trace that is, perhaps, no longer his own, but that remains as if (*quasiment*) his own. *Not, without, quasi* are three adverbs. *Quasiment.* Fable or fiction, everything happens as if I had wanted to ask, on the threshold of this lecture, what these three adverbs mean and whence they come.

P.S. One more word to conclude, and I ask your pardon for it. I am not certain that only rhetoric is at stake. But this also concerns the strange discursive modality, or rather the *step of* (not) *writing* (*pas d'écriture*), Heidegger's pass, impasse, or dodge. What does he do? He says to some students, in short: if I had to write a theology (I have always dreamed of this, but I didn't do it and know that I will never do it), I would not let the word *being* occur (*vorkommen*). It would not have a place, it would not have the right to a place in such a text. I mention this word here but I have never let it occur, it could not figure in all my work, except in *not doing it*—since I always said that Being is *not* (a being, that is) and that it *would have always had to* be written *under erasure*, a rule that I did not in fact always observe, but which I should have respected in principle, starting from the first word, *dès le premier verbe.* Understand me: this is an erasure that would above all have nothing negative about it! And even less of denegation! Etc.

What is thus the discursive modality of this *step of* (not) *writing* and of this abyss of denial? Is it first of all a modality, a simple modality among other possible ones, or rather a quasi-transcendental recourse of writing? We should not forget that we are dealing with an oral declaration, later recorded from memory by Beda Allemann. Heidegger indeed approved this protocol, but while remarking that it did not render present the atmosphere of the discussion, nor would a "complete shorthand report" have done this: no writing could have rendered what had been said *there.*

What was said *there* was addressed to colleagues and students, to disciples, in the very broad sense of this word. Like the address of Dionysius, in his apostrophe to Timothy, this text has a pedagogical or psychological virtue. It remains a text (written or oral; no matter) only in this measure: as repetition or repeatability on an *agogic* path.

But there is never a prayer, not even an apostrophe, in Heidegger's rhetoric. Unlike Dionysius, he never says "you":

neither to God nor to a disciple or reader. There is no place, or in any case there is no regularly assigned place, for these "neither true nor false" utterances that prayers are, according to Aristotle. This may be interpreted in at least two ways, which appear contradictory.

1. This absence signifies in effect that theology (in the sense in which Heidegger links it to faith and distinguishes it from theiology and from metaphysical onto-theology) is rigorously excluded from his texts. It is well defined there but excluded, at least in what ought to *direct* it, namely the movement of faith. And in fact, while thinking that solely the truth of Being can open onto the essense of the divinity and to what the word *god* means (one is familiar with the famous passage in the "Letter on Humanism"), Heidegger says no less: "At the interior of thought, nothing could be accomplished that would prepare for or contribute to determining what happens in faith and in grace. If faith summoned me in this manner, I would close down shop. —Of course, interior to the dimension of faith, one yet continues to think; but thinking as such no longer has a task."[33] In short, neither faith nor science, as such, thinks or has thinking as its task.

This absence of prayer, or of apostrophe in general, also confirms the predominance of the theoretical, "constative," even propositional form (in the third-person, indicative present: S is P) in the rhetoric, at least, of a text which yet forcefully questions the determination of truth linked to this theoreticism and to this judicative form.

2. But at the same time, on the contrary, one can read here a sign of respect for prayer. For the formidable questions evoked by the essence of prayer: can or must a prayer allow itself to be mentioned, quoted, inscribed in a compelling, *agogic* proof? Perhaps it need not be. Perhaps it must not do this. Perhaps, on the contrary, it must do this. Are there criteria external to the event itself to decide whether Dionysius, for example, distorted or rather accomplished the essence of prayer by quoting it, and first of all by writing it for Timothy? Does one have the right to think that, as a pure address, on the edge of silence, alien to every code and to every rite, hence to every repetition, prayer should never be turned away from its part by a notation or by the movement of an apostrophe, by a multiplication of addresses? That each time it takes place only once and should never be re-

corded? But perhaps the contrary is the case. Perhaps there would be no prayer, no pure possibility of prayer, without what we glimpse as a menace or as a contamination: writing, the code, repetition, analogy or the—at least apparent—multiplicity of addresses, initiation. If there were a purely pure experience of prayer, would one need religion and affirmative or negative theologies? Would one need a supplement of prayer? But if there were no supplement, if quotation did not bend prayer, if prayer did not bend, if it did not submit to writing, would a theiology be possible? Would a theology be possible?

## Notes

Translator's note: I shall avoid the customary apologies and excuses, denials and disclaimers, instead merely acknowledging the assistance of Barbara Caulk and Ora Wiskind in revisions of this translation.

1. Who has ever assumed the project of *the* negative theology *as such*, reclaiming it in the singular under this name, without subjugating and subordinating it, without at least pluralizing it? On the subject of this title, *the* negative theology, can one do anything but *deny* it? Jean-Luc Marion contests the legitimacy of this title, not only for the ensemble of Dionysius' oeuvre—which goes without saying—but even for the places where there is a question of "negative theologies" in the plural ("tines oi kataphatikai theologiai, tines ai apophatikai") in chapter 3 of the *Mystical Theology*. Concerning "what it is suitable to call 'negative theology,' " Jean-Luc Marion notes: "To our knowledge, Dionysius employs nothing which may be translated by 'negative theology.' If he speaks of 'negative theologies,' in the plural, he does not separate them from the 'affirmative theologies' with which they maintain the relationship which one describes here." (See the *Mystical Theology*, 1032 et seq.) Marion, *L'idole et la distance* (Paris: Grasset, 1977), pp. 189 and 244.

2. This occurred in diverse passages and contexts. I will cite only one in order to clarify a point and, perhaps, to respond to an objection which has the merit of not being stereotypical. In "Différance" (1968), contained in my *Margins of Philosophy*, trans. Alan Bass (Chicago: University of Chicago Press, 1982), p. 6, I wrote: "So much so that the detours, locutions, and syntax in which I will often have to take recourse will resemble those of

negative theology, occasionally even to the point of being indistinguishable from negative theology. Already we have had to delineate *that différance is not*, does not exist, is not a present-being (*on*) in any form; and we will be led to delineate also everything *that* it *is not*, that is, *everything;* and consequently that it has neither existence nor essence. It derives from no category of being, whether present or absent. And yet those aspects of *différance* which are thereby delineated are not theological, not even in the order of the most negative of negative theologies, which as one knows are always concerned with disengaging a hyperessentiality beyond the finite categories of essence and existence, that is, of presence, and always hastening to recall that God is refused the predicate of existence, only in order to acknowledge His superior, inconceivable, and ineffable mode of being" (translation modified slightly [KF]). After having quoted this last sentence, in *L'idole et la distance*, p. 318, Jean-Luc Marion objects: "What does 'one knows' mean here? We have seen, precisely, that the so-called negative theology, *in its depths* [my italics], does not aim to reestablish a 'hyperessentiality,' since it aims at neither predication nor at Being; how, *a fortiori*, could there be a question of existence and essence in Dionysius, who speaks a sufficiently originary Greek to see it in neither the idea nor the usage?" Here, too briefly, are some elements of a response. 1. In speaking of presence or absence, of existence or essence, I sought merely to specify, in a cursory manner, the different categories or modalities of presence in general, without precise historical reference to Dionysius. 2. Whatever may be the complex and quite enigmatic historicity of the distinction between essence and existence, I am not sure that it is simply ignored by Dionysius: how can one be certain of the *absence* of such a distinction at any stage of the Greek language? What does "a sufficiently originary Greek" mean? 3. What does "in its depths" mean here? What does it mean that "negative theology," in its depths, does not aim to reestablish a "hyperessentiality"? First of all, as Marion knows better than anyone else, it is difficult to consider accidental the reference to this hyperessentiality which plays a major, insistent, and *literal* role in so many texts by Dionysius—and by others, who I will cite later. Next—beyond this obvious case, the only one to which I had to refer in a lecture that was not devoted to negative theology and did not even name Dionysius—it is necessary to elaborate an interpretive discourse as interesting and original as that of Marion, at the crossing, in the wake, sometimes beyond thoughts like those of Heidegger, Urs von Balthasar, Levinas, and some others, to distinguish the "depths" (the thinking of the gift, of paternity, of distance, of celebration, etc.) from what in the so-called "negative theology" still seems to be very concerned with hyperessentiality. But without being able to develop this third point here, I will return to it below, at least in principle and in an oblique fashion.

3. Concerning a paradoxical writing of the word *without* (*sans*), notably in the work of Blanchot, I allow myself to refer to the essay "Pas" in *Gramma* (1976), nos. 3–4, reprinted in my *Parages* (Paris: Galilée, 1986). *Dieu sans l'être* is the magnificent title of a book by Jean-Luc Marion (Paris: Fayard, 1982), to which I cannot do justice in the space of a note or the time of a lecture. This title remains difficult to translate. Its very suspension depends on the grammatical vacillation that only French syntax can tolerate—precisely in the structure of a title—that is, of a nominal or incomplete phrase. *L'* may be the definite article of the noun *être* (*God without Being*), but it can also be a personal pronoun—object of the *verb* to be—referring to God, from God to God Himself who would not be what He is or who would be what He is *without being* (*it*) (*God without being God, God without being*): God with and without being. On the subject of a title's syntax, Levinas preferred to say—also in a most singular syntax, no doubt in order to avoid this ultimate precedence of Being or of the predicative sentence that would insinuate itself here—rather than "Being without Being," "God with or beyond Being," extra-essence, or hyperessence: *otherwise than Being.* Let us not forget these fairly recent, thought-provoking titles—*Dieu sans l'être* and *Autrement qu'être ou audelà de l'essence* (1974–78)—which seek, in two very different ways, to avoid what Levinas calls the contamination by Being, in order to "hear God not contaminated by Being" for example. Grammar does not suffice, but it never reduces to an accessory instrumentality; by the word *grammar* one designates a discipline and its history, or more radically the modalities of writing—how one writes of God. The two cited titles lead the way to two major responses to the question I would like to raise: how not to say or speak? Otherwise, and implicitly: how not to speak Being (how to avoid speaking—of Being?)? How to speak Being otherwise? How to speak otherwise (than) being? And so on.

4. Meister Eckhart, *Quasi stella matutina.* All translations of Meister Eckhart's sermons are based on *Meister Eckharts Predigten,* ed. Josef Quint (Stuttgart: W. Kohlhammer, 1936), vols. 1–3. The present passage appears in 1:145–46.

5. Pseudo-Dionysius, *The Mystical Theology*, in *The Divine Names and Mystical Theology,* trans. John D. Jones (Milwaukee, Wis.: Marquette University Press, 1980), ch. 1:998a et seq. References to these two works, cited in the text as *MT* and *DN,* are modified slightly from this translation [KF]. For obvious reasons, I will sometimes quote several words of the original text [JD].

6. Here the author alludes to the grammar of biblical Hebrew, which does not employ a present-tense form of the verb *to be;* the previous paragraph refers to a messianic motif in the Passover Haggadah [KF].

7. *Adolescens, tibi dico: surge,* in *Meister Eckharts Predigten,* 2:305.

8. Provenance of the call: Jerusalem. Sanford Budick had just called. He had to record a title, however provisory, on the program of the colloquium. I must associate the memory of this telephone call with that of a telegram. It also came from Jerusalem and was signed by Sanford Budick, who was then preparing the volume, which has since appeared, *Midrash and Literature* (New Haven, Conn.: Yale University Press, 1986). Having learned that in Seattle, during a colloquium devoted to Paul Celan, I had given what he called a "lecture on circumcision," he asked me: "could we have a portion of that lecture or some other piece you would be willing to give us however short stop midrash volume soon going to press."

9. Here it is not possible to become directly involved with this difficult problem of Hierarchy, in particular concerning relations of translation or analogy—or regarding the rupture and heterogeneity between hierarchy *as such,* namely "the sacred ordinance," the principle or origin of sanctity, and, on the other hand, the sociopolitical order. One may follow Jean-Luc Marion as far as possible when he dissociates the "*hierarchy,* understood from the Theandric mystery of which the Church offers us the unique place" and the "vulgar concept" or the "common concept" of hierarchy (*L'idole et la distance,* p. 209). One might even agree with certain of his more provocative formulations ("the political model of hierarchy has nothing to do with the mystery of the hierarchy which opens onto the communion of saints. The deliberate or naive equivocation betrays the perversion of the look, and does not even merit refutation. At issue is only seeing, or not seeing"; p. 217). No doubt, but what it is also *necessary to see* is the historic, essential, undeniable, and irreducible possibility of the aforementioned perversity which is perhaps only considerable by first having been observable, as one says, "in fact." How is the "vulgar concept" constituted? This is what it is also necessary to see or not to not see. How is it possible that "distance"—in the sense Marion gives to this word and which also makes up the distance between the two hierarchies—can have let itself be overstepped or "traversed" and *give place to the analogical translation of one hierarchy into another?* Can one proscribe here an "analogy" which appears nevertheless to support all of this construction? And if the translation is bad, erroneous, "vulgar," what would be the good political translation of the hierarchy as a "sacred

ordinance"? This is only a question, but it is not impossible that its matrix holds others of the same kind in reserve, on the subject of the trinitarian Thearchy of which the hierarchy would be "the icon, at once resembling and dissembling" (p. 224; and the entire exposition on pp. 207ff starting from the term "hierarchy" which "Dionysius mobilizes" and which "our modernity prohibits us from the outset from understanding correctly"); and thus on the subject of the trinitarian or patristic scheme sustaining a thinking of the gift that does not necessarily require it or that perhaps finds in it a strange and unfathomable *economy*, in other words a fascinating limit. Here I must interrupt this lengthy note on a noneconomy or an anarchy of the gift, which nevertheless has concerned me for a long time. In this regard I feel that Marion's thought is both very close and extremely distant; others might say opposed.

10. *Ecclesiastical Hierarchy*, p. 564a. Quotations from this work are translated from the French version cited by Derrida, as are a few short passages from the *Divine Names* and *Mystical Theology*.

11. "The infinite *différance* is finite." See Derrida, *Speech and Phenomenon and Other Essays*, trans. David Allison (Evanston, Ill.: Northwestern University Press, 1973), p. 102.

12. This allusion referred to a seminar on Jeremiah which had just taken place in Jerusalem (at the Institute for Advanced Studies), shortly before this colloquium, and to a large extent with the same participants. Concerning that which a question (be it the "piety of thought") must *already* contain in itself and which no longer belongs to the questioning, see my *De l'esprit: Heidegger et la question* (Paris: Galilée, 1987), pp. 147ff.

13. Despite this silence, or in fact because of it, one will perhaps permit me to interpret this lecture as the most "autobiographical" speech I have ever risked. One will attach to this word as many quotation marks as possible. It is necessary to surround with precautions the hypothesis of a self-presentation passing through a speech on the negative theology of others. But if one day I had to tell my story, nothing in this narrative would start to speak of the thing itself if I did not come up against this fact; for lack of capacity, competence, or self-authorization, I have never yet been able to speak of what my birth, as one says, should have made closest to me: the Jew, the Arab.

This small piece of autobiography confirms it obliquely. It is performed in all of my foreign languages: French, English, German, Greek, Latin, the philosophic, metaphilosophic, Christian, etc.

In brief, how not to speak of oneself? But also: how to do it without allowing oneself to be invented by the other? or without inventing the other?

14. A long introduction to this work in progress has appeared under the title *Chora*, in a volume in honor of Jean-Pierre Vernant.

15. See my essay "Le retrait de la métaphore," in *Psyché*, pp. 63–93.

16. Quoted by Jean-Luc Marion in *L'idole et la distance*, p. 249. Here I refer to this work, and in particular to the chapter "The Distance of the *Requisit* and the Discourse of Encomium: Dionysius." I must admit that I had not read this book at the time of writing this lecture. This book was in fact published in 1977, and its author had amicably sent it to me. Discouraged or irritated by the signs of reductive misunderstanding or injustice concerning me, which I thought I had immediately discerned, I made the mistake of not continuing my reading, thus allowing myself to be diverted by quite a secondary aspect (namely, his relationship to my work); today, after rereading Dionysius and preparing the present lecture, I better perceive the force and the necessity of this work—which does not always signify, on my part, an agreement without reservations. Since the limitations of this publication do not permit me to explain myself, I defer the matter until later. Nevertheless, the few lines in which I distinguish between prayer and encomium, like the references to *Dieu sans l'être*, were subsequently added to the exposition that I had devoted to prayer in the lecture read in Jerusalem. I did this in response and in homage to Jean-Luc Marion, who seems to me to give the impression all too quickly that the passage to the encomium is the passage to prayer itself, or that between these two the passage is immediate, necessary, and in some way analytic. Notably, when he writes: "Dionysius tends to substitute another verb for the *speaking* of predicative language, ὑμνεῖν, to praise. What does this substitution signify? It no doubt indicates the passage of the discourse to prayer, because 'prayer is a λόγος, but neither true nor false' (Aristotle)" (p. 232). What Aristotle says, as a matter of fact, in the *Peri Hermeneias* (17a), is that if all *logos* is significant (*semantikos*), only one in which one can distinguish the true and false is *apophantic*, and constitutes an affirmative proposition. And he adds: this does not appertain to all *logos;* "thus prayer [eukhè] is a discourse [logos], but neither true nor false [all'outè alethès oute pseudes]." But would Aristotle have said that the encomium (*hymnein*) is not apophantic? That it is neither true nor false? That it has no relationship to the distinction between the true and the false? One may doubt this. One may even doubt it in the case of Dionysius. For if the encomium or the celebration of

God indeed does not have the same rule of predication as every other proposition, even if the "truth" to which it lays claim is the higher truth of a hyperessentiality, it celebrates and names what "is" such as it "is," beyond Being. Even if it is not a predicative affirmation of the current type, the encomium preserves the style and the structure of a predicative affirmation. It says something about someone. This is not the case of the prayer that apostrophizes, addresses itself to the other and remains, in this pure movement, absolutely pre-predicative. Here it does not suffice to underscore the performative character of utterances of prayer and encomium. The performance itself does not always exclude predication. All the passages from the *Divine Names* or the *Mystical Theology*, to which Marion refers in a note (n. 65, p. 249) as "confirmation," involve an encomium or, as M. de Gandillac sometimes translates, a celebration that is not a prayer and that entails a predicative aim, however foreign it may be to "normal" ontological predication. One may even risk the following paradox: sometimes the celebration can go further than the prayer, at least in supplementing it where it cannot "accomplish" itself, namely, as Dionysius says, in the "union" (*DN*, ch. 2:680bcd). Even if the encomium cannot merely bring to light (*ekphainein*) or say, it says and determines —as that which it is — the very fact that it cannot show and know, and to which it cannot unite itself even by prayer. If prayer, at least according to Dionysius, tends toward union with God, the encomium is not prayer; it is at most its supplement. It is what is added to it, when union remains inaccessible or fails to occur, playing the role of substitute, but also determining the referent itself, which is also the cause (the Réquisit, Marion would say) of the prayer. It can incite to prayer, it can also follow it, but it is not identical with it. From many other possible examples, here I recall only the one Marion rightly quotes, underscoring a few words; "We must merely recall that this discourse does not aim to bring to light (εκφαινειν) the hyperessential essence insofar as it is hyperessential (because it remains unspeakable, unknowable, and thus entirely impossible to bring to light, *eluding all union*), but much rather to praise the procession which makes the essences and which comes before all the beings of the [trinitary] thearchy, a principle of essence" (*DN*, ch. 5:816c; cited by Marion on pp. 249–50). This passage may be found on p. 128 of the (often different) translation by Maurice de Gandillac in the (*Œvres Complètes of* Pseudo-Dionysius the Areopagite (Paris: Aubier-Montaigne, 1943). Not to bring to light, not to reveal (*ekphainein*), not to make access to it by a revelation reaching "union": this is not exactly not to speak, not to name, nor even to abstain from attributing (even if this is beyond Being). This is not to avoid speaking. It is even to start to speak in order to determine the addressee of the prayer, an addressee who is also *aitia*, of course, and cause or *requisit* of the prayer, according to a trinitary beyond of Being, a thearchy as principle of essence.

17. Marion, *L'idole et la distance*, p. 240.

18. *Quasi stella matutina*, in *Meister Eckharts Predigten*, 1;142.

19. Repetition appears at once proscribed, impossible and necessary, as if it were necessary to avoid the unavoidable. To analyze the law of these paradoxes from the viewpoint of writing (notably in the current sense of the word) or of a pedagogical initiation—which is much more than a "point of view"—it would be necessary to follow very closely such a passage in the *Divine Names*, for example, as that which explains to us why it would be "folly" to "repeat the same truths twice." For example, those of the *Theological Elements* of "our preceptor Hierotheus." If Dionysius undertakes to write other treatises, "and particularly that which one reads here [kai ten parousian theologian]," it is only to introduce *supplements* adapted to our forces (expositions, clarifications, distinctions), where Hierotheus had magisterially contented himself with a collective picture of fundamental definitions. Because these supplement do not fill a lack, they repeat without repeating what is already said, virtually. They follow the order given and obey a given order. They transgress no law; on the contrary, "everything happened as if he [Hierotheus] had prescribed that we, and all other preceptors of still inexperienced souls, introduce expositions and distinctions by a reasoning which was adapted to our forces." But the order, the prayer, or the request also come from the reader, from the immediate addressee, Timothy, *as if* he reflected Hierotheus' prescription ("everything happened as if he had prescribed that we . . . "): "And to this task you yourself have often committed us, and have sent back the book of Hierotheus, judging it to be too difficult." From the most difficult to the simplest, the *adjunction* of supplements only compensates for *our* weakness and not for a gap on the side of what there is to read. Even before determining our relationship to the major text of Hierotheus, the first master, this supplementarity will have marked the relationship of Hierotheus' writing to God's writing, or rather, to God's "dictation." And thus the elite or the hierarchy—and analogy—is constituted: "the instructions of his complete and presbyterial thoughts—which might be viewed as *new adjunct writings* in conformity with the writings of those anointed of God—are for those beyond the many. Thus, we will transmit what is divine according to our logos to those who are our equals . . . The eyewitness vision of the intelligible writings and a comprehensive instruction in these require the power of a presbyter, but the knowl-

edge and thorough learning of the reason which bear one to this are adapted to those dedicated and hallowed persons who are inferiors" (*DN*, ch. 3:681bc); my italics [translation modified slightly—KF]). Always in view of a greater sanctification, and thus of aging *well*, the consideration of age only takes on its sense from this analogy and this teleology.

20. This passage is translated directly from the French version cited by Derrida.

21. *Meister Eckharts Predigten*, 3:437.

22. *Ibid.*, 1:150.

23. Martin Heidegger, *Einführung in die Metaphysik* (Tübingen: Max Niemeyer, 1953), pp. 50–51. In English, see *An Introduction to Metaphysics*, trans. Ralph Manheim (New Haven, Conn.: Yale University Press, 1959), p. 66.

24. *Ibid.*, p. 6 in the German original and p. 7 in the English translation.

25. Although this distinction is essential and stable, it does not always receive a terminological equivalent as clear as, for example, in Martin Heidegger, *Hegel's Concept of Experience* (New York: Harper and Row, 1970), p. 135: "The science Aristotle has described—the science that observes beings as beings—he calls First Philosophy. But first philosophy does not only contemplate beings in their beingness [Seiendheit]; it also contemplates that being which corresponds to beingness in all purity: the supreme being. This being, το θειον, the Divine [das Göttliche], is also with a curious ambiguity called 'Being.' First philosophy, as ontology, is also the theology of what truly is. It should more accurately be called theiology. The science of beings as such is in itself onto-theological." See also Heidegger's course on *Schelling* (1936; Tübingen: M. Niemeyer, 1971), pp. 61–62. Insofar as it is distinct from the onto-theological theiology, theology had been defined in *Sein und Zeit* (p. 10): a "more originary making explicit" of the being of man in his relation to God, starting from the "meaning of faith." See Heidegger's *Nietzsche* (Pfullingen: Neske, 1961), 2:58–59. In the preceding chapter, "Nihilismus, *nihil* und Nichts," Heidegger defines the essence of nihilism (from which Nietzsche will not have escaped): not to take seriously the question of the Nothing, "the essential non-thinking of the essence of the Nothing [das wesenhafte Nichtdenken an das Wesen des Nichts]" (*ibid.*, pp. 53–54).

26. See, in particular, the resumé of a session of the *Académie évangélique*, early in December 1953, in Hofgeismar, *Heidegger et la*

*question de Dieu*, trans. Jean Greisch (Paris: Grasset 1980), p. 335.

27. *Es gibt die Zeit, es gibt das Sein*, says "Zeit und Sein" in 1962. Later printed in Martin Heidegger, *Zur Sache des Denkens* (Tübingen: Max Niemeyer, 1969), pp. 1–25. There is no question of reversing priority or a logical order and saying that the gift precedes Being. But the thinking of the gift opens up the space in which Being and time give themselves and give themselves to thought. Here I cannot enter into these questions, to which in the 1970s I devoted a seminar at the *École normale supérieure* and at Yale University ("Donner le temps"), which expressly orient all the texts I have published since about 1972.

28. Heidegger sometimes quotes Meister Eckhart, and frequently in regard to the thinking of the thing. "*As the old master of reading the living*, Meister Eckhart, says, in what is unspoken of their language [i.e., that of things] is God first God" (Martin Heidegger, *Der Feldweg* [Frankfurt am Main: Vittorio Klostermann, 1953], p. 4; my italics). It is always on the subject of the thing that he associates the name of Dionysius (who, to my knowledge, he cites nowhere else) with that of Eckhart: "Meister Eckhart employs the word *dinc* both for God and for the soul. . . . Thereby this *master of thought* [my italics] by no means wishes to say that God and the soul are similar to a boulder: a material object; *dinc* is here the cautious and reserved name for something that is in general. Thus Meister Eckhart says, following a passage of Dionysius the Areopagite: *diu minne ist der natur, daz si den menschen wandelt in die dinc, die er minnet* [the nature of love is that it transforms man into the things he loves]. . . . Like Meister Eckhart, Kant speaks of things and understands, by this word, something that is. But for Kant, what is becomes an object of representation [Gegenstand des Vorstellens]" ("Das Ding," *Vorträge und Aufsätze* [Pfullingen: Neske, 1954], p. 169). I quote this last phrase because, as we shall see, it is not without relation to the reason for which Heidegger writes the word *being* under erasure. Concerning the concept of *Gemüt* in Heidegger and a tradition that also leads back to Eckhart, among others, see my *De l'esprit: Heidegger et la question* (Paris: Galilée, 1987), p. 125 and passim.

29. By an analogous but no doubt radically different gesture, Jean-Luc Marion inscribes the name of God under a cross in *Dieu sans l'être*, "crossing G~~o~~d with the cross which reveals Him only in the disappearance, His death and resurrection" (pp. 152–153). This is another thinking of the gift and of the trace, a "theology" which would be "rigorously Christian" by sometimes opposing itself to the most kindred thoughts, those of Heidegger in particular: "these questions could join together in a topical, apparently modest ques-

tion: does the name of God, who crosses Himself with a cross because He crucifies Himself, arise from Being? We say nothing of 'God' in general, or of thought which takes its starting-point from the divine, hence also from the fourfold; we speak of the God who crosses himself with a cross because He reveals Himself by His being placed on the cross, the God revealed by, in, and as Christ; in other words, the God of rigorously *Christian* theology" (p. 107). By placing a cross on "God" rather than on "Being," Marion proposes to subtract the thinking of the gift, or rather of the *trace* of the gift, because there is also and still at issue a thinking of the *trace,* from the Heideggerian fourfold: "*God gives.* The giving *[donation],* giving one cause to guess how 'it gives,' a donation, provides the only accessible trace of Him who gives. Being/beings, like everything, if it is taken into view as a giving, can therein allow one to guess the trace of another gift. Here solely the model of the gift which one admits is important—appropriation or distance. In the former case, naturally, the agency of God could not intervene, since the giving *[donner]* is included in the fourfold. . . . There remains to be glimpsed—if not with Heidegger, at least from his reading and, if necessary, against him—that God does not belong to Being/beings, and even that Being/beings arises from distance" (pp. 153–54). This thinking of the trace is thus also that of a "distance" not reducible to the ontological difference.

30. See, among many other places, the first page of Martin Heidegger, "Die Sprache im Gedicht: Eine Erörterung von Georg Trakls Gedicht," in Martin Heidegger, *Unterwegs zur Sprache* (Pfullingen: Neske, 1959), p. 37. In English, see Martin Heidegger, *On the Way to Language*, trans. Peter D. Hertz (New York: Harper and Row, 1971), p. 159.

31. "Metaphysics is onto-theology. Whoever has experienced theology in its own roots—both the theology of the Christian faith and that of philosophy—today prefers, in the realm of thinking, to *remain silent* [schweigen] about God. For the onto-theological character of metaphysics has become questionable [fragwürdig] for thought, not on the basis of any atheism, but out of the experience of a thinking that has shown, in onto-theology, the as yet *unthought* unity of the essence of metaphysics." See the bilingual edition of Martin Heidegger's *Identity and Difference*, trans. Joan Stambaugh (New York: Harper and Row, 1969), pp. 54–55 and 121. I have underscored the words *remain silent.*

32. This seminar was translated and presented by F. Fédier and D. Saatdjian in the review *Po&sie* (1980), vol. 13, and the passage I quote was also translated in the same year by Jean Greisch in *Heidegger et la question de Dieu*, p. 334. The German text of the

privately circulated edition was quoted, for the passage that interests us, by J.-L. Marion, in *Dieu sans l'être*, p. 93.

33. Report of a session of the Evangelical Academy in Hofgeismar, December 1953, trans. Jean Greisch, in *Heidegger et la question de Dieu*, p. 335.

# FOUR

# *On Not Solving Riddles Alone*

Michel Despland

A strange necessity haunts the history of philosophy. Fresh conflicts periodically arise to remind readers that philosophy is more than the accumulation (or sifting) of true statements that can be found in books. To limit examples to the Platonic corpus, my teacher René Schaerer in 1938 wrote *La Question platonicienne* to "recall" the obvious: Plato wrote dialogues, and any examination of their content should also pay attention to their form. More recently, Jacques Derrida[1] broke with a long line of philosophers who found *Phaedrus* badly organized by examining attentively the way the dialogue was composed; not surprisingly, he was led to subtler thoughts than those commonly discerned by commentators who had concluded that Plato was not in good form when he wrote this piece (on grounds of being either too young or too old). All those who have gone some distance in the understanding of Plato now acknowledge that his philosophical dialogues are also works of art, and that the *logos* in them entertains constant (and varied) relations to *mythos*.[2] Besides being committed to the quest for knowledge and true opinions, Plato also strove to use language in a manner that makes it a good practice. (He accepts, even welcomes, public accountability on this point. His dialogues always invite third parties to assess the interaction of the protagonists.)

A similar necessity haunts the history of theology. In spite of its name (as some interpret it), theology is more than statements about God. The similarity, however, between the history of philosophy and that of theology may well stop here; for what else is there in theology? Service of the church, wrote Karl Barth, echoing Schleiermacher's statement to the effect that theologians are "princes of the church." (We may smile at the lack of modesty in such self-presentation, until we realize that princes may be made to give account of their use of power more easily than those who claim to be "servants of the servants of God.") Whether one insists that theologians must also be "committed Christians," or one requires the swearing of the antimodernist oath from them before allowing them to ply their trade, modern versions of the nature of Christian theology make it also, almost universally, a social praxis with a definite institutional context and obligations. It was not always like that. Edward Farley pointed out[3] that Divinity, as it was called in the early modern period, had a primarily sapiential meaning: to study theology was an endeavor of piety and led to growth in wisdom. This personal emphasis received a memorable expression in the last verses of Silesius's *Cherubinischer Wandersmann* (1657):

> Freund, es ist auch genug. Im Fall du mehr wilt lesen,
> So geh und werde selbst die Schrifft und selbst das Wesen.

At the end of the book, the reader is expected, not to review his reading the better to remember it, but to proceed with living, and write the rest in the language of deeds. The fateful turn, argues Farley, occurred with Schleiermacher: in his theory, theology became the basis for leadership in religious life, which he defined as an indispensible cultural practice. (Schleiermacher was determined to earn fairly a place for the theological faculty in the modern university and did not hesitate to jettison the older truth claims.) Theology was thus well on its way toward becoming the sum of professional skills a pastor needs to lead a church; when this point is reached, one is not far from admitting that good theology ensures the social duration of the institution and need not be of personal value to the student.[4]

Throughout the history of the church, negative theology appeared as an alternative to the mainstream. A weaker alternative for some; thus Derrida was accused of offering "only" a negative theology;[5] the implication was that he was obtaining only negative results and therefore was not contributing anything. But others have considered negative theology a higher, better alternative, correcting the inadequacies of the other theology. Most accounts today would consider these inadequacies to be mainly epistemological: positive theology claims to know more than one can in fact know. In contrast, on this view, negative theology has more rigorous standards of "truth"; it does not tell as much—it may even end up saying nothing—but what it says is more solid, "sounder." Such accounts are those I would like to urge you to set aside, with help from Jacques Derrida, because they hold on to the notion that theologians keep some ground under their feet.

The detour through the consideration of what philosophy (and theology) *also* are needs to be made a little more helpful. Philosophy, I said, is also the right use of words. In Plato this means a humanly appropriate use of words, different from the fanning of desires practiced (to their advantage and to that of their rich and ambitious pupils) by the Sophists; it is a nonmanipulative use of language, a therapeutic one.[6] Besides the example of the gentle questionner and narrator of apposite tales, the Socratic tradition gives concrete meaning to such right use of words by insisting on an inevitable choice: the speaker will have to choose—and the choice will depend on the context, of course—between either philanthropic eloquence (i.e., helping people in general as much as possible) or dialectic (i.e., helping the individual human being reach his or her fullest perfection).[7] Plato's philosophy of religion lands us upon a public piety, legislated about, and urges the individual on to further flight.[8]

Where our Christian theological heritage turns out to be most burdensome seems to me to be at this precise point: ordinarily Christians have not appropriated this distinction and thus have not been helped by it to see how problematic all their speaking might be.[9] Many reasons can serve to explain this state of affairs. The idea of revelation as ordinarily understood easily gives rise to the notion that human beings can have in their minds something of what God himself has in his, and thus can speak with the very words of God. Biblical notions of prophecy, apostolic authority in Peter's see, Protestant notions of biblical inerrancy, spiritualist notions of inner testimony of the Holy Spirit, all conspire to short-circuit reflectiveness about the human use of words and suspend ordinary notions of moral accountability. The vision of the new Jerusalem also tends to suspend pastoral prudence in public utterance with political ramifications. The resilience of providential (and postprovidential) views of history proves my point: as history unfolds, again and again some individuals claim to know its secret and use their voices to set forth in clear, understandable terms what God speaks (darkly) through the language of events.

One aspect of the Socratic philosophical tradition, currently skillfully retrieved by major studies,[10] further delineates what the right use of words consists of. One does philosophy to become better, a better and happier human being, to make the right choices in life and adhere only to reasonable opinions. (J. Bouveresse points out that the Enlightenment reversed the sequence: one learns sound knowledge in order to become happy[11]; as Derrida puts it, with Kant, wisdom is to be regulated by knowledge.[12]) "Facere docet philosophia, non dicere," repeats Seneca (*Epistulae morales*, 20.2). The Stoics, the Epicureans, and the Cynics were teachers like the Zen masters are. Unlike our university professors, they also worked on the body, and taught how to work on it oneself. "Examinations" were not the production of copy or of discourse, but tests of embodied persons. Art, logic, physics, and ethics were only means to the one important art, that of living well.[13]

Such priority commitment to furthering the actual well-being of the individual was constant. The ancient ideal of philosophy was "conscious work on the *psyche* in and through the body as its instrument."[14] Political obligation was acknowledged; the life course of the individual might well include periods of public office as well as of philosophical retreat. But the distinction between the art of speaking to the many and that of speaking with the few was never obliterated. In contrast, the Christian and post-Christian world keeps seeing vibrant, perfectionist ideologies at work, which effectively short-circuit the difference between the two manners of speaking. Ancient philosophers wanted to teach discipline and not just discuss ideas and inculcate opinion, but those who commended (and practiced) sexual abstinence never dreamt of enacting laws to prevent women who do not from terminating their unwanted pregnancies securely.

I can now advance my hypothesis: The promise of negative theologies comes from the fact that their patently recherché literary quality, their disruption of the rolling waves of ordinary theological rhetoric, alerts us to the matter of virtuosity in textual procedures and to the rapport with the reader that is being cultivated by any teacher.[15] The dramatic reversals of mood found in the Platonic dialogues, the shifting tones, puzzle the reader and encourage her or him to think that there is more to the book than meets the eye. Such procedures put us on the track of what makes "negative" theologies interesting.

Let us therefore clearly set aside vizualizations of large territories demarcated and occupied by "positive" theologies, contrasted with smaller but firmer grounds held by "negative" theologies. Neither should negative theologies be viewed as the "opposite" of the positive ones. They are rather moments of them, correctives one might perhaps say. "There is no purely negative discourse."[16] "Negative discourse on God is a phase of positive theology."[17] Such is the basic clue I get from the opening pages of "How to Avoid Speaking." Negative theologies have a familiar air because of an insistent rhetoric, that of negative determination.[18] As such, they can serve effectively to disengage Christian theologians from the habit of naively authoritative utterance. It makes it clearer, clearer than the other theology, that its text is "une autre mise en place des effets d'ouverture et de fermeture."[19]

Derrida makes a first contribution to such reading of negative theology by setting up a foil, by drawing a caricature:[20] the philosopher is someone "who habitually forgets s/he is writing."[21] What is now frequently labeled "logocentrism" aims at complete appropriation of all exteriority in masterful enunciation.[22] *Phallogocentrism* is, in my mind, a better, clearer label: it makes it clear that such art of the epistemic subject of positioning itself at the center and drawing everything in the horizon to itself is a move for power and was habitually done by men. Mark Taylor proposed yet another label, namely *monologism*;[23] this one also I welcome, since it makes clear the rejection of any decentering required by dialogue common in such views of rationality. All philosophical talk of being, all metaphysics and ontotheology, have been marred by such centrism. A call, when heard, is outside; hearing it does not put the call inside. As the essay "Of an Apocalyptic Tone" puts it, ontotheology "arraign[s]" *("arraisonne")* the call.[24]

Derrida's essay on translation, "Des tours de Babel," provides the clearest diagnosis of this marring (and clues to the overcoming of it). Significantly, it takes the form of a commentary on the story narrated in Genesis 11:1–9. Problems encountered in translation establish that languages are inadequate to each other. But even when taken by itself, each language is inadequate to itself and to meaning.[25] Language keeps making promises that it cannot keep.[26] Human beings, however, forgot this. God punished mankind (by dispersing it) because they wanted "to make a name for themselves"; their functioning with a common language caused them to forget they received their name from their father and made them think themselves capable of scaling the heavens.[27] Unaware of the nature of language and of the necessity of translation, these people "want to bring the world to reason."[28] They wanted to make of their language an instrument of mastery. The conclusion is clear: truth is not "representational correspondence."[29] And "no theorization, inasmuch as it is produced in a language, will be able to dominate the Babelian performance."[30]

> The writer writes *in* a language and *in* a logic whose proper system, laws, and life his discourse by definition cannot dominate absolutely. He uses them only by letting himself, after a fashion and up to a point, be governed by the system.[31]

Books too obey rules they cannot examine.

> The question about the origin of the book, the absolute interrogation, the interrogation of all possible interrogations, the "interrogation of God" will never belong to a book.[32]

The philosopher and the theologian, like all writers, are confined to the resources of a post-Babelian language and literary tradition (and usually of one of them at a time) and must learn to do their best with it.[33] "When we interrogate (*Anfragen*) the possibility of any question, i.e. language, we must be *already* in the element of language."[34]

And when it comes to doing his best with it, Derrida consistently sounds a political and moral note. At a decisive juncture in its argument, "Of an Apocalyptic Tone" states: "We cannot and we must not—this is a law and a destiny—forgo the *Aufklärung*."[35] In 1987, when the Heideggerian impact on the broad challenges flung at humanism ran high, Derrida refused to criticize "humanist teleology": "It has remained *up till now* . . . the price to be paid in the ethico-political denunciation of biologism, racism, naturalism etc."[36] Is there a union the free mind must pay dues to, before it can be authorized to philosophize?[37] There is a political duty to laugh some ideas off, but there is also one to discuss some topics with moral seriousness—Nazism, for instance.[38] Derrida singles himself out among the friendly commentators on Nietzsche by mentioning, en passant, but as something worth mentioning, that the only public school system that used Nietzsche was the Nazi one.[39]

But it is not enough to denounce phallogocentrism and monologism, and commend negative moments in theology. In "How to Avoid Speaking," Derrida examined closely the apophatic procedures in Pseudo-Dionysus[40] and contrasted them with Plato's text (*Timaeus*) on the *chora*. The opening statement was to the effect that there are many negative theologies, and that the various texts must be examined.[41] The attempt must be made to show forth, text in hand, what is involved in different textual virtuosities.

My intention therefore, in this section, is to examine some typically Greek virtuosities. Greek texts are at the origin of philosophy; they have launched a tradition of philosophy as a type of mental activity that I see as sharply distinct from thinking (as understood, for instance, by Heidegger or by Indian "philosophers"). As love of wisdom, philosophy is constituted by an incurable lack.[42] (See the *Symposium*) It proceeds by means of a critical examination of all languages that claim to convey wisdom. (This establishes at the outset a sharp distinction between philosophy and religion.) Thus the Greeks start a new model of mental activity: reflection on mental activity itself, and reflection undertaken in a fictitious ground where all opinions may be challenged and all moves are permitted. The Greeks thereby start a free look at all social linguistic practices.[43] But the language about the language is not the last word: Greek philosophers remain committed to a return to a language as real practice, responsible practice, enlightened by reflection and debate. There is no contradiction, thus, in seeing the Socratic tradition eventuate in use of texts for spiritual direction and seeing it shelter language as practice as well as language as examination of practice. As Plato puts it, an ignorant man speaks both the false and the true—but when he speaks the true, it is by chance; the expert also speaks both the false and the true—but the true, he speaks by choice (*Lesser Hippias* 367).

The Greek model of mental activity is not found only in philosophical texts.[44] My two examples will be drawn from literary texts, to make clear that Greek theory of mental activity is highly cognizant of the fullness of human interaction. (Socialized bodies are the best pictures of minds.)

1. Echoing (probably unwillingly) the Russian proverb to the effect that whoever has a trough never has difficulty in finding the swine, Sara Kofman wrote that "wherever there is a riddle, there is always a riddle-solver: Oedipus."[45] The errant young man meets the sphinx alone. I recall that, in French, she is now *la sphinge*; the monster is female. Oedipus solves her riddles by himself, without the help of any god. This properly heroic intellectual feat rids the city of its danger. The young man who comes out of nowhere starts a dynasty; he brings about a religious purgation without being religious; he starts a historical era without having a history. Defeated, the sphinx vanishes; she is miraculously excluded forever from the city that has in its midst the man who has answered the riddle about man.

When a plague breaks out in the city, royal Oedipus remains true to his masterful style: he promises to find the source of it. The trouble with truth is that, when one looks for it, one usually ends up finding it (it, or something like it). Relentlessly, the play works its series of reversals. The one who knows what man is does not know who he is. The savior-king is the pollution. The one who excluded the source of danger is the one to be excluded to make the city safe again. The one who reestablished social and cosmic order married his mother and ruined natural order by making himself the equal of his father. As Jean-Pierre Vernant pointed out,[46] it is his (short-lived) victory on the sphinx that made him the source of confusion and chaos.

The confusion is complete. A catharsis of sorts (horror and pity) occurs when the audience sees the blinded Oedipus. To the gesture of the city that banishes him, the king added his own self-punishment. The mutilation exhibits intelligence; it permits a grand metaphor: when Oedipus had his eyes, he did not see; blind, he may begin to see. Something regal, sublime, remains in this victim. (In contrast, Lear, punished, is completely humiliated and falls apart.) His self-punishment is one more act of mastery. While the sublimity of the hero remains suspect, the piety of the city is open to question. René Girard pointed out that the exclusion of Oedipus is a classic case of scapegoating.[47] True, Oedipus killed his father and married his mother; we can even add[48] that, too prompt at interpreting the meaning of oracles, negligent, Oedipus overlooked the fact that the god who made the prophecy did not answer the question he came to ask and did not tell him whether he was a bastard or not (*Oedipus Rex*, lines 779–93). So we (rightly) deem him in some sense guilty and accept the framework set up by the play; but must we accept it to the extent of believing that Oedipus is guilty of causing the plague? Must we conspire with those who framed him to the extent of abandoning our normal belief system, the one that would force us to state that the cessation of the plague at the time of his leaving the city is a coincidence? Must we be blinded to the point of not seeing him as socially useful victim?

The chaos and confusion are so complete that the play, at the end, manages to give the impression that a true, religiopolitical, ethicolegal solution has been found. But this is not the case. The collectivity of people are all in agreement, yet they are all wrong. This is one of those moments in which "there is absolutely no truth in culture."[49] King and people are each caught in panic.

Yet, only the king is heroic and deserves our pity. His self-mutilation forces him to some maturing: from now on he will have to trust what he hears rather than rely on what he sees. But that is not all: having proclaimed himself "son of Chance" (a way of saying he owes what he is primarily to himself), he took on divine proportions—he made himself *isotheos*, equal to god; he thus overstepped the limit and consequently paid the price; as Jean-Paul Vernant pointed out,[50] he became a scapegoat (*pharmakos*) because he embodied the evil that comes from trying to go too high (a sort of evil to be carefully differentiated from the more ordinary sort that consists in staying too low); thus the punishment is tragic, not pathetic. We still have admiration for him.

*Oedipus rex* (or, better, *Oedipus tyrant*) is a good example of monologism and phallogocentrism, because intelligence displays itself in verbal transactions (except for the appearance on stage of the mutilated ruler), in verbal transactions where the king remains the leader and does all he can to protect his leadership, and because intelligence, as it does its work, expels the wild female and takes possession of the tame one. What this intelligence is brought to, in the end, is the tragic acknowledgment of its limits.

2. The *Odyssey* provides us with a contrasting pattern. When Ulysses encounters Kirke, the attractive woman with an evil scheme in her head, he is protected by a god-given charm; naturally, he overcomes her evil intent; from then on, they carry their transactions in a mutually satisfactory manner. And when the hero arrives at Ithaka to regain possession of his kingdom and queen, not only must he wait until shepherds recognize and acknowledge him, but also he is tested by Penelope until, satisfied, she is willing to take possession of him.

Ulysses' meeting with the goddess Athena, as he lands on his home island, is particularly instructive (*Odyssey* 8.184ff). She first deceives him; she appears as a young shepherd, after pouring mist over the island and making it unrecognizable. He "used to every advantage the mind that was in him"—and "did not tell her the truth, but checked that word from the outset." Unlike Oedipus, he does not reveal his identity; he does not put his name forward, ahead of himself; he does not rush forward but steps back before considering moving in. Athena and Ulysses play with deceptions; they are both virtuosos in the language games appropriate to the situation. They thus come to position themselves cautiously within reality and come to know the reality (unlike those who speak to dominate others to prove their self-mastery). At the end comes the hard-earned recognition; Athena takes on the shape of a woman—he then knows who she is—and praises Ulysses. "You are fluent, and reason closely and keep your head always" (8.332)[51]. She also makes the land visible again. The goddess and the mortal man who became accomplices in the noble art of conversation and of establishing mutual acquaintance among total strangers, become allies in the serious task of ensuring the reentry of the legitimate monarch into his land and his family—and his reception by them.

Three features deserve closer examination in this display of intelligence. First, Ulysses and Athena spend time offering to each other a mix of deceptions and revelations. Something in the end is revealed because both shared the game of hiding and revealing. Second, the encounter entails a lot of aesthetic and social enjoyment. Athena and Ulysses have fun going through their range of conversational routines; each also quickly enjoys being in front of a worthy partner. Third, each is genial; what their communication achieves is the sense that they are both in the same world, the same geographical and social world, but also, and perhaps more importantly, the same world tout court. As they find each other's reality, they also find the reality of the world they are in. Kant argued in the *Critique of Judgement* (1.2.49) that the genius evokes the cosmological idea. He had previously admitted that the unity of the world cannot be known, that the worlds we actually live in are fractured. (As the romantic cliché puts it, each artist shapes his own.) But now, Kant adds that, nevertheless, the fact that we all live in the same world can be symbolically evoked[52] and that such symbolic evocation is an intrinsic part of the aesthetic achievement.[53]

Thus what we see in the *Odyssey* is a model of truth where truth does not lie in the correctness of mental representations but in the rectitude of the shared evaluation of reality and in the sharing of a (deserved) feeling of ease, of a morally earned sense of moral competence in the world. (In the ten years that elapsed between the end of the war and the landing upon Ithaka, Ulysses has been transformed from a heroic warrior into a master of the arts of peace.) After communicating with the goddess, Ulysses can see the world as it is, live with it and live with the people in it. While each person takes turn in speaking, this does not mean that each becomes, in her or his turn, the center of the transaction; each remains decentered, in relation to the other person, and in relation to the world. Each has one name, is one person, a centered self, but each is decentered by his or her relation with another centered self and his or her situation in the world.[54]

Other instances of nonphallogocentric and nonmonologic texts may be found in Greek literature. In the *Symposium*, for instance, Socrates, after refuting the most brilliant of a series of (manly) praises of love with his usual elenchos, displaces them, with a story. But his story does not place him at the center; he received it from another person, the priestess Diotima.[55]

How useful, then, is the notion of logocentrism, if numerous Greek examples show that inherent in the logos is a movement of decentering?[56] Should we not rather work with the hypothesis that it takes some hopefully recognizable perversion for the logos to become logocentric?

Clearly, irony, a common tool of those who speak the true by choice, is the best safeguard against perversion. Tragic irony forces the stubbornly centered self to recenter itself. In disastrous reversal, the one who claims to know is shown not to know. In comedies, blows are funny, not disastrous. More importantly, in comic irony, the one who knows does not say—at least not clearly and not right away. Comic irony suggests, even effects, reversals before it is too late: the winner of the Trojan war is put to the test by a woman who stayed at home doing embroidery. The expert is alert, and her expertise serves her, when it is needed.

My detour through Homer, Sophocles, as well as Plato should serve to establish that once a broad literary context has been set, the distinction between positive and negative theology can be replaced by the broader distinction between didactic (or scholastic) theology, and literarily crafted theology, such as is found, for instance, in Kierkegaard's writings. (The gap between the two kinds of theologies is now wide: When did one last teach rhetoric in theological schools?)[57] Negative theology, wrote Michel de Certeau, "signifie par ce qu'elle enlève."[58] What it singularly takes away is the pretence of directly communicating true opinion, such truths as may be assimilated by the acquisition and interiorization of language. In ensuring the absence of such a lesson to be learned, in disrupting the expectations of the docile reader, the writer achieves something more important than the formulation of memorable sentences; he or she prevents the establishment of the wrong relationship between writer and reader, and facilitates the sort of relationship genuine spiritual discipline requires. This characteristic application of virtuosity, this feature of withholding, of taking away, was practiced in Christianity before Pseudo-Dionysus, and, after him, by some who had never heard of him.

I do not think I need to labor the point that androcentrism is one of the most common perversions. Derrida has made the point in *Spurs: Nietzsche's Styles*,[59] especially in linking the openly misogynistic texts of Nietzsche to his polemics against claims to truth. But, taking a clue from "Of an Apocalyptic Tone," I might warn also against oracular solemnity. Longinus defined the sublime as an elevated tone that entrances the listener and is appropriate when we speak of mysteries we cannot fathom (*On the Sublime*, 1.35). The oracular speaker, whether archaic-religious, or modern-secular, speaks as if mandated by his source; there often is a pseudotragic heaviness to his tone. But along with this apparently higher mandate comes a withdrawal from accountability for his speaking. Such logos should never be allowed to seize the center. "The foundation of such authorities" cannot be allowed to stay "under cover in the unquestionable."[60]

> So we, *Aufklärer* of modern times, we continue to denounce the imposter apostles, the "so-called envoys" not sent [*envoyés*] by anyone, the liars and unfaithful ones, the turgidity and the pomposity of all those charged with a historic mission of whom nothing has been requested and who have been charged with nothing.[61]

Derrida's choice of topics keeps bringing us to the brink of archaic anxieties, keeps indicating contexts and withholding firm anchoring points.[62] But his unwillingness to become the shaman who lets us profit from the fruit of his exceptional spiritual travail does not land us upon the free market of opinion where all opinions are deemed equally legitimate and simply matters for subjective, preferential choices.[63] Methods for deciding the undecidable are honored. Agreement in a group need not become automatically conceived as proof of a successful bid for power on the part of a few. Derrida thus keeps returning us to something like the old public space of Kantian transcendental criticism. True, the late-twentieth-century public space is a noisier and less decorous space, has less rigid rules of order; tones clash—not everyone speaks like an elder statesman. Nevertheless, it is still a recognizable public space: in matters not subject to proof, dispute must yield to discussion, and, where discussion proceeds, agreement must be possible. There is a potentially universal tribunal in this forum.[64]

As Kofman and Norris took pains to show, to deconstruct metaphysics is not to become a positivist or a nihilist. Deconstruction is not demystification. Derrida rejects the notion that texts "contain" an abiding, self-present meaning and truth; he does not thereby invite us to "go beyond" philosophy and logocentric reason, but only invites us ever to test their limits.[65] There is a difference between the logos doing the saying and what is said, yet speakers must venture to leave something said. Lines drawn between representation and reality are suspect, but lines are to be drawn.[66] Interpretation is a free play. But, among humans, the rules one plays by are not what one plays with.

I think therefore I might be allowed to pick up a few straws I found in four of Derrida's texts to turn them into an invitation to theologians. I speak of ordinary, nonesoteric, rule-abiding theologians.

1. At the end of *Of Spirit: Heidegger and the Question*, the one work devoted to a steady discussion of Heidegger, Derrida imagines a contrast between two paths that takes the form of an exchange between Heidegger and Christian theologians. Heidegger is the first to establish a contrast by speaking of an original promise, which, while not being opposed to it, is foreign to Christianity.[67] To this the theologians respond that such contrast caricatures Christianity, gives it only a very conventional and doxic outline;[68] in fact, they say, we theologians also want to reach the dawn, hear the original call, and

sing the praise. Heidegger holds his ground: he does not listen to anything Christian or non-Christian, but tries to think "that *on the basis of which* all this is possible." And before the origin, there is not something that makes the origin possible, but something that "remains *origin-heterogeneous.*" The theologians agree with this heterogeneity; but Derrida still gives them a further point to make (and at this point, Derrida seems to join the theologians; at least he gives them the last word): while calling for continuing dialogue with Heidegger, Derrida has the theologians (?) state, "We are appealing to this entirely other in the memory of a promise or the promise of a memory."[69] The last word belongs not to an invitation to think but to something else, to an invitation to heed.

2. The essay "Des Tours de Babel" examines in what might consist truth in a translation from one language into another.[70] Translation is said to promise a kingdom in which languages are reconciled.[71] Links are established between such mundane considerations and sacred Scripture. Scripture is said to be the model and limit of all writing ("sacred writing as the model and the limit of all writing"). What-is-sacred and what-is-to-be-translated cannot be thought apart from each other.[72] The sacred text is the pure model, the absolute text, because as it requires and demands translation, it also announces itself as untranslatable.[73] (In the Islamic case, I might add, only the Arabic Koran is to be called the Koran; a qualifier must be added on the title page of translations; e.g. Arberry's *The Koran Interpreted.*) Still, when the sacred text receives fresh life through translation, a covenant and a promise are being realized. (Derrida quotes Walter Benjamin, who named God as he spoke of what guarantees the pact honored in the work of translation.)[74] It is appropriate here to recall with Norris[75] that, in Judaism, commentaries (another type of translation, although in the same language as the original text) are treated as sacred texts in their own right. The key to the particular characteristic of sacred texts may perhaps be found in the statement: "What comes to pass in a sacred text is the occurrence of a *pas de sens.*"[76] And yet, such text invites translation.

3. "Of an Apocalyptic Tone" demystifies the recourse to an apocalyptic tone (in proclamations of the death of philosophy, for instance). It demonstrates that attacks on the bibli-

cal apocalypse have usually unleashed new waves of apocalyptic talk.[77] Yet a limit is set to the demystification.[78] The scriptural apocalypse retains a singular status; its program still dominates the West;[79] we have not yet framed a metalanguage about it; in fact there cannot be "the metalanguage on the subject of eschatological language."[80] Its tonal imperative "Come!" cannot be subsumed under any category.[81] To deconstruct it, it is necessary to keep apocalyptic desire.[82] The voice of each writer in fact reduplicates the call, and also invites the reader to come, to heed the solicitation of an inconceivable other.[83] Here again Scripture is seen as model of all texts. And the question arises: Is not apocalypse the transcendental condition of all discourse, of all experience?[84] Taylor speaks of the co-dependent origination of all texts.[85] All writers are in a web that surpasses and encompasses them.

4. "How to Avoid Speaking: Denials" also brings us back to an absolute origin, "the thinking of an essential 'having-taken-place.' "[86]

> This call of the other, having always aready preceded the speech to which it has never been present a first time, announces itself in advance as a *recall*. Such a reference to the other will always have taken place. Prior to every proposition and even before all discourse in general—whether a promise, prayer, praise, celebration.[87]

Apophatic theology includes an address to God, a prayer.[88] The writer, in this case, heeds. (This is not the case when Plato accumulates his negatives on the *chora*.) The same essay also contains a tantalizing reference to the Jewish and Arab traditions, placed as two parallels to the Christian one, but left undescribed.[89] (A good occasion to bemoan the lacunae in our cultural transmission systems.)

In this blank, I find an invitation. I will try to indicate four features common to the Jewish, Christian, and Islamic traditions that deserve pondering.

Some prudence is called for, embarking on a topic that Derrida avoided. Not unlike Oedipus, I am rushing in where angels fear to tread. I hope, nevertheless, to keep in mind Derrida's warning against the drift of all commentators upon eschatological language "toward conductive violence, toward authoritarian 'duction.' "[90] So I must carefully warn the reader, first of all, by stating that I am leaving the philosophical ground (which is fictitious ground) and moving onto territories where human heeding is organized. I am discussing civilizations, these fictions that successfully made the many forget they were living in fictions. (I am moving onto the territory of what Plato called "laws"; Judaism and Islam would not feel ill at ease with such designation.[91]) I will therefore discuss scriptures as historically authoritative sources for positive, didactic theologies,[92] or as texts giving pattern to lives, not of texts helping us become conscious of patterns of mental life. And there is a second warning: to venture, in this way, into the discussion of civilizations may well be a salient characteristic of the West. As Julia Kristeva argued (on a psychoanalytic basis), human beings in the West are sure they can "translate" their mother and overcome (deny) through access to the symbolic world the incurable mourning that results from the loss of the Object. They are uniquely confident they can truly name.[93]

1. Each honors a sacred Scripture, not quite the same, but similarly honored. In each is kept a tradition of obedience to the text, which is somehow to be read at face value.[94] In each case the Author of the Text successfully resisted the metaphysical discussions heaped upon Him. Moves to go behind the appearance of the text, whether forbidden, discouraged, or allowed, are conceived as forgetting the point.[95]

2. In each case, the text is made accessible to all. One of the responses to the existence of the text is generalized alphabetization. In each case, women have encountered more obstacles in their access than men, or obtained only a reduced access.

3. Each tradition insists that the text is to be not just read and recited, but also commented upon. The text is thus taken into a process of ever-widening communicability. Trends in commentaries and their status vary, but the community is mandated to make the book its own by discussing it and writing on it. A forum is created, where tones clash and an appropriate tone struggled for. The revelation is heeded, and the logos not emasculated.[96] The web in which writers are caught is the supple web of public discussion.

4. In each case the call issued from the text has also led to a call to a publicly visible obedience.[97] Language is not adequate, but some trace must be left.[98] A history starts. The reality of "spiritual" freedom is made to join a realm of law

where obedience is enacted. Writers must write with precision. (Lawyers are usually more precise than poets.) What there is in the book that is more than meets the eye is not allowed to hide in authoritarian suggestiveness: it must be translated in public and private practice. Thus the original divine word reverberates amid the appearances of a tradition that has a visible history and a morality, is committed to civil living, keeps a record of its decisions, and keeps its memories in written form.

## *Notes*

1. Jacques Derrida, "Plato's Pharmacy," in *Dissemination*, trans. Barbara Johnson (Chicago: University of Chicago: University of Chicago Press, 1981), pp. 61–171.

2. In his *Lectures on the Philosophy of History*, Hegel holds that both features are indices of philosophical imperfection.

3. Edward Farley, *Theologia: The Fragmentation and Unity of Theological Education* (Philadelphia: Fortress, 1983), pp. ix–xii.

4. Ibid., pp. 86, 127.

5. Jacques Derrida, "How to Avoid Speaking: Denials," trans. Ken Frieden, in *Languages of the Unsayable: The Play of Negativity in Literature and Literary Theory* (New York: Columbia University Press, 1989), p. 75.

6. Michel Despland, *The Education of Desire: Plato and the Philosophy of Religion* (Toronto: University of Toronto Press, 1985), pp. 69–72, 117–120.

7. Hubert Kesters, *Plaidoyer d'un Socratique contre le Phèdre de Platon. XXVIème discours de Thémistius* Louvain Nauwelaerts, 1959, p. 22. Books in Plato's opinion, were useful to the many. Their objectives therefore had to be modest; they could not, for instance, convey knowledge of the Author of the Universe. See Borges, "Du culte des livres," in *Enquêtes* (Paris: Gallimard, 1957), p. 164.

8. Despland, *The Education of Desire*, pp. 207–217.

9. To be sure, Christian theology and pastoral practice knew the distinction between the many and the few. For centuries, the ability to practice asceticism separated the two groups. The few became viewed as a sacred elite, clearly something more than a wise or heroic one; as such they could and did transcend the

ordinary conditions of life. The Socratic tradition differs: as *Crito* makes clear, the wise man keeps his obligations to the city.

The distinction between the many and the few is useful, in my mind, only if strictly factual and quantitative. Talking with the few differs from talking to the many, but it is not revealing secrets to a group of initiates, nor meeting with a worthier elite. See Derrida, "How to Avoid Speaking," pp. 88–89.

10. Pierre Hadot, *Exercices spiritueles et philosophie antique*, 2nd ed. (Paris: Etudes augustiniennes, 1987); Michel Onfray, *Du cynisme. Portrait du philosophe en chien* (Paris: Grasset, 1990); Peter Sloterdijk, *Critique of Cynical Reason*, trans. Michael Eldred (Minneapolis: University of Minnesota Press, 1987).

11. Jacques Bouveresse, *Rationalité et cynisme* (Paris: Editions de Minuit, 1984), p. 10.

12. Jacques Derrida, "Of an Apocalyptic Tone Recently Adopted in Philosophy," *Semeia* 23 (1982); p. 32.

13. Horst Hutter, "Philosophy as Self-Transformation," *Historical Reflections/Réflexions historiques* 16 (1989); pp. 171–198.

14. Ibid., p. 176.

15. Negative theology is "a certain form of language, with its *mise en scène*." Derrida, "How to Avoid Speaking," p. 73.

16. Derrida, "How to Avoid Speaking," pp. 103–104; see also pp. 97–99.

17. Sara Kofman, *Lectures de Derrida* (Paris; Galilée, 1984), p. 37.

18. Derrida, "How to Avoid Speaking," p. 74.

19. Kofman, *Lectures de Derrida*, p. 11.

20. My speaking of a caricature should not be taken to imply that Derrida is somehow to be blamed, as not being accurate or fair. The popular "image," or misrepresentation, of the philosopher found in the *Theaetetus* is not given by Plato just to fan our indignation against those uncouth enough to hold this view. That Kierkegaard was caricatured is to his honor. The discourse of philosophy cannot ignore the nonphilosophic discourse on philosophy (nor can it simply nurse contempt for it).

21. Christopher Norris, *Derrida* (Cambridge: Harvard University Press, 1987), p. 21.

22. Kofman, *Lectures de Derrida*, p. 29.

23. Mark C. Taylor, *Erring: A Post-Modern A/Theology* (Chicago: University of Chicago Press, 1987), pp. 173, 175.

24. Derrida, "Of an Apocalyptic Tone," p. 65.

25. Derrida, "Des Tours de Babel," in *Difference in Translation*, ed. Joseph F. Graham (Ithaca and London: Cornell University Press, 1985), p. 165.

26. Jacques Derrida, *Of Spirit: Heidegger and the Question*, trans. Geoffrey Bennington and Rachel Bowlby (Chicago: University of Chicago Press, 1989), pp. 93–94.

27. Derrida, "Des Tours de Babel," p. 169.

28. Ibid., p. 174.

29. Ibid., p. 195. The impossibility of this view of truth is highlighted in Aristotle's statement that "names exist in finite number, while the number of things is infinite. It is inevitable therefore that a single name should have many meanings." *De Sophisticis Elenchus*, 1:165a:ii.

30. Ibid., p. 175.

31. Jacques Derrida, *Of Grammatology*, trans. Gyatri Chakravorty Spivak (Baltimore and London: Johns Hopkins University Press, 1976), p. 158.

32. Jacques Derrida, "Edmond Jabès and the Question of the Book," in *Writing and Difference*, trans. Alan Bass (Chicago: University of Chicago Press, 1978), p. 78.

33. As Norris points out (*Derrida*, p. 19), Derrida as philosophical reader seeks out those places where the author strains and exploits the resources of the language, "blindspots or moments of self-contradiction where a text involuntarily betrays the tension between rhetoric and logic, between what it manifestly *means to say* and what it is nonetheless *constrained to mean*."

34. Derrida, *Of Spirit*, p. 129 n. 5.

35. Derrida, "Of an Apocalyptic Tone," p. 59.

36. Derrida, *Of Spirit*, p. 56.

37. The same ethicopolitical necessity comes to the rescue of the subject in Derrida's *Of Spirit*, pp. 39–40.

38. Ibid., pp. 71–72, 109–110.

39. Norris, *Derrida*, p. 201.

40. Derrida, "How to Avoid Speaking," pp. 90–96.

41. Ibid., p. 82.

42. The finality of this incurability is expressed by the distrust of any god—or epiphany—that might bring the cure. See *Meno*.

43. A further salient fact is that such examination takes place in the context of the city-state: a limited social and political arena where the opinions of free men are often voiced in a decisional context and have visible practical consequences that may be assessed. Thucydides' *History of the Peloponnesian War* is the classical text here.

44. See René Schaerer, *L'homme antique* (Paris: Payot, 1958), and idem, *Le héros, le sage et l'événement* (Paris: Montaigne 1965).

45. Kofman, *Lectures de Derrida*, p. 88.

46. Jean-Pierre Vernant, "Ambiguity and Reversal. On the enigmatic stance of *Oedipus Rex*," in *Tragedy and Myth in Ancient Greece*, ed. Jean-Pierre Vernant and Pierre Vidal-Naquet, trans. Janet Lloyd (Atlantic Highlands, N.J.: Humanities Press, 1981), pp. 109–110.

47. René Girard, *The Scapegoat*, trans. Yvonne Freccero (Baltimore and London: Johns Hopkins University Press, 1986), and idem, *Job: The Victim of His People*, trans. Yvonne Freccero (Stanford: Stanford University Press, 1987), pp. 33–40.

48. Jean-Pierre Vernant, "Oedipus Without the Complex," *Tragedy and Myth*, ed. Vernant and Vidal-Naquet, p. 81.

49. René Girard, "Generative Scapegoating" in *Violent Origins: Ritual Killing and Cultural Formation*, ed. Walter Burkert, René Girard and Jonathan Z. Smith (Stanford: Stanford University Press, 1987), pp. 142, 185.

50. Vernant, "Ambiguity and Reversal," pp. 106–107. Quoted in Derrida, *Dissemination*, p. 131 n. 56.

51. "You are gentle, intelligent, discreet" says another translation. The range of existing translations is enormous: metaphors for mental excellence vary very widely across different cultures.

52. Luc Ferry, *Homo Aestheticus. L'invention du goût à l'âge démocratique* (Paris: Grasset, 1990), pp. 21, 121.

53. Such symbolic evocation of the unity of the world needs to be stressed, since our contemporary culture, with its emphasis on the autonomy of the subject, tends to lose reference to *the* world. Ferry, *Homo aestheticus*, p. 346.

54. Such decentering is nonthreatening: as the Aristotelian teaching puts it, humans are built to the same specifications as the universe. And vice versa. See Stephen R. L. Clark, *Aristotle's Man: Speculations upon Aristotelian Anthropology.* (Oxford: Clarendon Press, 1975), pp. 46–47. I owe this clue to correspondence with E. David Napier.

55. See my discussion of the *Symposium* in Despland, *The Education of Desire* pp. 230–39. For the unveiling of the alternative to phallogocentrism to be found in the *Laws*, see my article "The Heterosexual Body as Metaphor in Plato's Religious City," 1990–91, pp. 31–50 *Religion.*

56. Evidences of such decentering are gathered in Schaerer, *L'homme antique*, and in Marcel Detienne and Jean-Pierre Vernant, *Cunning Intelligence in Greek Culture and Society*, trans. Janet Lloyd (Atlantic Highlands, N.J.: Humanities Press, 1978).

57. Ever since Calvin, the alliance between persuasive rhetoric and theology has been deep, but, unfortunately, rarely explicit. See Benoît Girardin, *Rhétorique et Théologique. Calvin: le commentaire de l'Epître aux Romains* (Paris: Beauchesne, 1979), p. 360: "By inculcating belief, rhetoric rejects fragility."

58. de Certeau, quoted by Derrida in "Nombre de oui" in *Psyché* (Paris: Galilée, 1987), p. 649.

59. Jacques Derrida, *Spurs: Nietzsche's Styles*, trans. Barbara Harlow (Chicago: University of Chicago Press, 1978).

60. Derrida, "Of an Apocalyptic Tone," p. 59.

61. Ibid., p. 59.

62. Kofman, *Lectures de Derrida*, p. 20.

63. Thus we do not meet in his text the deep unbelief about all metastories that, in the eyes of Lyotard, is the characteristic of postmodernity. (See Bouveresse, *Rationalité et cynisme*, p. 124.)

64. See Ferry, *Homo aestheticus*, pp. 118, 122, 132. The rejection of the oracular tone should count heavily, in my mind, against the works of Heidegger, who warns, it seems to me, more severely of blasphemy against being than of crimes against mankind. The extraordinary courtesy Derrida extends to Heidegger is something I think I understand, but nevertheless resist. For an examination of the strange blend in Heidegger's works of principled overcoming of the moral point of view with sonorous moralisms, see Luc Ferry, and Alain Renault, "La question de l'éthique après Heidegger" in *Les fins de l'homme. A partir du travail de Jacques Derrida* (Paris: Galilée, 1981), pp. 23–54.

65. Taylor points out (*Erring*, p. 276) that the authors Derrida reads are usually shown to both extend and subvert the so-called traditional logocentric Western philosophy. I might add that many of the attacks on this "tradition" take over uncritically Hegel's view of the history of philosophy: they merely call "bad" what he called "good." Much in that tradition was ignored or caricatured by Hegel: there is more to Descartes than he found in him; the Spanish Jesuits deserve to be read (e.g., Baltasar Gracian).

66. Kofman, *Lectures de Derrida*, p. 39. Norris, *Erring*, pp. 54, 60, 130, 143.

67. Derrida, *Of Spirit*, p. 107.

68. Ibid., p. 108.

69. Ibid., pp. 111, 113.

70. Derrida, "Des Tours de Babel," p. 190.

71. Ibid., p. 200.

72. Ibid., p. 191.

73. Ibid., pp. 202–205.

74. Ibid., p. 182.

75. Norris, *Derrida*, p. 229.

76. Derrida, "Des Tours de Babel," p. 204.

77. Derrida, "Of an Apocalyptic Tone," p. 48.

78. Ibid., p. 59.

79. Ibid., p. 48.

80. Ibid., pp. 48–49.

81. Ibid., p. 65.

82. Ibid., p. 57.

83. Taylor, *Erring*, p. 303.

84. Derrida, "Of an Apocalyptic Tone," p. 57.

85. Taylor, *Erring*, p. 180.

86. Derrida, "How to Avoid Speaking," p. 109.

87. Ibid., pp. 97–98.

88. Ibid., pp. 103–104, 110.

89. Ibid., p. 122.

90. Derrida, "Of an Apocalyptic Tone," p. 66.

91. The antinomian theme so strong in Lutheran Christianity should not rule our preferences completely: life under laws is not inevitably inauthentic and enslaving. It depends on the laws.

92. Recent work on the parables makes clear that, at least in these texts, Scripture is not didactic in the usual sense: expectations are overthrown. Literary virtuosity is more involved in withholding than in giving.

93. Julia Kristeva, *Black Sun: Depression and Melancholy* trans. Leon S. Roudiey (New York: Columbia University Press, 1989), pp. 43–44, 66–68. I find the strongest expression of this commitment to honor all earnest affirmation in the Talmudic practice of recording all opinions, even the rejected ones. No publicly articulated discourse can safely be forgotten.

94. See Hans Frei, "The 'Literal Reading' of Biblical Narrative in the Christian Tradition: Does It Stretch or Will It Break?" *The Bible and the Narrative Tradition*, ed. Frank McConnel (New York: Oxford University Press, 1986), pp. 36–77. Frei identifies (p. 51) the unquestioned assumption present in all modern hermeneutics: "understanding" the Scriptures is an event in self-presence.

95. This question of sticking to appearances is politically important. Derrida deplores the move made by Fichte, who excludes from the German people those who seem to speak German without being German (*Of Spirit*, p. 70). Or by Hegel, who states that (at his point in history) philosophy may be found only in Germany, since non-Germans have excluded themselves from it (Ibid., p. 99). To make the contrast clear, I will quote General de Gaulle: "Est Français qui le veut." And is a philosopher whoever says he is one.

96. Derrida, "Of an Apocalyptic Tone," p. 78.

97. One of the best questions Derrida asks of Heidegger is about the philosophical Führung that issues a "call" but does not expect any obedience in particular (*Of Spirit*, p. 44). Derrida speaks appropriately of a romantic pathos: the call to thought does not issue *regulae ad directionem ingenii* (Ibid., p. 58).

98. Derrida, "How to Avoid Speaking," pp. 21–22.

# FIVE

# *nO nOt nO*

Mark C. Taylor

Who knows what we are doing when
we donnons au nom d'autre?

— Jacques Derrida

"*Viens* . . . Come!" "In the name of what?" In the name of what do we meet, linger, disperse? What calls? Calls us to gather here and now . . . in this time? At this place? What time? What place? What is the time and place of gathering? "What is the place, what takes place or gives place to thought?" In the name of what or of whom do we promise to speak and to write? Now and in the future? In the "name" of nothing? In the "name" of not? Perhaps. Perhaps we are called by nothing, in the "name" of a certain not, in order (if it is an order) not to speak and write "about" nothing. *Comment ne pas parler* . . . about nothing? How to avoid speaking . . . not? How to avoid speaking not without

> [the strange syntax of the *without* that would patiently interrogate us. . . . This I (without I) of the *without* in [Blanchot's] texts, you come to see that it disarticulates the entire logic of identity or of contradiction . . . *without* any dialectical reappropriation . . .
> without without without][1]

not speaking? When all is said and done (but when is [the] all said and done?), will all our speaking and writing have been for not/naught? Who can no or not no? To no and/or not to no? Either too much or too little.

Questions of excess . . . excessive questions.

o<br>
o<br>
o<br>
nO nOt<br>
nOt nO<br>
nO nOt nO<br>
o<br>
o<br>
o

## *(L)et(t)re(s)*

In the name of what . . . in the name of whom do we gather, linger, disperse? It is a certain negativity that draws us together while holding us apart and holds us apart while drawing us together. A certain negativity that is inscribed by (and, perhaps, *au nom de*) Jacques Derrida. Which negativity? What negativity? Whose negativity? Jacques', of course. Jacques' negativity that is neither precisely negative nor positive, neither exactly present nor absent.

"To leave this immense place empty" (122). There is an empty place at our table. The place is set, but the most important guest has not arrived. Jacques has not come. He was invited to our gathering but (politely) refused to come. In a letter dated 11 October 1989, he writes:

> *Cher Professeur Coward,*
>
> Votre project me paraît passionnant et je vous suis très reconnaissant de songer ainsi à m'y associer. Croyez bien que j'aurai à coeur de tout faire pour vous suivre. Malheureusement, il me sera impossible, pour des raisons quasiment physiques de participer directement au séminaire d'Octobre 1990.

How is this *quasiment* to be read? Is it, perhaps, the *quasiment* with which Derrida "ends" "How to Avoid Speaking: Denials"?

> *Not, without, quasi* are three adverbs. *Quasiment.* Fable or fiction, everything happens as if I had wanted to ask, on the threshold of this lecture, what these three adverbs mean and whence they come. (129)

The "quasi" will return.

"Unfortunately, it will be impossible . . . for me to participate directly." The qualification is important. While direct participation is impossible, indirect participation is possible. Derrida will participate *indirectly*—through texts. Though absent, Derrida is "present" in the texts he sends in his stead. Derrida's writings, in other words, re-mark the "presence" of his "absence."

Two texts: "How to Avoid Speaking: Denials" and "Of an Apocalyptic Tone Newly Adopted in Philosophy." Though both essays have been previously published at least twice, Derrida grants permission to reissue them yet again. No trace of original works here (or elsewhere). In addition to the refusal and the permission, Derrida makes a promise in his letter: "Bien entendu, je ferai aussi tout mon possible pour écrire le post-scriptum auquel vous faites allusion." Will Derrida keep his promise? There is a note of qualification in his pledge: "*tout mon possible.*" Will the postman deliver his message? Will promise lead to fulfillment? It remains uncertain.

Once—at least once—Jacques failed to fulfill a promise. "Of an Apocalyptic Tone Newly Adopted in Philosophy" is prefaced by a letter dated 2 January 1981. It is a "Dear John letter" in which Derrida confesses that he cannot fulfill a promise. The "solution" is again a repetition—the republication of a text that has already been delivered.

> Dear John,
>
> Despite the delays generously granted me, I could not write the text requested, whether it be a question of an essay or a response to the studies that are to appear in *Semeia*. . . .
>
> I am simultaneously sending you the text of the lecture I gave this summer at Cerisy-la-Salle. If you yourself and the editors of *Semeia* judge that it can, in whole or in the form of fragments, figure in the collection in preparation, you naturally have my agreement.

To whom is the letter sent? Who is the addressee? What is its destination? Who is John? The answer seems obvious: John is John Leavey, Jr., one of Derrida's most accomplished translators. But who or what is a translator? This question is too complex to be treated adequately in this context. Suffice it to say that the translator is one who transmits a message he has received from an other he might or might not know to others he can never know. The translator, in other words, does not exist in and for himself but is always for an other. He is a site of passage, something like a "sieve (*crible*)" that is forever straining, or a relay in a network of exchange whose currency is not fixed. Never speaking in his own voice, the translator echoes the discourse of an other. Which other? What other? For the moment, I delay responding.

But is the identity of the translator so obvious? After all, Derrida has taught us the impropriety of the proper. A name, it seems, can never be proper *sensu strictissimo*. An improper question for an improper noun: What is a john? More properly, I repeat: Who is John? John is, of course, the "author" of the Apocalypse, the Revelation of John. But John is not really the "author" of the Apocalypse, for the author is (always) an other, perhaps even the Other. Is "the Revelation of John" the revelation of John or of someone or something else? Rather than being an author, John is actually a translator who transmits a message from elsewhere.

> Disclosure of Yeshoua the messiah
> Elohim gives it to him
> to show to his servants
> what will come soon.
>
> He indicates it by sending it through his messenger
> to his servant Yohanan. (56)

Derrida comments:

> So John is the one who already receives some letters [*courrier*] through the medium yet of a bearer who is an angel, a pure messenger. And John translates a message already transmitted, testifies to a testimony that will be yet that of another testimony, that of Jesus; so many sendings, *envois*, so many voices,

> and this puts so many people on the telephone line. (56)

Is this a party line? Which party? Whose party?

Yet another John. A well-kept secret, though, like the purloined letter, publicly available for all to read. I believe the year was 1952—a little-noted entry in the student directory for *École Normale Supérieure*:

> Derrida, (Jackie)

Jackie! Jacques is Jackie? (*Aparté*: What's in a name? Would there ever have been deconstruction in America or elsewhere if Jacques had remained Jackie?) Jacques—*Maître Jacques*, Jack-of-all-trades, master of none? (But what does it mean to be master of none?) "Jack," of course, is the diminutive of John. Jacques, then, is Jack, and Jack is John.

Questions return: To whom is the letter sent? Who is its addressee? What is its destination? Who is John? The answer seems obvious: John is Jacques. Is Jacques writing to himself? For himself? Does the letter return to sender? Address unknown? Or address always already known before the (l)et(t)re is posted? Can the (l)et(t)re return without the message arriving?

Let us return to the "Dear John letter." John, we have discovered, is a translator: John Leavey, Jr., and John, "author" of the Apocalypse. Is Derrida also a translator? It would seem so. In his letter addressed to John, he writes:

> Modestly and in my own way, I try to translate (or let myself be involved, carried along, perhaps elsewhere, by and perhaps without) a thought of Heidegger that says: "If I were still writing a theology—I am sometimes tempted to do that—the expression 'Being' should not figure in it.

(Again problems of translation. In "How to Avoid Speaking," Derrida [or his translator] cites a different translation of this passage: "If I *were* yet to *write* a theology, as I am sometimes tempted to do, the word 'being' *ought* not to appear there [take place there, occur, figure, or happen there] [Wenn ich noch eine Theologie *schreiben würde*, wozu es mich manchmal reizt, dann *dürfte* in ihr das Wort 'Sein' nich vorkommen]." The most puzzling enigma created by these alternative translations concerns the time of writing or, more specifically, the time of writing theology. "If I were still writing a theology." "If I *were* yet to *write* a theology." Is the time of writing theology past or future? Or is it a past that returns as future?

A further problem of translation. It is not clear whether this published letter is "original" or a translation. It appears to be a translation, for Derrida (though it might be his translator) cites the French translation of this Heidegger text. Thus it seems that the critical Heidegger text is an English translation of a French translation of Heidegger's German.

What does it mean to translate Heidegger? Those who have tried frequently are forced to admit that Heidegger is untranslatable. The problem of translating Heidegger is, therefore, the problem of translating the untranslatable. By struggling to translate the untranslatable, Derrida approaches, albeit indirectly, the question of negative theology. Explaining the reasons for his failure to fulfill his promise, Derrida writes to John, who, we now know, might also be Jacques:

> I have nothing to say in addition or afresh. I found these texts lucid and rigorous; and in any case, I believe I have no objection to make to them, not even against some reservations or other regarding what I could say very insufficiently in the direction of negative theology. I am aware of this insufficiency and am quite convinced of the need for a rigorous and differentiated reading of everything advanced under this title (negative theology). My fascination at least testifies to this, right through my incompetence: in effect I believe that what is called "negative theology" (a rich and very diverse corpus) does not let itself be easily assembled under the general category "onto-theology-to-be deconstructed."

Derrida does not fulfill his promise, because he has "nothing to say." Is he, in effect, saying: "I have nothing left to say. Always nothing left to say. But how can I say it? Say it again? And again, and again?"[2] To say nothing is to speak not—to avoid speaking. But to avoid speaking by saying that one has nothing to say is to speak—to speak in order not to speak, to speak in order to say nothing. "In addition or afresh, I have nothing to say." Strange (l)et(t)re . . . strange message from this strange John. *Nothing arrives*!

> An apocalypse without apocalypse, an apocalypse without vision, without truth, without revelation, of *dispatches* [des envois] (for the "come" is plural in itself, in oneself), of addresses without message and without destination, without sender or decidable addressee, without last judgment, without any other eschatology than the tone of the "Come" itself, its very difference, an apocalypse beyond good and evil. (66)

Nothing *arrives*! *Without* arriving. Again, "the strange syntax of the without." How to avoid speaking not without not speaking? In the name of what or of whom do we promise (not) to speak and write? Now and in the future? In the "name" of nothing? In the "name" of not? Perhaps. Perhaps we are called by nothing, in the "name" of a certain not in order not to speak and write "about" nothing.

In not writing or almost not writing, Derrida makes, or almost makes, a promise: "The most diverse consequences and adventures *can* [emphasis added] await us—from completely other routes, completely other writings." Will Derrida follow these routes? Will he complete these writings? Where might these other routes and other writings lead? Perhaps to something like negative theology. To begin to answer these and other questions, we will have to wait at least five years. In June 1986, Derrida delivered a paper at a conference in Jerusalem. On this occasion, he was present to discuss "Absence and Negativity"—"in person," as it were. Whether absence and negativity are better approached in his absence or presence remains to be seen.

In the interval of the five years separating "Of an Apocalyptic Tone Newly Adopted in Philosophy" and "How to Avoid Speaking: Denials," as well as the four or five years following their republication along with the supplemental texts it now is generating, two further delays "appear": "Titles" and "Recuperation."

## *Titles*

"We are still on the threshold." A title is a threshold—a border, margin, or limit that brings together and holds apart the unwritten and the written. Neither inside nor outside the text, the title is, in a certain sense, untranslatable. The untranslatability of the title is not precisely the same as the untranslatability of the pre-text. Rather, the pretext is inscribed "within" the text through the repeated displacement of the title. In other words, the pretext, the before-text, always comes "after"—always follows the title and "its" text. Thus the pretext of the text is a before that is (always) yet to come.

It (what?) always begins with a question—a question of translation. How to translate—how to translate a title: *Comment ne pas parler*? First, the question of the question (which is, of course, a, or perhaps *the*, Heideggerian question). Is *Comment ne pas parler* a question or an assertion, an interrogation or a declaration? While the title bears no question mark, the text is nothing other than a sustained interrogation that raises questions without offering answers. In asking/asserting *Comment ne pas parler*, what is Derrida asking/asserting? Is he asking how not to speak, how to avoid speaking, or is he asserting how to speak not, how to speak the avoidance of speaking? Is he asking/asserting the impossibility of speaking or the unavoidability of speaking? Is he asking/asserting the impossibility of speaking not or the unavoidability of speaking not? No not . . . Not no . . . No not no?/.

The duplicity of the title is compounded by the single word that serves as the subtitle of the essay: *Dénégations*. At this point, translation becomes impossible. *Dénégation* is the word the French translators of Freud use for the German *Verneinung*. There is already a certain duplicity in *Verneinung*. The prefix *Ver-* can mean: removal, loss, stoppage, reversal, opposite, using up, expenditure, continuation to the end, alteration.[3] *Ver-nein-ung*, then, suggests both the presence and absence of negation, inclination, both the continuation and end of the no.[4] The complexity of *Verneinung* is not captured in the standard English translation of Freud's term as "negation." Difficulties are compounded by the choice of "denials" for the English translation of Derrida's *dénégations*. "Denial" is one of the English words used (the other is "disavowal") to translate Freud's *Verleugnung*. Though closely associated, *Verneinung* and *Verleugnung* are not equivalent.[5] To translate *dénégations* by *denials* is, therefore, a mistranslation. However, to translate *dénégations* "properly" (by way of *Verneinung*) by *negations* would also be a mistranslation. Moreover, the "proper" translation would be more misleading than the "mistranslation." Mistranslation, it seems, is unavoidable.

*Dénégation* captures the irresolvable duplicity of *Verneinung* in which affirmation and negation are conjoined without being united or synthesized. *Verneinung* is an affirmation that is a negation and a negation that is an affirmation. To de-negate is to un-negate. Un-negation is, of course, a form of negation. More precisely, denegation is an un-negation that affirms rather than negates negation. The affirmation of negation by way of denegation subverts the dialectical affirmation of negation by way of the negation of negation. To think or rethink negative theology with Derrida, it is necessary to think the negative undialectically by thinking a negative that is *neither* both negation and affirmation *nor* either negation or affirmation. To think this strange thought or unthought is to think the neither/nor implied in *dénégation*. All things considered, it seems better to leave the untranslatable untranslated. It is, after all, impossible to be sure whether "denegation" is or is not a translation. Thus a proposal for the retranslation of the title: "How to Avoid Speaking: Denegations."

Moving beyond the periphery, away from the peripheral . . . from margin toward . . . what? Certainly not the center. From title to text . . . text that is no longer (or perhaps is still) a pretext but is often called the "body proper" of the text . . . the body of the text that might be the word made "flesh" (but what word, which *Wort*? What is the *Ort* of the *W-Ort* . . . the place of the flesh of the word . . . of the text?) . . . in the body of the text, Derrida disavows a Freudian reading or merely a Freudian reading of *dénégation*. Pondering "*How not to divulge a secret*? How to avoid saying or speaking?," Derrida writes:

> Contradictory and unstable meanings give such a question its endless oscillation: what to do in order that the secret remain secret? How to make it known, in order that the secret of the secret—as such—not remain secret? . . . At one and the same time stable and unstable, this sentence allows itself to be carried by the movements that here I call *denial* (*dénégation*),

> a word that I would like to understand prior even to its elaboration in the Freudian context. (94–95)

Derrida is struggling to denegate Freud's denegation. But Freud, like Hegel (though in a different way), is inescapable. As we have discovered, according to the strange logic of denegation, un-negation repeats what it attempts to avoid, affirms what it tries to negate, owns what it seeks to disown. Thus, Derrida's effort to escape Freud denegates itself.

What secrets is Derrida not telling? What secrets is Jacques (or is it John?) telling by not telling? Before crossing the threshold (as if the threshold could ever be crossed), a (perhaps) final deferral.

## *Recuperation*

Negative theology is hot. Timely, one might say. But why? Why does negative theology return today—here and now, *ici et maintenant*? Has it ever gone away? If not, how can it return? What is the time of the timely? The time of the return of, or to negative theology? What is the place of the return of, or to negative theology? Is the time of the return the present—the here and now? Or is it another time? Another place?

The return of, or to, negative theology is, in most cases, a gesture of recuperation. After so many recuperative moves, one hesitates to sound an apocalyptic tone by calling such efforts final. Nonetheless, there is something desperate about these gestures of recuperation. All too often, the return to, or of, negative theology involves a dialectical move that is intended to negate negation. If apparent opposites are really one, then the negative is at the same time positive, and thus it becomes possible to discover resources for defense in criticism itself. Within this framework, deconstruction's interrogation of so-called ontotheology can be enlisted in support of a tradition that extends beyond the early church fathers to Neoplatonists and even Plato. It is precisely such gestures of recuperation that lead Derrida to deny that deconstruction is, in effect, a latter-day form of negative theology: "No, what I write is not 'negative theology.'" (Again, the strange logic of No . . . not.) Classical negative theology, Derrida insists, remains committed to the "ontological wager" that characterizes Western philosophy and theology.

"No . . . not. . . ." And yet. And yet, for Derrida, negation is always denegation; disavowal is in some sense avowal. Negative theology does not go away by simply negating or denying it. The repressed always re-turns. This is the source of its fascination. Derrida does not merely reject negative theology, for it continues to exercise a certain "fascination" for him. Is this the fascination of Blanchot's "*Viens*" with which "Of an Apocalyptic Tone Newly Adopted in Philosophy" ends and "How to Avoid Speaking" begins? For Blanchot, fascination is always "the fascination of the absence of time."

> The time of the absence of time is not dialectical. What appears in it is the fact that nothing appears, the being that lies deep within the absence of being, the being that is when there is nothing, that is no longer when here is something—as though there were beings only through the loss of being, when being is lacking. The reversal that constantly refers us back, in the absence of time, to the presence of absence but to this presence as absence, to absence as affirmation of itself, affirmation in which nothing is affirmed, in which nothing ceases to be affirmed, in the aggravation of the indefinite—this movement is not dialectical. . . . In the absence of time, what is new does not renew anything; what is present is not contemporary; what is present presents nothing, represents itself, belongs now and henceforth and at all times to recurrence. This is not, but comes back, comes as already and always past, so that I do not know it, but I recognize it, and this recognition destroys the power in me to know, the right to grasp, makes what cannot be grasped into something that cannot be relinquished, the inaccessible that I cannot cease attaining, what I cannot take but can only take back and never give up.[6]

The inaccessible . . . the unavoidable . . . the ungraspable. To recuperate is to recover. But to recover is to re-cover the irrecuperable. The irrecuperable is, of course, ungraspable. *Recuperate* derives from the stem *kap*, which means grasp, take, hold. The Germanic translation of *kap* is *haf* (Old English *helfeld*), which was a thread used for weaving. A heddle, by extension, is a device that grasps the thread. The threads of *recuperate* lead back to the problem of the text by way of *textere* (to weave). If the thread is ungraspable, the text unravels. This unraveling is the failure of recuperation. The impossibility of recooperation implies the inescapability of the irrecuperable. In the absence of recuperation, dis-ease grows, wounds fester, tears linger. Might this tear be the place or nonplace where "what is present presents nothing?" Might this "nothing" be the nothing that Derrida struggles to say or not to say? And might saying or not saying this nothing imply an opening in which it becomes possible to read negative theology otherwise—otherwise than ontotheologically?

## *Avoidances*

Derrida avoids negative theology as long as possible. That is to say, he avoids it until it becomes unavoidable. This avoidance, however, is never complete, for he remains *fascinated* by an unavoidable that remains ungraspable.

> As I have always been fascinated by the supposed movements of negative theology (which, no doubt, are themselves never foreign to the experience of fascination in general), I objected in vain to the assimilation of the thinking of the trace or of différance to some negative theology, and my response amounted to a promise: one day I would have to stop deferring, one day I would have to try to explain myself directly on this subject, and at last to speak of "negative theology" itself, assuming that some such thing exists.
>
> Has that day come? (82)

Is "How to Avoid Speaking: Denegations" the fulfillment of a promise or yet another promissory note? In this text, does Derrida "explain himself directly" on negative theology? Or is his language still something like what Kierkegaard describes as "indirect discourse?" Either promise or fulfillment . . . both promise and fulfillment . . . neither promise nor fulfillment? And what if "fulfilling" a promise means not fulfilling it? What if to talk or write "directly" is to talk or write indirectly?

What if Derrida in this text writes more directly, which means indirectly, about what he is always not talking and writing about?

To begin to answer these questions, an additional query must be posed: What is a promise? A promise is, in Austin's terms, a performative utterance. In contrast to constative utterances, which assert or describe facts or antecedent conditions, a performative utterance is a speech act that realizes a state of affairs that did not exist prior to the language event. An effective speech act presupposes that the participants are fully conscious of their deeds and clearly understand not only their own intentions but the intentions of each other. For Austin and his followers, a promise must always be made in the present and with full self-presence.

If, however, a promise presupposes the full presence of the present, then is a promise possible? From Derrida's perspective, there is *always* a remainder that escapes totalization, and hence the present can never be totally present. Inasmuch as it requires the presence of self-consciousness and the self-consciousness of presence, the promise would seem to be impossible. And yet, Derrida insists, promising is unavoidable. Commenting on the writings of Paul de Man, Derrida argues that "the promise is impossible but inevitable. . . . Even if a promise could be kept, this would matter little. What is essential here is that a pure promise cannot properly take place, in a proper place, even though promising is inevitable as soon as we open our mouths—or rather as soon as there is a text."[7] Language, in other words, is unavoidably promissory. Derrida notes the twist of Freud's polyvalent prefix *ver-* that de Man uses to transform Heidegger's famous "*Die Sprache spricht*" into "*Die Sprache verspricht.*" "Language promises" . . . always promises . . . unavoidably promises . . . more and/or less than it delivers. But why must language promise? How can language promise if a promise cannot take place? How can language be unavoidably promissory if promising is impossible? It is a matter of time and space, or of a certain absence of time and space.

The promise, which cannot properly take place, has always already occurred. Language, like Lacan's symbolic order, precedes those who speak it or those through whom it speaks. Inscription within the symbolic order or linguistic system entails a "primal" lack that leaves an irrecuperable remainder. Language, therefore, is always lacking, which does not mean that we simply fall silent. To the contrary, lack releases the event of language. In this linguistic event, to speak is to say the impossibility of saying by promising what cannot be delivered.

> Discourse on the promise is already a promise: *in* the promise. I will thus not speak of this or that promise, but of that which, as necessary as it is impossible, inscribes us by its trace in language—before language. From the moment I open my mouth, I have already promised; or rather, and sooner, the promise has seized the *I* that promises to speak to the other. . . . This promise is older than I am. Here is something that appears impossible, the theoreticians of speech acts would say: like every genuine performative, a promise must be made in the present, in the first person (in the singular or plural). It must be made by one who is capable of saying *I* or *we*. (84)

Though inseparable from language, the trace "in language—before language" is nonetheless "older" than language. Language is constituted by *not saying* the trace. Since such not saying is necessary rather than contingent, the unspeakable trace is unavoidable. To speak, it is necessary to avoid speaking the trace. The avoidance of language, however, is not merely negative but is at the same time the *saying* of not-saying. This saying *without* saying is an unsaying that is, in effect, the denegation of language.

The promise is unavoidable and impossible. To speak is to promise, and yet the promise is never present; it never takes place but has always already occurred or is always about to occur. The place of the promise is not here, and its time is not now. Never here and now, the time and place of the promise are past or future. The issue is tense. The tense of the promise is past or future . . . or, through a metalepsis, a past that returns as a future in an eternally deferred future perfect. The past that haunts language is a strange, even uncanny past. As that which is always already lacking, this past was never present and thus cannot be re-presented. Though never experienced, the trace of the past is unforgettable.

> Thus, at the moment when the question "How to avoid speaking?" arises, it is already too late. There was no longer any question of not speaking. Language has started without us, in us and before us. This is what theology calls God, and it is necessary, it will have been necessary to speak. This "it is necessary" (*il faut*) is *both* the trace of undeniable necessity—which is another way of saying that one cannot avoid denying it, one can only deny it—*and* of a past injunction. Always already past, hence without a past present. Indeed, it must have been possible to speak in order to allow the question "How to avoid speaking?" to arise. Having come from the past, language before language, a past that was never present and yet remains unforgettable—this "it is necessary" thus seems to beckon toward the event of an order or of a promise that does not belong to what one currently calls history, the discourse of history or the history of discourse. (99)

In this case, that which does not belong to history is not eternal, though it is immemorial. Rather, the not-historical is, in Blanchot's terms, *le pas au-delà*.

> Time, time: *le pas au-delà*, which is not accomplished in time, would lead outside of time, without this outside being timeless, but there where time would fall, fragile fall, according to this "outside of time in time" toward which writing would draw us, if it were permitted of us, vanished from us, writing the secret of the ancient fear.[8]

Blanchot names this unnamable time the "terrifyingly ancient." In Levinas's terms, the irrecuperable past is the "unrepresentable before." This past that was never present is undeniably *provocative*; it provokes by calling (*vocare*) forth (*pro*). From whom does this call come? To whom is it directed? Origin and destination remain uncertain, and yet the call is both undeniable and unavoidable. This provocation that approaches from elsewhere disrupts and displaces by sending us on our way—a way from which there is no return. Such sending creates a debt (*Schuld*) that is in a certain sense our guilt (*Schuld*), and this guilt creates responsibility (*Schuld*). Like the translator named John (or Jacques), we are always already in debt.

> The translator is indebted, he appears to himself as translator in a situation of debt; and his task is to *render*, to render that which must have been given.[9]

The words and (speech) acts with which the translator attempts to discharge this debt are promissory notes (*Schuldschein*). As the word *Schuldschein* suggests, the promissory note is the appearance (*Schein*) of debt and/or guilt (*Schuld*). If *die Sprache verspricht*, then language implies a debt that entails an impossible responsibility.

To speak is to be indebted or subjected to an other for whom and to whom every subject is unavoidably responsible. As Levinas insists, responsibility is antecedent to freedom. The subject's responsibility is actualized in its response-ability, that is, in its ability to respond to the provocation of the other. "*Viens* . . . Come!" We forever live in thc *Wake* of this call.

> Stay awake!
> Strengthen what is left, so near death.
> If you do not stay awake,
> I shall come like a thief:
> You will not know at what hour I shall come to you.
>
> I shall come: the coming is always to come. . . . *I come* means: I am going to come, I am to-come in the imminence of an "I am going to come," "I am in the process of coming," "I am on the point of going to come." (54)

Who calls: "Come?" "I shall come?" God, perhaps? No, not . . . not precisely God.

And yet, the re-cited words are, of course, those of John, the translator, who is forever in a situation of debt to an Other. Without the gift, which is also *ein Gift*, from beyond, there would be no translation. The debt of the translator is always secondary—secondary not only to a certain creditor but also to a more "original" debtor.

> Nothing is more serious than translation. . . . For if the structure of the original is marked by the require-

> ment to be translated, it is that in laying down the law the original begins by indebting itself *as well* with regard to the translator. The original is the first debtor, the first petitioner; it begins by lacking and by pleading for translation. . . . In giving his name, God also appealed to translation, not only between the tongues that had suddenly become multiple and confused, but first *of his name*, of the name he had proclaimed, given, and which should be translated as confusion to be understood, hence to let it be understood that it is difficult to translate and to understand.[10]

Why is *nothing* more serious than translation? Is translation (and what is not translation?) for nothing? What gives itself to be translated? What does not give itself to be translated? What allows, indeed forces us to translate? What am I trying to translate—here and now—in this text? Derrida, of course. But Derrida is himself a translator whose writings we all know are untranslatable. To translate Derrida is to try (and unavoidably to fail) to translate his untranslatable translations of the untranslatable.

That which is untranslatable must remain secret. Perhaps the untranslatable secret is "the secret of the ancient fear" . . . the terrible secret that might be *provoked* by "*l'effroyablement ancien*." Who can tell? Who could tell such a secret? Any secret? Can a secret be told—told in such a way that it remains—remains (a) secret? In telling, does a secret remain? Or must a secret be told in order to be (a) secret? Would a secret that no one knows be a secret? Is the secret that remains in telling the remains that always remain, the remainder that is always to be told, whose telling is always yet to come?

Perhaps Derrida is struggling to tell us a secret. Perhaps it is precisely the telling or nontelling of the secret that secretes the texts written in his name or the name of an other. Derrida's fascination with the secret is no secret; it is *there* clear as day in his texts for anyone with eyes to see.

> Under this title, "How to avoid speaking," is it necessary to speak of the secret. . . . *How not to divulge a secret*? How to avoid speaking or saying? . . . How to make it known in order that the secret of the secret—as such not remain secret? . . . There is a secret of

> denial and a denial of the secret. The secret as such, *as secret*, separates and already institutes a negativity; it is a negation that denies itself. It de-negates itself. This denegation does not happen to it by accident; it is essential and originary. And in the *as such* of the secret that denies itself because it appears to itself in order to be what it is, this de-negation gives no chance to dialectic. (95)

Promise and secret intersect in the activity of denegation. The terrifyingly ancient seems to be the secret that renders all speech and writing promissory. In the wake of the "ancient of ancients," words promise but do not fulfill. Language always implies a "profound formerly [*profond jadis*, Levinas]" or "unprepresentable before" that never was, is, or will be present. Since "the genesis of secrecy" is always missing, there is nothing to tell. I repeat: There is *nothing* to tell. The secret is that there is no secret.

> There is no secret *as such*; I deny it. And this is what I confide in secret to whomever allies himself to me. This is the secret of the alliance. If the theo-logical necessarily insinuates itself there, this does not mean that the secret itself is theo-logical. But does something like the secret *itself*, properly speaking, ever exist? The name of God (I do not say God, but how to avoid saying God here, from the moment when I say the name of God?) can only be *said* in the modality of this secret denial: above all, I did not want to say that. (95)

Denials of denials; negations of negations. No not no. How to not to speak? How to speak? How to avoid speaking—*that*?

It is, of course, possible that the title is *both* interrogation *and* assertion, *both* question *and* answer: "How to avoid speaking?" "Denegations." Denegation, however, is an answer that is no answer, for it *neither* asserts *nor* denies. Denegation *performs* in a way other than the performative utterance of speech act theory. When understood in terms of denegation, promising and telling (a secret) accomplish nothing. Such "accomplishment" is a failure to accomplish. The text in which this unaccomplishment is accomplished becomes a performative utterance that "says" the "unsayable" by unsaying all saying and every said. Neither autonomous nor reflexive, such a text does not refer to things or narrate events beyond itself but inscribes a more radical "beyond" that is nevertheless inscribed "within" the text itself. This is the "beyond" that Blanchot (improperly) names *le pas au-delà.* The step (*pas*) toward the not (*pas*) that is forever beyond (*au-delà*) can be taken (if at all) only in a textual "event" that performs an impossible "event." In a text entitled simply "Not [*Pas*]," Derrida offers an analysis of Blanchot's writing that indirectly describes (while performing) his own textual practice.

> This "terrifyingly ancient" time binds one to the *récit*, makes of the *récit*, thus determined, the sole text that places us in relation (without relation) to what passes with this past of the not [*pas*], which no concept, no poem would any longer even be able to cite. Thus to recite, since it can only be a question of that: to cite a "Come," which still has not called, which is called, after a "Come," an *already* more ancient than time, an absolute crypt. This *récit* destroys the *récit* (the one that pretends to relate, according to the current logic of these words, an event) but it does not do it in the name of the concept as a philosophical gesture, but rather in the name of an other (dissimulated) *récit*, according to the other-event [*l'autre-événement*], to the not of the concept. It "would" be the coming of this other-event called "Come" if this would not arrive from a simple step/not [*pas*]. Thus it would not suffice to say that the *récit* (of Blanchot [and of Derrida]) is not the relation of the event but the event itself. Rather, it "would have been" the labyrinthian and snared structure of the not of event. . . . It, the necessity, the chance, still marks the chance, the risk: that the other of language takes place in the not beyond of language. No not *its* other but the other without it.[11]

"L'autre de la langue se passe dans le pas au-delà de la langue. Non pas son autre mais l'autre sans elle." "The task of the translator" is infinite! Perhaps translation is the play of the infinite itself. "The other of language takes place [or passes away, fades, decays] in the not [or the step] beyond of language." "The not beyond of language" must be read in at least two conflicting ways at once: the not that *is* the beyond of language, and the not that *is not* beyond language, that is, the not-beyond of language. "*Pas* non" also remains questionable. Does it negate or not negate? Both negate and not negate? Or neither negate nor not negate? Furthermore, the *de* does not denote ownership but a certain dispossession. "No not *its* other but the other without it [i.e., language]." The *pas* that is *au-delà* language, as an other that does not even belong to language as *its* other, *is not the not* of (classical) negative theology. No, not that, no but an other no that is at the same time not no. A *quasi* no, a no *without* no—this is the *not* that obsesses Derrida in "How to Avoid Speaking: Denegations" and elsewhere. "As if I had wanted to ask, on the threshold of this lecture, what these three adverbs mean and whence they come."

Does "How to Avoid Speaking: Denegations" fulfill Derrida's promise to speak directly about negative theology? It is impossible to say . . . always impossible to say. Not only for us but also for Derrida.

> Will I do it? Am I in Jerusalem? This is a question to which one will never respond in the present tense, only in the future or in the past. Why insist on this postponement? Because it appears to me neither avoidable nor insignificant. One can never decide whether deferring, as such, brings about precisely that which it defers and alters (*diffère*). It is not certain that I am keeping my promise today; nor is it certain that in further delaying I have not, nevertheless, already kept it. (83)

Whether to fulfill or defer, Derrida develops a tightly structured argument that mimes the dialectical machinations of Hegel's speculative logic. Three stages or moments: Greek, Christian, and a third that is undecidable—perhaps both Greek and Christian, perhaps neither Greek nor Christian. There is, however, something missing. Derrida is (yet again) avoiding something. In fact, his whole argument is a complex strategy of avoidance. This is no secret, for he tells us directly what he is *not* talking about.

> Three stages or three places in any case to avoid speaking of a question that I will be unable [N.B., not unwilling but *unable*] to treat; to deny it in some way,

> or to speak of it without speaking of it, in a negative mode: what do I understand by negative theology and its phantoms in a tradition of thought that is neither Greek nor Christian? In other words, what of Jewish and Islamic thought in this regard? By example, and in everything that I will say, a certain void, place of an internal desert, will perhaps allow this question to resonate. (100)

This internal desert is the space in which the withdrawal of the terrifyingly ancient destines its followers to err.

First Greek. But the beginning is already double. Derrida identifies two strands of "negative theology" in the Greek tradition: one dominant, one repressed. On the one hand, something like what will become negative theology appears in Plato's *Republic* and reappears in a variety of Neo-platonisms. Within this framework, the idea of the Good "has its place beyond Being or essence. Thus the Good is not, nor is its place. But this not-being is not a non-being" (100). To the contrary, the beyond-Being of the Good is a Being-beyond that is "surreal" or "hyperreal." Since this hyperessentiality surpasses both beings and Being, it resists positive predication. One can only express the surreal in negative terms. In this case, negation is at the same time affirmation. The surreality that is affirmed through the process of negation does not break with Being but is its eternal origin and goal. The Go(o)d is the Alpha and Omega of everything that *is*.

On the other hand, there is a repressed "tropic of negativity" that insinuates itself within the Platonic text at pivotal points. The return of the repressed implies a "third species" that "is" *neither* being *nor* nonbeing. It is crucial to distinguish this nondialectical third from the dialectical third that also inhabits the Platonic corpus. Though Plato's dialectical third is "beyond" the opposites it unites, it still "concerns Being." It "gathers" or "interweaves" the terms of every relationship. This gathering is the labor of the *logos*.

Beyond the gathering of the *logos*, Plato glimpses a different third that is resolutely nondialectical. He associates this third with the strange space or spacing of the *khora*. In the *Timaeus*, the *khora* "appears" as the place or nonplace into which the Demiurge introduces the images of the paradigms that are essential to the process of creation. As such, the *khora* "must have been *there*, as the 'there' itself, beyond time or in any case beyond becoming, in a beyond time without common measure with the eternity of the ideas and the becoming of sensible things" (104). The *khora* marks the margin of the neither/nor that "is" *neither* either/or *nor* both/and. "It is necessary to avoid speaking of *khora* as of 'something' that is or is not, that could be present or absent, intelligible, sensible, or both at once, active or passive, the Good . . . or the Evil, God or man, the living or the nonliving" (106). Neither being nor nonbeing, the *khora* involves a negativity that escapes both the positive and negative theological register. As such, the *khora* is *atheological.*

> Radically nonhuman and atheological, one cannot even say that it *gives* place or that *there is* the *khora*. The *es gibt*, thus translated, too vividly announces or recalls the dispensation of God, of man, or even that of the Being of which certain texts by Heidegger speak (*es gibt Sein*). *Khora* is not even *that* (*ça*), the *es* or *id* of giving, before all subjectivity. It does not give place as one would give something, whatever it may be; it neither creates nor produces anything, not even an event insofar as it takes place. It gives no order and makes no promise. It is radically ahistorical, because nothing happens through it and nothing happens to it. (106)

In the Platonic text and the traditions to which it gives rise, the thought of the *khora* remains oblique and unstable. Neither/nor tends to slip into both/and in a move intended to reappropriate the *khora* within an ontotheological economy. But this domesticating gesture fails, for the *khora* is irrepressible and thus repeatedly returns.

Then Christian. Though Derrida's account of Christian negative theology is extensive, his point is simple. Among the Christian writers Derrida considers are Pseudo-Dionysius, Meister Eckhart, Bernard of Clairvaux, and Augustine. In each case, Derrida maintains, the via negativa turns out to be implicitly affirmative. Christians have, for the most part, extended and elaborated the dominant strand in the Platonic tradition. In Christian theology, God, who is beyond Being, is not discontinuous with it. The apophatic God, like the Platonic Good, is surreal, hyperreal, hyperessential, or "supereminent Being." When carried to completion (and completion *is* possible for the *theologian*), the negative becomes positive. This form of negation, according to Derrida, is a "negativity without negativity" (113). As Eckhart stresses, the goal of the via negativa is the uninhibited enjoyment of the "pure, clear, limpid One, separated from all duality." Eckhart speaks of this One as "Nothing" or "hyperessential nothingness." "We must," Eckhart insists, "eternally sink ourselves in this One, from the Something to the Nothing" (121). This Nothing, however, is a nonbeing that is actually identical with the fullness of Being. As Eckhart's successor, Hegel, argues in his *Science of Logic*, Being and Nothing are One. When *dialectically* understood, nothing and nonbeing turn out to be every bit as ontological as beings and Being. Within the dialectics of christo-logic, negation implies affirmation, death leads to life, and crucifixion harbors resurrection.

> Contrary to what seemed to happen in the "experience" of the place called *khora*, the apophasis is brought into motion—it is *initiated*, in the sense of initiative and initiation—by the event of a revelation that is also a promise. This apophasis belongs to a history; or rather, it opens up a history and an anthropo-theological dimension. (117–18)

The history that the event of revelation opens is the history of salvation whose goal is the re-covery of the "absolute crypt" of the *khora*.

The empty tomb can, however, be understood in at least two ways: as a sign of the reality of resurrection or as a sign of the impossibility of resurrection. Even in the midst of the Christian effort to re-cover the "absolute crypt"[12] of the *khora*, Derrida espies an irrecuperable trace. What is Eckhart *not* saying? Or what is he saying by not saying? Is denegation quietly at work in Eckhart's text? In the text of all apophatic theology? Derrida comments on Eckhart's text:

> This is to speak in order to command not to speak, to say what God is not, that he is a non-God. How may one hear the copula of being that articulates this singular speech and this order to be silent? Where

> does it have its place? Where does it take place? It is the place, the place of this writing, and more precisely, a threshold. (121)

Remember, "we are still on the threshold." Not just here and now but always. The threshold is the site (or nonsite/nonsight) of passage. But does a threshold permit translation (*trans*, across + *latus*, carried)? Can a passage—any passage—be translated? Eckhart's text attempts to translate the threshold by carrying the reader beyond the limit.

> The place is only a place of passage, and more precisely, a threshold. But a threshold, this time, to give access to what is no longer a place. A subordination, a relativization of the place, and an extraordinary consequence; the place is Being. What finds itself reduced to the condition of a threshold is Being itself, Being as a place. Solely a threshold, but a sacred place, the outer sanctuary (*parvis*) of the temple. (121)

Which temple? What if Eckhart's temple stands in the midst of "The Origin of the Work of Art"? Or what if Heidegger's temple, which is really Greek, stands in the midst of Eckhart's temple? It is well known that Heidegger sustained a lifelong interest in Eckhart. If Eckhart's temple is Heideggerian and Heidegger's temple is Greek, then which strand of the Greek tradition is woven into the text of the via negativa? As we have seen, Derrida argues that Christian negative theology extends and expands the domination of Greek ontology. Domination, however, always requires repression, and the repressed never goes away but always returns to disrupt, interrupt, dislocate. The origin of the work of art, in whose cleft Heidegger's Greek temple stands (and falls), is a certain *Riss*—tear, tear, fissure, gap, flaw, crack. Perhaps this *Riss*, which rends the text of negative theology, points toward a different space and a different time. "Temple," after all, derives from the Latin *templum*, which, like *tempus* (time), comes from the Greek *temnos*. While *temno* means "cut," *temnos* designates that which is "cut off." Accordingly, *templum* is a section, a part cut off. What, then, is the time and place of the severed part—*la part madudite*?[13] Perhaps the time/place of the *templum* is the time/place of a threshold that cannot be crossed or erased. Something like an invisible sieve, a filter that permits the eye to see.

> The soul, which exercises its power in the eye, allows one to see what is not, what is not present;[14] it "works in nonbeing and follows God who works in nonbeing." Guided by this *psyche*, the eye thus passes the threshold of Being toward nonbeing in order to see what does not present itself. Eckhart compares the eye to a sieve [*crible*]. Things must be "passed through the sieve [*gebiutelt*]." This sieve is not one figure among others; it tells us the difference between Being and nonbeing. There is no text, above all no sermon, no possible predication, without the invention of such a filter. (121–22)

So understood, the sieve is, in effect, a figure for Heidegger's "ontological difference."

*Un crible*, however, is not only a sieve; it is also a riddle. To riddle is to pierce with holes, to perforate. But to riddle can also mean to speak enigmatically. A riddle, of course, is a puzzle, conundrum, insoluble problem, or mystery. In some cases, however, a riddle is actually a sieve—a coarse-meshed sieve, used for separating wheat from chaff, sand from gravel, ashes from cinders. And what of the "rid" in *rid-dle*? Of what does the riddle rid us? What of the wheat? In which book is it to be found? What of the sand? Is this the sand of a certain interior desert? Or the sand of another "book"—an "older," perhaps terrifyingly ancient testament? And what of the ashes? Whose ashes? Of what, of whom are riddled ashes the trace?

> Ash.
> Ash. Ash.
> Night.
> Night-and-Night.[15]

Riddles. Riddles that riddle the Heideggerian text.

First Greek. Then Christian. Then "neither Greek nor Christian." But first a further delay—a supplementary deferral in which Der-rid-a again tells us what he is not telling us or is telling us by not telling us.

> I thus decided *not to speak* of negativity or of apophatic movements in, for example, the Jewish or Islamic

> traditions. To leave this immense place empty, and above all that which cannot connect such a name of God with the name of the Place, to remain thus on the threshold—was this not the most consistent possible apophasis? (122)

By re-citing the avoidance to which his *récit* is devoted, Derrida refigures the third in a nondialectical and nonsynthetic way. Is the *aparté* with which the third (non)moment of Derrida's argument begins really a deferral? Or is he telling us what he will be addressing when he writes about Heidegger?

How is Heidegger to be read? Derrida has always insisted that Heidegger must be read with "two hands" at once. But whose hands are these? What is the place of the hand in the Heideggerian text? "Two texts, two hands, two visions, two ways of listening. Together simultaneously and separately."[16] Two texts, two hands: On the one hand, but on the other hand.

> My first paradigm was Greek and the second Christian, without ceasing to be Greek. The last will be neither Greek nor Christian. If I were not afraid of trying your patience, I would recall that which, in Heidegger's thinking, could resemble the most questioning legacy, both the most audacious and the most liberated repetitions of the traditions I have just invoked. (122)

Again it is a question of tense. The tense is conditional—always conditional: "*Ce qui, dans la pensée de Heidegger, pourrait ressembler.*" Not *does* but *could* resemble. Heidegger repeats the traditions that Derrida has just invoked: Greek and Christian. It is possible to argue, indeed many have already argued, that Heidegger brings together—perhaps even synthesizes—the Greek and Christian traditions in a way that creates new possibilities for theology. When so understood, Heidegger perpetuates the very ontotheological tradition he attempts to dismantle. The arguments are too well known to be repeated here.

But there are gaps in Heidegger's position. And these gaps suggest other traditions. As we have discovered, the Greek and Christian versions of apophatic thought are themselves riddled. Philosophers and theologians from Plato on have repeatedly said something other than they intended or thought they were saying. From time to time, Heidegger glimpses this *other* that inhabits the theologic-philosophical text. At one point, he writes:

> If Plato takes the *khorismos* into consideration, the difference of place [*die verschiedene Ortung*] between Being and beings, he thus poses the question of the wholly other place [*nach dem ganz anderen Ort*] of Being, by comparison with that of beings. (123)

Derrida notes the importance of Heidegger's observation: "I merely underscore this movement toward a *wholly other* place [*un lieu* tout autre], as place of Being or *place of the wholly other*: in and beyond a Platonic or Neoplatonic tradition. But also in and beyond a Christian tradition of which Heidegger—while submerged in it, as in the Greek tradition—never ceased claiming, whether by denial or not, that it could in no case entertain a philosophy" (123). The question that remains is whether the place of the wholly other is a place of Being or is a wholly other "place."

In probing this problem, Derrida returns to the task of the translator defined in his letter to John: "Modestly and in my own way, I try to translate . . . a thought of Heidegger." Near the end of "How to Avoid Speaking: Denegations," Derrida repeats Heidegger's thought: "If I *were* yet to *write* a theology, as I am sometimes tempted to do, the word 'being' *ought* not to appear there." The question that Derrida poses is whether Heidegger has not, in fact, done what he said he had not done, done what he said he ought to avoid doing.

> Hasn't Heidegger written what he says he would have liked to write, a theology *without* the word *being*? But didn't he also write what he says should not be written, what he should not have written, namely a theology that is opened, dominated, and invaded by the word *being*?
>
> With and without the word *being*, he wrote a theology with and without God. He did what he said it would be necessary to avoid doing. He said, wrote, and allowed to be written exactly what he said he wanted to avoid. He was not there without leaving a trace of all these folds. He was not there without allowing a trace to appear, a trace that is, perhaps,

> no longer his own, but that remains as if (*quasiment*) his own. (128–29)

The trace that is neither Heidegger's nor not Heidegger's, is the trace that Derrida follows. If Derrida's writings are translations of the Heideggerian text, then Derrida's questions of Heidegger can be turned back on the Derridean text. "Hasn't [Derrida] written what he says he would have liked to write? . . . Didn't he also write what he says should not be written?" In the midst of his text on Heidegger's text, Derrida offers another important parenthetical re-mark: "(*To say nothing*, once again, of the mysticisms or theologies in the Jewish, Islamic, or other traditions)" (124). Is Derrida saying nothing once again? Saying nothing by what he is not saying? Isn't his nonsaying nonetheless a saying? A denegation? Isn't his avoidance of speaking the only way he has to speak about that which he knows he cannot speak about? Isn't the unspoken third that is *neither* Greek *nor* Christian not Heidegger's third but the third of "the Jewish, Islamic, or other traditions"? "I do not intend to respond to these questions nor even to conclude with them" (128).

## *"Autobiography"*

A final note that is not, of course, final. On the threshold of his account of Greek, Christian, and neither Greek nor Christian, at the precise moment he tells us what he is *not* going to tell us (i.e., "Jewish and Islamic thought in this regard"), Derrida adds an unexpected note—note 13.

> Despite this silence, or in fact because of it, one will perhaps permit me to interpret this lecture as the most "autobiographical" speech I have ever risked. One will attach to this word as many quotation marks as possible. It is necessary to surround with precautions the hypothesis of a self-presentation passing through a speech on the negative theology of others. But if one day I had to tell my story, nothing in this narrative would start to speak of the thing itself if I

> did not come up against this fact: for lack of capacity, competence, or self-authorization, I have never been able to speak of what my birth, as one says, should have made closest to me: the Jew, the Arab. (135)

"If one day I had to tell my story." "If I *were* yet to *write* a theology." The tense remains conditional. Might Derrida's story be a retranslation of Heidegger's neither/nor? Are Derrida's denials to be believed? Is he not speaking of his birth and of what is closest to him—the Jew, the Arab? And what could be more important today than speaking of the Jew and the Arab here and now?

For many years—at least since *Glas* and I suspect long before, perhaps even from the beginning—Derrida has been struggling with the question of autobiography. As time passes and texts accumulate, I begin to suspect that Derrida's deepest *desire* is to write an "autobiography." But how could he fulfill this desire? How could he write an autobiography without at the same time writing a theology? Derrida could (or would) no more write an autobiography than he could (or would) write a theology. If, however, he were to write (or were always already writing) an "autobiography," it would seem that he must write (or have always already been writing) an *atheology*. Atheology "has nothing to do with negative theology; there is reference neither to an event nor to a giving, neither to an order nor to a promise, even if, as I have just underscored, the absence of promise or of order—the barren, radically nonhuman and atheological character of this 'place'—obliges us to speak and to refer to it in a certain and unique manner, as to the wholly other who is neither transcendent, absolutely distanced, nor immanent and close" (108). Neither transcendent nor immanent, the wholly other is traced in an immemorial past, which, though never present eternally returns as an outstanding future that never arrives. As we have seen, the trace of this strange altarity haunts the western theologico-philosophical tradition—from Plato's *khora*, to Eckhart's sieve, to Heidegger's *Riss*, and beyond. It is not impossible that this wholly other is the "terrifyingly ancient" that approaches from another yet more ancient tradition. This *tout autre* might imply the denegation of Jewish and Islamic traditions that Derrida's quasi-"autobiographical," atheological text performs. Perhaps.

The riddle remains . . . remains unanswered.

*P.S.*

o

o

o

Have *I* delivered? Have I fulfilled my promise to write on or about "Derrida and negative theology"? Or have I delivered something else? A different text? An other text? Is the text promise of fulfillment? Or neither? I *cannot* tell.

o

o

o

*Will* Derrida deliver? Will he write the P.S. he has pledged to write? Will he fulfill his promise? Even if he delivers, will he fulfill his promise? Or will his "fulfillment" be another promise? Another promise that might be the only possibility of "fulfilling" a promise? It remains to be seen. *It* always remains . . . to be seen.

o

o

o

## *Notes*

1. Jacques Derrida, "*Pas*," *Gramma* 3/4 (1976), pp. 180, 139, 152, 189.

2. Mark C. Taylor, "Unending Strokes," *Theology at the End of the Century: A Dialogue on the Postmodern*, ed. Robert Scharlemann (Charlottesville: University of Virginia Press, 1990), p. 136.

3. A network of terms bearing the prefix *Ver-* plays a crucial role in Freud's theories: *Verarbeitung, Verdichtung, Verdrangte, Verdrangung, Verfullung, Verkehrung, Versagung, Verschiebung, Verwerfung,* etc.

4. In his brief essay entitled "Negation," Freud writes: "To negate something in a judgment is, at bottom, to say: 'This is something which I should prefer to repress.' A negative judgment is the intellectual substitute for repression; its 'no' is the hallmark of repression, a certificate of origin—like, let us say, 'Made in Germany.' With the help of the symbol of negation, thinking frees itself from the restrictions of repression and enriches itself with material that is indispensable for its proper functioning" (*The Standard Edition of the Complete Psychological Works of Sigmund Freud,* vol. 19, trans. James Strachey (London: Hogarth Press, 1961), p. 236).

5. The most important difference between these two terms concerns the problem of castration and the correlative question of fetishism. "The mechanism of *Verleugnung,*" Laplanche and Pontalis explain, "is first described by Freud in the course of his discussion of castration. Confronted by the absence of a penis in the girl, children 'disavow (*leugnen*) the fact and believe that they *do* see a penis, all the same'. . . . [T]he fetishist perpetuates an infantile attitude by holding two incompatible positions at the same time: he simultaneously disavows and acknowledges the fact of feminine castration" (J. Laplanche and J.-B. Pontalis, *The Language of Psychoanalysis,* trans. D. Nicholson-Smith [New York: Norton, 1973], pp. 118, 119).

6. Maurice Blanchot, "The Essential Solitude," *The Gaze of Orpheus and Other Essays,* trans. Lydia Davis (Barrytown, NY: Station Hill Press, 1981), p. 73.

7. Jacques Derrida, *Memories for Paul de Man,* trans. Cecile Lindsay, Jonathan Culler, and Eduardo Cadava (New York: Columbia University Press, 1986), p. 98.

8. Maurice Blanchot, *Le Pas au-delà* (Paris: Gallimard, 1973), p. 8.

9. Jacques Derrida, "Des Tours de Babel," *Difference in Translation,* ed. Joseph Graham (Ithaca, N.Y.: Cornell University Press, 1985), p. 176.

10. Derrida, "Des Tours de Babel," p. 184.

11. Derrida, "*Pas,*" pp. 168–69.

12. For a detailed analysis of the crypt, see: "Fors: The Anglish Words of Nicholas Abraham and Maria Torok," which appears as

the foreword to Abraham and Torok's *The Wolfman's Magic Word: A Cryptonomy*, trans. Nicholas Rand (Minneapolis: University of Minnesota Press, 1986).

13. See: Georges Bataille, *La Part madudite* (Paris: Les Éditions de Minuit, 1967).

14. The problematic of the "part cut off" could be extended to the issue of castration, which plays such an important role in "Of an Apocalyptic Tone Recently Adopted in Philosophy." Always playing on many registers at once, Derrida suggests an association between Eckhart's argument and castration by way of the issue of vision. The fetish allows one to see "what is not present." This is, of course, one strategy for dealing with the problem of castration. As Derrida has long insisted, logocentrism and phallocentrism are inseparable. Eckhart's "Nothing that is Being" is a fetish constructed to repress the inescapability of lack.

15. These lines from a poem by Paul Celan are quoted by Derrida in "Shibboleth," *Midrash and Literature*, eds. Geoffrey Hartman and Sanford Budick (New Haven: Yale University Press, 1986), p. 336.

16. Jacques Derrida, "*Ousia* and *Gramme*: Note on a Note from *Being and Time*," *Margins of Philosophy*, trans. Alan Bass (Chicago: University of Chicago Press, 1987), p. 65.

# SIX

# *A Hindu Response to Derrida's View of Negative Theology*

Harold Coward

To present a Hindu response to Derrida's view of negative theology requires first that we are clear on what his viewpoint is. In his essay "Différance," Derrida admits that the detours, locutions, and syntax that he uses often resemble those of negative theology, "even to the point of being indistinguishable from negative theology."[1] Yet he wants to clear a space for his approach as not negative theology—at least not the negative theology of the Christian tradition of Dionysius the Areopagite, Augustine, and Meister Eckhart. He admits to having had to resort to negation to delineate *différance*:

> *Différance is not*, does not exist, is not a present being (*on*) in any form . . . it has neither existence nor essence. It derives from no category of being, whether present or absent. And yet those aspects of *différance* which are hereby delineated are not theological, not even in the order of the most negative of negative theologies, which are always concerned with disengaging a superessentiality beyond the finite categories of essence and existence, that is, of presence, and always hastening to recall that God is refused the predicate of existence, only in order to acknowledge

> his superior, inconceivable, and ineffable mode of being.[2]

Unlike the hyper- or superessentiality that Christian negative theology seems to produce, differance, claims Derrida, in its negative delineation "is not only irreducible to any ontological or theological—ontotheological—reappropriation, but as the very opening of the space in which ontotheology—philosophy—produces its system and its history, it includes ontotheology, inscribing it and exceeding it without return.[3] In short, Derrida's negative delineation of differance, he claims, does not result in a reestablishment of itself as "hyper-differance," but simply clears a space in which the unfolding of negative theology and its hyperessentialism can take place.

Since these statements were first made and published by Derrida in 1968, he has continued to wrestle with the issue on two sides. First, is his characterization correct that Christian negative theology always ends up in a reappropriation of the essence that has been negated in a hyperessentialism? Second, does his own delineation of differance manage to escape ending up as hyper-differance? Both of these worries Derrida finally addresses almost twenty years later in his essay "How to Avoid Speaking: Denials."[4] In his essay Derrida notes an objection raised by Jean-Luc Marion against his earlier assessment that Christian negative theology ends in hyperessentialism. Derrida responds by offering a careful reading of Dionysius, Augustine, and Eckhart that suggests that the negative theology of these Christian thinkers (and the Greek thought they appropriate) still ends up in hyperessentiality.[5] In the course of the essay Derrida offers the oblique comment that he has decided not to speak of negativity in any other traditions, for example, in Judaism or Islam. Instead he leaves "this immense place empty"[6] for others to study. This chapter widens that immense empty place to include the via negativa of Hinduism, especially with regard to the hyperessentiality problem.

## *I. Via Negativa and Hyperessentiality in Hinduism*

Derrida is very clear in his view of hyperessentiality. To the extent that negative theology reserves beyond all negation some hyperessentiality of the sort one finds in Dionysius and Eckhart, says Derrida, I could not put my writing under the heading of negative theology. Would this clear distancing also hold between Derrida and the frequent Hindu formulations of the via negativa?

Although the earliest Hindu scriptures, the Vedas, contain mainly affirmative statements about the Divine, there is one hymn, Ṛgveda 10.129, that contains elements of both skepticism and negation. The passage reads, "The sages searching in their hearts with wisdom found out the bond of being in non-being."[7] It is in the later Upaniṣads, however, that negation is given full development until it becomes a major means of enlightenment and release. The premise assumed in the Upaniṣads according to Advaita is that Brahman, the Divine or the Real, is always present but obscured by a beginningless covering of ignorance. To reveal or to know Brahman, then, one need only remove the obscuring ignorance. And negation was a favorite technique, used by the Upanisadic teachers with their students, for removing ignorance. This is especially true of the Bṛhadāraṇyaka Upaniṣad, where the negation formula *neti, neti* (not this, not that) is effectively employed. For example, when the student Śākalya asks, "What is the Brahman that you know? What is the basis of your Self (*Ātman*)?" the teacher Yājñavalkya replies, "The Ātman can only be described as *neti, neti*—not this, not that—for it is ungraspable, unattached and irreducible."[8] In his commentary on the passage, Śaṇkara notes that Brahman is incomprehensible because it goes beyond the attributes of effects (*sarva-kārya-dharmātītaḥ*).[9] In the same Upaniṣad we find another example of when King Janaka questions the teacher Yājñavalkya as to the nature of the true self and is told: "The self (*ātman*) is *neti, neti* (not this, not that). He is incomprehensible for he is never comprehended."[10] Again Śaṇkara comments that, in such passages treating of Brahman, what is meant is a Brahman devoid of all attributes and distinctions.[11]

The suggestion that the via negativa ends in nihilism also came up in India, in the discussion of these Upanisadic passages. In Śaṇkara's commentary on the Brahman Sūtra, an objector suggests that the *neti, neti* formula has the result of denying Brahman altogether. To this Śaṇkara replies that it is impossible that the phrase *neti, neti* denies Brahman, for that would lead to a doctrine of a general void. Śaṇkara comments:

> Whenever we deny something unreal, we do so with reference to something real; the unreal snake, e.g., is denied with reference to the real rope. But this (denial of something unreal with reference to something real) is possible only if some entity is left . . .
>
> Brahman is that whose nature is permanent purity, intelligence, and freedom; it transcends speech and mind, does not fall within the category of "object," and constitutes the inward Self of all. Of this Brahman our text denies all plurality of forms; but Brahman itself leaves untouched.
>
> . . . the clause ["*neti, neti!*"] denies not absolutely everything but only everything but Brahman.[12]

Śaṇkara thus demonstrates that the Upaṇisadic *neti, neti* denies everything but Brahman. He goes on to suggest that Brahman is experienced by yogis in meditation, a suggestion that may functionally parallel the role of prayer in negative theology. But we will come back to that later (in section 4).

Derrida's critique of Christian negative theology was that it seemed to reserve beyond all positive predication and beyond all negation, even beyond Being, some hyperessentiality, a Being beyond being.[13] To the extent that it privileged some indestructible unity or presence, then, said Derrida, it must be subject to deconstruction. Derrida quotes an example from Meister Eckhart: "When I said that God is not being and that he is above Being, I have not denied Him being but, rather, I have exalted Being in Him."[14] Does the Advaita use of *neti, neti* end up in the same position of privileging Being in Brahman? If so, it too would be subject to deconstruction.

It is clear from the Upanisadic texts and commentaries examined above that *neti, neti* is applied to all predications of Brahman, whether positive or negative in nature. But it is equally true that, as Śaṇkara puts it, the application of *neti, neti* leaves Brahman itself untouched. That there is a Brahman is provisionally accepted on the evidence of scripture (the Vedas) and of reason, which argues that negation could not function unless it were grounded, ultimately, on the Real. In the famous rope-snake analogy, the unreal snake can only be negated with reference to the real rope. Similarly the predications of Brahman (even those in the affirmative, as may be found in the Vedas) can only be negated as unreal with reference to a real Brahman. Is this the kind of result that Derrida describes as "a supreme Being who remains incommensurate to the being of all that is, which is nothing, neither present nor absent, and so on"?[15] Perhaps, but we need to examine Hindu thought more closely before accepting it as equivalent to Derrida's "supreme Being."

Bṛhadāraṇyaka Upaniṣad 2.3.1–6 is a key passage in Hindu thought, both because its interpretation provides the foundational difference between Śaṇkara and Rāmānuja, and because it sets the stage for the two-level understanding of Brahman. It begins by stating that there are two forms of Brahman, the formed and the formless. The formed Brahman is described as the mortal, the actual, the essence of which is the sun, which gives forth warmth. The formless Brahman is the immortal, the space within the self (*ātman*). Verse 6 concludes:

> He who knows it thus attains splendour like a sudden flash of lightening. Now therefore there is the teaching *neti, neti* for there is nothing higher than this, that he is not this. Now the designation for him is the truth of truth. Verily, the vital breath is truth, and He is the truth of that.[16]

According to Śaṇkara this passage contrasts the characterization of the subtle body as being like a flame of fire or a white lotus with the Absolute transcendent Brahman that can only be negated. Thus all the description (including all action or movement) applies to the formed, or *saguṇa*, Brahman, the Brahman with qualities, and *neti, neti* applies to the formless, or *nirguṇa*, Brahman, the Brahman without qualities. Radhakrishnan compares Śaṇkara's *nirguṇa* or *neti, neti* Brahman to Dionysius's calling God "the absolute Nothing which is above all existence" and to Hooker's "our safest eloquence concerning him is our silence."[17] Rāmānuja, however, rejects the notion of *nirguṇa* Brahman completely, maintaining that there can be no object without qualities—not even Brahman. He interprets the *neti, neti* of the text as negating any evil qualities as being in Brahman,[18] and not meaning that Brahman has no qualities at all. It is clear from the two interpretations that the via negativa is to be found in Śaṇkara's Advaita Vedanta and not in Rāmānuja's Viśiṣtādvaita Vedānta, even though the latter was much more influential upon the masses of Hindus.

Śaṇkara clearly distinguishes a higher (*nirguṇa*) from a lower (*saguṇa*) Brahman in his *Brahmasūtrabhāṣya* and elsewhere. The higher Brahman is free form all adjuncts, all name and form, and it is knowledge of this Brahman that constitutes liberation (*mokṣa*) according to Śaṇkara. *Saguṇa* Brahman is the lower Brahman and is Brahman viewed from ignorance (*avidyā*). One cannot speak about the higher Brahman positively. So the texts use negative adjectives, such as "without qualifiers" (*nirviśeṣa*), "without form" (*arūpa*), "without parts and without end" (*advaita*). But the most important is *neti, neti*. In his commentary on the above passage from the Bṛhadāraṇyaka Upaniṣad, Śaṇkara asks, "How is it that by the expression 'not this, not this' the truth of truth is to be described?" and answers "To be sure Brahman is sometimes described by expressions such as 'knowledge, bliss, Brahman, Ātman', etc., but if we wish to describe its true nature it is impossible. Thus we are reduced to 'not this, not this,' eliminating all positive characteristics that might be thought to apply to it."[19] In his commentary on Guaḍapāḍa's Kārikā on the Māṇdūkya Upaniṣad, Śaṇkara adds that the function of *neti, neti* is to remove the obstructions produced by ignorance (*avidyā*), which preclude us from the better state of the characterlessness of the pure. Ātman.[20] Further clarification is added by Śaṇkara's pupil Sureśvara, who points out that the negation *neti, neti* in the Bṛhadāraṇyaka Upaniṣad does not have negation as its purpose; rather, it purports *identity*.[21] Where does this leave us in regard to the question of hyperessentialism? The Upaniṣad quoted above not only negates with *neti, neti* but then goes on and states that Brahman is the truth of truth and that vital breath (*prāṇa*) is truth. This might well be judged as hyperessentialism. However, Śaṇkara's interpretation of the passage is a thoroughgoing via negativa. Higher Brahman is *nirguṇa*, or completely without characteristics, all of which are ignorance (*avidyā*). The purpose of the negation *neti, neti* is to remove ignorance so as to reveal the underlying pure Ātman-Brahman. Ultimately then, as Sureśvara pointed out, *neti, neti* ends not in negation but in *identity*. While Derrida might argue that this is still hyperessentialism, I would suggest that it is *functionally* not much different from Derrida ending up with différance after everything else is negated. Derrida's defense, "What différance, the trace, and so on 'mean'—which hence *does not mean anything*—is 'before' the concept, the name, the word, 'something' that would be nothing, that no longer arises from Being . . . and even less from some hyperessentiality."[22] This defense could, I would argue, equally apply to Śaṇkara. The *identity* referred to by Sureśvara means nothing in conceptual terms. It is, as Derrida puts it, before any conceptualization in terms of name and form takes place.

Śaṇkara, however, does evoke three positive properties in alluding to Brahman. These are truth (*sat* or *satya*), consciousness (*cit* or *caitanya*), and bliss (*ānanda*). They allude to but do not define Brahman.[23] They are merely hints, pointers, or clues. The term *sat* occurs in the earliest Vedic texts in debates as to whether the universe sprang from *sat* or *asat*, being or nonbeing. Texts are found on each side of the issue, but Advaitins have viewed *sat* as the more fundamental of the two. As we have seen above, the Bṛhadāraṇyaka Upaniṣad declares that the Self is "truth of truth" (*satyasya satya*), and Śaṇkara and Sureśvara treat this as a parallel pronouncement to *neti, neti*.[24] As Potter helpfully summarizes, the term *cit* suggests that the highest, or *nirguṇa*, Brahman is pure consciousness, or awareness (*jñāna*), or the Witness (*sākṣin*), which is not itself an object of thought. Brahman is the self-luminous source of all consciousness. By its light everything else is known to awareness. But it is not a relational consciousness between knower and known. The closest approximation to pure consciousness in our ordinary experience comes in deep sleep, which according to the Māṇḍūkya Upaniṣad and Advaita Vedanta is a state of consciousness without any objects.[25] As Potter points out "when objects appear to this witnessing consciousness, they are the work of beginingless *avidyā*, or ignorance; they are superimposed on pure consciousness, which remains unaffected by that relationship."[26] The term *ananda*, or bliss, in the Upaniṣads suggests that Brahman is "full" (*pūrṇa*), not lacking in anything.[27] Thus, the negation of all *avidyā*, which leaves only Brahman, cannot be taken as void or nihilism. From the Advaita Vedanta perspective these three terms *sat*, *cit*, and *ananda* do not define *nirguṇa* Brahman but simply act like the pointer on a weather vane in pointing us toward Brahman. Ultimately our only way of knowing Brahman is by direct intuition.

## *II. The Direct Intuition of Brahman and Hyperessentiality*

To Derrida the Hindu claim of a direct intuition of Brahman, the Absolute, would sound like an intuition of presence and therefore of hyperessentiality. There might also be a question from Derrida as to just how far the negation of language can progress in the process of revealing the direct intuition. Derrida's much-quoted phrase *il n'y a pas de hors-texte* (there is nothing outside the text)[28] would suggest that whatever revelation takes place via the process of negation must somehow take place within language. On this point there is a very definite split within Hindu thought. Śaṇkara, perhaps like the Buddhist Nāgārjuna, maintains that the negation of language must be complete in order for the revelation to arise. This would suggest a consciousness free from all difference, something Derrida would seem bound to reject. However, Hindu thinkers such as Bhartṛhari, the Advaitin Maṇḍana Miśra, and more recently Aurobindo argue that the divine consciousness of Brahman necessarily involves language, even at the highest level of direct intuition after all negation has occurred. Of these Hindu thinkers, however, only Śaṇkara makes substantial use of the technique of negation, and so our analysis will focus mainly on his approach in relation to Derrida.

Śaṇkara would clearly disagree with Derrida. For Śaṇkara there is a Real that exists over and above language, namely, Brahman. Yet when we place Śaṇkara's thought in close proximity with the thought of Derrida, new aspects of Derrida are highlighted, especially in regard to negation. Just as for Śaṇkara the Real, Brahman, is fully seen only when language is negated, so also Derrida, in "Edmond Jabès and the Question of the Book," comments that for Judaism God is not known directly through the Book but when we keep still. Then God comes to us in action, questioning us, demanding a moral response. Unlike the perfect stillness of the Greek logos or Śaṇkara's intuition of Brahman, Derrida following Jabès, talks of a God who constantly questions out of silence. This questioning comes from a rupture within God as the origin of history. Derrida quotes Reb Lema, "Do not forget that you are the nucleus of a rupture," and goes on to say:

> God separated himself from himself in order to let us speak, in order to astonish and to interrogate us. He did so not by speaking but by keeping still, by letting silence interrupt his voice and his signs, by letting the Tables be broken. In *Exodus* God repented . . . between original speech and writing and, within Scripture, between the origin and the repetition (*Exodus* 32:14; 33:17). Writing is, thus, originally hermetic and secondary. Our writing, certainly, but already His, which starts with the stifling of his voice and the dissimulation of his Face. This difference, this negativity in God is our freedom, the transcendence and the verb which can relocate the purity of their negative origin only by the possibility of the Question.[29]

There is a dynamism, an originary force, here in the negation that is not found in the Greek logos or in Śaṇkara's Brahman. Rather than a direct intuition, it starts with God's silent desire to speak. Out of that silence comes not only God's speech and ours but also, because of the questioning silence, our freedom to act. But with this freedom comes the responsibility interrogated in God's written and silent questioning. But to be heard, language, both God's and ours, must be silenced or negated.

Śaṇkara would agree with Jabès and Derrida that our language and even the revealed language of the Veda ultimately must be silenced for the Real, Brahman, to be "heard" or "seen." This is indeed the goal of Śaṇkara's disciplined meditation—to hear (*śravaṇa*), think (*manana*), and reflect (*nididhāsana*).[30] But Śaṇkara takes pains to make clear that hearing, thinking, and reflecting are not activities nor are they to be understood as injunctions from Scripture. Śaṇkara's concern here is to separate the realization of Brahman from any motivated action, since in his system all such action is necessarily tainted with egoism's desire for a result—which itself will obstruct the Real. For Śaṇkara, Brahman, the Real exists separate from language and action and reveals itself only when language, its actions, and its questionings are canceled out—as in the final direct perception prompted by meditation on the Upanisadic phrase *tat tvam asi* (that thou art)—so that Brahman alone remains.[31]

But the intuition of Brahman is experienced as something like pure being and pure bliss rather than the kind of freedom-giving but ever-disturbing divine questioner of Jabès and Derrida.

But what exactly is involved in this final meditation on *tat tvam asi*, such that it turns into the final negation that, so to speak, pole-vaults us out of ordinary experience of language and the world (*māyā*, or *saguṇa* Brahman) into the direct experience of *nirguṇa*, or higher, Brahman? Śaṇkara's position is that one cannot be liberated into a direct intuition of Brahman merely by hearing a "great sentence" like *That Thou art* without understanding what it means. If the meanings are not understood, the negation of *māyā*, including *tat tvam asi*, will not take place, and Brahman will not be realized. For example, one may wrongly think that the words *That thou art* directly denote Brahman or that the *art* in the phrase *is* the *is* of predication, when really it is the *is* of identity: That (Brahman), Thou (Ātman) art; therefore, Ātman = Brahman. What is negated by the phrase is the devotee's ignorance that his or her self is something different from Brahman. The negation of the ignorance simultaneously opens up the experience of Self (Ātman) as nothing different from Brahman. Śaṇkara's pupil Sureśvara explains the negative function of *That thou art* as follows:

> That the sentence cannot be interpreted literally should be evident when one reflects that the designation of "that" excludes thou and the designation of "thou" excludes that and yet they are identified in the same sentence. So we are immediately led to forget the literal meaning as well as the figurative one inasmuch as this is an identity statement, and given proper preparation we should immediately grasp the sense of the statement even though no literal "translation" is possible. This grasping will necessarily be accompanied by a realization that no words, which is to say no properties, properly apply to that which is conveyed through the sentence.[32]

The negative function of *tat tvam asi* is to negate its literal meaning of difference and induce an intuition of identity.

For Śaṇkara, language is a part of *māyā* (our worldly experience) and is ultimately unreal, for it disappears when

Brahman, the Real, is "seen." But this does not mean that language is not to be valued.

Indeed, for Śaṇkara, language as Veda is the only means by which Brahman can be realized. But even the best language, the great sentences of the Upaniṣads, must be left behind for the *anubhava*, or direct intuition, of Brahman to occur. This is clearly evidenced by Śaṇkara's theory of error, in which the realization of Brahman is simultaneous with the canceling itself out of *tat tvam asi*—or, to evoke the favorite Vedantin analogy, the snake disappears completely when the rope is seen. Ultimately, then, for Śaṇkara, it is the Upanisadic *neti, neti* (not this, not that), speech as a via negativa to the Real, that characterizes Śaṇkara's theory of language in relation to the Real.

By contrast, even though he too stresses the need for silence, Derrida never ends up in a silence totally transcendent of language. Derrida, in his reading of Jabès, describes God's silence as that which both speaks and stifles itself so that we may have freedom to hear and be heard. Meanings and questions for us "ooze out" from around the letters and spoken sounds to emerge not in propositions but in silences—blanks.[33] Language, even the language of the Book, ends in silence (both agree on this), but a silence filled with tension of divine interrogation rather than Śaṇkara's direct intuition of identity with Brahman in which all cognition ceases. While there is no direct intuition for Derrida, there is a silence that is not a void or a nihilism but that is filled with the insistent stirrings of God. Thus even in the ultimate silence there is the experience of difference for Derrida.

At this point Derrida would apparently be offering a critique of Śaṇkara's emphasis on identity. However, on closer analysis the two are seen to be engaged in a similar philosophical tactic. Just as Śaṇkara would use the conceptual term *identity* as simply a hint or pointer to the nature of the real (we use "real" here as simply a functional or generic term for comparative purposes, and not to indicate any sense of essence or presence), so also Derrida admits that his use of differance to indicate the nature of the real must be constantly deconstructed. Both Śaṇkara and Derrida agree that the conceptual oppositions that make up language are the obstacles that get in the way of the experience of the real. Identifying oneself with either of the terms that make up these oppositions (e.g., *identity* for Śaṇkara; *differance* for Derrida) is the trap of language that must be overcome.

For Śaṇkara the only way out is to transcend language altogether, so that all of the opposites, and indeed all conceptualizing, are canceled by the direct intuition (*anubhava*) of the real. By contrast, Derrida thinks this trap may be escaped by staying within language but on the middle path between the pairs of opposites. When the opposites of language are maintained in dynamic tension, through a continual deconstruction of first one opposite and then the other, the real is experienced. For the moment the real is spoken, it is tending to swing the pendulum of language toward either one or the other of the opposites. Only by a continual deconstructing and reversing of each pendulum swing may we experience the real. For Derrida, the constant change and challenge that this deconstruction requires is not a cause for lament—it is rather the recognition that such a process, with its ongoing need for deconstruction, is itself the real. Derrida's position is clearly revealed in his critical reading of Rousseau. In spite of his attempt to maintain an original "natural" order of values for humanity, language, and society, Rousseau is forced, as Derrida demonstrates, to admit that there is never a moment of pure being or presence—as the Western logocentric tradition and Śaṇkara attempt to maintain. Always at the source Derrida is able to find a moment of differance, a rupture of the divine, a falling away from nature, the origins of speech, or even the experience of pure melody in music without the implicit presence of harmony.[34] Thus the impossibility of the everpresent desire to experience the real as pure presence.[35] Śaṇkara would agree with Derrida that so long as one stays in the lower realms of language and music, the bliss of pure presence, so desired by Rousseau, is an impossibility. But although Derrida stops with the revelation of the divine rupture and the impossible possibility that results from the experience of the real as difference, Śaṇkara goes on to a *nirguṇa*, or qualityless, level of experience where the existential frustrations of difference that characterize *māyā*, or this world, are totally transcended. One gets completely out of all the obstructions of language, with the help of language—the revealed words of the Veda—to the pure intuition of Brahman. In Śaṇkara's view Derrida's description of the real is quite correct for the lower level of reality, the level of *māyā*. Derrida's failure, in Śaṇkara's view, is his unwillingness to study the special words of the Veda with such seriousness and intensity that he is "pole-vaulted" right out of the realm of language and difference into the direct *anubhava*, or self-realization, of Brahman. Even when Derrida discusses the silence of God in his reading of "Jabès and the Question of the Book," he remains in the realm of a divine questioning that betrays the lower (*saguṇa*) level of knowledge of Brahman. For his part Derrida would maintain that Śaṇkara's so-called lower, or *saguṇa*, level exhausts our experience of the real. To think of a higher level of pure identity or pure Brahman is foolishly to attempt to escape the dynamic existential tension and demands of difference to be found in the barest melody or even in the silent questioning of God that squeezes itself between the letters and words of scripture.

## *III. The Reality behind All Negations*

Negative theology presumes some reality as existing behind all negations—a reality that the negations reveal. That reality for Dionysius, Eckhardt, and Augustine is God, for Derrida it is the call of the Other that precedes all speech, and for Hindu thought it is Brahman. Derrida put it this way.

> Even if one speaks and says nothing, even if an apophatic discourse deprives itself of meaning or of an object, it takes place. That which is committed or rendered it possible *has taken* place. The possible absence of a referent still beckons, if not toward the thing of which one speaks (such as God, who is nothing because He takes place, *without* place, *beyond Being*), at least toward the other (other than Being) who calls or to whom this speech is addressed. . . . This call of the other, having always already preceded the speech to which it has never been present a first time, announces itself in advance as a *recall*.[36]

Such a beginningless reference to the other is seen by Derrida as a precondition for all language—whether a promise, a prayer, praise, or celebration. Even the most negative discourse presupposes and preserves a trace of the other.[37] In the case of the Christian apophatics of Dionysius, the power of all speaking in general, as well as all affirmations and negations, proceeds as a gift and an effect of God. Even the very possibility of speaking the *Divine Names*, Derrida points out, and of speaking them in a correct manner, returns to God.[38] This idea that there is a beginningless trace or gift that precedes and establishes the possibility for all language, including all negations, is also present in Hinduism.

As mentioned earlier there are speculations in the Vedas that identify speech with the Absolute. These speculations are given systematic development by the Grammarian school of Indian philosophy, with Bhartṛhari as its leading exponent.[39] Unlike Śaṇkara, who sees language, including even scriptural language, as part of *māyā* or the worldly obscuration and therefore completely separate from the Real (*nirguṇa* Brahman), Bhartṛhari sees the real as *Śabdabrahman*—a unity of language and consciousness.[40] Consequently language is not something to be completely negated and transcended (Śaṇkara) but rather is an inescapable part of the nature of reality even in its highest form. If Derrida thinks that, even with the ingenious negations of the via negativa, one can never get out of a language, Bhartṛhari agrees. This means that whatever reality exists behind the negations of the via negativa, it will be experienced and known through language. But how can this be? From the point of view of logic, Śaṇkara would seem to be right. Language in its cognitive forms necessarily limits or filters our experience and knowledge of Brahman and consequently must be transcended for a full and unfiltered experience. Bhartṛhari disagrees. If we examine consciousness, we can never find a state in which some trace of language is not present. Indeed, Bhartṛhari, following some scriptures, is bold to maintain that Brahman, at the highest level, eternally has within, in pregnant form, the trace or seed of all language and all consciousness—for Bhartṛhari language and consciousness are eternally intertwined, you cannot have one without the other.[41] This means that in moving toward Brahman, what is negated is not language per se, but its corrupt and obscuring forms (*avidyā*, or ignorance, for Bhartṛhari). Once these are purified, language functions as an open channel to Brahman. Thus Bhartṛhari's Grammarian philosophy is really a kind of spiritual linguistic therapy—a label that might also be appropriate for Derrida' Grammatology.

There is no uncertainty as to the reality of the goal at the end of Bhartṛhari's spiritual therapy,—it is the direct experience of *Śabdabrahman* (Divine Word-Consciousness). But what is the reality at the end of Derrida's process of therapeutic deconstruction? Although Derrida keeps his spiritual self well hidden, a comparison with Bhartṛhari from the perspective of what is being negated, and what is left, may prove enlightening. Unlike Śaṇkara, who requires the negation of all language including even the great scriptural passages of *neti, neti* or *tat tvam asi*, Bhartṛhari negates only those forms of language use that are obscuring in nature. What are they? First, there is the use of incorrect grammar, which serves to obscure our understanding of language—all language, but particularly the criterion revelation of the Veda. After such elementary purification has taken place, the focus shifts to obstacles that would prevent one from understanding the deeper meaning of the Vedas, the preeminent obstacle being our own egotism.[42] All attempts or temptations to use language for our own pleasure, fame, or fortune will, even if we use it with grammatical correctness, obscure from us its deeper or true meaning. We may hear and speak words correctly, even beautifully, but without an engagement of our inner selves. Only when we negate our own self-centered karmic desires and allow the words themselves to command our full attention is their true inner meaning revealed. This is true for all words but especially true for those of the Veda. For Bhartṛhari the Veda is not one book among others but is the criterion revelation of the Absolute, *Śabdabrahman* itself. Since *Śabdabrahman* is nothing but word-consciousness, this means that the words of the Veda are the primary structures of consciousness (both our own and that of the Absolute) that are obscured by *karma* or ignorance. When we lose ourselves in a completely clear experience of the Vedic words and sentences, what we are experiencing is nothing but *Śabdabrahman*. As Bhartṛhari puts it:

> After having purified speech and after having rested it on the mind, after having broken its bonds and made it bond-free.

> After having reached the inner light, he with his knots cut, becomes unified with the Supreme Light.[43]

Although the "cutting of knots" is not defined by Bhartṛhari, Vṛṣabha describes it as a cutting of the bonds and knots of "ego-sense." In Indian thought, egotism is the largest, most resistant, and most obscuring karma to be overcome. For Bhartṛhari it is intimately tied up with impure language use. Once one's ego-knots are cut or negated, then one sees without error the power of words and knows the true nature of things.[44] The word-forms are seen for what they are, namely, partial manifestations of the one Divine Word. The direct experience of the whole of *Śabdabrahman*, the whole unity of all word-consciousness, is gradually realized as more and more of one's deeply rooted ego-sense is negated.[45] The means by which this is achieved is called by Bhartṛhari *Śabdapūrvayoga* (the yoga of the Word) and is a meditational exercise in which the mind is concentrated on the unity of the Divine Word, the Absolute, and turned away from the diversity of thoughts and sounds that manifest it.[46] Unlike Śaṇkara's all-or-nothing enlightenment in which all language disappears in the final *neti, neti* or *tat tvam asi* negation before Brahman is realized, Bhartṛhari describes a series of progressively clearer intuitions until a clear and correct apprehension finally takes place.[47] The error of *avidyā*, or ignorance, is negated gradually rather than all of a sudden as with Śaṇkara.

We have already mentioned Derrida's notion of a beginningless trace of the other as a precondition that establishes the possibility for all language, but what else can be said about his via negativa? Derrida's deconstruction attempts to negate the whole system of metaphysical opposition that has characterized Western philosophy and theology. He criticizes not only the logoecentric view but any philosophy that privileges one opposite or extreme over the other. Derrida establishes his critique by deconstructing the viewpoint that has dominated Western metaphysics; namely, that a separate Being or Presence is immediately reflected in speech and then given secondary representation in writing. Derrida deconstructs this argument as it is presented in Plato, Rousseau, and others, by finding that writing, when understood as differance, contains all of spoken language and all inscribed language.[48] Differance does not depend on sound or writing, but is their precondition. Although it does not exist, its possibility is anterior to all expressions (signified-signifier, content-expression, etc.). This intrinsic differance permits the articulation of speech and writing, and founds the metaphysical opposition between signifier and signified. Differance, therefore, is the formation of form and the being imprinted of the imprint.[49] Deconstruction is needed when one side of a metaphysical opposition is privileged by the suppression of the differance that is inherent within itself—as for example, in Western philosophy's suppression of differance in the establishment of an unchanging logos, presence, or Self. Once the privileging or suppression is negated, language recovers its pure possibility for signification.

We see, then, that behind Derrida's deconstruction there is something more than nihilism or mere playfulness. Indeed, like Bhartṛhari, there is a teleology inherent in Derrida's philosophy of language. In *Of Grammatology,* Derrida discusses the nature of the arche-trace or differance. This trace, like the *Śabdabrahman* of Bhartṛhari, contains the primordial differance. This differance is the inherent teleological force within us that leads to self-manifestation.[50] And this self-manifestation is structured according to the diverse possibilities of the trace. The general characteristic of the manifested trace is that of temporal becoming. Within this becoming, the teleological is but one moment of the total movement of the trace.[51] It is the direct experience of this dynamic process of becoming, not as a process of static reflection or metaphysical opposition, that would for Derrida be the functional parallel of spiritual realization.[52] The sensitive deconstruction of the illusions of permanence, of stasis, or presence (which our ordinary experience and many of our philosophies have superimposed on the becoming of a language) is Derrida's prescription as the means for spiritual realization. We cannot name this realization "spiritual," for that is already to engage the vocabulary of metaphysical opposition. But to understand it as manifestation of the inherent differance of the trace is for Derrida the goal. To go from the inscribed trace (writing) to the spoken word and the arche-writing that prefigures and predisposes both, only to be thrown back again, in a continual deconstructive reverse, would seem to be Derrida's use of language as a spiritual discipline. Although this may look like a Madhyamikan Buddhist answer, it is not. The deconstructive reverse does not result in the silence (*śūnya*) of a language, but rather in the realization that the dynamic tension in the becoming of language is itself the whole. For Derrida, all of this cannot be understood as abstract theorizing. The language we are deconstructing is our own thinking and speaking—our own consciousness. We ourselves are the text we are deconstructing. That is why, for Derrida, there is nothing outside of texts. Deconstruction is the process of becoming self-aware, of self-realization.

Can we say that this Derridean deconstruction of language is a means for spiritual realization? A comparison of Derrida and Bhartṛhari helps us to see why we can answer this question in the affirmative. Like Derrida, Bhartṛhari maintains that the analysis of linguistic experience is an examination of the very nature of our consciousness. Just as for Derrida consciousness is nothing but trace or writing, so for Bhartṛhari consciousness is nothing but *Śabdabrahman*—the inextricable intertwining of consciousness with the word. But one difference that must be acknowledged immediately is that, although Derrida deconstructs all books, all scriptures, privileging none, Bhartṛhari explicitly states that the Veda is the means for the realization of Brahman.[53]

Bhartṛhari is not simply privileging one book or one scripture over all the others. His thought is more complex and subtle than that. On the one hand, as we have seen earlier, Bhartṛhari has said that the Veda is the normative form (*anukāra*) of the manifested *Śabdabrahman*. All other language is merely a further elaboration of the criterion manifestation of the *Śabdabrahman* as the Veda. The Veda is not one book among others, it is the true manifestion of the *Śabdabrahman*. This is why Bhartṛhari describes it as both the form and the means of the realization of Brahman. Like Derrida, however, Bhartṛhari analyzes the individual's inner experience not as the static presence of a set of divine words or forms (the logos model), nor as a superimposition of epistemological forms (Śaṇkara's *māyā*), but as an inner word that is primarily productive of activity and only secondarily productive of knowledge.[54] Bhartṛhari's *Śabdabrahman*, the Word-Principle is primarily an ontological principle and only secondarily epistemological.

More clues as to what is behind Derrida's relentless negation of all theology, philosophy, and ordinary language that objectifies our experience into fake gods and unreal presences are found in his essay "Of an Apocalyptic Tone Newly Adopted in Philosophy."[55] A vision and spiritual source rooted in the Hebrew prophets is suggested. This essay is a reading of the New Testament "Revelation or Apocalypse of John" in which Derrida suggests that the apocalyptic be considered "a transcendental condition of all discourse, of all experience even, of every mark or every trace."[56] The Apocalypse of John, he suggests, could be taken as "an *exemplary* revelation of this transcendental structure." And the theme of the Johannine Apocalypse he identifies as the recurrent and imperative "Come" of the text (Revelation 22:17–20). "Come" evokes both the imminent coming of the Lord and the imperative that the hearer come quickly. The call beyond being or logos itself comes from beyond being. It cannot come from a voice that is given any personification in our hearing of it—for that would be to "package" it in categories of presence. " 'Come' is plural in itself, in oneself." Its only content, says Derrida, is its resounding imperative tone[57] that calls forth action from us. The other characteristic of this exemplary book of Apocalypse is indicated in its final words, " 'Do not seal [close] the words of the inspiration of this volume.' " To seal is to encapsulate or close off the inherent "Come" of language and religion. The "Come" from beyond being and the imperative "Come" within oneself never close. The action of coming to the call that never ceases is the end to be realized. All of this fits well with the prophetic impulse of the Hebrew Bible. Its relentless negation of any conceptualization or speaking of the divine (the sin of idolatry), its prophetic hearing of the call to obedience that must always translate into action and its open-ended future that calls us to be-come to an end that is always simultaneously a new beginning—all of this seems to justify our rooting of Derrida in the spiritual critique of the Hebrew prophets, which Derrida has reformulated as a negation of all idolatrous use of language.

Like Derrida, Bhartṛhari's science of grammar is also a call to action, to *dharma*. Bhartṛhari reinterprets Vedic *dharma* as the *dharma* of *Śabdabrahman*. This shift means that the *dharma* that one seeks to realize is no longer outside oneself, one's language, or the Veda, but is the very essence of one's consciousness. Just as for Derrida the voice of the prophetic "Come" becomes the "Come let us go," the inner voice of language, so also for Bhartṛhari, the Vedic *dharma* as the *Śabdabrahman* becomes the *dharma* of "correct" language within individual consciousness. The purification of speech, the task of the traditional Vedic discipline of grammar, becomes the means for inner spiritualization.

One of the places in Derrida's writing where his emphasis on moral action as the end goal of deconstruction is most clearly seen in his brilliant essay "Violence and Metaphysics: An Essay on the Thought of Emmanuel Levinas."[58] In Levinas Derrida finds a clear analysis of the epistemological emphasis of the Greek tradition of metaphysics (which has largely determined Western philosophy), and its violent encounter with an alien mode of thought—the ethical thrust of Hebrew thought.[59] Levinas presents us with a summons to move from the Greek metaphysics of presence, which seeks to absorb all differences into identity, toward prophetic speech with its strong ethical impulse. For Levinas the ethical relationship is "the only one capable of opening the space of transcendence and of liberating metaphysics."[60] Rather than ethics being seen as a second-order consideration arising from and founded on epistemology (the dominant view of Western philosophy), Levinas proposes an ethics that would not be subject to the governing interests of epistemology but be grounded in a recourse to experience as understood within the context of Hebrew messianic eschatology.[61] Within the analysis of experience the Other, and our ethical relationship with the Other, is the imperative.

In Derrida's essay Levinas is described as exploring the limits of the Greek tradition by placing it in dialogue with the ethical imperative of the Hebrew tradition. Rather than a metaphysics of logos and light, Levinas finds himself led by the Hebrew paradigm of relationship with the Other to a kind of discourse that can be grasped only between the self and the human other. It is this human encounter that is fundamental, and not the Greek method of knowing by the relationship between the mind and its object, which produces ethics only as a secondary consideration. All philosophy must take its rise from the face-to-face context. The foundation of metaphysics for Levinas is found in the resemblance between humans and God, between the human visage and the face of the Divine. For us, the Other in our relationships resembles God. Thus human discourse is properly understood only if it is seen as discourse with God. Such discourse presupposes separation rather than identity with God.[62]

For Levinas, and I think for Derrida, all of this is grounded in God who appears to us as difference, as other.[63] Without this difference, this God who breaches space, there would be no time or history, for the unbroken identity of the Greeks would be the sole existent. God, as the infinitely Other, creates the context for all relationship that is also the context for all language.[64] And the fundamental philosophical content of this language of human relationship is a call for ethical action. But Derrida pushes Levinas's thought even further. The separation required for discourse with God means that we are created in his image not "in terms of communion or knowledge, nor in terms of participation and incarnation. . . . [Rather] we are 'in the Trace of God.' "[65] This trace shows itself not in the presence but in the absence of God.

> The face of God disappears forever in showing itself. . . . The face of Yahweh is the *total* person and the *total* presence of "the Eternal speaking face to face with Moses," but saying to him also: "Thou canst not see my face: for there shall be no man see me and live . . . thou shalt stand upon a rock and it shall come to pass, while my glory passeth by, that I will put thee in a cleft of the rock, and will cover thee with my hand while I pass by: And I will take away mine hand, and thou shalt see my back parts: but my face shall not be seen (Exodus 33:20–23). The face of God which commands while hiding itself is at once more and less a face than all faces.[66]

Derrida goes on to suggest that Levinas is perhaps coming very close to Jabès when he says, "All faces are His; this is why HE has no face?"[67] It is in our relationship with other faces that we encounter the God who is otherwise absent to us.[68]

## *IV. Silence*

Negation in Hinduism ends in silence. This especially true of Śaṇkara's philosophy, where the goal of both *neti, neti* and *tat tvam asi* is to totally transcend language. Silence is not only the ultimate end but, in the form of silent meditation upon negations such as *neti, neti,* is also the means for the final realization of release (*mokṣa*). Meditation (*nididhyāsana*) upon the negative texts is part of the spiritual discipline prescribed by Śaṇkara until the direct awareness of Brahman shines forth.[69] In that final state, all language and cognition, including even the negative formulations themselves, completely disappear. Or to use the rope-snake analogy: For the rope (Brahman) to be seen, snake (*māyā*, including even the negations of the Veda) must completely disappear. In his commentary on the Brahma Sūtra, Śaṇkara refers to a Upaniṣad that has since become lost. Bahva, asked by Baskali to expound Brahman, kept silent. The student prayed, "Teach me, Sir." But the teacher remained silent. When asked by the student a second and third time, the teacher said, "I am teaching but you do not follow. The self is silence."[70]

Although Śaṇkara's silence at the *nirguṇa* level is devoid of language, this does not mean that it is a void. Rather it is the realization of a one-sided identity relation between Brahman and the world *māyā* (including all language, even the Veda). Brahman can exist without *māyā*, but *māyā* cannot exist without Brahman. Language as a part of *māyā* has epistemological but not ontological status. Rather than being thought of as emptiness, it should be likened to fullness. In the experience of *mokṣa* one has realized that oneself and everything is nondifferent from the Brahman—thus the name "Advaita" or nonduality." After the Advaita negation, what is left is bare identity with Brahman, which has been there always, but, because of the obscuration of beginningless ignorance, has never been realized. All of this is the "content" of Śaṇkara's silence. In many ways this approach of Śaṇkara is opposite that of Derrida. For Śaṇkara language is purely epistemological in function. For him self-realization is not the realization that we ourselves are the text (Derrida's position), but rather the realization that language is the *māyā* that is totally transcended when the Real, Brahman, is seen. For Śaṇkara the goal is not to be impelled into action by language (Derrida's view) but to transcend language and action, even moral action, to the silent direct realization of Brahman.

In contrast to Śaṇkara, Bhartṛhari's final realization occurs within, rather than outside of, language. In this sense Bhartṛhari is much closer to Derrida. Bhartṛhari conceives of three levels of language: *vaikharī*, *madhyamā*, and *paśyantī*.[71]

*Vaikharī* is spoken speech. *Madhyamā* is language at the inner level of mental thought. *Paśyantī* is the unified silent idea that is evoked by or precedes both inner thought and spoken speech. When, through negation and meditation, the last remaining ego-knots are removed, *paśyantī* reveals the Absolute *Śabdabrahman.* But for Bhartṛhari, *Śabdabrahman* does not just remain in pure silence. The Absolute word-consciousness has within itself a trace, an impulse, toward differentiation into thought and spoken speech. As the *Vākyapadīya* puts it, there is a pent up pregnancy within *Śabdabrahman* that predisposes the silence of *paśyantī* to burst forth in thought and speech.[72] The ultimate silence, after all negation and purification has occurred, remains within the unity of language. And that unity contains within itself the seeds of difference which create the possibility for the multiplicity of language to burst forth.

Silence is seen by Derrida as by Bhartṛhari, to be dynamic in nature. Rather than being the cessation of language, as suggested by Śaṇkara and Mādhyamika, Derrida's silence is the origin, the source of all speaking, and yet a source that locates itself in the quiet between the sounds of God's voice and the spaces between the letters of his writing. Language, both ours and God's, originates not in God's speaking but in God's keeping still—it "starts with the stifling of his voice and the dissimulation of his face. This difference, this negativity in God is our freedom, the transcendence and the verb which can relocate the purity of their negative origin only in the possibility of the Question."[73] But for this Question to be heard requires the negation or deconstruction of our usual language patterns and the privileging in terms of power, politics, and sexuality that they constitute. Derrida evokes the image of going into the desert, of negating our popular patterns of privileging, and experiencing an emancipation and silence out of which language can speak afresh. Just as it is God's silence, God's absent presence in the desert, that creates an opening, a moment of freedom for something other than God to exist, so also, on our human side, it is in our silence that we become sensitive to the other. More than that, however, is the content of this opening, this silence. It is that of a God who astonishes and questions us, demanding moral action from the midst of silence. Unlike the perfect stillness of the Greek logos or Śaṇkara's Brahman, Derrida following Levinas,[74] Jabes, and the Jewish tradition, talks of a God who constantly questions out of silence.

For Derrida the ultimate silent experience of the divine does not cancel out ordinary language, as it does for the language of Śaṇkara's *māyā;* rather, it throws us back into our experience of wordly language. Freed from entrapment in the privileging of one of the pairs of opposites, we are infused with a divine demand for moral action. In Derrida's silence is a dynamism, a divine difference, that is not found in the Greek logos or the pure consciousness, pure being, and pure bliss of Śaṇkara's Brahman but has a parallel in Bhartṛhari's *Śabdabrahman.* It is a reality that starts with God's silent desire to speak. Out of that silence comes not only his speech and ours but also, because of the questioning inherent in the silence, our freedom and imperative to act. The responsibility accompanying this freedom is found in God's written and silent questioning of us. But to be heard, his speaking and ours must be silenced. This is the paradox of language for Derrida, a paradox in some ways similar to, and in other ways quite different from, the paradoxes of Śaṇkara and Bhartṛhari.

## Notes

1. Jacques Derrida, *Margins of Philosophy*, trans. Alan Bass (Chicago: University of Chicago Press, 1982), p. 6.

2. Ibid.

3. Ibid.

4. Jacques Derrida, "How to Avoid Speaking: Denials," trans. Ken Frieden (Chapter 3), pp. 73–142. On p. 82, Derrida notes that he has objected in vain to the assimilation of trace and of *differance* to negative theology.

5. Ibid., p. 64 n. 2.

6. Ibid., p. 53.

7. *Ṛgveda* 10.129 as translated by Macdonell in *A Source Book in Indian Philosophy*, ed. S. Radhakrishnan and C. A Moore (Princeton University Press), 1967, p. 23.

8. *Bṛhadāranayaka Upaniṣad* 3.9.26, trans by Radhakrishnan.

9. As quoted by S. Radhakrishnan, *The Principal Upanisads* (London: Allen & Unwin, 1968), p. 243.

10. *Bṛhadāranayaka Upaniṣad* 4.2.4, trans by Radhakrishnan.

11. *The Vedānta Sūtras with Commentary by Śaṅkarākārya*, trans. George Thibaut, *Sacred Books of the East* (Delhi: Motilal Banarsidass, 1968), part 1, p. 327.

12. Ibid., pt. 2, 3.2.22, pp. 168–71.

13. Derrida, "How to Avoid Speaking," pp. 79–80.

14. Ibid., p. 78.

15. Ibid., p. 79.

16. Translation by S. Radhakrishnan, *The Principal Upanisads*, p. 194.

17. Ibid., pp. 194–5.

18. Ibid., p. 195.

19. Śaṇkara's *Bṛhadāraṇyakabhāṣya*, in *Advaita Vedānta up to Saṃkara and His Pupils*, ed. by Karl Potter, trans. by Karl Potter (Princeton: Princeton University Press, 1981), p. 193. It should be noted, however, that there is a tradition that does attempt to speak of the higher, or *nirguṇa*, Brahman positively (see Sureśvara in his *Naiskarmasiddhi* or Dharmaraja in the *Vendāta Paribhāṣā*).

20. The *Māṇḍūkyopaniṣad with Gauḍapāda's Kārikā and Saṇkara's Commentary*, trans. Swami Nikjhilananda (Mysore: Sri Ramakrishna Ashrama, 1968), pp. 117–20.

21. Sureśvara, *Bṛhadāraṇyakopaniṣadbhāṣyavārttika* in Karl Potter, *Advaita Vedānta up to Śaṃkara and His Pupils*, p. 483.

22. Derrida, "How to Avoid Speaking," p. 79.

23. In Advaita, it is a commonplace that there are two "definitions" (*lakṣaṇas*) of Brahman. The *tatastha-lakṣanṣa* just implies the presence of Brahman as the unconditioned ground of all phenomena. It does not give insight into the nature of Brahman. This is done by the *svarūpa-lakṣaṇa*, a nonrelational definition that uses the three terms of *sat*, *cit*, and *ānanda* to provide hints as to the nature of Brahman. (See T. R. V. Murti's classical essay on this question "The Two Definitions of Brahman in The Advaita" in *Studies in Indian Thought*, ed. Harold Coward (Delhi: Motilal Banarsidass, 1983), pp. 72–87).

24. *Advaita Vedānta up to Śaṃkara and His Pupils*, p. 75.

25. *Māṇḍūkya Upaniṣad* 5.

26. *Advaita Vedānta up to Śaṃkara and His Pupils*, p. 76.

27. Ibid.

28. See Christopher Norris, *Deconstruction: Theory and Practice* (London: Methuen, 1982), p. 41.

29. Jacques Derrida, "Edmond Jabès and the Question of the Book" in *Writing and Difference*, trans. Alan Bass (Chicago: University of Chicago Press, 1978), p. 67.

30. *Advaita Vedānta up to Śaṃkara and His Pupils*, p. 52.

31. Śaṇkara, *Bṛhadāranyakabhāṣya* 1.4.7.

32. As summarized by Karl Potter, *Advaita Vedānta up to Śaṃkara and His Pupils*, p. 61.

33. Derrida, "Edmond Jabès," p. 71.

34. Jacques Derrida, Of *Grammatology*, trans. Gayatri Chakravorty Spivak (Baltimore: Johns Hopkins University Press, 1976), p. 212.

35. Ibid., p. 244.

36. Derrida "How to Avoid Speaking," p. 25.

37. Ibid.

38. Ibid. See also Pseudo-Dionysius Areopagite, *The Divine Names and Mystical Theology*, trans. John D. Jones (Milwaukee: Marquette University Press, 1980), p. 206: "Thus if what we have said is right and we have really attained in our thinking to the unfolding of divine names in a way which is possible for us, we must attribute this to the cause of all goods which has first given up the gift to speak and, then, to speak well."

39. See Harold Coward and K. Kunjunni Raja, *The Philosophy of the Grammarians* (Princeton: Princeton University Press, 1990).

40. *The Vākyapadīya of Bhaṛtrhari with the Vrtti*, trans. K. Subramania Iyer (Poona: Deccan College, 1965), 1.1 (hereafter cited V.P.).

41. V.P. 1.4,1.51,1.123.

42. V.P. 1.131.

43. Ibid., *Vṛtti.*

44. V.P. 1.143, *Vṛtti.* See also V.P. 1.14.

45. V.P. 1.142 with *Vṛtti.*

46. V.P. 1.14.

47. *Sphoṭasiddhi of Maṇḍana Miśra,* trans. K. A. Subramania Iyer (Poona: Deccan College, 1966), *Kārikā* 19–20.

48. See Derrida, Of *Grammatology*, and Derrida, "Plato's Pharmacy," in *Dissemination,* trans. Barbara Johnson (Chicago: University of Chicago Press, 1981).

49. Derrida, *Of Grammatology*, pp. 57–63.

50. Ibid., pp. 46ff.

51. Ibid., p. 47.

52. Derrida's writing is purposely not systematic. But he does give a fair hint as to the shape that the becoming of the trace takes:

> Representation mingles with what it represents, to the point where one speaks as one writes, one thinks as if the represented were nothing more than the shadow or reflection of the representer. . . . In this play of representation, the point of origin becomes ungraspable. There are things like reflecting pools, and images, an infinite reference from one to the other, but no longer a source, a spring [source]. There is no longer simple origin. For what is reflected is split in *itself* and not only as an addition to itself of its image. The reflection, the image, the double, splits what it doubles. The origin of the speculation becomes a difference. What can look at itself is not one; and the law of addition of the origin to its representation, of the thing to its image, is that one plus one makes at least three. (*Of Grammatology,* p. 36)

53. V.P. 1.5.

54. V.P. 1.51.

55. Jacques Derrida,"Of An Apocalyptic Tone Newly Adopted in Philosophy," (Chapter 2), pp 25–71.

56. Ibid., p. 57.

57. Ibid., p. 66.

58. Derrida, *Writing and Difference*, pp. 79–153.

59. See Christopher Norris, *Derrida* (Cambridge: Hrvard University Press, 1987), pp. 230–37.

60. Derrida, *Writing and Difference*, p. 83.

61. Ibid.

62. Ibid., p. 108.

63. Ibid., p.116.

64. Ibid., p. 151.

65. Ibid., p. 108.

66. Ibid.

67. Ibid., p. 109.

68. Ibid.

69. *Bṛhadāraṇyakopaniṣādbhāṣyavārttika* 899–920, as summarized in *Advaita Vedānta up to Śaṃkara and His Pupils*, p. 465.

70. As quoted by S. Radhakrishnan, *The Principal Upanisads*, p. 67.

71. V.P. 1.142.

72. V.P. 1.2, 1.3.

73. Derrida, "Edmond Jabès," *Writing and Difference*, p. 67.

74. See Emmanuel Levinas, *Otherwise than Being or Beyond Essence*, trans. Alphonso Lingis (The Hague: Martin Nijhoff, 1981). The distinctive feature of Levinas's ethical philosophy is that its locus is in the other who faces, the face of the other (p. xiii).

# SEVEN

# *The Deconstruction of Buddhism*

David Loy

What is interesting about Buddhism, from a Derridean point of view, is that it is both ontotheological (therefore what needs to be deconstructed) and deconstructive (providing a different example of how to deconstruct). What is interesting about Derrida's type of deconstruction, from a Buddhist point of view, is that it is logocentric.

What Derrida says about philosophy, that it "always reappropriates for itself the discourse that delimits it," is equally true of Buddhism. Like all religions, Buddhism includes a strong ontotheological element, yet it also contains the resources that have repeatedly deconstructed this tendency. Thanks to sensitivities that Derrida's texts have helped to develop, it is possible to understand the Buddhist tradition as a history of this struggle between deconstructive delimitation and metaphysical reappropriation, between a message that undermines all security by undermining the sense-of-self that seeks security, and a countervailing tendency to dogmatize and institutionalize that challenge. According to this version of deconstruction, however, Derrida's approach is still logocentric, for what needs to be deconstructed is not just language but the world we live in and the way we live in it, trapped within a cage of our own making—"bound by our own rope," to use the Zen phrase.[1]

The consequence of this struggle has been a self-consciousness about those *aporias* of negative theology that Derrida points out in "How to Avoid Speaking: Denials": hyperessentiality; the secret society's secret that there is no secret; "the homology of hierarchy which leads to that which situates itself beyond all position"; the promise, the order, and the waiting. All these aspects are to be found in Buddhism, but rather than their being tendencies that need to be exposed, the development of Buddhist thought is the history of making these problems central and deconstructing them by revealing the logocentricity that motivates them. As we shall see, Buddhist philosophy has been preoccupied with refuting any tendency to postulate a transcendental-signified, including any "hyperessentialism." The Buddha himself emphasized that he had no secret, although that did not stop later generations from attributing one to him; insofar as the solution to Zen koans might be considered a secret, Zen teachers emphasize that that answer is always quite obvious; in fact, our inability to see the obvious is precisely the point. The sangha (community of monks and nuns) that the Buddha established has been called the world"s first democracy; in contrast to the Hindu caste system, hierarchy was determined solely by when one joined. There is no "order" from any transcendental being that requires one to practice Buddhism; in contrast to Mosaic law, the Buddhist precepts (to avoid killing, stealing, etc.) are vows one makes *to oneself* to try to live in a certain way. The "promise" of Buddhism is quite pragmatic; in his talk to the Kalamas (praised as the first "charter of free inquiry"), the Buddha emphasized that they should not accept any religious doctrine until they had tried it out for themselves and seen how it changed their lives. Finally, "waiting" (more generally, any expectation) has been repeatedly identified as the most problematic tendency in meditative practice.[2]

Buddhism begins with the Buddha (literally, "the Awake"), c. 563–483 B.C. The usual problem of legendary origins is further complicated by the fact that the Buddha, like Socrates and Christ, wrote nothing; I don't know why, since as far as I know he had no objections against writing. (Given the problematics of translation, the Buddha's attitude is noteworthy: When two disciples sought permission to translate his vernacular teachings into classical Sanskrit verse, he refused, saying that in each region the teachings should be presented in the local language.) Unlike the brief career of Christ, the Buddha lived for forty-five years after his enlightenment, and left behind extensive oral teachings later recorded in the Pali Canon, which is approximately eleven times the length of the Bible. One of the most striking things about this voluminous material is that it says so much about the path to nirvāṇa and so little about nirvāṇa itself. The Buddha's attitude seems to have been that it is not helpful to talk about it very much; so that if you want to know what nirvāṇa is, you must experience it yourself. Except for some terms of praise, the few descriptions are negative: they say what nirvāṇa is not.

The Pali Canon contains several different accounts of exactly what the Buddha realized in his paradigmatic enlightenment under the Bo tree. Perhaps most significant from a deconstructive approach is that none of these earliest accounts invokes an inexpressible "self-presence." According to the most common story, the Buddha realized the Three Knowledges: he was able to remember his past lifetimes as far back as he wanted, to see the karmic connections between those lifetimes, and to understand the Four Truths: how life is *duḥkha* (the usual translation, "suffering," is too limited; better is something like "dissatisfaction/frustration"), that the cause of *duḥkha* is desire and ignorance, that there is an end to *duḥkha*—nirvāṇa—and an eightfold path leading to that end, which he himself had reached. "Ignorance was dispelled, knowledge arose." According to another account, the Buddha realized the truth of *pratītya-samutpāda*, "dependent origination," which was to become the most important doctrine of Buddhism; according to a third, he realized that there is no persisting self, and that the impersonal physical and mental processes whose interaction creates the illusion of self are impermanent and cause suffering.[3]

In contrast to the other main Indian tradition, the Upaniṣadic, which emphasizes the identity of self, substance, and transcendental Absolute, the Buddha emphasized that there is no self, that everything without exception arises and passes away according to conditions, and that hence there is no personal God or impersonal Absolute. The Buddha's mostly impromptu talks were in response to questions, but there were some questions he would not answer, because they "are not conducive to enlightenment." These included whether or not the world had an origin or will have an end, whether or not it is spatially finite, whether or not a Buddha exists after death, and whether or not the life-principle (*jīva*) is identical with the body. Buddhism postulates no "golden age" of plenitude before a fall into the suffering of history and self-consciousness, and therefore harbors no dream of returning to any such pure origin. There is no attempt to explain (and without a God there is no need to explain) suffering as a result of original sin; nor is there any Last Judgment.

The Buddha emphasized that he who understands *pratītya-samutpāda* understands the *dharma* (his teaching) and vice versa. "Dependent-origination" explains our experience by locating all phenomena within a set of twelve factors, each conditioned by and conditioning all the others. The twelve links of this chain (which integrates shorter chains that the Buddha elaborated on different occasions) are traditionally explained as follows:

The presupposition of the whole process is (1) *ignorance*. Our basic problem is ignore-ance, because something about experience is overlooked in the impulse to gratify desires. Due to this ignorance, (2) *volitional tendencies* from a person's previous lifetime survive physical death and tend to cause a new birth. The original Sanskrit term *saṃskārah* is especially difficult to translate; literally something like "preparation, get up," it refers to acts of will associated with particular states of mind. The continuation of these volitional tendencies explains how rebirth is possible without a permanent soul or persisting self: they survive physical death to affect the new (3) *consciousness* that arises when they influence a fertilized egg to cause conception. But there is no substance here: both volitional tendencies and the resulting rebirth-consciousness are impermanent, conditioned by earlier factors and conditioning later ones, in an apparently ceaseless cycle.

Conception causes (4) *mind-body*, the fetus, to grow, which develops (5) the *six sense organs*, including the mental organ of mind, understood as that which perceives mental objects.

The sense organs allow (6) *contact* between each organ and its respective sense object, giving rise to (7) *sensation*, which leads to (8) *craving* for that sensation. Craving causes (9) *grasping*, or attachment to life in general. Such clinging is traditionally classified into four types: clinging to pleasure, to views, to morality and external observances, and to belief in a soul or self. This classification is striking because it denies any difference in kind between physical sense grasping and mental attachment; it is the same problematic tendency that manifests in all four. Grasping leads to (10) *becoming*, the tendency after physical death to be reborn, causing (11) another *birth* and therefore (12) *old age and death and the suffering* associated with them. And so the cycle continues.

These twelve links are usually understood to describe three lifetimes: the first two factors give causes from the past that have led to our present existence; the next five are their effects in the present; the following three are causes in the present life that will lead to another birth; the last two are their effects in a future life. However, these three "lifetimes" have also been taken metaphorically, as referring to the various factors conditioning every moment of our existence. In neither case is ignorance a "first cause" that began the whole process in some distant past. Although ignorance is presented as if it were a precondition, the important point is that there is no first cause. All the twelve factors are interdependent, each conditioning all the others, and there is no reference in Buddhism to some past time before this cycle was operating. In response to the problem of how rebirth can occur without a permanent soul or self that is reborn, rebirth is explained as a series of impersonal processes, which occur without any self that is doing or experiencing them. In one Pali sutra, a monk asks the Buddha to whom belong, and for whom occur, the phenomena described in *pratītya-samutpāda*. The Buddha rejects that question as misguided; from each factor as its preconditions arises another factor; that is all. *Duḥkha* occurs without there being anyone who causes or experiences the *duḥkha*.

When the Buddha died, he did not appoint a successor: "Let the *dharma* be your guide." Predictably, and "according to a law that can be formalized," that *dharma* was soon canonized from a guide (a raft that can be used to cross the river of suffering, but not afterward to be carried around on our backs, to use the Buddha's own analogy) into an ontotheology. Within a few generations, the Buddha's clearly nonmetaphysical approach yielded to the desire to abstract an *abhidharma*, or "higher dharma," from his extensive and repetitious talks. Since the sense-of-self is due to interaction among the various factors constituting *pratītya-samutpāda*, the abhidharmikas concluded that reality is plural: what exists are these various elements, which they enumerated and classified. This process of extricating a core teaching transformed the Buddhist path of liberation into an atomism nonetheless ontotheological: in place of the one substance of Vedānta, Buddhism was now understood to assert that there are in effect innumerable momentary substances.[4]

The reaction to this philosophical development and other tendencies was the development of Mahāyāna, a revolution as important to Buddhism as the Protestant Reformation for Christianity, although curiously split in apparently incompatible directions: in popular religious terms, the paradigmatic but very human Buddha (when asked whether he was a man or a god, he answered: "I am a man who has awakened") was elevated into a metaphysical principle, in fact the ground of the universe, and granted a pantheon of bodhisattvas who help others attain salvation. Philosophically, however, there was a thoroughgoing self-deconstruction of the Buddhist teachings that has continued to reverberate through all subsequent Buddhist thought, so radical and influential it has never been completely reappropriated. The locus classicus of this Mādhyamika school is in the *Mūlamadhyamikakārikā* (hereafter "MMK") of Nāgārjuna, who is believed to have lived in the second century A.D. The MMK offers a systematic analysis of all the important philosophical issues of its time, not to solve these problems but to demonstrate that any possible philosophical solution is self-contradictory or otherwise unjustifiable. This is not done to prepare the ground for Nāgārjuna's own solution: "If I were to advance any thesis whatsoever, that in itself would be a fault; but I advance no thesis and so cannot be faulted" [*Vigrahavyāvartanī*, verse 29]. The best way to bring out the similarities and differences between Nāgārjuna and Derrida is to consider separately what the MMK says about *śūnyatā*, nirvāṇa and the two-truths doctrine.

## Śūnyatā

> The spiritual conquerors have proclaimed *śūnyatā* to be the exhaustion of all theories and views; those for whom *śūnyatā* is itself a theory they declared to be incurable.
>
> The feeble-minded are destroyed by the misunderstood doctrine of *śūnyatā*, as by a snake ineptly seized or some secret knowledge wrongly applied.
>
> We interpret *pratītya-samutpāda* as *śūnyatā*. *Śūnyatā* is a guiding, not a cognitive, notion, presupposing the everyday. (MMK, 12.8, 24.11, 18)[5]

The first verse of the MMK proclaims its thoroughgoing critique of *being*. "No things whatsoever exist, at any time or place, having risen by themselves, from another, from both or without cause." Paralleling the poststructuralist radicalization of structuralist claims about language, Nāgārjuna's argument merely brings out more fully the implications of *pratītya-samutpāda*, showing that dependent-origination should rather be understood as "nondependent nonorigination." *Pratītya-samutpāda* does not teach a causal relation between entities, because the fact that these twelve factors are mutually dependent means that they are not really entities; none could occur without the conditioning of all the other factors. In other words, none of the twelve phenomena—which are said to encompass all experience—self-exists, because each is infected with the traces of all the others: *none is "self-present"* for they are all *śūnya*. Or better: that none is self-present is the meaning of *śūnya*. The important terms *śūnya* and its substantive *śūnyatā* are also very difficult to translate. They derive from the Sanskrit root *śū*, which means "to be swollen," both like a hollow balloon and like a pregnant woman; therefore the usual English translation "empty" and "emptiness" must be supplemented with the notion of "pregnant with possibilities." (Sprung's translation uses the cumbersome "absence of being in things.") Rather than *śūnyatā* being solely a negative concept, however, Nāgārjuna emphasizes that it is only because everything is *śūnya* that any change, including spiritual transformation, is possible.

The point of *śūnyatā* is to deconstruct the self-existence/ self-presence of things. Nāgārjuna was addressing not only the self-sufficient atomic elements of the Abhidharma analysis, but most of all the repressed, unconscious metaphysics of "common sense," according to which the world is a collection of existing things (including us) that originate and eventually disappear. The corresponding danger was that *śūnyatā* would itself become reappropriated into a metaphysics, so Nāgārjuna was careful to warn that *śūnyatā* was a heuristic, not a cognitive, notion. Although the concept of *śūnyatā* is so central to Mādhyamika analysis that the school became known as *śūnyāvāda* ("the way of śūnya"), there is no such "thing" as *śūnyatā*. Here the obvious parallel with Derrida's *différance* runs deep. *Śūnyatā* , like *différance*, is permanently "under erasure," deployed for tactical reasons but denied any semantic or conceptual stability. It "presupposes the everyday" because it is parasitic on the notion of things, which it refutes. "If there were something not *śūnya* there would be something *śūnya*, but there is nothing not *śūnya*, so how can anything be *śūnya?*" (MMK 12.7) Likewise, to make the application of *śūnyatā* into a *method* would miss the point of Nāgārjuna's deconstruction as much as of Derrida's. Derrida is concerned that we not replace the specific, detailed activity of deconstructive reading with some generalized idea about that activity that presumes to comprehend all its different types of application. For Nāgārjuna, however, *śūnyatā* aims at "the exhaustion of all theories and views," because he has another ambition, as we shall see; the purpose of *śūnyatā* is to help us "let go" of our concepts, in which case we must let go of the concept of *śūnyatā* as well.

For both, *différance/śūnyatā* is a "nonsite" or "non-philosophical site" from which to question philosophy itself. But, as Derrida emphasizes, the history of philosophy is the metaphysical reincorporation of such nonsites. Nāgārjuna warned, as strongly as he could, that *śūnyatā* was a snake that, if grasped at the wrong end, could be fatal; yet that is precisely what happened—repeatedly—in later Buddhism. If "those for whom *śūnyatā* is itself a theory" are "incurable," the question why so many people seem to be incurable must be addressed. The other important philosophical school of Mahāyāna Buddhism was Yogācāra, which became known as the "Mind-only" *(Vijñānavāda)* school. I shall not review the controversies about whether or not Yogācāra is an idealism (therefore a reversion to logocentrism) and how compatible it is with Mādhyamika, except to emphasize that its methodology was different: rather than offering a logical analysis of philosophical categories, it attempted to work out the implications of certain meditative experiences. But later Chinese permutations of Yogācāra did effect such a philosophical "transcendentalization" of "Mind" and "Buddha-nature," which had occurred even earlier on the popular level. Thus what happened in Buddhism parallels what occurred in other traditions such as Yoga and Vedānta in India, Taoism in China: contrary to what we might expect, in each case the theistic and devotional tendency evolved relatively late, for the most part after the philosophical developments that are of greater intellectual interest. Perhaps this is a warning to those such as Kant who believe in philosophical progress. Is eternal vigilance the price of freedom from ontotheology, as Derrida implies?

Saussure taught that meaning in a linguistic system is a function not of any straightforward relationship between signifier and signified, but of a complex set of differences. Barthes pointed out that the text is a tissue of quotations, not a line of words releasing the single "theological" meaning of an author-god but a multidimensional space in which a variety of writings blend and/or clash. Today Derrida shows that the meaning of such a line of words can never be completely fulfilled or totalized, hence the text never attains self-presence; the continual circulation of signifiers signifies that meaning has no firm foundation or epistemological ground. *What would we end up with if these claims about textuality were extrapolated to the whole universe?* Nāgārjuna's logical and epistemological analysis did not appeal to the Chinese Buddhists, who preferred a more metaphysical (and therefore ontotheological) way to express the interconditionality of all phenomena: the metaphor of Indra's net described in the Avataṃsaka Sutra and developed in the Hua-yen school of Mahāyāna.

> Far away in the heavenly abode of the great god Indra, there is a wonderful net that has been hung by some cunning artificer in such a manner that it stretches out infinitely in all directions. In accordance with the

> extravagant tastes of deities, the artificer has hung a single glittering jewel in each "eye" of the net, and since the net itself is infinite in all dimensions, the jewels are infinite in number. There hang the jewels, glittering like stars of the first magnitude, a wonderful sight to behold. If we now arbitrarily select one of these jewels for inspection and look closely at it, we will discover that in its polished surface there are reflected all the other jewels in the net, infinite in number. Not only that, but each of the jewels reflected in this one jewel is also reflecting all the other jewels, so that there is an infinite reflecting process occurring. . . . It symbolizes a cosmos in which there is an infinitely repeated interrelationship among all the members of the cosmos. This relationship is said to be one of simultaneous mutual identity and mutual inter-causality.[6]

Every "individual" is at the same time the effect of the whole and the cause of the whole, and the totality is a vast, infinite body of members, each sustaining and defining all the others. "The cosmos is, in short, a self-creating, self-maintaining, and self-defining organism." This world is nonteleological: "There is no theory of a beginning time, no concept of a creator, no question of the purpose of it all. The universe is taken as a given." Such a universe has no hierarchy: "There is no center, or, perhaps if there is one, it is everywhere."[7]

If "even today the notion of a center lacking any structure represents the unthinkable itself,"[8] is Indra's net an "unthinkable structure"? Nāgārjuna would not approve of such an ontotheological trope any more than Derrida would, but the metaphor is not without value. *Of Grammatology* criticizes the system of *s'entendre-parler* [hearing/understanding oneself speak] which has "produced the idea of the world, the idea of world-origin, arising from the difference between the worldly and the non-worldly, the outside and the inside, ideality and non-ideality, universal and non-universal, transcendental and empirical, etc." (8). In Indra's net those categories and binary oppositions do not apply. That *this* "textuality" extends beyond language means that right now you are reading more than the insights of Nāgārjuna and Derrida, and more than the effects of Professor Coward's invitation to contribute this paper: for in this page is the entire universe. The Vietnamese Zen master Thich Nhat Hanh makes this point best:

> If you are a poet, you will see clearly that there is a cloud floating in this sheet of paper. Without a cloud, there will be no rain; without rain, the trees cannot grow, and without trees we cannot make paper. The cloud is essential for the paper to exist. If the cloud is not here, the sheet of paper cannot be here either. . . .
>
> If we look into this sheet of paper even more deeply, we can see the sunshine in it. If the sunshine is not there, the tree cannot grow. In fact, nothing can grow. Even we cannot grow without sunshine. And so, we know that the sunshine is also in this sheet of paper. The paper and the sunshine inter-are. And if we continue to look, we can see the logger who cut the tree and brought it to the mill to be transformed into paper. And we see the wheat. We know that the logger cannot exist without his daily bread, and therefore the wheat that became his bread is also in this sheet of paper. And the logger's father and mother are in it too. . . .
>
> You cannot point out one thing that is not here—time, space, the earth, the rain, the minerals in the soil, the sunshine, the cloud, the river, the heat. Everything co-exists with this sheet of paper. . . . As thin as this sheet of paper is, it contains everything in the universe in it.[9]

To emphasize Nāgārjuna's point, the metaphor of Indra's net does not actually refer to our interdependence, for that would presuppose the existence of separate things that are related together. Rather, just as every sign is a sign of a sign, so everywhere there are only traces, and those traces are traces of traces.

If such is the case here and now, there is nothing that needs to be attained or could be lost; in that sense it is a past that has *always* been present. Then what is our problem? Why do we suffer? Buddhism provides no "first cause" to explain *duḥkha*, but accounts for our dissatisfaction by relating it back to the delusive sense-of-self, which like everything else is a manifestation of this web yet feels separate from it. The basic difficulty is that insofar as I feel separate, (i.e., a self-existing, Cartesian-like consciousness), I am insecure, for the ineluctable trace of nothingness in my fictitious (because not self-existing/self-present) sense-of-self is experienced as a sense-of-lack; in reaction, the sense-of-self becomes preoccupied with trying to become self-existing/self-present, in one or another symbolic fashion. The tragic irony is that the ways we attempt to do this cannot succeed, for the delusive sense-of-self can never expel the trace of *lack* that constitutes it; while in the most important sense we are already self-existing, insofar as the infinite set of differential traces that constitutes each of us is the whole net. "The self-existence of a Buddha is the self-existence of this very cosmos. The Buddha is without a self-existent nature; the cosmos too is without a self-existent nature." (MMK 22.16) I think this touches on the enduring attraction of logocentrism and ontotheology, not just in the West but everywhere: Being means security, the grounding of the self, whether it is experiencing something transcendent or intellectually sublimated into a metaphysical *archē*. We want to meet God face to face, or see our essential Buddha-nature, but trace/*śūnyatā* means we never catch it. The sense-of-self wants to gain nirvāṇa/enlightenment, but trace/*śūnyatā* means it can never attain it. The problem, again, is our desire for self-presence, emphasis here being as much on the *self-* as on the *-presence*.

Then the solution somehow has to do with not-catching, with no longer needing to bring these fleeting traces to self-presence. It is the difference between a bad infinity and a good infinity: a shift in perspective that changes everything.

> Subhūti: How is perfect wisdom *[prajñāpāramitā]* marked?
>
> The Lord: It has non-attachment for its mark. . . . To the extent that beings take hold of things and settle down in them, to that extent there is defilement. But no one is thereby defiled. And to the extent that one does not take hold of things and does not settle down in them, to that extent can one conceive of the absence of I-making and mine-making. In that sense

> can one form the concept of the purification of beings, i.e., to the extent that they do not take hold of things and do not settle down in them, to that extent there is purification. But no one is therein purified. When a Bodhisattva courses thus, he courses in perfect wisdom.[10]

The most famous line in the *Diamond Sutra* encapsulates this as an injunction: "Let the mind come forth without fixing it anywhere." Nāgārjuna sees the consequences of all this: "When there is clinging perception *(upādāne)*, the perceiver generates being. When there is no clinging perception, he will be freed and there will be no being" (MMK 26.7) As long as I am motivated by *lack*, I will seek to *real-ize* myself by fixating on ("settling down in") something that dissolves in my grasp, for everything is an elusive trace of traces. *Lack* is " 'self-hunger,' " that seeks fulfillment in " 'the absolute phantasm' " of " 'absolute self-having.' "[11]

What might a Buddhist teacher, concerned to help his students realize this freedom, say about Derrida's deconstruction? That Derrida's freedom is too much a *textual* freedom, that it is overly preoccupied with language because it seeks liberation through and in language—in other words, that it is logocentric. The danger is not only that we will try to find a "fully meaningful" symbol to settle down with, but that we will live too much symbolically, inscribed within an endless recirculation of concepts even if we do not grasp at the ones that are supposed to bring Being into our grasp. This remains a source of *duḥkha* because we still try to retain a ground: in language as a whole. It is the difference between a restricted and a general economy.

## The Two Truths

> The teaching of the Buddhas is wholly based on there being two truths: that of a personal everyday world and a higher truth which surpasses it.
>
> Those who do not clearly know the true distinction between the two truths cannot clearly know the hidden depths of the Buddha's teaching.

> Unless the transactional realm is accepted as a base, the surpassing sense cannot be pointed out; if the surpassing sense is not comprehended *nirvāṇa* cannot be attained. [MMK 24.8–10].

At the end of "The Ends of Man," Derrida declares the importance of a double strategy: on the one hand, to "attempt an exit and a deconstruction without changing terrain," which uses the instruments of language against language, at the risk of ceaselessly consolidating at a deeper level that which one allegedly deconstructs. On the other hand, to "decide to change terrain, in a discontinuous and irruptive fashion, by brutally placing oneself outside, and by affirming an absolute break and difference"—at the risk, again, of inhabiting more naively than before that which one claims to have deserted, for "language ceaselessly reinstates the new terrain on the oldest ground."[12] Derrida writes often about "the necessity of lodging oneself within traditional conceptuality in order to destroy it," for "we cannot give up this metaphysical complicity without also giving up the critique we are directing against this complicity."[13] The resources to make one's critique of metaphysics must be borrowed from that which one wants to undo. Notice, however, that both strategies are threatened by the same fate: the metaphysical dilemma is between reinscribing the new on the old terrain or having one's new terrain be reinscribed on the old, a negligible difference. The danger is being trapped somewhere within language; the possibility is "the joyous affirmation of the play of the world and of the innocence of becoming, the affirmation of a world of signs without fault, without truth, and without origin which is offered to an active interpretation"[14]—a Nietzsche-like, but only *textual*, liberation from Being. The difference is between being stuck somewhere within language and being free within language.

Lyotard defines postmodernism as suspicion of all metanarratives, yet it is when we think we are escaping metanarratives that we are most susceptible to them. This is the basic problem not only with "discontinuous and irruptive" works such as *Anti-Oedipus*[15] but also with such "nonmetaphysical" theories as empiricism, pragmatism, and, even more fundamentally, the unconscious metaphysics that passes as "common sense." Nāgārjuna's analyses address the main philosophical theories of his day, but his real target is that automatized, sedimented metaphysics disguised as *the world we live in.* If philosophy were merely the sport of philosophers, one could ignore it, but we have no choice in the matter. "It was a Greek who said, 'If one has to philosophize, one has to philosophize; if one does not have to philosophize, one still has to philosophize (to say it and think it). One always has to philosophize.' "[16] The fundamental categories of "everydayness" are self-existing/self-present things—including us—that are born, change, and eventually pass away; in order to explain the relations among these things, space, time, and causality are also necessary. And the vehicle of this commonsense metaphysics, creating and sustaining it, is language, which presents us with a set of nouns (self-subsistent things) that have temporal and causal predicates (things arise, change, and disappear). But, given that we find ourselves inscribed within language—that "language has started without us, in us and before us" ("How to Avoid Speaking")—how shall we proceed? Thus the double strategy of Buddhism, the "two truths." On the one hand, language must be used to expose the traps of language: in addition to Nāgārjuna's deconstruction of self-existent things, there are, for example, all the binary dualisms (purity vs. impurity, life vs. death, being vs. nothingness, success vs. failure, women vs. men, self vs. other) whereby we "tie ourselves without a rope" as we vainly try to valorize one half and reject the other. The danger with this strategy is that, as long as my sense-of-*lack* motivates me to seek Being in some sublimated form, I shall escape from one trap merely to fall into another. So the other strategy is a more disruptive one: a "higher" or "surpassing truth" that points beyond language and therefore beyond truth, raising the question of "the truth of truth" and the very possibility of truth in philosophy.

In "Of an Apocalyptic Tone Newly Adopted in Philosophy," Derrida analyzes Kant's critique of certain "self-styled mystagogues" and questions Kant's attempt to distinguish what they do from what he does. If such mystagoguery is due to a deterioration in the true essence of philosophy, then the problem is that philosophy lost its first signification very early, since Kant must distinguish between Plato the "good" Academician and Plato the presumed author of the letters, "the father of the delirium, of all exaltation in philosophy"

(39). It is another instance where a pure origin turns out to be already infected with the supplement that supposedly corrupts it.

But Derrida is more interested in the truce Kant proposes between the two parties: a concordat acknowledging that the difference between them is their different manner of presenting the same moral law. Philosophy didactically leads the moral law in us back to distinct concepts according to logic, whereas the other procedure is to personify this moral law in an esthetic manner. Derrida wonders whether this really exorcises the "apocalyptic tone" that Kant found objectionable in the "mystagogues," or rather reveals it within Kant's own discourse:

> Can not one say then that all the parties of such a concordat are the subjects of eschatological discourses? . . . If Kant denounces those who proclaim that philosophy is at an end for two thousand years, he has himself, in marking a limit, indeed the end of a certain type of metaphysics, freed another wave of eschatological discourses in philosophy. His progressivism, his belief in the future of a certain philosophy, indeed of another metaphysics, is not contradictory to this proclamation of ends and of the end. And I shall now start again from this fact: from then on . . . the West has been dominated by a powerful program that was also an untransgressible contract among discourses of the end. The themes of the end of history and the death of philosophy represent [*figurent*] only the most comprehensive, massive, and gathered forms of this. (47–48)

Derrida acknowledges the difference between Hegelian, Marxist, and Nietzschean eschatology:

> But aren't these differences measured as deviations in relation to the fundamental tonality of this *Stimmung* audible across so many thematic variations? Haven't all the differences [*différends*] taken the form of a going-one-better in eschatological eloquence, each newcomer, more lucid than the other, more vigilant and more prodigal too, coming to add more to it: I tell you

> this in truth; this is not only the end of this here but also and first of that there, the end of history, the end of the class struggle, the end of philosophy . . . And whoever would come to refine, to say the finally final, [*le fin du fin*], namely the end of the end, [*la fin de la fin*], the end of ends, that the end has always already begun, that we must still distinguish between closure and end, that person would, whether wanting to or not, participate in the concert. For that is also the end of metalanguage on the subject of eschatological language. With the result that we can wonder if eschatology is a is a tone, or even the voice itself. Isn't the voice always that of the last man? (48–49)

We do not need to ask where Derrida himself fits into all this. The tone Derrida identifies within all Western philosophical discourse is even more audible from outside, especially from the Indian (including Buddhist) tradition, which, in contrast, consists of a set of more-or-less distinct schools that developed side by side, as commentators added their notes to subcommentaries to commentaries on sacred texts. From the Western perspective, the Asian respect for tradition (e.g., Confucian gerontocracy) may look, and often is, stultifying, but from the other side the Western need to revolutionize tradition *is* the tradition. Despite recent critiques of Oedipus and patriarchy, there is still the same tendency to kill the father; and, as Derrida implies, to kill the myth of Oedipus is to reenact the myth. I think Derrida's phrase puts a finger on it: Whence this need to be "the last man"? The one who stands on everyone else's shoulders, on whose shoulders no one stands, with whom history stops, through whom signifiers do not recirculate because *his/hers* grasp the Truth? Why is it that philosophers can accept their own physical death more readily than the refutation of their ideas? The issue, as we are beginning to understand, is that there are many ways to seek Being.

> Whoever takes on the apocalyptic tone comes to signify to, if not tell, you something. What? The truth, of course, and to signify to you that it reveals the truth to you; tone is revelatory of some unveiling in process. . . . Truth itself is the end, the destination,

> and that truth unveils itself is the advent of the end. Truth is the end and the instance of the last judgment. . . . And that is why there would not be any truth of the apocalypse that is not the truth of truth. (53)

Nietzsche and Heidegger point out that nihilism is the essence of metaphysics because metaphysics seeks to ground itself in being and therefore is preoccupied with nonbeing; the truth, for them, is that there is no such ground. The problem with this realization is that even such apparently modest truth claims are just as much an attempt to ground oneself and therefore are disrupted by the inability of language to attain any self-presence in the sublimated form of self-contained meaning. Even as "the secret is that there is no secret," so for Buddhism the "higher truth" (and by saying this we shall make it the lower truth) is that there is no truth (and now we can appreciate why it is necessary to accept the "transactional realm" in order to point to the surpassing truth: that is, why Nāgārjuna insists there are two truths). There is no problem with "your lunch is in the refrigerator," but there is a problem insofar as philosophy is our attempt to grasp the concepts that grasp Being. If the truth is that conceptual place where we may rest, the search for truth is also the search for that which will fill up our *lack,* and philosophy is the conceptual attempt to find God in the net of our concepts. Then philosophy can never escape its apocalyptic tone insofar as its destiny is to seek truth. If it were possibile for our sense-of-*lack* to be resolved, for our bad infinity to be transformed into a good infinity, then truth too would be transformed: from nothing (our *lack* allows us no rest) into *everything.* According to a famous Zen story, the Buddha sat before a large audience who expected him to speak, but he said nothing, twirling a flower between his fingers. No one "understood" except Mahākāśyapa, who "cracked a smile"—whereupon the Buddha acknowledged his realization.

"Shall we thus continue in the best apocalyptic tradition, to denounce the false apocalypses?" (59). The fact—the truth—is that all philosophy, including Derrida's and including mine, cannot escape this apocalyptic "tone" insofar as it is motivated by sublimated *lack.* And not just philosophy. Derrida wonders if the apocalyptic tone is "a transcendental condition of all discourse, of all experience itself, of every mark or of every trace." And not only a tone: insofar as we hope to overcome our *lack*, we are thrust into the future, toward that awaited moment when self-presence will be gained; as Derrida implies, belief in progress, in the future itself, is a version of it.

There is another way to make this point about truth, which has implications for the future of the conversation between Western philosophy and Buddhism. According to the established myth, Western philosophy begins with the Greek discovery of reason, with the emancipation of thought from myth and religion, in an awakening that (according to Plato and Aristotle) observes the world with wonder and curiosity. In India, however, philosophy is said to begin with *duḥkha;* the fact of our suffering motivates the search for a way to end it. But this is also the origin of religion, which is why there is no sharp distinction between the two in India; the path to liberation encompasses both. From the Indian perspective, then, the originary Greek distinction between philosophy and religion is suspect; and if there is something unnatural about their bifurcation, we should expect to detect "traces" of each in the other. If their common ground is the need to end *duḥkha* and overcome *lack*, we shouldn't be surprised by a religious tone, an apocalyptic urgency at the very heart of philosophy itself. No wonder, then, that a secularized rationalism will have to keep revolutionizing itself and killing its fathers: only in that way can it avoid the fact that philosophy cannot grant the Truth that is sought from it.

Furthermore: What does this tone infecting its innermost core imply about reason? I am wondering about this: Was the *discovery* of reason more a matter of *creating* a place of self-grounding as thinking? *Cogito ergo sum.* Or rather *trying* to make thinking into such a "space" of self-grounding, given Derrida's and Buddhism's point about the impossibility of self-presence?[17] If the larger meaning of deconstruction is that *language/reason is deconstructing itself as our place of self-grounding,* the full consequences of deconstruction remain to be seen. This puts us on delicate ground, since we don't want to "lose our reason" in the way that, for example, Nietzsche did. But Buddhism offers other ways to do so.

Derrida concludes by announcing "an apocalypse without apocalypse, an apocalypse without vision, without truth, without revelation, of dispatches (for the 'come' is plural in itself, in oneself), of addresses without message and without destination, without sender or decidable addressee, without last judgement, without any other eschatology than the tone of the 'Come' itself, its very difference, an apocalypse beyond good and evil" (66). A Buddhist apocalypse, congenial to any jewel in Indra's net that isn't trying to fixate itself. "Here the catastrophe would perhaps be *of* the apocalypse itself, its *pli* and its end, a closure without end, an end without end" (67). The sense-of-self can never fill up its sense-of-*lack*, but it can realize that what it seeks it has never lacked. "And what if this outside of the apocalypse was within the apocalypse? What if it was the apocalypse itself, what precisely breaks-in in the 'Come'?" (67). Perhaps this is what we have always sought: not to become real but to realize that we don't need to become real. In the end, is there any difference between them?

## Nirvāṇa

> There is no specifiable difference whatsoever between *nirvāṇa* and the everyday world; there is no specifiable difference whatever between the everyday world and *nirvāṇa*.
>
> The ontic range of *nirvāṇa* is the ontic range of the everyday world. There is not even the subtlest difference between the two.
>
> That which, taken as causal or dependent, is the process of being born and passing on, is, taken non-causally and beyond all dependence, declared to be *nirvāṇa*.
>
> Ultimate serenity is the coming to rest of all ways of taking things, the repose of named things; no truth has been taught by a Buddha for anyone, anywhere. [MMK, 25.19, 20, 9, 24]

The climactic chapter of the MMK addresses the nature of nirvāṇa in order to prove that there is no transcendental-signified: since nothing is self-existent, nirvāṇa, too, is *śūnya*. The everyday world, which is the process of things (including me) being born, changing, and passing away, is for that reason a world of suffering, *saṁsāra*. Yet there is no specifiable difference between this world and nirvāṇa. There is, however, a difference of perspective, or rather a difference in the way they are "taken," which has not yet been brought out fully in our discussions of *pratītya-samutpāda* and Indra's net. The irony of Nāgārjuna's approach to *pratītya-samutpāda* is that its use of causation refutes causation: after the deconstruction of the self-existence or being of things (including us) into their conditions and interdependence, causality itself then disappears, because without any*thing* to cause/be effected, the world will not be experienced in terms of cause and effect. Once causality has been used to refute the apparent self-existence of objective things, the lack of things to relate together refutes causality. If things originate (change, cease to exist, etc.), there are no self-existing things; but if there are no things, then there is nothing to originate and therefore no origination.

It is because we see the world as a collection of discrete things that we superimpose causal relationships, to "glue" these things together. Therefore the victory of causality is Pyrrhic, for if there is only causality, there is no causality. This self-refutation has religious consequences: Cause-and-effect is essential to our project of attempting to secure ourselves "within" the world; its evaporation leaves behind it not chance (its binary opposite) but a sense of mystery, of being part of something that we can never grasp, since we are a manifestation of it. When there is no need to defend a fragile sense-of-self, such mystery is not threatening, and rather than attempt to banish it, one is able to yield to it.

In Derrida's terms, the important thing about causality is that it is the equivalent of textual *différance* in the world of things. If *différance* is the ineluctability of textual causal relationships, causality is the *différance* of the "objective" world. Nāgārjuna's use of interdependence to refute the self-existence of things is equivalent to what Derrida does for textual meaning, as we have seen. But Nāgārjuna's second and reverse move is one that Derrida doesn't make: the absence of any self-existing objects refutes causality/*différance*. The aporias of causality are well known; Hume's version, which points out that we can never perceive any necessary connection between cause and effect, was anticipated by the Mahāyāna philosopher Dharmakīrti in the seventh century A.D. Nāgārjuna's version points to the contradiction necessary for a cause-and-effect relationship: the effect can be neither the same as the cause nor different from it. If the effect is the same as the cause, nothing has been caused; if it is different, then any cause should be able to cause any effect.[18]

Therefore *pratītya-samutpāda* is not a doctrine of dependent origination but an account of nondependent nonorigination. It describes, not the interaction of realities, but the sequence and juxtaposition of "appearances"—or what could be called appearances if there were some nonappearance to be contrasted with. Origination, duration, and cessation are "like an illusion, a dream, or an imaginary city in the sky" (MMK 7.34). What is perhaps the most famous of all Mahāyāna scriptures, the Diamond Sutra, concludes with the statement that "all phenomena are like a dream, an illusion, a bubble and a shadow, like dew and lightning." As soon as we abolish the "real" world, "appearance" becomes the only reality, and we discover

> a world scattered in pieces, covered with explosions; a world freed from the ties of gravity (i.e., from relationship with a foundation); a world made of moving and light surfaces where the incessant shifting of masks is named laughter, dance, game.[19]

For both Nietzsche and Buddhism, our way of trying to solve a problem turns out to be what maintains the problem. We try to "peel away" the apparent world to get at the real one, but that dualism between them *is* our problematic delusion, which leaves, as the only remaining candidate for real world, the apparent one—a world whose actual nature has not been noticed because we have been so concerned to transcend it. This allows us to see more clearly how "everydayness" and "common sense" are not alternatives to metaphysical speculation but a disguised—because automatized and unconscious—version of it. As Berkeley pointed out, no one has ever experienced matter; from the other side, it is "common sense" that is idealist in postulating minds-inside-bodies; and, as Nāgārjuna would emphasize, the refutation of either does not imply the truth of the other.

One such "appearance"—no more or less so than anything else—is what is called "a Buddha." Derrida points to the "hyperessentiality," the being (or nonbeing—an hypostatized *śūnyatā* can work as well) beyond Being whose trace lingers in most negative theologies, infecting them with a more subtle transcendental-signified. Nāgārjuna is also sensitive to this issue. Like other negative theologies, Nāgārjuna begins by dedicating the MMK to the Buddha, but then he devotes the most important chapter to proving there can be no such thing as a Buddha, just as there is no other self-present transcendental-signified. Instead, the serenity (or "beatitude": *śiva*) we seek is the coming-to-rest of all ways of taking things, the repose of named things *(sarvopalambhopaśamaprapañcopaśamah).* His commentator Candrakīrti (seventh century A.D.) glosses the verse as follows: "The very coming to rest, the non-functioning, of perceptions as signs of all named things, is itself *nirvāṇa* . . . . When verbal assertions cease, named things are in repose; and the ceasing to function of discursive thought is ultimate serenity."[20] Contrast this to Derrida's problematization of the difference between signifier and signified: "From the moment that one questions the possibility of such a transcendental signified, and that one realizes that every signified is in the position of a signifier, the distinction between signified and signifier becomes problematical at its root."[21] For Derrida, what is problematic is the relationship between name and concept; so it is not surprising that he concludes with an endless recirculation of concepts. But notice what is signifier and what is signified, for Candrakīrti: The nonfunctioning of preceptions as signs for named things is nirvāṇa. The problem is not merely that language acts as a filter, obscuring the nature of things. Rather, names are used to objectify appearances into the "self-existing" things we perceive *as* books, tables, trees, you, and me. In other words, the "objective" world of material things, which interact causally "in" space and time, is metaphysical through and through. It is this metaphysics that most needs to be deconstructed, according to Buddhism, because this is the metaphysics, disguising itself as commonsense reality, that makes me suffer—especially insofar as I understand myself to be such a self-existing being "in" time that will nonetheless die. (Our fundamental *duḥkha* may be expressed as this contradiction: on the one hand, we feel that we are *or should be* self-existent, a self-sufficient self-consciousness, on the other hand, we know that we were born, are growing old, and will die.) The important thing in Buddhism is that the coming-to-rest of our using names to take perceptions as self-existing objects actually deconstructs the "objective" everyday world. Since that world is as differential, as full of traces, as the textual discourse Derrida works on, the Buddhist response is to use those differences/deferrals to deconstruct that objectified world, including ourselves, since we sub-jects are the first to be ob-jectified. If there are only traces of traces, what happens if we stop trying to arrest those elusive traces into a self-presence? If we do not take perceptions as signs of named things, the most fundamental and problematic dualism of all—that between my fragile sense of being and the nothingness that threatens it—is conflated; if we do not need to fixate ourselves, if we can "let go" of ourselves, we *un*find ourselves "in" the dreamlike world that the Diamond Sutra describes, and plunge into the horizontality of moving and light surfaces where there are no objects, only an incessant shifting of masks; where there is no security and also no need for security, because everything that can be lost has been, including oneself. Especially oneself.

In order for this to occur, however, another strategy is necessary: a discontinuous, irruptive one that does not constitute a different philosophical approach but a nonphilo–sophical one because it lets go of thoughts. I refer, of course, to the various meditative practices that are so important in Buddhism. Are such practices the "other" of philosophy, feared and ridiculed because they challenge the only ground philosophy knows? When we are not so quick to grasp at thoughts (truth as grasping the concepts that grasp Being), there is the possibility of another praxis besides conceptualization, a more unmediated way of approaching that issue. I do not see how, within language, it can be proven or disproven that we remain inscribed within the circulations of its signifiers. Derrida shows only that language cannot grant access to any self-present meaning; his methodology cannot settle the question whether our experience of language and the so-called objective world is susceptible to a radical transformation. The other possibility is that what all philosophy seeks, insofar as it cannot escape its apocalyptic tone, may be accessible in a different fashion. The fact that other, nonconceptual forms of mental discipline and concentration have been so significant, not only in Buddhism but in many other non-Western and Western traditions, suggests that we need to find out what they may contribute to these issues.[22]

## Notes

1. Derrida, like Heidegger, has been careful to confine to the Western tradition his conclusions about the continual attraction of ontotheology, but the case of Buddhism suggests how they can and perhaps must be generalized. Buddhism is a religious/philosophical tradition not originating in or overtaken by Greek presence (e.g., Plato's *eidos*), yet Sanskrit and Pali are also Indo-European languages whose categories (in contrast with Chinese and Japanese) tend toward a strong transcendental-phenomenal distinction. One of the most striking things about Buddhism in its Indian context is how it both reflects and resists this bifurcation.

2. As an example of the last problematic, here is a famous story about Ma-tsu (709–788 A.D.), one of the most important Chinese Ch'an (Zen) masters:

Abbot Huai-jang visited the young Ma-tsu in his cell and asked: "In practicing sitting-meditation, what do you aspire to attain?" "To attain Buddhahood," was the answer. Huai-jang took up a piece of brick and began to grind it against a rock. After some moments Ma-tsu became curious and asked: "What are you grinding that for?" "I want to grind it into a mirror." Amused, Ma-tsu said, "How can you hope to grind a piece of brick into a mirror?" Huai-jang replied, "Since a piece of brick cannot be ground into a mirror, how can you sit yourself into a Buddha?" "What must I do then?" Ma-tsu asked. "Take the case of an ox-cart," said Huai-jang. "If the cart does not move, do you whip the cart or the ox?" Ma-tsu remained silent. "In learning sitting-meditation, do you aspire to learn the sitting-Ch'an, or do you aspire to imitate the seated Buddha? If the former, Ch'an does not consist in sitting or in lying down. If the latter, the Buddha has no fixed postures. The Buddha-way goes on forever, and never abides in anything. You must not therefore be attached to nor abandon any particular phase of it. To sit yourself into a Buddha is to kill the Buddha. To be attached to the sitting posture is to fail to comprehend the essential principle." When Ma-tsu heard these instructions, he felt as though he were drinking the most exquisite nectar. (From John C. H. Wu, *The Golden Age of Zen* [Taipei: United Publishing Center, 1975], p. 92.)

3. According to the most common Mahāyāna account, however, the Buddha attained enlightenment when he looked up from his meditations and saw the morning star, whereupon he exclaimed: "Now I realize that all beings have the Buddha-nature."

4. A similar and equally predictable formalization occurred with the rules that monks and nuns followed. In order to create the best

environment for meditative practice, numerous regulations evolved in this fashion: Some problem in daily life arose, which made disciples ask the Buddha, what should be done in such a case? His answers were along the lines of "Let's do it like this." Shortly before his death the Buddha said that the sangha might, if it wished, abolish the minor disciplinary rules (which constituted the vast majority); instead, these several hundred rules of thumb became canonized into the *vinaya*, the complicated "discipline" that came to constitute the main (for many monks and nuns, the only) form of spiritual practice. (*Dīgha Nikāya* 16.6.3)

5. The translation used in this paper is Mervyn Sprung's in his edition of *Lucid Exposition of the Middle Way* (Boulder, Colo.: Prajñā Press, 1979), Candrakīrti's classic commentary on the MMK.

6. Francis H. Cook's description in his *Hua-yen Buddhism: The Jewel Net of Indra* (University Park: Pennsylvania State University Press, 1977), p. 2.

7. Cook, ibid.

8. Derrida, *Writing and Difference*, trans. Alan Bass (Chicago: University of Chicago Press, 1978), p. 279.

9. Thich Nhat Hanh, *The Heart of Understanding* (Berkeley, Calif.: Parallax Press, 1988), pp. 3–5.

10. *The Perfection of Wisdom in Eight Thousand Lines and its Verse Summary*, trans. Edward Conze (Bolinas, Calif.: Four Seasons Foundation, 1973), pp. 237–38. A key Mahāyāna term is *apratiṣṭhita-nirvāṇa*, usually understood as "not dwelling in nirvāṇa": that is, the bodhisattva's compassion causes him/her to reject entry into final nirvāṇa in order to help all suffering sentient beings. But it may also mean "nondwelling nirvāṇa" or "non-abiding cessation."

11. In "An Apocalyptic Tone," Derrida quotes his own *Glas*. " 'The apocalyptic, in other words, capital unveiling, in truth lays bare the self-hunger.' " " 'The absolute phantasm as an absolute self-having in its most mournful glory' " (p. 61). For more on the sense-of-*lack* as "shadow" of the sense-of-self, see David Loy, "The Nonduality of Life and Death: A Buddhist View of Repression," *Philosophy East and West* 40, no. 2 (April 1990), pp. 151–174.

12. Derrida, *The Margins of Philosophy*, trans. A. Bass (Chicago: University of Chicago Press, 1982), p. 135.

13. *Writing and Difference*, pp. 111, 281.

14. *Writing and Difference*, p. 292.

15. Gilles Deleuze and Felix Guattari, *Anti-Oedipus*, trans. H. R. Lane, Robert Hurley, and Mark Seem (New York: Viking Press, 1977).

16. Derrida, *Writing and Difference*, 152. Traditionally attributed to the *Protrepticus* of Aristotle, but now disputed. See Anton-Hermann Chroust, *Aristotle: Protrepticus, A Reconstruction* (Notre Dame: University of Notre Dame Press, 1964) pp. 48–49.

17. "*Reason*, n., an imaginary process onto which the responsibility for thinking is off-loaded." (Rene Daumal, *A Night of Serious Drinking*, trans. David Coward and E. A. Lovatt [Boston: Shambhala, 1979], p. 51)

18. MMK 10:19, 22. Cf. Nietzsche, *The Gay Science*, no. 112: "Cause and effect: such a duality probably never exists; in truth we are confronted by a continuum out of which we isolate a couple of pieces, just as we perceive motion only as isolated points and then infer it without ever actually seeing it. . . . An intellect that could see cause and effect as a continuum and a flux and not, as we do, in terms of an arbitrary division and dismemberment, would repudiate the concept of cause and effect and deny all conditionality." For more on this issue, see my *Nonduality* (New Haven: Yale University Press, 1988), chap. 6.

19. Michel Haar, "Nietzsche and Metaphysical Language," in *The New Nietzsche: Contemporary Styles of Interpretation*, ed. David B. Allison (New York: Delta, 1977), p. 7.

20. In Sprung's *Lucid Exposition*, p. 262.

21. Derrida, *Positions*, trans. A. Bass (Chicago: University of Chicago Press, 1981), p. 20.

22. The relation between Nāgārjuna's Mādhyamika and Ch'an (Zen) Buddhism is a fascinating one. From one perspective, Ch'an may be said to put into practice the approach of Nāgārjuna. From another, Ch'an practice is a deconstruction of Mādhyamika theory, whose antimetaphysics is still philosophical. If the dualism between inside and outside is a construct, the result of an "invagination" of the outside (which is therefore not an outside), it raises the possibility of a "devagination." The Japanese Zen master Dōgen (1200–1253) described his experience thus: "I came to realize clearly that my mind is nothing other than rivers and mountains and trees, the sun and the moon and the stars."

# EIGHT

# *Conclusion: Divine Reservations*

Morny Joy

This may not be the place to explore the intricacies of women's spirituality in the thirteenth century, particularly that of the Beguines,[1] but their exploration of certain themes of negative theology adds a specific dimension to our discussion.[2] The women mystics I have in mind are Mechthild of Magdeburg (ca. 1207–82), and Hadewijch,[3] as well as Marguerite of Porete (d. 1310). Within the neoplatonic dispensation they followed, the desire of these women was to become "what God is."[4] Though there are variations in their descriptions of the means by which one attains this state and of the nature of the experience itself, the prevailing imagery of these descriptions is of a negative variety. And while their concern may not be to observe the niceties of philosophical differentiation that is found in the later work of Meister Eckhart, their evocations are all the more poignant. This is because the flavor of immediacy informs all their writings. Primacy is given to affective rather than to intellectual knowledge. It is not a rational *deus absconditus* that they seek, but a God whose infinity far surpasses any human attempt at containment. In the hands of the Beguines the apophatic tradition takes on a particular quality.

From this perspective, the postulates of negative qualification indicating divine superessentiality become a correlate of their own insignificance. The two types of negativity operating here are not necessarily of the same order. Negative theology is one thing; negation of self is another. Yet, in Beguine spirituality, the two forms of negation are often inextricably linked.

For instance, to become "what God is" one must first become nothing. This virtual elimination of any initiative on one's part is a prerequisite of unitive mysticism and the experience of immersion in those fathomless depths that defy description. Scholastic sclerosis this is not. The apophatic nature of the divine is invoked, as is their own abandonment, but more often than not it is by the imagery of the desert. So it is that the symbol of the desert can circumscribe the wasteland of the human will and desire as well as the bankruptcy of theoretical designations. Renunciation of all that is human both precedes and follows the encounter with the All that is Nothing.

As an illustration, Mechthild of Magdeburg, in her poem "The Desert Has Twelve Things," commences with the salutation, "You must love nothingness."[5] Likewise Hadewijch delineates the appropriate demeanor:

> It is like a desert
> To be here below,
> For here,
> Neither sense nor words
> Can reach or penetrate.[6]

Again Marguerite of Porete extemporizes on the same paradoxical theme:

> And so such a soul, having become nothing,
> possesses all and yet possesses nought,
> wishes all and wishes nothing,
> she knows everything and knows nought.[7]

The unwritten assumption in these writings is that love and reason initially interact and fuel this quest, but at a certain juncture there is a recognition that it is love, alone and unadorned, that can penetrate the obscurity of the infinite. Reason can only resort to negative qualifications in its adoption of images, symbols, and formulations. Words are always suspect. They are frail and erratic implements, never completely capable of conveying the nature of that presence that is absence. Theoretical constructs are seen for what they are—artificial and makeshift categories—and are to be treated accordingly.

All this must seem a far cry from the work of Nietzsche and Heidegger, who I believe posed the fundamental questions that also inform the agenda of this conference. Nietzsche instigated the logistics of the death of God when he declared: "I am afraid we are not rid of God because we still have faith in grammar."[8] Heidegger intensified the project as he sought to move beyond the traditional concept of God or the ontological difference that had delimited Being within a metaphysical straitjacket. Yet both Nietzsche and Heidegger, though not, strictly speaking, advocates of negative theology, were still haunted by the ghost of God. Nietzsche, in his last year of productivity, identified himself as a disciple of Dionysus, the god who not only danced, but who decadently reveled on the ruins of all systems and structures. Heidegger, in a posthumously published interview, declared:

> Only a god can save us. The sole possibility that is left for us is to prepare a sort of readiness, through thinking and poetizing, for the appearance of the god or for the absence of the god in the time of foundering; for in the face of the god who is absent, we founder.[9]

The echoes of Nietzsche's and Heidegger's struggles with the absolute and its designations still reverberate. Is it nihilism or anarchic celebration? Are we floundering in primal chaos or flaunting the erratic nature of our existence? Or both at once? Or neither? Ambiguous, absurd, cynical, elusive, irrational, equivocal, sophistic, undecidable. Derrida himself is no stranger to these terms, or rather, the reception of the work of Derrida runs the gamut of these designations. Is Derrida's refusal to conform to logocentric norms a symptom of a fatal metaphysical disease or a cure for what ails the Western mind-set? Is Derrida's strategy of deconstruction the *pharmakon* that can either kill or cure? It would seem that in wrestling with Nietzsche and Heidegger, Derrida's work avoids prescribing a solution. It remains deliberately indeterminate.

Derrida's own response to Nietzsche and Heidegger is at once an acknowledgment of their respective excavations of metaphysical foundations; yet it is also an excursus that places their work, as well as his own, into question. Derrida realizes that there are no clear-cut answers, no final solutions, for the conundrums of existence. There are especially no conceptual formulas that can define/reveal all. So his work itself becomes part of an interpretative process. Except that interpretation has now become the point of interrogation. So do we interpret Derrida, or do we imitate him? Do we undo him what he has done unto us? And what of God, anyway? Dionysus, *Dasein,* or a constant disappearing act? Or do we discern in the death of the purported God of metaphysics, beyond all ontological embarrassments, a silent space of infinite possibility, the god of negative theology? Is Derrida, in spite of his own proclivities, a devotee of divine negation?

As David Loy observes in chapter 7, Derrida himself proposes a double strategy. One form could be described as deconstruction "without changing terrain, by repeating what is implicit in the founding concepts and the original problematic, by using against the edifice the instruments or stones available in the house." The other goes further: "To decide to change terrain, in a discontinuous and irruptive fashion, by brutally placing oneself outside, and by affirming an absolute break and difference."[10] It is in the second, more negative or Nietzschean, mode that Derrida is most usually interpreted within the contemporary religious debate. Here all of deconstruction's destabilizing strategies are but "the death of God put into writing." As Carl Raschke has also observed: "Deconstruction is the dance of death on the tomb of God."[11] In Raschke's Derridean scenario, theologically we have reached the end of the line.

On the other hand, in his book *Radical Hermeneutics,*[12] John Caputo will go a Heideggerian route, discerning in *différance,* as it disrupts ontic plenitude, a type of excess, that is, an inevitable exclusion that is an impetus for further discovery. It is a type of parthenogenetic process, born of the very multiplicity and indeterminacy of meaning. However, this is Caputo's, not Derrida's, solution to the theological dilemma. It is Caputo's response to the purely negative reading of the erstwhile grammar of theology: a grammar that both named and framed God.

Yet there is another possible scenario, that of the later Heidegger's poetics of disclosure/withdrawal, which signifies a new type of grammar. Although former preordained constructs are deemed inappropriate, there may remain an unthought Being whose time has yet to come—has yet to be deciphered. In fact, Derrida, in his enigmatic fashion, flirts with such a possibility in an early exploration of Heidegger, "Ousia and Grammē":

> There may be a difference still more unthought than the difference between Being and beings. We certainly can go further toward naming it in our language. Beyond Being and beings, this difference, ceaselessly differing from and deferring (itself), would trace (itself) (by itself)—this *différance* would be the first or last trace if one still could speak, here, of origin and end.
>
> Such a *différance* would at once, again, give us to think a writing without presence and without absence, without history, without cause, without *archia*, without *telos*, a writing that absolutely upsets all dialectics, all theology, all teleology, all ontology. A writing exceeding everything that the history of metaphysics has comprehended in the form of the Aristotelian *grammē*, in its point, in its line, in its circle, in its time, and in its space.[13]

This description, written by Derrida in the late sixties, evokes the ethos of the God of the apophatic tradition, the God beyond language, beyond thought, the God of negative theology that differentiates while remaining undifferentiated. It is this particular statement of Derrida's that most commentators refer to in drawing a comparison between deconstruction and negative theology. And this is probably as close as Derrida has dared to express himself on the matter, that is, until he realized that he had to call a halt to his own and his commentators' hypothesizing. And so, it is in the light of Derrida's own program, specifically his reflections in "How to Avoid Speaking: Denials"[14] and "Of an Apocalyptic Tone Newly Adopted in Philosophy,"[15] that I will review the papers of this conference. At the same time, I shall investigate the possibility of a space in deconstruction that may or may not permit the notion of negative theology.

It is in "Denials" that I believe Derrida approaches a confessional mode for the first time in his work. Derrida, as dissimulator, has perhaps met his match in the delicate maneuverings of negative theology. How is he to speak of a movement that, as his own, negates any intentionality, disclaims all concepts and categories within a system of infinite regress. Derrida, as dissembling dissimulator, is nonetheless in his element, as he interrogates the possibilities not only of his own discourse, but of negative theology.

Derrida's initial reservations are concerned with his own promise (to speak of negative theology) both to himself and to the organizer of the conference. What are the conditions of fulfilling this promise? Expanding the context, so that he deals not just with this specific instance, but with promise as always already symptomatic of language, Derrida positions himself within the matrix of displacement that is his signature. Here, although promise is always implicit in language, it marks the radical deconstructive economy of endless proliferation of possibility, of promise. One's sayings, or situation, can never again be sure. Language itself is always assured, yet because of its indefinite nature, how could it ever be possible to ascertain whether Derrida has or has not kept his promise? Committed inevitably to speech, to discourse, Derrida investigates with gleeful enthusiasm the convolutions of speaking, or not speaking, about negative theology within the constraints of discourse.

In his investigation of the logic, rhetoric, and grammar of negative theology, Derrida is fascinated by the risks of double-dealing within negative language—and by its corollaries of secrecy and silence. If one speaks at all, what sort of language is appropriate? Is denial alone legitimate? What do affirmations intend? When does the rhetoric of negative capability introduce intimations of divine intercession? When does speech become ineffectual? Where lies the difference between speaking and saying? Derrida traverses, transgresses, these various forms of language with evident relish. For him the ultimate enigma of negative theology dwells in the complicity of secrecy—a cipher of sorts that disclaims its own mystery. The disclosure is the absence of any presence—of any secret. Its secret, as such, can therefore never be affirmed or denied. The negation at its core will nonetheless function as a lure, as a process of denegation, yet as an ultimate destabilizer of any definite pronouncements as to its contents, its identity. It is in this sense that negative theology could be considered similar to the displacements of deconstruction.

But Derrida won't have this. For him, behind the seeming disaffirmations of negative theology lurks an ontological telos, the ultimate deus ex machina who informs the whole undertaking. This absolute Nonpresence is indeed an instance of an anathema to Derrida—for it has all the earmarks of an originary presence. All its indeterminate calculations are in the service of a form of signification, though it contravenes all traditional rules of procedure. "Neither/nor" in this context does not indicate a parenthesis in proceedings with indeterminable reverberations, as it does for Derrida. It signals instead a complete break, in both the level and the manner of discourse. It signals another modus operandi altogether.

Derrida, however, does not rest content with this differentiation. In his customary manner he will pursue the conditions of negative theology itself. He does this by juxtaposing its discourse with similar depositions in Western philosophy. This exercise in textual interpolation places negative theology as an expression within the text of Western ontotheology per se. In "Denials" the interaction and juxtaposition of Platonic, Dionysian and Heideggerian moments highlight a similar type of speculative dialectics without a stable resolution. The intent is an informal cross-examination of the multiple examples of avoidance of that resonant space that marks the inexpressible. The topology of the trace throws into relief the deconstructive concern with inscription itself, with the impossibility of defining the trace. This Derridean tactic of using one text to interrogate another is employed in this instance with specific reference to that entity that can only be written under erasure: ~~Being~~, or ~~God~~. Such a strategy risks, as always, absurdity or exhaustion. Derrida's impatience with univocal gestures, with irreducible systems, cannot but leave us with conundrums of possible meanings, of impossible answers, of endless interplays. And so, a question to mirror his own meanderings: Has Derrida fulfilled his promise to speak of negative theology?

Of the four respondents, it is Mark Taylor who emphatically wants to remind us of the hypothetical nature of all verbal inscriptions. These would naturally include Derrida's own statements regarding his commitment to the proceedings of this conference. But knowing the nature of the deconstructive species, are we not naïve nowadays if we ever make the mistake of taking a person at her or his word? Derrida could indeed mean many things, mostly of an indeterminate nature, for ultimately his messages have no fixed abode, no final destination . . . words adrift, unrelated to any form, so that all forms are suspect. It seems there is nothing left to say. So why the continued clatter, the seeming reductio ad absurdum of any attempt at meaning.

Perhaps it is because Derrida does have something to say, but he wants to make sure that it is not placed upon a conveyor belt that will deposit it at an allotted site. Derrida has derided Lacan for his psychoanalytic determinism of desire and does not want to be caught in the same predictable trap. But Derrida speaks. He acknowledges the negative capability of language to convey a semblance of that about which nothing can be said. Taylor elaborates specifically on this aspect in his discussion, observing that Derrida's moves of negation/avowal are akin to the negative element in Platonic-type metaphysics.

But is this structural comparison all there is? Is Derrida simply pointing to the incapacity of language to fulfill the promise with which we have endowed it? If that is so, he need say no more. The point is made. For, as observed above, Derrida would not in his wildest dreams be caught imputing the existence of any ontological composite above and beyond his logocentric frolics. But it is the very vehemence, as it were, of his denials—his excessive convolutions of approach and avoidance—that still make me suspicious that something more is at stake.

Taylor also detects an avoidance here, in Derrida's "nondialectic" presentation in "Denials" of the Greek, Christian, and Heideggerian moments that he sees as constituting metaphysical moments. In this triad, according to Derrida, the last moment of the purported dialectic could alternatively be Judaic or Islamic mysticism. But this possibility will remain unexplored. This potential, yet unsaid, element is the undeterminable *trace* that could undermine the whole procedure. The trace that could instigate another line of questioning altogether. Or it could put an end to all questions, for there are no answers, only further questions. The possibilities are infinite. Then why delimit them in this fashion? It appears that to posit a potential Jewish or Islamic solution is a somewhat gratuitous plot on Derrida's part. This ruse points to a deliberate use of deconstruction as a type of *agent provocateur*, a prod in the soft underbelly of all traditional mainstream assumptions. Would it not be more consistent to leave the trace unsaid? To leave it to its own wayward devices? Does not Derrida reveal/conceal himself by such deliberate delimitations? If so, Taylor does not call him on this move, but proceeds in the very same provocative vein in a purposeful deflation of Christian and Western metaphysical assumptions.

But to return to the crucial question. What is Derrida intimating by his position "on the threshold"? As Taylor notes, to move beyond this threshold means, in Meister Eckhart's account, to acquire a new eye. As mystics, including the Beguines, would name it, this new eye is the eye of love. With access to these new vistas, one need no longer speak in negatives, in riddles. One in fact need not have recourse to language. This is perhaps the greatest secret of them all. Here is home: a wordless sanctuary. But Derrida remains on the threshold.

He cannot come home—though it seems he is enticed, fascinated. Derrida is the exile, the outsider, tempted by words to burst his bounds, yet circumscribed within their limitations. The eye of love is foreign to the forays of his deconstruction. Lashed to the masthead of reason, he will not succumb to the siren song of experience. Yet Derrida has found a home of sorts. He has placed himself forever in the site of the other—not in the simplistic style of the Hegelian negation of negation, but the site of the wandering signifier, the elusive other, the erratic and errant element that haunts all our presences—perhaps even his own. In this guise, will he remain the wandering Reb Derrida to all Greek and Christian ontological homecomings?

And yet it is Derrida's own trajectory that has confined him to his logocentric wanderings. David Loy, in his comparison of *différance* and *śūnyatā* (as described by Nāgārjuna within the Mādhyamika school) plots a similar deconstructive ploy at work in these Western and Buddhist operations, but allows that *śūnyatā* is more radical in its effects.[16] In fact *śūnyatā*, in its reverse strategy, emphasizes a form of reinscription that counterquestions the logocentric system itself in a way that eludes Derrida.

Buddhist philosophy, specifically as elaborated by Nāgārjuna, wishes to relieve us of our ontological burdens, particularly of our need to philosophize. It puts into question not only language and its dualist conundra, but also the very nature of the type of existence that requires such manipulation. Ultimately, of course, it is ourselves, our ways of being, that are interrogated. To achieve this, the constructs of perception and mind are subjected to rigorous scrutiny. The basic procedure is communicated by a dialectical critique of any metaphysical statement in an effort to demonstrate not only its intractable duality but also its utter insubstantiality. This process is not found not only in Nāgārjuna's *Mūlamadhyamikakārikā*, but also in other Buddhist Sutras, e.g., the Vimalakīrti Sutra:

> The bodhisattva Parigūḍha declared, " 'Self' and 'selflessness' are dualistic. Since the existence of self cannot be perceived, what is there to be made 'selfless'? Thus, the nondualism of the vision of their nature is the entrance into nonduality."[17]

The dualist, or everyday, way of perception must give way to a nondual awareness. To achieve this, the form as well as the content of any idea or sensation must undergo a two-way movement of a deconstructive variety. Then, and only then, is a nondual experience possible. One has passed beyond the pairs of opposites. The presumption is, of course, that "what metaphysics has sought in language can be found in some other way."[18] But as Loy is the first to admit, "in language, such a possibility cannot be proven or disproven."[19]

There are many ways that nonduality can be expressed, as well as many corollaries that follow its initial premise. David Loy has explored the alternatives in detail in his book *Nonduality*.[20] In this particular instance I will concentrate solely on the form that Loy describes with specific reference to *śūnyatā* as central to Nāgārjuna's logic. It is here that Loy deftly explicates the basic differences between Buddhism and deconstruction. A initial comparison of *śūnyatā* and *différance* on a formal level indicates that they spring from the same impulse. *Śūnyatā*, as a guiding principle, is empty. It is not an entity that exists apart from phenomena, yet it serves to illustrate their inherent limitations. In Loy's words, there is no such thing as *śūnyatā*. But Nāgārjuna is not content to prescribe *śūnyatā* simply as a device that destabilizes textual pretensions. A change in the very manner of our perceiving is required, though the exact nature of this change is variously described. Inevitably, verbal diagnoses are not efficacious in enabling this breakthrough. And it is in connection with this particular aspect that Loy delineates the reverse strategy that characterizes most Buddhist operations. For not only does the form have no content (a perspective shared with Derrida), but the content has no form. As Loy succinctly states:

> Having deconstructed the self-existence or being of things (including us) into their conditions and inter-dependence, causality itself then disappears, because without anything to cause/be effected, the world will not be experienced in terms of cause and effect. (247)

As with causality, so with all concepts. Within Buddhism, one could say that there is indeed something outside the text, though its expression is problematic, since it pertains to a state that defies ordinary description. It is all in the nature of perception as it obtains in a nondual state, and here the texts of Buddhism vary enormously. The ultimate depiction, in a paradoxical play, decrees that from the standpoint of enlightenment, the subject and object become one and the same. The subject/object dichotomy has always been a false imposition of conventional metaphysics. There is actually no distinction between self and the world. From a nondual perspective, *nirvāṇa* and *saṁsāra* (the everyday world) are one. Such a statement should not be understood in any naïve way, for this subtle observation carries with it the full panoply of Buddhist insight into the human condition. This perspective also should not be mistaken for either epistemological or ontological pronouncements of a traditional sort, though undoubtedly claims are being made for the existential reverberations of certain logical and psychological practices.

The basis of the Buddhist program seems to be that it discerns a lack that impels our search for a self-presence that can never be obtained. Whereas Derrida would read this as a desire that is forever inscribed in the text as symptom—manifested most significantly in an apocalyptic tone—Buddhists do not. It is not an "originary lack," it is a contingent type of dissatisfaction that motivates desire. It can be described along the lines of an endemic human orientation, constituted by ignorance/desire, which in turn influences our dualist proclivities. Without the apparatus of any sophisticated psychoanalytic theory, this Buddhist continuum of ignorance/desire can seem a gratuitous postulate. But the point is not to get caught up in any absolute definitions. In Buddhist practice, the aim is to dissolve these bonds of desire and their concomitant structures. The dialectical exercises are part of a concerted program. The verbal assaults destroy any monolithic claims. They illustrate that nothing has an independent, intrinsic nature. Thus, there is no causality. All is mutually interdependent, without any subsisting discrete or absolute reality. To realize this, after an extensive period of meditation and mindfulness, is to achieve *nirvāṇa.* The scales of dualism and deception, allied to desire, are dissolved. With such a drastic alteration in the manner of understanding the world, our manner of processing these perceptions is also changed. This liberation, or *nirvāṇa,* also frees us from the constraints of needing to resort to words to prove, disprove, or escape conventions. As Buddha, one can simply hold up a flower.

I do not feel, however, that the West wants enlightenment of this Eastern variety—cussed logocentric creatures that we are. But if we in the West are not on the path to enlightenment in the Buddhist sense, are we, like Derrida, condemned to a lopsided deconstruction of linguistically based knowledge? Admittedly, with this device comes insight into the dualistic deceptions that have been perpetrated by the agents of truth—but there is nowhere else to go. Our desires laid bare, the apocalyptic urge to proclaim the ultimate order is defused. In their stead, unfortunately, there is not the silence of the sage. Prescriptions abound, of either the nihilistic or the exuberant variety. When Mark Taylor and Carl Raschke interpret the deconstructive impulse as the interment of the God who has been dying a lingering death since Nietzsche, their logocentric affiliation is all too palpable. Words upon words, word after word, ad infinitum, the continuing logomachy of the Western mind-set, proclaiming in profusion a point that could be made succinctly.

Yet the awareness of the duplicitous nature of all ontological constructs need not lead to such profligacy. This seemingly devastating indictment of logocentrism can also be read within a heuristic, rather than a destructive, framework. John Caputo, in *Radical Hermeneutics*, would read this diagnosis as a prescription for "living in the flux," or "dancing on the edge of the abyss."[21] Thus, if one is not prepared for the ruthlessness of nihilism (however extravagant the consequent frolics as cited by Raschke, Taylor, and company) Caputo's route is a feasible one, though I am not sure that it would receive Derrida's unequivocal approval, as Caputo's work is still suffused with a nostalgia for presence. Caputo, in his buoyant reading of Derrida, relates the breaching of metaphysics by deconstructive sorties to moments of conceptual discontinuity. Here he makes a qualitative leap, without the benefit of any Buddhist regime of dislocation, and discerns a sacred space in the disruptive excess of deconstruction that can foster further disclosure. Caputo detects such moments in the work of other philosophers in the Western tradition: "What breaks down in the breakthrough is the spell of conceptuality."[22] While these conceptual collapses would simply indicate the bankruptcy of their former claims for Derrida, they indicate something more radical for Caputo. It is similar to the Buddhist insight into the nature of our pretences to control, but lacks the Buddhist method of dismantling of all notions of self, reality, as unsubstantial figments. Yet the identity that Caputo envisages does echo the Buddhist discovery, behind and beyond conventional appearances, of another reality:

> After tracing out this deconstructive course, after allowing the disseminating drift its full play, we are in an odd way led *back* to ourselves, not in a moment of recovery and self-presence but in a deeper less innocent way.[23]

On a basic level Caputo prescribes the remedy of radical hermeneutics as one that moves beyond the confines of traditional paradigms. In his view, abstractions have always obscured the matter they describe. For Caputo, awareness of their ultimate futility to capture the absolute permits a chastened acknowledgment of an unconditioned, unthematized ground that forever eludes description. This is a mystery that can never be deciphered. Neither deconstruction nor radical hermeneutics can prove or disprove the existence of this realm. For Caputo, this mystery encompasses the existence of God, as well as those personal potentialities that can never be predicted. It is thus never be to be considered as an original innocence or as an ideal identity. It is what emerges if we do not seek to control the process. So it is that the dance on the abyss need not a dithyramb to the forces of dissolution, but a paean to the nimble of mind and foot who celebrate the recognition of the breakdown/breakthrough of human presumptions to capture the mystery. It is from this perspective that Caputo can say:

> I do not think that Derrida undoes the very idea of religious revelation but that he undoes a lot of the ideas of revelation that religious writers have preferred for some time now.[24]

Caputo's work also introduces an interesting hypothesis that I will not be able to pursue fully in this context. Toward the end of *Radical Hermeneutics* he states:

> The best we can do, after "owning up" to the elusiveness which envelops us all, is to let all things—gods, earth, and mortals—be.[25]

His main exemplar of this condition of living "without a why" is Meister Eckhart, who adapted this very prominent theme of the Beguines.[26] As described earlier, this total abandonment of all creaturely efforts and conventions was a prerequisite for the mystical experience that, for descriptive purposes within the Western worldview, has been depicted in the negative epithets of the apophatic tradition. In this sense it could be alleged that the Buddhist dialectic of Nāgārjuna has a formal intent similar to Western attempts to clear away the debris of wrongheaded approaches. It is in their schemas and modes of description that difficulties of comparison arise.

This is compounded when Caputo points out that a central idea in his procedure, *Gelassenheit*—"living without a way"—is a term that Heidegger borrowed from Eckhart. Caputo does not agree with the Derridean view that Heidegger was still in quest of an originary presence or essence. Instead, he believes that Heidegger was aware that the ontotheological heritage obfuscated the human predicament and did not let us see ourselves as we are in a nonqualified way. Hence *Gelassenheit* for Caputo is not an ontological restoration of some primordial essence, but the recognition of "that which we have been all along." This explains Caputo's predilection for the work of Eckhart and Heidegger, for it would appear that, in their quest for an unconditioned, they are also attempting to break those logocentric chains that bind us. All conceptual crutches are to be removed, so that one can see the world just as it is. A Buddhist would describe this as *"Tathatā."* Though similar in description, there is not an actual equivalence involved here. For unlike the Buddhist discipline, Caputo's modest proposal stops short of calling for a drastic reorganization of our lifestyle. Caputo is content to invoke an intellectual breakthrough. It is the mind that is free to play, unfettered by conceptual restrictions. The scrupulous and exacting demands involving the complete eradication of any reliance on notions of the self, as in Buddhist discipline, is not required.

Still Caputo is not the only one to catch a glimpse of these connections, though I don't believe he perceives their full implications. Controversial though his associations may be, Mahāyāna Buddhist scholar Daisetz T. Suzuki also grasped a similarity between his own ideas and those of Eckhart. The introductory chapter of his *Mysticism: Christian and Buddhist* is entitled "Meister Eckhart and Buddhism," and further comparisons are pursued in later chapters.[27] Suzuki's principal insight concerns "the circular and contradictory movement [that] characterizes our spiritual experience."[28] Suzuki discusses the misunderstanding that could arise if one were unaware of the interplay between what he terms the "absolute" and "relative" forms of knowledge. (This is the same assumption within the Buddhist orientation presented by Loy in the section of his paper entitled "The Two Truths.") Suzuki describes this interplay:

> To know God is "to go out" as the Biblical nobleman does according to Eckhart, and his "returning '" means knowing oneself as creature by knowing God. When the soul knows God it becomes conscious of its one-

> ness with God and at the same time it realizes how "dissimilar" it is.[29]

Suzuki is not concerned so much with the specific doctrinal contents of this insight as with its formal structures. The descriptions of Eckhart depend on a distinction between the God of revelation and the Godhead, which far surpasses any limited historical revelation. The Godhead, beyond any symbolic literalisms, is a living in the mystery that defies any intellectualizations. Expanding on this position, Suzuki alleges that by living out the implications of this ontological revolution one "comprehends" the gulf that separates the two dimensions. At the same time one realizes the relativity of any language, or system of knowledge, that tries to bridge the gap.

It is seeing, not defining, that is central to knowing in Buddhism. As Suzuki describes the process, what needs to be perceived is this very interplay of relative and absolute knowledge. "Enlightenment is seeing the absolute ego as reflected in the relative ego and acting through it."[30] It is achieving awareness of this manipulation as a product of one's own limited understanding. What the Buddha discovered were the machinations of the *gahakāraka* (the builder of the house) and his own entrapment in its wiles. In Suzuki's view then, *nirvāṇa* is not simply the eradication of the chains of desire, but insight into its effects on knowledge. In this way one is freed of its control.[31]

It is not the aim of this short exercise to determine whether Eckhart, Heidegger, and Suzuki are describing the same phenomena. What does seem possible to affirm is that each, in his own way, sought to express the inexpressible, beyond conventional formulas of knowledge. They all also posited another way of "knowing" that escaped the dilemmas of dualistic language. Ultimately this was impossible to describe, not necessarily because of the limitations of human language, though this was not a negligible consideration. Rather it was because the insights they achieved illuminated the utter futility of language. Language, as symptomatic of desire, impeded and distorted this perception.

Whether such unmediated vision is possible becomes a moot point. Nonetheless, what is at issue here is to what extent this modality of being is different from Derrida's logocentric and metaphyscial musings. Derrida himself admits that for all his maneuverings he remains within a metaphysical world. This is Heidegger's world of the twofold. Perhaps faith and belief are modes that should never be defined, let alone the "object" of their orientation. Grammars of assent always betray their origins. As we have seen, for various motivations, there are those who believe experience is all. The rest is silence.

The same dynamic of nonduality and its modes of expression is illustrated by Harold Coward's examination of Advaita Vedānta as expounded by Śaṅkara. Coward is accurate in his detecting an evident formal comparison of deconstruction with Vedānta's negative dialectic of *neti, neti,* as well as its subsequent dissolution of subject/object dichotomy, exemplified in *tat tvam asi.* But his conclusions as regards a virtual identification of its thematic intent with Derrida's agenda are questionable. Of course, such conjectures are plausible, but one could argue it either way—that is, either all forms of negative dialectic are simply deconstructive of any metaphysical assumptions, or all negative dialectics presuppose another order of consciousness.

Within Advaita Vedānta, this other modality of consciousness is referred to often as the Real, and *mokṣa,* or enlightenment, is its mode of access. Numerous articles, including one by Loy, have been devoted to the similarities/dissimilarities of *mokṣa* in Hinduism and *nirvāṇa* in Buddhism, as well as their appropriate rules and regulations.[32] Though both systems are in search of nonduality, their respective emphases differ. Advaita Vedānta distinguishes between *saguṇa* Brahman, the qualified world of everyday perception, and *nirguṇa* Brahman, or the Real, the unmediated world of direct discernment. The progress from one level of knowledge to another, together with its theoretical underpinnings, provide an interesting variant to the Buddhist approach. Both systems intend to deny the ontological status of the world of appearances. Buddhism does this by refuting theoretically, in a manner comparable to deconstruction, its cognitive claims, but it takes its conclusions further to dismantle even the existence of the world of appearances. Advaita Vedānta, in contrast, presupposes that, though all empirical knowledge of the world of appearances has value, it is ultimately illusory *(māyā).* Thus, once this "veil of ignorance" *(māyā)* is dispersed, nondual perception is possible, and one can have knowledge of Brahman. An addendum to this presupposition, which echoes Buddhist logic, allows that in the final analysis, there is no distinction between Atman (as that which underlies the everyday) and Brahman. As in Buddhism, such a conclusion can only be asserted from a nondual perspective.

This seeming contradiction would appear to fall into the trap of essentialism, of positing a Real that subsumes the world of appearances. However, this is not the case. Hinduism asserts that it is only from within the world of appearances that such a binary version of Reality is postulated. Once this fallacious worldview is exposed with its dubious dualisms, the undistorted Reality that pervades all is revealed. Obviously a much more discriminating inquiry can be undertaken as to the differences between the negative constructs of Nāgārjuna and those of Śaṅkara.[33] Suffice it to say, for present purposes, that after a detailed examination, David Loy concludes that their divergences are (phenomenologically speaking) obverse images:

> Because our linguistic categories and ordinary ways of thinking are inherently dualistic, it is natural to try to describe nondual experience by eliminating either the subject or the object. So we have seen how Vedānta makes absolute the unchanging Self-substance, Buddhism the impermanent world that is experienced.[34]

It would seem, nonetheless, that the category of Brahman/Atman, or Reality, within Hinduism could be deconstructed by Derrida as long as he believes it remains within a metaphysical mind-set, despite its adherents' protestations to the contrary. Coward, however, takes the opposite tack, arguing that Derrida's differential ordering can be construed as in the service of the Real, that is, that deconstruction is an operation of removing the rubble of false comprehension so that an undistorted vision may result. Ultimately Coward's comparison is not just formal but substantive.

Now Derrida, I am sure, would disown any formal resemblance to Vedānta. I do not think he would acquiesce to the implication made by Coward that Derrida himself is deconstructing the poles of opposition, from the perspective of difference, so as to move beyond the dualist nature of all language and concepts. The nature of the real, however described, must indeed be deconstructed, according to Derrida, but not in order liberate language for the benefit of another dimension. There is no Real for Derrida, merely endless proliferation, constant deferral of meaning. Nor do I believe that this process itself constitutes the real/Real in any way.

Coward's other point of comparison is between Derrida and Bhartṛhari. Now it seems to me that Bhartṛhari's version of enlightenment does not subscribe to the tenets of negative theology. For Bhartṛhari, as for Derrida, the linguistic domain is inescapable. However, for Bhartṛhari, it is hypostatized as Word. In one sense, this mystical identification of word/Word is not unrelated to that of the Logos of John's Gospel. As such, it is not immune to Derrida's deflations. But again Coward would see it otherwise. In his view, Bhartṛhari, as a grammarian, undertakes a type of spiritual therapy so as to refine the proper use of words—to render them worthy vehicles of transcendence. Coward understands Derrida to be engaged in a similar purgatory exercise. The Veda is the exemplary form by which all other articulations are judged. However, in Coward's opinion, this process of refinement cannot be considered just a static apotheosis of language, for it has ontological, rather than simply epistemological, repercussions. The implication is that this purification of language is also the practical path to self-realization.

By analogy, Coward thus believes that he can assert: "Deconstruction is the process of becoming self-aware, of self-realization" (216). But this seems a confusion of means and ends. For Derrida, deconstruction may indeed effect insight into the status of knowing, but that insight is concerned with the conditions of possibility/impossibility that circumscribe all modes of knowledge. If there is no self, there cannot be self-knowledge. We are indeed always already delimited by the very logocentric circumstances that are our only means of definition. Illusion, for Derrida, is to believe we can escape them.

Derrida's proliferation of language—the site of all speech and writing—is the inscription of the *trace,* of *différance*—that marks the condition of language. And while deconstruction may permit the clarification of this situation, there are no ontological resonances. This is not a spiritual insight. It is the recognition that we are bounded by words, and that these words will get us nowhere. There is no end, no whole, no origin. The process may be all, but this neither reifies or deifies it.

Coward's final insight is to remark on Derrida's prophetic, as opposed to apocalyptic, tone, a position he develops in "Of an Apocalyptic Tone Newly Adopted in Philosophy." The prophetic, in this instance, is viewed specifically as a call to action within a world whose future is not predetermined. Coward views this ethical imperative as common to both Derrida and Bhartṛhari, echoing his earlier comparison of their similar spiritual endeavors. In this connection, moral activity is regarded as the aim of deconstruction, and the formative influence on Derrida of the work of Levinas, with his emphasis on the trace and otherness, is cited. The underlying principles of Levinas do indeed imply the locus of absence as the source of reflection, and the subtle nuances of negation as the impulse of response, but I don't believe these can be identified with prophetic injunctions of the traditional variety.

For Levinas the human face, as the trace of the absent divine, as the locus of the ever-elusive Other, does establish the grounds of relationship. But Derrida is not interested in this paradigm of personal interaction. What captivates him is the idea of the absence of God. Divine Alterity is evoked not so much by prophetic exportations, nor by moral injunctions, as by rabbinic interpretation.

Derrida indeed is, as Susan Handelman depicts him, within a rabbinic tradition of heretic hermeneutics.[35] This brand of hermeneutics, with its deliberate inversions and deviations, mirrors the Jewish estrangement from easy solutions. It is a hermeneutics of exile, of absence, of constant interrogation. It is the form of Scripture that can occur only if God is absent, if God is silent, if God is a stranger even to himself. As Derrida suggests in his discussion of Jabès' *Book of Questions:*

> God separated himself from himself in order to let us speak, in order to astonish and to interrogate us. He did so not by speaking but by keeping still, by letting silence interrupt his voice and signs, by letting the Tables be broken.[36]

It does seem fitting that, if Derrida believed in a God, it would only be in a God whose very existence was a question mark, an enigma, whose (non)existence echoed through all human deliberations of his purported signs. In these procedures, signs are never symbols. Hermeneutics does not attain definitive meaning. Any utterance reflects the indeterminate situation of a displaced people, a people who never have the certainties of Greek metaphysics. The rupture between Athens and Jerusalem. Hegel's bad infinity. Derrida at once seeks to elude and to expose Hellenic-Christian convictions. The fact of the nonadvent of the Messiah is not a calamity. It marks instead the Judaic disposition that constantly explores the limits of any reconciliation, any expectation.

Derrida's affinity is with this *Book of Questions* as an indicator of subversive practices, as a symptom of his own dislocation. His exilic companions are Jabès and Levinas. Derrida finds within their hesitations, within their intimations of obscurity, the inevitable paradox of displacement where one may forever be a stranger to that which one desperately seeks. Yet what does Derrida seek, if anything? For finally it would seem to identify with a book, however subject to the play of *différance* within its covers, is to establish a form of identity. And here again Derrida will equivocate. Insofar as the book is symptomatic of writing, it remains indeterminate, but even so, to guard his flanks, Derrida will speculate about a principle that could exist prior to any book.

But before we explore these farther reaches of discontinuity, Michael Despland, on another tack, invites us to consider certain possible concordances with the idiom of deconstruction that could exist within our Greek inheritance. Despland proposes the option that perhaps Western thought has not always been susceptible to apocalyptic inclinations, perhaps there exist other avenues of ordering ourselves and our world. Now Derrida in "Of an Apocalyptic Tone" associates the apocalyptic with the mystagogic and situates both positions as the eternal alternative of the clear light of reason. The two delineate an interminable struggle, whereby false or obscure claimants will be continually disabused of their eschatological pretensions by the agents of enlightenment. These functionaries of reason with their apocalyptic tone nonetheless impose their sense of (an) ending(s). Derrida describes the inevitability, the insolubility of this omnipresent predicament. As Loy describes the situation, this condition of finitude without finality characterizes the human predicament.

In one sense, Despland would acquiesce with this state of affairs, but he does not wish to have Western philosophy and theology circumscribed completely by ordinances of an authoritarian nature. Phallogocentrism need not be the whole story. According to Despland there is a stand, discernible in the Greek operations, that realizes the limits of language. This manifests itself in two different ways.

One is the emphasis on action. Philosophy, on Despland's reading, was not merely uplifting dialogue but the means to the practical realization of the good life. While I do find Despland's attempted retrieval of the tradition from mere pompous verbosity appealing, I am aware of an equally formidable ascetic current from Plato onward. This preached that the good could only be obtained by eliminating the material, by attaining a higher spiritual state. I would have to admit this conflict, delineated in the struggle of mind/spirit with the wayward body (though it has practical implications), is but another manifestation of the apocalyptic impulse.

Despland also appeals to the distinction between didactic theology/philosophy and poetic illustrations of endorsed behavior within literary genres. In distinctive ways, Ulysses and Oedipus are personifications of conduct that is punished or rewarded. Specifically, the cunning of Ulysses and his encounters with Athena and Kirke win Despland's approval. But these contacts, however their metamorphoses upset the expected order, are tests of the hero. By his own guile, Ulysses at once deflates yet participates in many-layered subterfuges. He has a wily way with words and women. He is in one sense a prototypical deconstructive (anti)hero. Yet, in the end, he comes home. Order is restored. Rewards and punishments are apportioned.

Though aware of our inescapable involvement in this apocalyptic need for closure, Derrida would want us to remain alert to any restorations, to any reconciliations. Our suspicions should not be bought off by promises of security. For Derrida, all our deliberations, however public, must always occur within an orbit of continual testing, of constant vigilance. So it is that Despland's final invitation to theologians, while it involves the notions of heterogeneity and untranslatability, is weakened by his own unintentional apocalyptic disposition. And though he concedes that all writers are inextricably entangled in a web of language, he nonetheless proposes avenues of escape.

But is attitude all, as Despland suggests? Is irony sufficient? I would be very sympathetic to a reading or interpretation that incorporated the canny complicity of the Ulysses/Kirke/Athena encounters—but to my mind, the proponents still think they know the score. I would propose an alternate example of uncanny knowing, of suspicious yet open procedure, that nevertheless is evidence of the type of declaration (if not liberation) that can be made in the light of postmodern suspicion. It is Umberto Eco who delineates such an avowal in a time of easy entanglements, of fragile commitments:

> I think of the postmodern attitude as that of a man who loves a very cultivated woman and knows he cannot say to her, "I love you madly," because he knows that she knows (and that she knows that he knows) that these words have already been written by Barbara Cartland. Still, there is a solution. He can say, "As Barbara Cartland would put it, I love you madly." At this point, having avoided false innocence, having said clearly that it is no longer possible to speak innocently, he will nevertheless have said what he wanted to say to the woman: that he loves her, but he loves her in an age of lost innocence. If the woman goes along with this, she will have received a declaration of love all the same. Neither of the two speakers will feel innocent, both will have accepted the challenge of the past, of the already said, which cannot be eliminated, both will consciously and with pleasure play the game of irony. . . . But both will have succeeded, once again, in speaking of love.[37]

It would be an easy thing to play infinitely, to backtrack, to redouble one's efforts, to discredit any affirmation, to prevaricate without cessation. And, in this sense, Derrida is a *magister ludi.* But the play is serious. For, as he intimates at the end of the essay "Structure, Sign and Play, in the Discourse of the Human Sciences," it is "The as yet unnameable which is proclaiming itself." This disclosure, in the present circumstances, can only proclaim itself "under the species of the nonspecies, in the formless, mute, infant, and terrifying form of monstrosity."[38] Portentous nonsense or pious platitude? Obviously Derrida's appeals to negativity, otherness, and absence overturn the law of opposition as well as any negative dialectic. Equally obviously, the rule of undecidability must preside. And though he appeals to writing as the locus of this play of indetermination, Derrida nonetheless refuses to be confined even to its irresolute borders as drawn by Judaic tradition of disputation of the word.

Yet how to evoke this nonsite, the always already otherwise. For if, as Derrida intimates, language has indeed started without us, this process must not be associated, as it has mistakenly been by logocentrism, with God. On the other hand, this principle of absence, this alterity, is not to be confused with nonexistence. Nor, finally, should it succumb, as Derrida reads it, to the pretensions of negative theology, which negates only to confirm (though this confirmation can be detected by Derrida only because of the ambience of prayer within which it occurs).

And so, how is Derrida to avoid speaking of a question that is beyond him to formulate? For indeed, as he observes:

> The question about the origin of the book, the absolute interrogation, the interrogation about all possible interrogations, the "interrogation of God" will never belong to any book.[39]

And how is he to speak without speaking in a negative mode. For the possibility of the question can find its basis only in the absence of God, in a rupture, in a mode of negativity that defies, yet defines, conditions of language.

Derrida's ellipses would seem to be able to operate merely in an interrogative voice that undermines, yet remains within, its metaphysical qualifications. In this sense, deconstruction and negative theology traverse the same territory. But just as the ultimate positive intent of negative theology is disclosed for Derrida by its prayerful framework, so Derrida's own parallel interventions are situated within a (non)teleology of ultimate uncertainty.

With reference to writing, this ambience of indetermination is conveyed by the principle of illegibility.

> Prior to the book (in the nonchronological sense), original illegibility is therefore the very possibility of the

> book and, within it, of the ulterior and eventual opposition of "rationalism" and "irrationalism."[40]

And with reference to God, this indefinite modality is described by the (non)parameter of a "negative atheology,"[41] for the infinite is "doubtless neither one, nor empty, nor innumerable."[42] For according to the practice of deconstruction, the infinite cannot be affirmed or denied, neither accounted for nor dismissed. It stands forever irreducible. In this sense, it is perpetually under erasure: the ultimate question for which there is no answer, the answer with which no question is commensurate.

In this attempt to situate what could be described as the condition of (non)possibility for his strategy, Derrida's scheme corresponds to Kevin Hart's understanding of negative theology.[43] Hart's position is similar to that of Jean-Luc Marion, which Derrida discusses in "Denials." For Hart, as for Marion, the concept of God is always under erasure. Negative theology, on this reading, is not an overture to statements about God's mode of existence. In Hart's view it is, on the contrary,

> a supplement which is, strictly speaking, prior to all the statements of positive theology . . . [it] performs the deconstruction of positive theology . . . [it] reveals a non-metaphysical theology at work within positive theology.[44]

So rather than deconstruction being a form of negative theology, negative theology is itself a form of deconstruction. Negative theology has the intention, as does deconstruction, of deflating metaphyscial presumptions. In a further qualification Hart insists that mysticism must not be conflated with metaphysics, and that any rational suppositions to this effect must be foiled. Hart believes that Derrida unfortunately senses such a collusion of mysticism (specifically negative theology) with the methods of reason, so as to provide a solid grounding for faith. In contrast, Hart argues that negative theology disabuses mysticism of any claims by reason to supply the dimensions of God's existence. What God is will thus always remain a question. Negative theology, according to Hart, is always already the locus of that question.

The interrogative mode thus marks for both Derrida and Hart the domain of God's existence. But where Derrida will remain sceptical, faith will intervene for Hart. Which brings me back full circle, to the Beguines with whom I introduced my commentary. Ontotheology has traditionally employed the devices of reason, logic, and grammar to bring its constructs to the support of faith. The mystical tendency, with its experiential accent, has always been suspicious of this agenda. Its emotional elements presume another order of operation where reason is, in the end, irrelevant. Utter abandonment to love and its consequences is disconcerting. Perhaps this explains the readiness of ratiocinators throughout history to meet its challenges with charges of heresy or insanity. Perhaps it also explains Derrida's reluctance to meet it, even in its apophatic guise, on any other grounds than those of logocentrism.

## Notes

1. For an introduction, see *Beguine Spirituality*, ed. F. Bowie, trans. O. Davies (New York: Crossroad, 1990).

2. I am aware that my synthesis of these currents of thirteenth-century mysticism are somewhat cursory and are prone to the type of generalization that a discriminating reading of each woman would avoid. Unfortunately, the constraints of this assignment preclude such an undertaking. For more detailed studies, I would recommend: E. Zum Brunn and G. Epiney-Burgand, *Women Mystics in Medieval Europe*, trans. S. Hughes (New York: Paragon, 1989), and P. Dronke, *Women Writers of the Middle Ages* (Cambridge: Cambridge University Press, 1984). I am indebted to Ursula King and Peter Dronke, respectively, for recommending these volumes.

3. The identity of the author of the various works that have been attributed to Hadewijch is still the subject of speculation. There were no less 111 women named "Hadewijch" composing spiritual writings in the twelfth and thirteenth centuries.

4. For the expression, I am indebted to Zum Brunn and Epiney-Burgard, *Women Mystics*, p. xviii.

5. Ibid., p. 60.

6. Ibid., p. 138. In Zum Brunn and Epiney-Burgard, this work is attributed to Hadewijch II, not as usual to Hadewijch of Antwerp. The authors cite various reasons for this decision. See pp. 129–31.

7. Ibid., p. 166.

8. F. Nietzsche, "Twilight of Idols," in *The Portable Nietzsche*, ed. W. Kaufmann (New York: Viking, 1963), p. 483.

9. M. Heidegger, "Only a God Can Save Us," *Philosophy Today* (Winter 1976), p. 277.

10. J. Derrida, "The Ends of Man," in *Margins of Philosophy*, trans. Alan Bass (Chicago: University of Chicago Press, 1982), p. 135.

11. Carl A. Raschke, "The Deconstruction of God," in *Deconstruction and Theology* (New York: Crossroad, 1982), p. 28.

12. J. Caputo, *Radical Hermeneutics* (Bloomington: Indiana University Press, 1987).

13. J. Derrida, "Ousia and Grammē," *Margins of Philosophy*, p. 67.

14. J. Derrida, "How to Avoid Speaking: Denials," Chapter 3, pp. 73–142.

15. J. Derrida, "Of an Apocalyptic Tone Newly Adopted in Philosophy," Chapter 2, pp. 25–71.

16. In this response I do not wish to appear to be playing fast and loose with Buddhist categories, knowing that understandings of *śūnyatā* and *nirvāṇa* differ widely from school to school. Nor do I wish to appear to be making sweeping generalizations. Unless otherwise stated, my remarks will confine themselves within the parameters set by David Loy in his paper.

17. *The Holy Teaching of Vimalakīrti*, trans. Robert A. F. Thurman (University Park: Pennsylvania State University Press, 1981), p. 74.

18. David Loy, "The Clôture of Deconstruction: A Mahāyāna Critique of Derrida," *International Philosophical Quarterly* 27/1, no. 105 (March 1987), p. 80.

19. Ibid., p. 80.

20. D. Loy, *Nonduality* (New Haven: Yale University Press, 1988).

21. J. Caputo, *Radical Hermeneutics* (Bloomington: Indiana University Press, 1987), pp. 271–94.

22. Ibid., p. 270.

23. Ibid., p. 97.

24. J. Caputo, Review of books by Derrida, *Religious Studies Review* 16, no. 1 (Jan. 1990), p. 25.

25. Caputo, *Radical Hermeneutics*, p. 293.

26. Zum Brunn and Epiney-Burgard, *Women Mystics*, p. xxxi.

27. D. T. Suzuki, *Mysticism: Christian and Buddhist* (London: Unwin Hyman, 1970 [1988]).

28. Ibid., p. 63.

29. Ibid., p. 62.

30. Ibid., p. 34.

31. Suzuki's interpretation of Eckhart's experience as one that lets God be at the same time as letting oneself and all things be, is not without its critics. Reiner Schürmann contests this identification. He alleges that whereas Eckhart's 'isness' "is rooted in God as Being which is at once being and not-being. . . . the Buddhist 'isness' seems to refer to a thing's fact of being." Reiner Schürmann, *Meister Eckhart* (Bloomington: Indiana University Press, 1978), p. 221.

32. D. Loy, "Enlightenment in Buddhism and Advaita Vedānta: Are *Nirvāṇa* and *Mokṣa* the Same?" *International Philosophical Quarterly* 22, no. 1 (1982), pp. 65–74.

33. Loy, *Nonduality*, pp. 50–69; 191–201; 202–60.

34. Ibid., p. 261.

35. Susan Handelman, *The Slayers of Moses* (Albany: State University of New York Press, 1982), pp. 163–78.

36. J. Derrida, "Edmond Jabès and the Question of the Book," in *Writing and Difference*, trans. Alan Bass (Chicago: University of Chicago Press, 1978), p. 67.

37. U. Eco, *Postscript to the Name of the Rose* (New York: Harcourt Brace Jovanovich, 1984), pp. 67–68.

38. J. Derrida, "Structure, Sign, and Play in the Discourse of the Human Sciences," in *Writing and Difference*, pp. 278–93.

39. Derrida, "Edmond Jabès," p. 78.

40. Ibid., p. 77.

41. J. Derrida, "Ellipsis," in *Writing and Difference*, p. 297.

42. Ibid., p. 299.

43. Kevin Hart, *Trespass of the Sign* (New York: Cambridge University Press, 1989).

44. Ibid., p. 104.

NINE

# *Post-Scriptum: Aporias, Ways and Voices*

Jacques Derrida

Translated by John P. Leavey, Jr.

—More than one, it is necessary to be more than one to speak, several voices are necessary for that . . .

—Yes, and *par excellence,* let us say exemplarily, when it's a matter of God . . .

—Still more, if this is possible, when one claims to speak about God according to the apophatic [*l'apophase*], in other words, according to the voiceless voice [*la voix blanche*], the way of theology called or so called negative. This voice multiplies itself, dividing within itself: it says one thing and its contrary, God that is without being or God that (is) beyond being. The *apophatic* is a declaration, an explanation, a response that, taking on the subject of God a negative or interrogative form (that is also what *apophasis* means), at times resembles a profession of atheism as to be mistaken for it. All the more because the modality of *apophasis,* despite its negative or interrogative value, is often that of the sentence, verdict or decision, of the *statement.* I would like to speak to you, don't hesitate to interrupt me, of this multiplicity of voices, of this quite initial, but interminable as well, end of monologism—and of what follows . . .

—Like a certain mysticism, apophatic discourse has always been suspected of atheism. Nothing seems at once more merited and more insignificant, more displaced, more blind than such a trial [*procès*]. Leibniz himself was inclined to this. Heidegger recalls what he said of Angelus Silesius: "'With every mystic there are some places that are extraordinarily bold, full of difficult metaphors and inclining almost to Godlessness, just as I have sometimes seen in the German poems—beautiful besides—of a certain Angelus Silesius. . . .'"[1]

Inclining, but not going beyond incline or inclination, not even or almost (*beinahe zur Gottlosigkeit hinneigend*), and the oblique slope [*penchant*] of this clinamen does not seem separable from a certain boldness of language [*langue*], from a poetic or metaphoric tongue . . .

—And besides beautiful, don't forget, Leibniz notes this as if it were a matter of an addition or an accessory (*im übrigen schönen*), but I wonder if it isn't a matter there, beauty or sublimity, of an essential trait of negative theology. As for the example of Angelus Silesius . . .

—Let's leave this question aside for the moment: does the *heritage* of Angelus Silesius (Johannes Scheffler) belong or not to the tradition of negative theology in the strict sense? Can one speak here of a "strict sense"? You couldn't deny, I think, that Angelus Silesius keeps an evident kinship with apophatic theology. His example signifies for us, at this moment, only this affinity between the atheism suspected by Leibniz and a certain apophatic boldness. This apophatic boldness always consists in going further than is reasonably permitted. That is one of the essential traits of all negative theology: passing to the limit, then crossing a frontier, including that of a community, thus of a sociopolitical, institutional, ecclesial reason or *raison d'être*.

—If the apophatic inclines almost toward atheism, can't one say that, on the other hand or thereby, the extreme and most consequent forms of declared atheism will have always attested the most intense desire of God? Isn't that from then on a program or a matrix? A typical and identifiable recurrence?

—Yes and no. One apophatic [*apophase*] can in effect respond to, correspond to, correspond with the most insatiable *desire of God*, according to the history and the event of its manifestation or the secret of its nonmanifestation. The other apophatic, the other voice, can remain radically foreign to all desire, in any case to every anthropotheomorphic form of desire.

—But isn't it proper to desire to carry with it its own proper suspension, the death or the phantom of desire? To go toward the absolute other, isn't that the extreme tension of a desire that tries thereby to renounce its own proper movement, its own movement of appropriation?

—Attest, you were saying, attest the desire *of* God. The phrase is not only equivocal, of an equivocity essential, signifying, decisive in its very undecidability, to wit, the equivocity that the double genitive marks ("objective" and "subjective," even before the grammatical or ontological upsurge of a subject or an object), in other words, that of the origin and of the end of such a desire: does it come from God in us, from God for us, from us for God? And as we do not determine ourselves *before* this desire, as no relation to self can be sure of preceding it, to wit, of preceding a relation to the other, all reflection is caught in the genealogy of this genitive. I understand by that a reflection on self, an autobiographical reflection, for example, as well as a reflection on the idea or on the name of God. But your phrase is otherwise equivocal: when it names the testimony. For if atheism, like aphophatic theology, attests the desire of God, if it avows, confesses or indirectly signifies, as in a symptom, the desire of God, in the presence of whom does it do this? Who speaks to whom? Let us stay a little while with this question and feign to know what a discourse of negative theology is, with its determined traits and its own proper inclination. To whom is this discourse addressed? Who is its addressee? Does it exist before this interlocutor, before the discourse, before its actualization [*son passage à l'acte*], before its performative accomplishment? Dionysius the Areopagite, for example, articulates a certain prayer, turned toward God; he links it with an address to the disciple, more precisely to the becoming-disciple of him who is thus called to hear. An apostrophe (to God) is turned toward another apostrophe in the direction of him. . .

—Never of her . . .

—Not to my knowledge, of *him* who exactly does not yet know what he knows or should know, but should know with a nonknowledge, according to a certain nonknowledge. The hymn and the didactic become allied here according to a mode whose essential and thus irreducible originality would have to be recaptured. It is a matter of a singular movement of the soul or, if you prefer, of a conversion of existence that accords itself to, in order to reveal in its very night, the most secret secret. This conversion turns (itself) toward the other in order to turn (it) toward God, without there being an order to these two movements that are in truth the same, without one or the other being circumvented or diverted. Such a conversion is no doubt not without relation to the movement of the Augustinian confession . . .

—whose autobiographical character and what that confession inaugurates in this regard it would be as useless to recall; it would be naive to think that one knows what is the essence, the provenance, or the history of autobiography outside events like Augustine's *Confessions* . . .

—When he asks (himself), when he asks in truth of God and already of his readers why he confesses himself to God when God knows everything, the response makes it appear that what is essential to the avowal or the testimony does not consist in an experience of knowledge. Its act is not reduced to informing, teaching, making known. Stranger to knowing, thus to every determination or to every predicative attribution, confession shares [*partage*] this destiny with the apophatic movement. Augustine's response is inscribed from the outset in the Christian order of love or charity: as fraternity. The response is addressed to "brotherly and devout ears" (X, 34, 51), to a "brotherly mind," in order to make them better in charity (X, 4, 5). Confession does not consist in making known—and thereby it teaches that teaching as the transmission of positive knowledge is not essential. The avowal does not belong in essence to the order of cognitive determination; it is quasi-apophatic in this regard. As act of charity, love, and friendship in Christ, the avowal is destined to God and to creatures, to the Father and to the brothers in order to "stir up" love, to augment an affect, love, among them, among us (XI, 1, 1). For Augustine does not respond only to the question: why do I confess to you, God, who know all in advance? Augustine speaks of "doing the truth" (*veritatem facere*), which does not come down to revealing, unveiling, nor to informing in the order of cognitive reason. He responds to the question of public and written testimony.

I want "to do the truth," he says, "in my heart, in front of you, in my confession," but also "in my writing before many witnesses (*in stilo autem meo coram multis testibus*)" (X, 1, 1). And if he confesses in writing (*in litteris, per has litteras*) (IX, 12, 33; X, 3, 4), it is because he wants to leave a trace for his brothers to come in charity in order to stir up also, at the same time as his, the love of readers (*qui haec legunt*) (XI, 1, 1).[2] This moment of writing is done for "afterwards" ["*après*"]. But it also follows the conversion and remains the trace of a present moment of the confession that would have no sense without this trace, without this address to the brother readers: as if the act of confession and of conversion having *already* taken place between God and him, being as it were written (it is an *act* in the sense of archive or memory), it was necessary to add a *post-scriptum*—the *Confessions*, nothing less—addressed to brothers, those who are called to recognize one another as sons of God and brothers. But the address itself to God already implies the possibility and the necessity of this *post-scriptum* that is originarily essential to it. Its irreducibility is interpreted finally, but we won't elaborate on that here, in accord with Augustinian thought of revelation, memory, and time.

—Would you say that every *post-scriptum* necessarily lets itself be interpreted in the same horizon? And that it has the same structure?

—No, not without numerous precautions. But can a *post-scriptum* ever *be interpreted*, in the sense of hermeneutic reading as well as of musical performance, for example, without composing at least indirectly with the Augustinian scansion or score [*partition*]? An analogous question could be posed for all that we in the West call autobiography, whatever the singularity of its "here and now."

—Do you mean that every "here and now" of a western autobiography is already in memory of the *Confessions'* "here and now"?

—Yes, but the *Confessions* themselves were already, in their wildest present, in their date, in their place, an act of memory. Let us leave Augustine here, although he always haunts certain landscapes of apophatic mysticism (Meister Eckhart cites him often; he often cites the "without" of Saint Augustine, that quasi-negative predication of the singular without concept, for example: "God is wise *without* wisdom, good *without* goodness, powerful *without* power"). In this place of retreat you invited me to, in this town of familial exile where your mother has not finished dying, on the shore of the Mediterranean, I was able to carry with me, for this two weeks, only extracts from the *Cherubinischer Wandersmann* of Angelus Silesius[3] and the manuscripts of this volume here. All the time I am wondering if this work of Silesius indeed comes under negative theology. Are there sure criteria available to decide the belonging, virtual or actual, of a discourse to negative theology? Negative theology is not a genre, and first because it is not an art, a literary art, even if, as Leibniz justly remarked on Silesius, it is a matter there also of "German—beautiful besides—poems" full of "difficult metaphors." Is there, to take up again an expression of Mark Taylor, a "classic" negative theology?[4] One can doubt this, and surely we shall have to go back over this serious and limitless question. If the consequent unfolding of so many discourses (logic, onto-logic, theo-logic or not) inevitably leads to conclusions whose form or content is similar to negative theology, where are the "classic" frontiers of negative theology? The fact remains that the finale, the conclusion (*Beschluß*) of this book, and this leads us back to the question of the addressee, is a final address that says something of the end of discourse itself and is an address to the friend:

> Freund es ist auch genug. Jm fall du mehr wilt lesen,
> So geh und werde selbst die Schrifft und selbst das Wesen.
>
> Friend, let this be enough; if you wish to read beyond,
> Go and become yourself the writ and yourself the essence.
> [6:263]

The friend whose sex is not specified is asked, recommended, enjoined, *prescribed* to render itself, by reading, beyond reading: beyond at least the legibility of what is currently readable, beyond the final signature—and for that reason to write. Not to write this or that that falls outside his writing as a note, a *nota bene* or a *post-scriptum* letting writing in its turn fall behind the written, but for the friend itself to become the written or Writing, to become the essence that writing will have treated. (No) more place, starting from there, beyond, but nothing more is told us beyond, for a *post-scriptum*. The *post-scriptum* will be the debt or the duty, will have to (should) be resorbed into a writing that would be nothing other than the essence that would be nothing other than the being-friend or the becoming-friend of the other. The becoming (*Werden*), the becoming-friend, the becoming-writing, and the essence (*Wesen*) would be the same here.

—Certainly, but this essence (*Wesen*) that, in wanting to read more, the friend would become, writing itself, scripting itself, in writing [*dans l'écriture, en s'écrivant, en s'écriturant*], this essence will have *been* nothing before this becoming, that is, before this writing prescribed to the friend-reader. This essence is born from nothing and tends toward nothing. For earlier, didn't Silesius say . . .

—By what right are these aphorisms, these sententious fragments, or these poetic flashes linked together, as if they formed the continuous tissue of a syllogism? The final *Beschluß* is not the conclusion of a demonstration, but an *envoi*. Each speaking [*parole*] is independent. In any case, you cannot logically connect them in any manner without posing this problem of logic, form, rhetoric, or poetics. You cannot treat this peregrination of writing as a treatise of philosophy or theology, not even as a sermon or a hymn.

—Certainly, but in what remains the same book, one also read:

> *Nichts werden ist GOTT werden.*
> Nichts wird was zuvor ist: wirstu nicht vor zu nicht,
> So wirstu nimmermehr gebohrn vom ewgen Licht.
>
> *To become Nothing is to become God*
> Nothing becomes what is before: if you do not become nothing,
> Never will you be born of eternal light.
>
> (6:130)

How is this *becoming* to be thought? *Werden:* at once birth and change, formation and transformation. This coming to being starting from nothing and *as nothing, as God and as Nothing,* as the Nothing itself, this birth that carries itself without premise, this becoming-self as becoming-God—or Nothing—that is what appears impossible, more than impossible, the most impossible possible, more impossible than the impossible if the impossible is the simple negative modality of the possible.

—This thought seems strangely familiar to the experience of what is called deconstruction. Far from being a methodical technique, a possible or necessary procedure, unrolling the law of a program and applying rules, that is, unfolding possibilities, deconstruction has often been defined as the very experience of the (impossible) possibility of the impossible,[5] of the most impossible, a condition that deconstruction shares with the gift,[6] the "yes," the "come," decision, etc.

—The becoming-nothing, as becoming-self or as becoming-God, the becoming (*Werden*) as the engendering *of* the other, *ever since* the other, that is what, according to Angelus Silesius, is possible, but as more impossible still than the impossible. This "more," this beyond, this *hyper* (*über*) obviously introduces an absolute heterogeneity in the order and in the modality of the possible. The possibility of the impossible, of the "more impossible" that as such is also possible ("more impossible than the impossible"), marks an absolute interruption in the regime of the possible that nonetheless remains, if this can be said, in place. When Silesius writes:

> *Das überunmöglichste ist möglich.*
> Du kanst mit deinem Pfeil die Sonne nicht erreichen,
> Jch kan mit meinem wol die ewge Sonn bestreichen.
>
> *The most impossible is possible*
> With your arrow you cannot reach the sun,
> With mine I can sweep under my fire the eternal sun.
> (6:153)

The "*über*" of "*überunmöglichste*" moreover can signify just as well "most" or "more than": the most impossible or the more than impossible.

Elsewhere:

> Geh hin, wo du nicht kanst: sih, wo du sihest nicht:
> Hör wo nichts schallt und klingt, so bistu wo Gott spricht.
>
> Go there where you cannot; see where you do not see;
> Hear where nothing rings or sounds, so are you where God speaks.
> (1:199)

—The possibility of the impossible, of the "most impossible," of the more impossible than the most impossible, that recalls, unless it announces, what Heidegger says of death: "die Möglichkeit der schlechthinnigen Daseinsunmöglichkeit" ["the possibility of the absolute impossibility of Dasein"].[7] What is, for *Dasein*, purely and simply impossible is what is possible, and death is its name. I wonder if that is a matter of a purely formal analogy. What if negative theology were speaking at bottom of the mortality of *Dasein?* And of its heritage? Of what is written after it, according to [*d'après*] it? We shall no doubt come back to this.

—All the apophatic mystics can also be read as powerful discourses on death, on the (impossible) possibility of the proper death of being-there that speaks, and that speaks of what carries away, interrupts, denies, or annihilates its speaking as well as its own *Dasein*. Between the existential analytic of being-for-death, in *Sein und Zeit*, and the remarks of Heidegger on the theological, the theiological, and above all on a theology in which the word "being" would not even appear, the coherence seems to me profound and the continuity rigorous.

—What would this hyper-impossibility have to do, in the singular obscurity of this sun, with friendship? With the address to the friend?

—The questions of address and destination, of love and friendship (beyond even determinations of *philia* or charity) could lead us in numerous directions. In our place here and in the little time at our disposal, allow me to privilege one, only one, of these questions. What reunites us here, the two of us, after the Calgary colloquium on negative theology? Mark Taylor often questioned himself on the experience of what gathers or reunites, of *gathering*.[8] This colloquium has already taken place. A colloquium is a place one goes to (as to a synagogue, that place one comes to to gather together) to address oneself to others. At this colloquium in which we were not able, despite our desire, to participate directly, we had promised, you recall, to bring ourselves together in a certain form, with some delay, and by writing. In any case, the possibility of a colloquium—and then of speaking with one another—was indeed announced to *us*, a colloquium whose title bore the words "negative theology." Under what conditions was this project able to be announced? What can one desire to share there? What was one already able to share? Who then addresses whom? And what does "friendship" signify in this case?

—From the very beginning, and from the first word of our promise, you remember, we had thought we had to forgo, for countless reasons, a *post-scriptum* that was a long and detailed response. We have had above all to forgo an original discussion that is on the same scale as so many contributions whose richness and rigor, diversity too, we have admired and that we will still have much to learn from and to meditate on. Every immediate response would be hasty and presumptuous, in truth irresponsible and not very "*responsive.*" It will be necessary to *postpone* once more a true *post-scriptum.*

—What you seemed to care about, you said to me, was to manifest a gratitude whose meaning would not be without relation to what is called here negative theology and that in its turn would not risk, *not too much*, becoming ingratitude, an inversion that lies in wait to threaten all apophatic movements. And then no doubt you have more affinity, at the outset, an immediate affinity, given or cultivated, with particular participants, with particular discourses held here . . .

—What's the use of denying it? But also what's the use of remarking or underlining it? These shared portions [*partages*], these common inclinations, or these crossd paths appear from the reading of our respective texts, in particular those that are published right here. And if I have not yet ever met the other participants of the colloquium, it is also true that my friendship and my admiration, my gratefulness to Mark Taylor are not separable from his thought or his writings—from this one here.

Nevertheless, I would like to speak of another "community" (a word I never much liked, because of its connotation of participation, indeed fusion, identification: I see in it as many threats as promises), of another being-together than this one here, of another gathering-together of singularities, of another friendship, even though that friendship no doubt owes the essential to being- or gathering-together. I mean the friendship that permits such a meeting, and that very polylogue through which are written and read those for whom "negative theology," through the enigma of its name and its original lack of meaning, still signifies something and pushes them to address one another *under this name, in this name, and by this title.*

How, today, can one speak (that is, speak together, address someone) on the subject of and in the name of negative theology? How can that take place today, today still, so long after the inaugural openings of the *via negativa?* Is negative theology a "topic"? How would what still comes to us under the domestic, European, Greek, and Christian term of negative theology, of negative way, of apophatic discourse, be the chance of an incomparable translatability in principle without limit? Not of a universal tongue, of an ecumenism or of some consensus, but of a tongue to come that can be shared more than ever? One should wonder what signifies in this regard the friendship of the friend, if one withdraws it, like negative theology itself, from all its dominant determinations in the Greek or Christian world,[9] from the fraternal (fraternalist) and phallocentric schema of *philia* or charity, as well as from a certain arrested form of democracy.

—Friendship and translation, then, and the experience of translation as friendship, that is what you seem to wish we were speaking about. It is true that one imagines with difficulty a translation, in the current sense of the term, and whether it is competent or not, without some *philein*, without some love or friendship, without some "lovence" [*"aimance"*], as you would say, borne [*portée*] toward the thing, the text, or the other to be translated. Even if hatred can sharpen the vigilance of a translator and motivate a demystifying interpretation, this hatred still reveals an intense form of desire, interest, indeed of fascination.

—Those are experiences of translation, it seems to me, that make up this "Colloquium," and almost all the authors even give this to be remarked. Let it be said in passing, a translation (the nonoriginal version of a textual event that will have preceded it) also shares that curious status of the *post-scriptum* about which we are going around in circles.

—In which, rather, we discuss [*nous débattons*], we flounder [*nous nous débattons*]. How does negative theology always run the risk of resembling an exercise of translation? An exercise and nothing but? And an exercise in the form of a *post-scriptum?* How would this risk also give it a chance?

—Let's start again from this proposition, if you like: "What is called 'negative theology,' in an idiom of Greco-Latin filiation, is a language [*langage*]."

—Only a language? More or less than a language? Isn't it also what questions and casts suspicion on the very essence or possibility of language? Isn't it what, in essence, exceeds language, so that the "essence" of negative theology would carry itself outside of language?

—Doubtless, but what is called "negative theology," in an idiom of Greco-Latin filiation, is a language, at least, that says, in one mode or another, what we have just specified on language, that is, on itself. How does one leap out of this circle?

—Consequently, to believe you, an admissible disputing of this proposition of the type S is P ("what is called 'NT' . . . is a language," etc.) could not take the form of a refutation. It could not consist in giving a critique of its falseness, but in suspecting its vagueness, emptiness or obscurity, in accusing it of not being able to determine either the subject or the attribute of that judgment, of not even proving this learned ignorance, in the sense ennobled by Nicolas of Cusa or certain supporters of negative theology. The proposition ("what is called 'negative theology' . . . is a language") has no rigorously determinable reference: neither in its subject nor in its attribute, we just said, but not even in its copula. For it happens that, however little is known of the said negative theology . . .

—You avow then that we do indeed know something about it, we don't speak of it in the void, we come after this knowledge, however minimal and precarious. We pre-understand it . . .

—The pre-understanding then would be the fact from which we should indeed start, in relation to which we would be placed-after [*post-posés*]. We come *after the fact* [après le fait]; and the discursive possibilities of the *via negativa* are doubtless exhausted, that is what remains for us to think. Besides, they will be very quickly exhausted; they will always consist in an intimate and immediate analytic exhaustion [*exhaustion*] of themselves, as if they could not have any history. That is why the slightness of the reference corpus (here *The Cherubinic Wanderer*, for example) or the rarefaction of examples should not be a serious problem. We are in absolute exemplarity as in the aridity of the desert, for the essential tendency is to formalizing rarefaction. Impoverishment is de rigueur.

—These discursive possibilities are exhausted as formal possibilities, no doubt, and if we formalize to the extreme the procedures of this theology. Which seems feasible and tempting. Then nothing remains for you, not even a name or a reference. You can speak of exhaustion [*d'épuisement*] only in the perspective of this complete formalization and in posing as extrinsic to this formal or conceptual completeness those "difficult metaphors . . . inclining almost to Godlessness," that poetic beauty too that Leibniz speaks about concerning Angelus Silesius. Thus you would oppose one form to the other, that of onto-logical formalism to that of poetics, and would remain prisoner of a problematic opposition between form and content. But this so traditional disjunction between concept and metaphor, between logic, rhetoric, and poetics, between sense and language, isn't it a philosophical pre-judgment that not only one can or must deconstruct, but that, in its very possibility, the event named "negative theology" will have powerfully contributed to calling into question?

—I only wanted to recall that we pre-understood *already* and then that we write *after* pre-understanding negative theology as a "critique" (for the moment let's not say a "deconstruction") of the proposition, of the verb "be" in the third person indicative and of everything that, in the determination of the essence, depends on this mood, this time, and this person: briefly, a critique of ontology, of theology, and of language. To say "What is called 'negative theology,' in an idiom of Greco-Latin filiation, is a language" is then to say little, almost nothing, perhaps less than nothing.

—Negative theology means (to say) very little, almost nothing, perhaps something other than something. Whence its inexhaustible exhaustion . . .

—That being the case, can one be authorized to speak of this apparently elementary *factum*, perhaps indeterminate, obscure or void and yet hardly contestable, to wit, our pre-understanding of what is "called 'negative theology' . . . ," etc.? What we are identifying under these two words, today, isn't it first of all a corpus, at once open and closed, given, well-ordered, a set of statements [*un ensemble d'énoncés*] recognizable either by their family resemblance or because they come under a regular logicodiscursive type whose recurrence lends itself to a formalization? This formalization can become mechanical . . .

—All the more mechanizable and easily reproducible, falsifiable, exposed to forgery and counterfeit since the statement of negative theology empties itself by definition, by vocation, of all intuitive plenitude. *Kenōsis* of discourse. If a phenomenological type of rule is followed for distinguishing between a full intuition and an empty or symbolic intending [*visée*] forgetful of the originary perception supporting it, then the apophatic statements *are, must be* on the side of the empty and then of mechanical, indeed purely verbal, repetition of phrases without actual or full intentional meaning. Apophatic statements represent what Husserl identifies as the moment of *crisis* (forgetting of the full and originary intuition, empty functioning of symbolic language, objectivism, etc.). But in revealing the originary and final necessity of this crisis, in denouncing from the language of crisis the snares of intuitive consciousness and of phenomenology, they destabilize the very axiomatics of the phenomenological, that is also, the ontological and transcendental, critique. Emptiness is essential and necessary to them. If they guard against this, it is through the moment of prayer or the hymn. But this protective moment remains structurally exterior to the purely apophatic instance, that is, to *negative* theology as such, if there is any, in the strict sense, which can at times be doubted. The value, the *evaluation* of the quality, of the intensity, or of the force of events of negative theology would then result from this *relation* that articulates *this* void [*vide*] on the plenitude of a prayer or an attribution (theo-logical, theio-logical, or onto-logical) negated [*niée*], let's say denegated [*déniée*]. The criterion is the measure of a *relation*, and this relation is stretched between two poles, one of which must be that of positivity de-negated.

—From what does this redoubtable mechanicity result, the facility that there can be in imitating or fabricating negative theology (or as well a poetry of the same inspiration, of which we indeed have examples)? From the fact, I believe, that the very functioning of these statements resides in a formalization. This formalization essentially does without, tends essentially to do without all content and every idiomatic signifier, every presentation or representation, images and even names of God, for example, in this tongue or that culture. In brief, negative theology lets itself be approached (pre-understood) as a corpus largely archived with propositions whose logical modalities, grammar, lexicon, and very semantics are already accessible to us, at least for what is determinable in them.

—Whence the possibility of a canonizing monumentalization of works that obey laws, that seem docile to the norms of a genre and an art, that repeat traditions, that present themselves as iterable, influential or influenceable, objects of transfer, of credit and of discipline. For there are masters and disciples there. Recall Dionysius and Timothy. There are exercises and formations, there are schools, in the Christian mystical tradition as well as in an ontotheological or meontological (more Greek) tradition, in its exoteric or esoteric forms.

—Certainly, and he is already a disciple, however inspired, the one who wrote that not only God but the deity surpasses knowledge, that the singularity of the unknown God overflows the essence and the divinity, thwarts the oppositions of the negative and the positive, of being and nothingness, of thing and nonthing, and thus transcends all the theological attributes:

*Der unerkandte GOtt.*
Was GOtt ist weiß man nicht: Er ist nicht Licht, nicht Geist,
Nicht Wonnigkeit, nicht Eins [Derrida's version: Nicht Wahrheit, Einheit, Eins], nicht was man Gottheit heist:
Nicht Weißheit, nicht Verstand, nicht Liebe, Wille, Gütte:
Kein Ding, kein Unding auch, kein Wesen, kein Gemütte:
Er ist was ich, und du, und keine Creatur,
Eh wir geworden sind was Er ist, nie erfuhr.

*The Unknowable God*
What God is one knows not: He is not light, not spirit,
Not delight, not one [Not truth, unity, one], not what is called divinity:
Not wisdom, not intellect, not love, will, goodness:
No thing, no no-thing either, no essence, no concern:
He is what I, or you, or any other creature,
Before we became what He is, has never come to know.
(4:21)

—The following maxim [*sentence*] is precisely addressed to Saint Augustine as if to someone close, a master and a predecessor that he can amicably or respectfully challenge: "Stop, my *Augustine:* before you have penetrated God to the bottom (*ergründen*), one will find the entire sea in a small pit (*Grüblein*)" [4:22].

—Angelus Silesius had his own peculiar genius, but already he was repeating, continuing, importing, transporting. He would transfer or translate in all the senses of this term because he already *was writing after.* He kept the archive, kept in memory the teaching of Christoph Köler. He had read Tauler, Ruysbroeck, Boehme, and above all Eckhart.

—What we ought to start from, if I understand you right (and this would be the a *priori* of our *a posteriori,* to wit, of this *post-scriptum* we are engaged in), is this astonishing *fact* [fait], this *already done* [déjà fait], this *all done* [tout fait]: while negating or effacing all, while proceeding to eradicate every predicate and claiming to inhabit the desert . . .

—The desert is one of the beautiful and difficult metaphors that Leibniz was no doubt speaking of, but I am also struck by its recurrence, in other words, by the *typical striking* that reproduces the metaphor like a seal. Thus:

*Man muß noch über GOtt.*
. . . Wol sol ich dann nun hin?
Jch muß noch über GOtt in eine wüste ziehn.

*One must go beyond God*
. . . What should my quest then be?
I must beyond God into a desert flee.

(1:7)

Or again:

*Die Einsamkeit.*
Die Einsamkeit ist noth: doch sey nur nicht gemein:
So kanstu überall in einer Wüsten seyn.

*Solitude*
Solitude is necessary, but be only not (in) public,
So you can everywhere be in a desert.

(2:117)

And elsewhere it is a question of "desert times (*in diser wüsten Zeit*)" (3:184). Isn't the desert a paradoxical figure of the *aporia?* No [*pas de*] marked out [*tracé*] or assured passage, no route in any case, at the very most trails that are not reliable ways, the paths are not yet cleared [*frayés*], unless the sand has already re-covered them. But isn't the uncleared way also the condition of *decision* or *event*, which consist in opening the way, in (*sur*)*passing*, thus in going *beyond?*

—Despite this desert, then, what we call negative theology grows and cultivates itself as a memory, an institution, a history, a discipline. It is a culture, with its archives and its tradition, and accumulates the *acts* of a tongue [*langue*]. That in particular is what the phrase "What is called 'negative theology,' in an idiom of Greco-Latin filiation, is a language" would suggest. However much one recalls (one precisely must recall and recall that that proves the possibility of the memory kept) that negative theology "consists," through its claim to depart from all consistency, in a language that does not cease testing the very limits of language, and exemplarily those of propositional, theoretical, or constative language . . .

—By that, negative theology would be not only a language and a testing of language, but above all the most thinking, the most exacting, the most intractable experience of the "essence" of language: a discourse on language, a "monologue" (in the heterological sense that Novalis or Heidegger gives to this word) in which language and tongue speak for themselves and record [*prennent acte de*] that *Die Sprache spricht.* Whence this poetic or fictional dimension, at times ironic, always allegorical, about which some would say that it is only a form, an appearance, or a simulacrum. . . . It is true that, simultaneously, this arid fictionality tends to denounce images, figures, idols, rhetoric. An iconoclastic fiction must be thought.

—However much one says, then, that beyond the theorem and constative description, the discourse of negative theology "consists" in exceeding essence and language, it *remains. . .*

—What does "remain" mean here? Is it a modality of "being"?

—I don't know. Perhaps this, precisely, that this theology would be nothing . . .

—To be nothing, wouldn't that be its secret or declared vow? What do you believe you are thus threatening it with? Our discussion still supposes that this theology is something (determinable) and not nothing and wants to be or become something rather than nothing. Now we meant, just a moment ago too, to claim the contrary . . .

—A question of reading or hearing [*l'oreille*]. In any case, negative theology would be nothing, very simply nothing, if this excess or this surplus (with regard to language) did not imprint some mark on some singular events of language and did not leave some remains on the body of a tongue . . .

—A corpus, in sum.

—Some trace remains right in this corpus, becomes this corpus as *sur-vivance* of the apophatic (more than life and more than death), survivance of an internal ontologicosemantic auto-destruction: there will have been absolute rarefaction, the desert will have taken place, nothing will have taken place but this place. Certainly, the "unknowable God" (*"Der unerkandte GOtt,"* 4:21), the ignored or unrecognized God that we spoke about says nothing; of him there is nothing said that might hold . . .

—Save his name . . .

—that names nothing that might hold, not even a divinity (*Gottheit*), nothing whose withdrawal [*dérobement*] does not carry away every phrase that tries to measure itself against him. "God" "is" the name of this bottomless collapse, of this endless desertification of language. But the trace of this negative operation is inscribed *in* and *on* and *as* the *event* (what *comes*, what there is and which is always singular, what finds in this kenosis the most decisive condition of its coming or its upsurging). *There is* this event, which remains, even if this remnance is not more substantial, more essential than this God, more ontologically determinable than this name of God of whom it is said that he names nothing that is, neither this nor that. It is even said of him that he is not what *is given there* in the sense of *es gibt:* He is not what gives, he is beyond all gifts ("*GOtt über alle Gaben,*" 4:30).

—Don't forget that that is said in the course of a prayer that asks God to give himself rather than gifts: "Giebstu mir dich nicht selbst, so hastu nichts gegeben": "If you don't give yourself to me, then you have given nothing." Which interprets again the divinity of God as gift or desire of giving.

*In* and *on,* you said, that implies, apparently, some *topos* . . .

— . . . or some *khōra* (interval, place, spacing). Everything is played out here. For this emplacement displaces and disorganizes also all our ontotopological prejudices, in particular our objective science of space.

—You well know that, in nearly all its Greek, Christian, or Jewish networks [*filières*], the *via negativa* conjugates reference to God, the name of God with the experience of place. The desert is also a figure of the pure place. But figuration in general results from this spatiality, from this locality of the word [*parole*].

—Yes, Angelus Silesius writes this about the word (*das Wort*), that is to say, about the divine word as well, and some translate *Wort* here just simply by God:

> *Der Ort ist das Wort.*
> Der ort und's *Wort* ist Eins, und wäre nicht der ort
> (Bey Ewger Ewigkeit!) es wäre nicht das *Wort.*
>
> *The Place is the word*
> The place and the *word* is one, and were the place not
> (of all eternal eternity!) the *word* would not be.
>
> (1:205)

—Not objective nor earthly, this place comes under no geography, geometry, or geophysics. It is not *that in which* is found a subject or an object. It is found in us, whence the equivocal necessity of recognizing it and at once of getting rid of it:

> *Der Orth ist selbst in dir.*
> Nicht du bist in dem Orth, der Orth der ist in dir!
> Wirfstu jhn auß, so steht die Ewigkeit schon hier.
>
> *The place is itself in you*
> It is not you in the place, the place is in you!
> Cast it out, and here is already eternity.
>
> (1:185)

—The here (*hier*) of eternity is situated there, already (*schon*): already there, it situates this throwing [*jet*] or this throwing up [*rejet*] (*Auswerfen* is difficult to translate: at once exclusion, putting aside, throwing out [*rejet*], but first of all throwing that puts outside, that produces the outside and thus space, separates the place from itself). It is from this already that the *post-scriptum* finds its place—and fatally.

—As if in response, it is already in correspondence with what Mark Taylor will have written of the "pretext of the text" which "is a before that is (always) yet to come." Or again with his question: "What is the *Ort* of the *W-ort?*"[10]

—The event remains at once in and on language, then, within and at the surface (a surface open, exposed, immediately overflowed, outside of itself), in and on the mouth, on the tip [*bout*] of the tongue, as is said in English and French, or on the edge of the lips passed over by words that *carry* themselves toward God. They are *carried* by a movement of *ference* (transference, reference, differance) toward God. They name God, speak of him, speak *him*, speak *to him*, *let him speak in them*, let themselves be carried by him, make (themselves) a reference to just what the name supposes to name beyond itself, the nameable beyond the name, the unnameable nameable.

—Certainly, but *in* and *on* a language that, while being opened by this *ference*, says the inadequation of the reference, the insufficiency or the lapse of knowing, its incompetence as to what it is said to be the knowing of. Such an inadequation translates and betrays the absence of a common measure between the opening, openness [*apérité*], revelation, knowledge on the one hand and on the other a certain absolute secret, nonprovisional, heterogeneous to all manifestation. This secret is not a reserve of potential [*potentiel*] knowing, a potential [*en puissance*] manifestation. And the language of ab-negation or of renunciation is not negative: not only because it does not state in the mode of descriptive predication and of the indicative proposition simply affected with a negation ("this is not that"), but because it denounces as much as it renounces; and it denounces, enjoining; it prescribes overflowing this insufficiency; it orders: *it is necessary* to do the impossible, *it is necessary* to go (*Geh*, Go!) there where one cannot go. A question of place, again. I shall say in French: *il y a lieu de* (which means "*il faut*," "it is necessary," "there is ground for") rendering oneself *there where* it is impossible to go. To go where it is possible to go would not be a displacement or a decision, it would be the irresponsible unfolding of a program. The sole decision possible passes through the madness of the undecidable and the impossible: to go where (*wo*, *Ort*, *Wort*) it is impossible to go:

Geh hin, wo du nicht kanst: sih, wo du sihest nicht:
Hör wo nichts schallt und klingt, so bistu wo Gott spricht.

(1:199)

—According to you, it is this normative denunciation on the ground of impossibility, this sweet rage against language, this jealous anger of language within itself and against itself that leaves the mark of a scar in that place where the impossible takes place, isn't it?

—Is there some other thing, ever, that may be legible? Some other thing than the trace of a wound? And some other thing that may ever take place? Do you know another definition of event?

—But nothing is more illegible than a wound, as well. I suppose that in your eyes legibility and illegibility do not equal two in this place. According to you, it is this trace in any case that becomes legible, renders and renders itself legible: in and on language, that is, at the edge of language . . .

—There is only the edge in language. . . . That is, reference. From the supposed fact that there is never anything but reference, an irreducible reference, one can *just as well* conclude that the referent is or is not indispensable. All history of negative theology, I bet, plays itself out in this brief and slight axiom.

—"At the edge of language" then would mean: "at the edge as language," in the same and double movement: withdrawing [*dérobement*] and overflowing [*débordement*]. But as the moment and the force, as the *movements* of the injunction take place *over the edge* [pardessus bord], as they draw their energy *from having already taken place*—even if it is as a promise—the legible-illegible text, the theologico-negative maxim [*sentence*] remains as a *post-scriptum.* It is originarily a *post-scriptum,* it comes after the event . . .

—an event, if I understand right, that would have the form of a seal, as if it were committed to keeping a secret, the event sealed with an indecipherable signature.

—The sealed event corresponding to the experience of a *trait* (drawn line, *Zug,* edge, border, overflowing, relation to the other, *Zug, Bezug,* ference, reference to some *other* thing than self, differance), the deferred action [*l'après-coup*] is indeed the coming of a writing after the other: *post-scriptum.*

—The trace of this wounded writing that bears the stigmata of its own proper inadequation: signed, assumed, claimed . . .

— . . . of its own proper disproportion also, of its *hubris* thus countersigned: that cannot be a simple mark identical to self . . .

— . . . as if there ever were any . . .

—That cannot be a signature uneffaced, ineffaceable, invulnerable, legible for what it is on a surface, right on a support that would only equal one with (it)self. The very support remains improbable. This mark takes place after taking place, in a slight, discreet, but powerful movement of dis-location, on the unstable and divided edge of what is called language. The very unity of what is called language becomes enigmatic and uncertain there.

—And so the phrase "What is called 'negative theology' . . . is a language" says at once too much and too little. It no longer has the intelligibility of a sure axiom, no longer gives the chance of a consensus, the charter of a colloquium or the assured space of a communication.

—Let's not yet discedit the phrase. Let's provisionally keep it, as a guiding thread, as if we had need of it and need of going further.

—Don't all the apophatic theologemes have the status or rather the movement, the instability of this trajectory? Don't they resemble arrows, darts [*traits*], a grouped firing of arrows destined to point in the same direction? But an arrow is only an arrow; it is never an end in itself.

—Silesius says this well when he speaks precisely of the possibility of the most impossible or of the more than the most impossible (*"Das überunmöglichste ist möglich"*). It specifies, you recall:

> With your arrow you cannot reach the sun,
> With mine I can sweep under my fire the eternal sun.
> (6:153)

—Let's keep this proposition ("What is called 'negative theology' . . . is a language"). Let's try to question it in its most manifest meaning, *at face value*. And let's come back to the theme of *philein*, let's say rather of lovence [*aimance*] as transfer or translation.

—These themes are not localizable, but let's go on.

—Do you want us to act as if they were? Appearance gives us the impression that the expression "negative theology" has no strict equivalent outside two traditions, philosophy or ontotheology of Greek provenance, new-testament theology or Christian mysticism. These two trajectories, these two paths [*trajets*] thus arrowed would cross each other in the heart of what we call negative theology. Such a crossing . . .

—Everything here, you realize, seems crucial: the crossroads of these two paths, the *kreuzweise Durchstreichung* under which Heidegger erases the word being (which his theology to come would have had, he says, to dispense with), and the *Gevier* to which he claims then to refer, the Christian cross under which Marion himself erases the word God . . .

—That's true. In any case, the expression "negative theology" names most often a discursive experience that is situated at one of the angles formed by the crossing of these two lines. Even if one line is then always *crossed*, this line is situated in that place. Whatever the translations, analogies, transpositions, transferences, metaphors, never has any discourse expressly given itself this title (negative theology, apophatic method, *via negativa*) in the thoughts of Jewish, Muslim, Buddhist culture.

—Are you sure that this title has never been claimed by any author for his very own discourse, even in the traditions you invoke?

—I was only wanting to suggest that in the cultural or historical zone in which the expression "negative theology" appears as a sort of domestic and controlled appellation, the zone in sum of that Christian philosophy whose concept Heidegger was saying was as mad and contradictory as that of a squared circle, the apophatic has always represented a sort of paradoxical hyperbole.

—That's a name quite philosophical and quite Greek.

—From this paradoxical hyperbole, let's retain here the trait necessary to a brief demonstration. Let's be more modest, to a working hypothesis. Here it is. What permits localizing negative theology in a historial site and identifying its very own idiom is also what uproots it from its rooting. What assigns it a proper place is what expropriates it and *engages* it thus in a movement of universalizing translation. In other words, it is what engages it in the element of the most shareable [*partageable*] discourse, for example, that of this conversation or of this colloquium in which are crossed thematics Christian and nonchristian, philosophical and nonphilosophical, European and noneuropean, etc.

—Do you see in this *engagement* something that is allied with this singular friendship you spoke about just a moment ago with gratefulness—and apropos gratitude?

—I don't know. All this remains very preliminary, as preliminary as a *post-scriptum* can be. If I use words as philosophical and Greek as "paradoxical hyperbole," I do so first of all, among other things, to point [*faire signe*] toward a well-known passage of Plato's *Republic. Huperbolē* names the movement of transcendence that carries or transports *epekeina tēs ousias.* This excessive movement, the firing of this displacing arrow [*cette flèche en déplacement*] encourages saying: X "is" beyond what is, beyond being or beingness [*étantité*]. Let X here be the Good, it matters little for the moment, since we are analyzing the formal possibility of saying: X "is" beyond what "is," X is without being [*sans (l')être*]. This hyperbole *announces.* It announces in a double sense: it signals an open possibility, but it also provokes thereby the opening of the possibility. Its event is at once revealing and producing, *post-scriptum* and inaugural writing. Its event announces what comes and makes come what will come from now on in all the movements in *hyper, ultra, au-delà, beyond, über,* which will precipitate discourse or first of all existence.

—You said "existence," if I understand right, in order not to say "subject," "soul," "spirit," "ego," nor even *Da-sein.* And yet *Dasein* is open to being as being through the possibility of going beyond the present of what is.

—To be sure, and Heidegger does indeed understand *Dasein* thus; he describes the movement of its transcendence by explicitly citing the Platonic *epekeina tēs ousias.* But then he seems to understand/hear the beyond as the beyond of the totality of beings and not as the beyond of being itself, in the sense of negative theology. Now the hyperbolic movements in the Platonic, Plotinian, or Neoplatonic style will not only precipitate beyond being or God as he is (the supreme being), but beyond God even as name, as naming, named, or nameable, as reference is made there to some thing.

—Besides, the beyond as beyond God is not a place, but a movement of transcendence that surpasses God himself, being, essence, the proper or the selfsame, the *Selbst* or *Self* of God, the divinity of God (*Gottheit*)—in which it surpasses positive *theology* as well as what Heidegger proposes to call *theiology*, discourse on the divinity (*theion*) of the divine. Angelus Silesius, again:

*Man muß noch über GOtt.*
. . .
Jch muß noch über GOtt in eine wüste ziehn.

(1:7)

*Die über-GOttheit.*
Was man von GOtt gesagt, das gnüget mir noch nicht:
Die über-GOttheit ist mein Leben und mein Liecht.

*The beyond divinity*
What was said of God, not yet suffices me:
The beyond divinity is my life and my light.

(1:15)

—In this movement that carries itself beyond, being and knowing, existence and knowledge are radically dissociated. It is as it were a fracture of the *cogito* (Augustinian or Cartesian) as the *cogito* gives me to know not only *that*, but *what and who* I am. This fracture is as valid for me as for God and extends its crack into the analogy between God and me, creator and creature. This time the analogy does not repair, nor reconcile, but aggravates the dissociation.

*Man weiß nicht was man ist.*
Jch weiß nicht was ich bin. Jch bin nicht was ich weiß:
Ein ding und nit ein ding: Ein stüpffchin und ein kreiß.

*One knows not what one is*
I know not what I am. I am not what I know:
A thing and not a thing: a point and a circle.

(1:5)

And here is, hardly much farther, the analogy, the "*wie*":

*Jch bin wie Gott, un Gott wie ich.*
Jch bin so groß als GOtt: Er ist als ich so klein:
Er kan nicht über mich, ich unter Jhm nicht seyn.

*I am as God, and God as I*
I am as big as God: He is as small as I:
He cannot be over me, I cannot be under him.
(1:10)

—I am always sensitive to this unusual alliance of *two powers* and of *two voices* in these poetic aphorisms or in these declarations without appeal, above all when the *I* advances there in this way, at once alone with God and as the example that is authorized to speak for each one, without waiting for any response or fearing discussion. Contrary to what we said at the beginning of our conversation, there is also a monologism or soliloquy in these imperturbable discourses: nothing seems to disquiet them. These two powers are, *on the one hand,* that of a radical critique, of a hypercritique after which nothing more seems assured, neither philosophy nor theology, nor science, nor good sense, nor the least *doxa,* and *on the other hand,* conversely, as we are settled beyond all discussion, the authority of that sententious voice that produces or reproduces mechanically its verdicts with the tone of the most dogmatic assurance: nothing nor no one can oppose this, since we are in the element of assumed contradiction and of claimed paradox.

—The double power of these two voices is not without relation with the *double bind* of ex-appropriation or of the uprooting rooting I spoke about just before. On one hand, in effect, this theology launches or carries negativity as the principle of auto-destruction in the heart of each thesis; in any case the theology suspends every thesis, all belief, all *doxa* . . .

—In which its *epokhē* has some affinity with the *skepsis* of scepticism as well as with the phenomenological reduction. And contrary to what we said a few minutes ago, transcendental phenomenology, as it passes through the suspension of all *doxa,* of every positing of existence, of every thesis, inhabits the same element as negative theology. One would be a good propaedeutic for the other.

—If you like, but this is not incompatible with what we said about the language of crisis. But let's leave that. *On the one hand,* then, placing the thesis in parenthesis or in quotation marks ruins each ontological or theological proposition, in truth each philosopheme as such. In this sense, the principle of negative theology, in a movement of internal rebellion, radically contests the tradition from which it seems to come. Principle against principle. Parricide and uprooting, rupture of belonging, interruption of a sort of social contract, the one that gives right to the State, the nation, more generally to the philosophical community as rational and logocentric community. Negative theology uproots itself from there after the fact [*après coup*], in the torsion or conversion of a second movement of uprooting, as if a signature was not countersigned but contradicted in a codicil or in the remorse of a *post-scriptum* at the bottom of the contract. This contract rupture programs a whole series of analogous and recurrent movements, a whole outbidding of the *nec plus ultra* that calls to witness the *epekeina tēs ousias*, and at times without presenting itself as negative theology (Plotinus, Heidegger, Levinas).

But *on the other hand*, and in that very way, nothing is more faithful than this hyperbole to the originary ontotheological injunction. The *post-scriptum* remains a countersignature, even if it denies this. In the most apophatic moment, even when one says: God is not, or is not either this or that, not this nor its contrary; or again, being is not, etc.; even then it is still a matter of saying the entity [*étant*] such as it is, in its truth, even were it meta-metaphysical, meta-ontological. It is a matter of holding the promise of saying the truth at any price, of rendering oneself to the truth of the name, to the thing itself such as it must be named by the name, that is, beyond the name. It is a matter of recording the referential transcendence of which the negative way is only one way, one methodic approach, one series of stages. Angelus Silesius, among others, specifies this well when he adds, in a sort of note or *post-scriptum* to sentence 1:7, *"Man muß noch über GOtt":* "beyond all one knows of God or can think of him, according to negative contemplation (*nach der verneinnenden beschawung*), about which search through the *mystics*."

—Then you wouldn't say that the *Cherubinic Wanderer* comes under negative theology.

—No, certainly not in any sure, pure, and integral fashion, although the *Cherubinic Wanderer* owes much to it. But I would no more say that of any text. Conversely, I trust no text that is not is some way contaminated with negative theology, and even among those texts that apparently do not have, want, or believe they have any relation with theology in general. Negative theology is everywhere, but it is never by itself. In that way it also belongs, without fulfilling, to the space of the philosophical or ontotheological promise that it seems to break [*renier*]: to record, as we said a moment ago, the referential transcendence of language; to say God such as he is, beyond [*par delà*] his images, beyond this idol that being can still be, beyond what is said, seen, or known of him; to respond to the true name of God, to the name to which God responds and corresponds beyond the name that we know him by or hear. It is to this end that the negative procedure refuses, denies, rejects all the inadequate attributions. It does so in the name of a way of truth and in order to hear the name of a just voice. Its authority we spoke about a few minutes ago comes from the truth in the name and on the way of which it raises the voice—and that speaks through its mouth: *alētheia* as the forgotten secret that sees itself thus unveiled or the truth as promised adequation. In any case, desire to say and rejoin what is *proper* to God.

—But what is this proper, if the proper of this proper consists in expropriating itself, if the proper of the proper *is* justly having nothing of its own [*en propre*]? What does "is" mean here?

—That's Silesius's question:

*GOttes Eigenschafft.*
Was ist GOtts Eigenschafft? sich in Geschöpff ergiessen
Allzeit derselbe seyn, nichts haben, wollen, wissen.*

*God's own proper*
What is God's own proper? to pour forth in creation,
To be the same in all times, to have, want, know nothing.*
(2:132)

But the *post-scriptum* adds a decisive philosophical precision: a remorse reinscribes this proposition within the ontology that opposes essence to accident, necessity to contingency:

> *Understand this *accidentaliter* (*Verstehe* accidencialiter) or in a contingent way (*oder zufälliger weise*); for what God wants and knows, he knows and wants essentially (*wesentlich*). Thus he has nothing else (by way of property [or quality: *mit Eigenschafft*]).

Now this revolution, at once interior and exterior, that makes philosophy, ontotheological metaphysics, pass over the other edge of itself, is also the condition of its translatability. What makes philosophy go outside itself calls for a community that overflows its tongue and broaches [*entame*] a process of universalization.

—What makes it go outside itself would come to it thus already from the outside, from the absolute outside. That is why the revolution could not be only internal [*intestine*].

—That's exactly what the revolution says, what the mystics and the theologians of the apophatic say when they speak of an absolute transcendence that announces itself within. All that comes down to the same or, indifferently, to the other. What we've just said about philosophical Greece is also valid for the Greek tradition or translation of the Christian revelation. *On the one hand,* in the interior, if one can say this, of a history of Christianity . . .

—But for a while now I have the impression that it is the idea itself of an identity or a self-interiority of every tradition (*the one* metaphysics, *the one* ontotheology, *the one* phenomenology, *the one* Christian revelation, *the one* history itself, *the one* history of being, *the one* epoch, *the one* tradition, self-identity in general, the one, etc.) that finds itself contested at its root.

—In effect, and negative theology is one of the most remarkable manifestations of this self-difference. Let's say then: in what one *could believe* to be the interior of a history of Christianity (and all that we have read of Silesius is through and through overdetermined by the themes of Christian revelation, other citations would have demonstrated this at any moment), the apophatic design is also anxious to render itself independent of revelation, of all the literal language of New Testament eventness [*événementialité*], of the coming of Christ, of the Passion, of the dogma of the Trinity, etc. An immediate but intuitionless mysticism, a sort of abstract kenosis, frees this language from all authority, all narrative, all dogma, all belief—and at the limit from all faith. At the limit, this mysticism remains, after the fact [*après coup*], independent of all history of Christianity, *absolutely* independent, detached even, perhaps absolved, from the idea of sin, freed even, perhaps redeemed, from the idea of redemption. Whence the courage and the dissidence, potential or actual, of these masters (think of Eckhart), whence the persecution they suffered at times, whence their passion, whence this scent of heresy, these trials, this subversive marginality of the apophatic current in the history of theology and of the Church.

—Thus, what we analyzed a few minutes ago, this rupture of the social contract but as a process of universalization, is what would be regularly reproduced . . .

—You could almost say normally, inevitably, typically . . .

—as dissidence or heresy, *pharmakos* to be excluded or sacrificed, another figure of the passion. For it is true that, *on the other hand,* and according to the law of the same *double bind,* the dissident uprooting, *responding* thus to the call and to the gift of Christ, such as they would resound everywhere, in the ages of ages, and rendering itself responsible for them before him, that is, before God, can claim to fulfill, in its most historic essence, the vocation or the promise of Christianity.

Besides, hidden or visible, metaphoric or literal (and with regard to the apophatic vigilance, this rhetoric on rhetoric moves itself as if into a state of dogmatic somnambulism), the reference to the Gospel is most often constitutive, ineffaceable, prescribed. See, for example, this "figure" of Christian interiorization that makes here of the heart a Mount of Olives, as Saint Paul speaks elsewhere of the circumcision of the heart:

> *Der Oelberg.*
> Sol dich deß Herren Angst erlösen von beschwerden,
> So muß dein Hertze vor zu einem Oelberg werden.
>
> *Mount of Olives*
> Should the Lord's agony redeem you of your sin,
> Your heart must become first a Mount of Olives.
>
> (2:81)

—But don't you believe that a certain Platonism—or Neoplatonism—is indispensable and congenital here? "Plato, in order to dispose to Christianity" [*Pensées* 612/219], said Pascal, in whom one could at times discern the genius or the machine of apophatic dialectics . . .

—As is the case everywhere. And when Silesius names the eyes of the soul, how is one not to recognize there a vein of the Platonic *heritage?* But that can be found again elsewhere and without filiation. One can always affirm and deny a filiation; the affirmation or the assumption of this *inherited* debt as de-negation is the *double truth of filiation,* like that of negative theology.

—But isn't it more difficult to replatonize or rehellenize creationism? Now creationism often belongs to the logical structure of a good many apophatic discourses. In this way, creationism would also be their historic limit, in the double sense of this word: the limit *in* history and the limit *as* history. Like that of hell, the concept of creature is indispensable to Angelus Silesius. When he says to us, "Go there where you cannot go," it is to develop the title, in a way, of this maxim [*maxime*], to wit, "*GOtt ausser Creatur,*" "God outside the creature" (1:199). If the proper of God is not to have properties, it is, as we heard, because God pours forth "in creation (*ins Geschöpf*)" . . .

—But what if that signified, in place of being a creationist dogma, that creation means expropriating production and that everywhere there is ex-appropriation there is creation? What if that were only a redefinition of the current concept of creation? Once more, one should say of anything or anybody what one says of God or some other thing. One would respond thus in the same way to the question "Who am I?" "Who are you?" "What is the other?" "What is anybody or anything as other?" "What is the being of beings as completely other?" All the examples are good ones, even if they all show that they are singularly though unequally good.

—I have no objection to this hypothesis. Everything would remain intact after the passage of the *via negativa.* That explains, besides, if not a certain quietism, at least the role that *Gelassenheit plays* in the thought of Silesius, and first of all the role that *play* itself does not fail to play in the thought of divine creation:

*GOtt spielt mit dem Geschöpffe.*
Diß alles ist ein Spiel, das Jhr die GOttheit macht:
Sie hat die Creatur umb Jhret willn erdacht.

*God plays with creation.*
All that is play that the deity gives itself:
It has imagined the creature for Its pleasure.

(2:198)

—Negative theology then can only present itself as one of the most playful forms of the creature's participation in this divine play, since "I" am "as" "God," you recall. There remains the question of what gives rise and place to this play, the question of the place opened for this play between God and his creation, in other terms, for ex-appropriation. In the maxim "*GOtt ausser Creatur,*" the *ad-verb* that says the place (*wo*) gathers the whole enigma:

> Geh hin, wo du nicht kanst: sih, wo du sihest nicht:
> Hör wo nichts schallt und klingt, so bestu wo Gott spricht.
> [1:199]

This adverb of place says the place of the word [*verbe*] of God, of God as word, and "*Der Ort ist das Wort*" (1:205) indeed affirms the place as word [*parole*] of God.

—Is this place created by God? Is it part of the play? Or else is it God himself? Or even what precedes, in order to make them possible, both God and his Play? In other words, it remains to be known if this nonsensible (invisible and inaudible) place is opened by God, by the name of God (which would again be some other thing, perhaps), or if it is "older" than the time of creation, than time itself, than history, narrative, word, etc. It remains to be known (beyond knowing) if the place is opened by appeal (response, the event that calls for the response, revelation, history, etc.), or if it remains impassively foreign, like *Khōra,* to everything that takes its place and replaces itself and plays within this place, including what is named God.

—Do we have any choice? Why choose between the two? Is it possible? But it is true that these two "places," these two experiences of place, these two ways are no doubt of an absolute heterogeneity. One place excludes the other, one (sur)passes the other, one does without the other, one is, absolutely, *without* the other. But what still relates them to each other is this strange preposition, this strange with-without or without-with, *without.* The logic of this junction or of this joining (conjunction-disjunction) permits and forbids at once what could be called exemplarism. Each thing, each being, you, me, the other, each X, each name, and each name of God can become the example of other substitutable Xs. A process of absolute formalization. A name of God, in a tongue, a phrase, a prayer, becomes an example of the name and of names of God, then of names in general. *It is necessary* (*il faut*) to choose *the best* of the examples (and it is necessarily the absolute good, the *agathon*, that finds itself to be, then, *epekeina tēs ousias*), but it is the best *as example:* for what it is and for what it is not, for what it is and for what it represents, replaces, exemplifies. And the "it is necessary" (the best) is also an example for all the "it is necessary"s that there are and can be.

—"Il faut" does not only mean it is necessary, but, in French, etymologically, "it lacks" or "is wanting." The lack or lapse is never faraway.

—This exemplarism joins and disjoins at once, dislocates the best as the indifferent, the best as well as the indifferent: *on one side*, on one way, a profound and abyssal eternity, fundamental but accessible to the teleo-eschatological narrative and to a certain experience or historical (or historial) revelation; *on the other side*, on the other way, the nontemporality of an abyss without bottom or surface, an absolute impassibility (neither life nor death) that gives rise to everything that it is not. In fact, two abysses.

—But the two abysses Silesius speaks about are two examples of the first abyss, the profound, the one that you have just defined first, although it is not in any way first, precisely. Silesius writes:

*Ein Abgrund rufft dem andern.*
Der Abgrund meines Geists rufft immer mit Geschrey
Den Abgrund GOttes an: Sag welcher tieffer sey?

*One abyss calls the other*
The abyss of my spirit always invokes with cries
The abyss of God: say which may be deeper?

(1:68)

—It is just this singular exemplarism that at once roots and uproots the idiom. Each idiom (for example, Greek ontotheology or Christian revelation) can attest for itself and for what it is not (not yet or forever), without this value of testimony (martyr) being itself totally determined by the inside of the idiom (Christian martyr, for example). There, in this testimony offered not to oneself but to the other, is produced the horizon of translatability—then of friendship, of universal community, of European decentering, beyond the values of *philia*, of charity, of everything that can be associated with them, even beyond the European interpretation of the name of Europe.

—Are you implying that it is on this condition that one can organize international and intercultural colloquiums on "negative theology" (I would now put quotation marks on this expression).

—For example. It is necessary in any case to think the historial and a-historial possibility of this project. Would you have imagined such a colloquium only a century ago? But what seems possible becomes by that very way infinitely problematic. This double paradox resembles a double aporia: simultaneous negation and re-affirmation of Greek onto-theology and metaphysics, uprooting and expansion of Christianity, in Europe and outside of Europe, at the very moment when vocations, some statistics tell us, seem on the wane there . . .

—I am thinking of what is happening in Europe itself in which the Pope appeals to the constitution or to the restoration of a Europe united in Christianity—which would be its very essence, and its destination. He tries to demonstrate, in the course of his voyages, that the victory over the totalitarianisms of the East has been carried off thanks to and in the name of Christianity. In the course of the so-called Gulf war, the allied western democracies often kept up a Christian discourse while speaking of international law. There would be too much to say here, and that is not the subject of the colloquium.

—On one hand, this negation, as reaffirmation, can seem to double bolt the logocentric impasse of European domesticity (and India in this regard is not the absolute other of Europe). But on the other hand, it is also what, working on the *open* edge of this interiority or intimacy, *lets* (laisse) passage, *lets the other be.*

—*Laisser* is a difficult word to translate. How are they going to translate it? By "to leave," as in the phrase that won't be long in coming shortly when we will have to go our separate ways (I leave you, I am going, *I leave*) or else "to let"?

—Here it is to the German idiom that we shall have to have recourse. Silesius writes in the tradition of the *Gelas-*

*senheit* that goes from Eckhart, at least, to Heidegger. It is necessary to leave all, to leave every "something" through love of God, and no doubt to leave God himself, to abandon him, that is, at once to leave him and (but) let him (be beyond being-something):

*Das etwas muß man lassen.*
Mensch so du etwas liebst, so liebstu nichts fürwahr:
GOtt ist nicht diß und das, drumb laß das Etwas gar.

*One must leave the something*
Man, if you love something, then you love nothing truly:
God is not this and that, leave then forever the something.
(1:44)

Or again:

*Die geheimste Gelassenheit.*
Gelassenheit fäht GOtt: GOtt aber selbst zulassen,
Jst ein Gelassenheit, die wenig Menschen fassen.

*The most secret abandon*
Abandon seizes God; but to leave God Himself,
Is an abandonment that few men can grasp.
(2:92)

—The abandonment of this *Gelassenheit*, the abandonment *to* this *Gelassenheit* does not exclude pleasure or enjoyment; on the contrary, it gives rise to them. It opens the play *of* God (of God and with God, of God with self and with creation); it opens to the enjoyment *of* God:

*Wie kan man GOttes genissen.*
GOtt ist ein Einges Ein, wer seiner wil geniessen,
Muß sich nicht weniger als Er, in Jhn einschlissen.

*How one can enjoy God*
God is a unique One; whoever wants to enjoy Him
Must, no less than He, be enclosed in Him.
(1:83)

—To let passage to the other, to the totally other, is hospitality. A double hospitality: the one that has the form of Babel (the appeal to universal translation but also the violent imposition of the name, of the tongue, and of the idiom) *and* the one (another, the same) of the deconstruction of the

Tower of Babel. The two designs are moved by a certain desire of universal community, beyond the desert of an arid formalization, that is, beyond economy itself. But the two must deal [*traiter*] with what they claim to avoid: the untreatable itself. The desire of God, God as the other name of desire deals in the desert with radical atheism.

—In listening to you, one has more and more the feeling that *desert* is the other name, if not the proper place, of *desire*. And the at times oracular tone of the apophatic, to which we alluded a few minutes ago, often resounds in a desert, which does not always come down to preaching in the desert.

—The movement toward the universal tongue oscillates between formalism, or the poorest, most arid, in effect the most desertlike technoscientificity, and a sort of universal hive of inviolable secrets, of idioms that are never translated except as untranslatable seals. In this oscillation, "negative theology" is caught, comprised and comprehensive at once.

But the Babelian narrative (construction and deconstruction at once) is still a (hi)story. Too full of sense. Here the invisible limit would pass less between the Babelian project and its deconstruction than between the Babelian place (event, *Ereignis*, history, revelation, eschatoteleology, messianism, address, destination, response and responsibility, construction and deconstruction) and "something" without thing, like an indeconstructible *Khōra:* the place that gives rise and place to Babel would be indeconstructible, not as a construction whose foundations would be sure, sheltered from every internal or external deconstruction, but as the very spacing of de-construction. There is where that happens and where there are those "things" called, for example, negative theology and its analogs, deconstruction and its analogs, this colloquium here and its analogs.

—What do you mean, by reassuring yourself in these "analogies"? That there is a singular chance in the transfer or the translation of that of which negative theology would be a sort of *analogon* or general equivalent, in the translatability uprooting but also returning this *analogon* to its Greek or Christian economy? That this chance would be that of a singularity doing today some other thing than losing itself in the community?

—Perhaps. But I would not yet speak of human, nor even anthropotheocentric, community or singularity, nor even of a *Gevier* in which what is called "animal" would be a mortal passed over in silence. Yes, the *via negaiva* would perhaps today be the passage of the idiom into the most common desert, as the chance of law [*droit*] and of another treaty of universal peace (beyond what is today called international law, that thing very positive but still so tributary of the European concept of the State and of law, then so easy to arraign [*arraisonner*] for particular States): the chance of a promise and of an announcement in any case.

—Would you go so far as to say that today there is a "politics" and a "law" of negative theology? A juridico-political lesson to be drawn from the possibility of this theology?

—No, not to be drawn, not to be deduced as from a program, from premises or axioms. But there would no more be any "politics," "law," or "morals" *without* this possibility, the very possibility that obliges us from now on to place these words between quotation marks. Their sense will have wavered.

—But you admit at the same time that "without" and "not without" ["*pas sans*"] are the most difficult words to say and to hear/understand, the most unthinkable or most impossible. What does Silesius mean, for example, when he leaves us the inheritance of this maxim:

> *Kein Tod ist ohn ein Leben.*
>
> *No death is without life*
>
> (1:36)

and better:

> *Nichts lebet ohne Sterben.*
> GOtt selber, wenn Er dir wil leben, muß er sterben:
> Wie dänckstu ohne Tod sein Leben zuererben?
>
> *Nothing lives without dying*
> God himself, if He wants to live for you, must die:
> How do you think, without death, to inherit his own life?
> (1:33)

—Has anything more profound ever been written on inheritance? I understand that as a thesis on what *inherit* means (to say).

—Yes, as the "without," heritage, inheritance, filiation, if you prefer, is the most difficult thing to think and to "live," to "die." But don't forget that these maxims of Silesius, notably those that immediately surround them (1:30, 31, 32, 34, etc.), have a Christian sense, and the *post-scripta* of maxims 31 and 32 ("*God dies and live in us* / I do not die nor live: God himself dies in me," etc.) cite saint Paul in order to explain how it is necessary to read. A *post-scriptum* of Christian reading or self-interpretation can command the whole perspective of the *Cherubinic Wanderer,* and of all the "without"s, including "*GOtt mag nichts ohne mich*" (1:96), including "*GOtt ist ohne Willen*" (1:294), and including, whether Heidegger likes it or not, the "*Ohne warumb*" of "Die Ros' ist ohn warumb . . . " (1:289). If Heidegger doesn't like this, it is necessary for him to write another *post-scriptum,* which is always possible, and represents another experience of inheritance-syllabification.

The difficulty of the "without" spreads into what is still called politics, morals, or law, which are just as threatened as promised by the apophatic. Take the example of democracy, of the idea of democracy, of democracy to come (neither the Idea in the Kantian sense, nor the current, limited, and determined concept of democracy, but democracy as promise). Its path passes perhaps today in the world through (across) the aporias of negative theology that we just analyzed so schematically.

—How can a path pass through aporias?

—What would a path be without aporia? Would there be a way [*voie*] without what clears the way there where the way is not opened, whether it is blocked or still buried in the nonway? Would there be a way without the necessity of deciding there where the decision seems impossible? Would there be a decision there where the decision is possible and programmable? And would one speak, could one only speak of this thing? Would there be a voice [*voix*] for that?

—You recognize that the possibility then of speaking or walking seems just as impossible. So difficult in any case that this passage through aporia seems first of all (perhaps) reserved as a secret for a few. This esoterism seems strange for a democracy, even for this democracy to come that you define no more than the apophatic defines God. Its to-come would be jealously thought, watched over, hardly taught by a few. Very suspect.

—Understand me, it's a matter of maintaining a double injunction. Two concurrent desires divide apophatic theology, at the edge of nondesire, around the gulf and chaos of the *Khōra*: the desire to be inclusive of all (community, *koinē*) and the desire to keep or entrust the secret within the very strict limits of those who hear/understand it *right*, as secret, and are then capable or worthy of keeping it. The secret, no more than democracy or the secret of democracy, must not, besides cannot be entrusted to just anyone. Again the paradox of the example: the post-scriptum anyone (example as sample) must also give the *good* example. Understand me right when I say that, I am still citing Silesius, in this sort of *post-scriptum* that he adds to the maxim on "*The blessed silence* (*Das seelige Stilleschweigen*)" (1:19). It is a matter of understanding right a silence, as elsewhere the *Gelassenheit:*

> Wie seelig ist der Mensch, der weder wil noch weiß!
>
> How blessed the man who neither wishes nor knows!

And here is the Nota Bene as *post-scriptum:*

> Der GOtt (versteh mich recht) nicht gibet Lob noch Preiß.
>
> To God (understand me right) give neither praise nor glory.

And you remember that "few men" are ready to grasp the exemplary *Gelassenheit*, the one that not only grasps, but knows how to abandon God (2:92). The reserved, the most refined, the rarest secret is that of one *Gelassenheit* and not of the other, of this *Gelassenheit* here and not of another that resembles it, of this leaving-the-other-here and not of the other.

—But Angelus Silesius does not represent the whole, nor even the best example of "classic" or canonic negative theology. Why bring everything back to him?

—That is the accident or the contingency of my (hi)story, an autobiographical chance [*aléa*], if you like. It is the *Cherubinic Wanderer* (and still extracts only) that I chose to carry with me to this family place. At once because Silesius begins to be more familiar and friendly to me (I am recently interested in him because of sentences I have not cited today) and because it takes up little room in traveling (70 pages). Negative theology, we have said this enough, is also the most economical and most powerful formalization, the greatest reserve of language possible in so few words. Inexhaustible literature, literature for the desert, for the exile, always saying too much and too little, it holds desire in suspense. It always leaves you without ever going away from you.

Nice-Berlin, August 1991

## Notes

1. " 'Ben jenen Mystikern gibt es einige Stellen, die außerordentlich kühn sind, voll von schwierigen Metaphern und beinahe zur Gottlosigkeit hinneigend, so wie ich Gleiches bisweilen in den deutschen—im übrigen schönen—Gedichten eines gewissen Mannes bemerkt habe, der sich Johannes Angelus Silesius nennt . . .' " (Leibniz, Letter to Paccius, 28 January 1695, in *Leibnitii opera*, ed. L. Dutens [Geneva: 1768]: 6:56). Cited by Martin Heidegger, *Der Satz vom Grund* (Pfullingen: Neske, 1957), p. 68; *The Principle of Reason*, trans. Reginald Lilly (Bloomington: Indiana University Press,1992), p. 35 [modified].

2. Aurelius Augustine, *Confessionum*, ed. Martin Skutella (Stuttgart: Teubner, 1981); *The Confessions of St. Augustine*, trans. Rex Warner (New York: New American Library, 1963), pp. 243, 212, 257, 210 (modified), 207, 212, 257 respectively—Trans.

3. Angelus Silesius (Johannes Scheffler), *Cherubinischer Wandersmann*, ed. Louise Gnädinger (Stuttgart: Philipp Reclam, 1984); *The Cherubinic Wanderer*, trans. Maria Shrady (New York: Paulist, 1986). [*Trans.*—The translation by Shrady, which is a selection, does not contain all the maxims cited and has been modified in the translations cited. Concerning the editions he uses, Derrida states: "*La rose est sans pourquoi* (extracts from *Pélerin Chérubinique*, trans. Roger Munier [Paris: Arfuyen, 1988]). I nearly always modify the translation and reconstitute the original transcription in old Gerrnan, as it is found published in the complete edition of *Cherubinischer Wandersmann*, by H. Piard (Paris: Aubier, 1946) (bilingual ed.). Some of the maxims cited refer to this edition and are not found in the extracts proposed by Roger Munier." In this English translation I have followed Gnädinger's critical edition and indicated the one significant difference of versions in brackets in sentence 4:21.]

4. Mark Taylor, "nO nOt nO," pp. 176 and 186 above.

5. See notably J. Derrida, "Psyché: Invention de l'autre," in *Psyché: Inventions de l'autre* (Paris: Galilée, 1987), notably p. 59 and *passim;* "Psyche: Inventions of the Other," trans. Catherine Porter, in *Reading de Man Reading,* ed. Lindsay Waters and Wlad Godzich (Minneapolis: University of Minnesota Press, 1989), p. 60; and *Memoires, for Paul de Man,* rev. ed., trans. Cecile Lindsay, Jonathan Culler, Eduardo Cadava, and Peggy Kamuf (New York: Columbia University Press, 1986, 1989).

6. Numerous references to this subject are gathered in J. Derrida, *Donner le temps, 1. La fausse monnaie* (Paris: Galilée, 1991); translation by Peggy Kamuf forthcoming, University of Chicago Press, 1992.

7. Martin Heidegger, *Sein und Zeit,* 16th ed. (Tubingen: Niemeyer, 1986), § 50, p. 250; *Being and Time,* trans. John Macquarrie and Edward Robinson (New York: Harper, 1962), p. 294.

8. For example, pp. 168 and 187 above.

9. See J. Derrida, "The Politics of Friendship," trans. Gabriel Motzkin, *The Journal of Philosophy* 85:11 (November 1988): 632–44. That is the very schematic resumé of ongoing research on the history and the major or canonic traits of the concept of friendship.

10. Pp. 174 and 175 above.

# Index

*abhidharma (higher dharma)*, 232, 234. See also *dharma*
Academy, 89
Advaita Vedānta, 203, 205, 271
Advaitin, 205
affirmation, 7, 90–91, 189
affirmative theology, 11, 131. *See also* positive theology; theology
*agapè*, 109
*agogic* path, 129
Allemann, Beda, 129
analogical, 47; mediation, 103
analogy, 2, 3, 41–42, 74, 111, 112, 131, 318; Vedantin, 209
animal(s), 13,14,17, 86–88, 319
*Anti-Oedipus*, 240
*anubhava*, 209, 211
apocalypse, 25, 27, 31, 38, 40, 50, 53, 55, 56, 59, 61, 66, 67, 158, 170, 173, 244, 245–46; Buddhist, 246; Horsemen of, 62
apocalyptic, 36, 47, 51, 53, 57, 60, 64; desire, 158;—disclosure, 56;—talk, 158;—tone, 52, 53, 57, 60, 242, 243, 250, 266, 275;—voice, 58; Western, 50
*apokalupsis*, 25, 27
*apokalupō*, 26
Apollo, 103
apophantics, 53
apophasis, 6, 8, 88, 110, 114, 117–18, 119, 283
apophatic, 74, 114, 256, 283, 285, 318, 320;—atheology, 20;—discourse, 4. 76, 88, 98, 284, 293;—movement, 81, 122;—mysticism, 287, 291;—oracular tone, 318;—procedures, 97; theology, 3, 4,103,124,158, 284, 321;—thought, 6;—tradition, 100, 255; —utterances, 75, 296;—voyage, 79;—wager, 5
apophaticism, 2, 21
*aporia*, 105, 113, 228, 247, 316, 320
apostrophe, 116–17, 121, 130
appropriation, 10, 14, 18, 19, 68n, 285
Arab, 158
Arabic, 157
Arberry, Arthur J., *The Koran Interpreted*, 157
archetypes: theory of, 114
Aristotle, 44, 45, 105, 130, 136n, 139n 245; *Peri Hermeneias*, 136n; *Physics*, 105
atheism, 75, 76, 77, 284–85
Athena, 152–53, 276–77
atheological, 108
atheology, 195; negative, 279
*Ātman/ātman*, 19, 201, 204–5, 208, 272. *See also* Self/self
*atopos*, 96
Augustine, Saint, 78, 113, 120–21, 188, 199, 200, 211, 298; *Confessions*, 286–87
Augustinian, 307

Aurobindo, 206
Austine, J. L., 179
autonomy, 1, 2, 37, 99
Avatamsaka Sūtra, 235–36. *See also* Indra's net

Babel, 54, 63. *See also* Tower of Babel
Barth, Karl, 144
Barthes, Roland, 235
Bataille, Georges, 20
becoming (*Werden*), 289–90
Beguine(s), 255–56, 263, 268, 280
Being/being, 2,12, 74, 77–80, 90, 96, 97, 100–3, 105, 110, 113–14, 116, 118, 120–30, 177, 187, 188–90, 193, 214, 238, 240, 241, 243, 244, 250; God, as without, 77. *See also* nonbeing
Benjamin, Walter, 25, 157
Berkeley, George, 248
Bernard of Clairvaux, 113, 188
Bhartṛhari, 21, 206, 212–17, 222, 273–74; *Vākyapadīya*, 221
Blanchot, Maurice, 20, 55, 62, 64, 67, 133n, 167, 181, 185; *Last Man*, 49; *The Madness of the Day*, 50; "Viens", 177
bliss *(ānanda)*, 205, 208
bodhisattva(s), 232, 239
Boehme, Jacob, 298
Bouveresse, J, 146
Brahman Sutra, 201,220
Brahman, 19, 201–21, 271–72; formed (saguṇa), 203; formless (nirguṇa), 203, 205. See also nirguṇa; saguṇa
Bruno, Giordano, 100
Buddha, 228–32, 238, 239, 249, 270; nature, 235, 238
Buddhism, 19, 21, 227, 245, 248, 249, 265, 270, 305. *See also* Mahāyāna; philosophy, Buddhist
Buddhist apocalypse, 246

Candrakīrti, 249
Caputo, John, 267–69; *Radical Hemeneutics*, 258–59, 268
Cartesian, 106,123, 238, 307. *See also* Descartes, René
Cartland, Barbara, 277
castrating, 45
castration, 40, 42;—as metaphor, 43;—of reason, 43
causality, 247, 266
Cause, 91, 98
censorship, 59–60
Certeau, Michel de, 154
Ch'an. See Zen
*Cherubinic Wanderer, The*. *See* Silesius, Angelus, *Cherubinischer Wandersmann*
China, 235
Chouraqui, André, 25, 55, 68n, 71n; "Liminaire pour l'Apocalypse", 26–27
Christ, 62, 228–29, 286, 311
Christian, 40, 89, 100, 102, 108, 114, 116, 122, 123, 124, 144, 147, 186, 191, 194, 199, 262, 263;—apophases, 109;—apophatics, 97, 192, 211; Helenic–, 275; Judeo–, 16;—mysticism, 297, 305, 311;—negative theology, 100, 144, 145, 188, 190, 200, 202;—prayer, 111;—revelation, 315;—theologians, 147
Christianity, 18, 155, 156, 311, 316; end of, 48
Church, 19, 134n, 145, 312; seven, of Asia, 55
clitoris, 43
co-dependent origination, 158
*cogito*, 307
"Come", 62–67, 182, 185, 217, 245–46

consciousness, 12, 13, 17, 87, 88, 212, 216, 230, 271; as *caitanya*, 205; Cartesian, 238; divine, 206; end of, 51; human, 14; modality of, 271; pure, 222; witnessing, 205. *See also Śabdabrahman*
Copernican revolution, 47
Coward, Harold, 19, 20, 168, 271–74; "A Hindu Response to Derrida's View of Negative Theology", 21
creation, 313–14, 317
Cynics, 146

de Man, Paul, 179
(de)constitution, 10,11,13,18, 19
deception, 152–53
deconstruction, 2, 3, 4, 11, 12, 13, 20, 21, 51, 77, 88, 156, 176, 210, 215–16, 221, 227, 239, 240, 245, 250, 257–58, 261, 263, 264, 267, 271, 273, 279, 290, 317–18; Nāgārjuna's, 234, 247; therapeutic dimension to, 21
delerium, 36, 53, 241. See also *Verstimmung*
demiurge, 104, 187
demystification, 57, 59, 156, 158
demystifing desire, 58
demystify, 51, 60
denegation/*dénégation*, 7, 8, 9, 10, 12, 14, 19, 88, 129, 174–75, 184, 261
denial *(dénégation,)*, 95
Derrida, Jacques: "Désistance", 8, 9; "Des tours de Babel", 148; *Dieu sans être*, 12; "Différance", 2, 3, 4, 199; "Economimesis", 40; "Edmond Jabès and the Question of the Book", 206, 208–09, 211; Glas, 32, 40, 61,195; "How to Avoid Speaking: Denegations". *See* "How to Avoid Speaking: Denials"; "How to Avoid Speaking: Denials", 2, 4, 5, 9, 11, 12, 17, 19, 20, 147, 149, 158, 168–69; 171, 173, 177, 178, 186, 193, 200, 228, 241, 259–62, 279; "Living On", 20; "At This Very Moment in This Work Here I Am", 62; "Of an Apocalyptic Tone Newly Adopted in Philosophy", 19, 20, 148–49, 155, 157, 169–70, 173, 177, 217, 241, 259, 274, 275; *Of Grammatology*, 77, 215, 236; *Of Spirit: Heidegger and the Question*, 156; "Pas", 62, 133n, 185–86; *Spurs: Nietzsche's Styles*, 155; "Structure, Sing and Play, in the Discourse of the Human Sciences", 277; "The Ends of Man", 240; *The Post Card: From Socrates to Freud and Beyond*, 32, 38, 61, 62; "Violence and Metaphysics: An Essay on the Thought of Emmanuel Levinas", 217
Descartes, René, 105. *See also* Cartesian
desire(s), 15–16, 17, 18, 36, 51, 65, 229, 262, 266, 285, 321; appetitive, 18; apocalyptic, 158; secret, 19; sublimation of, 16
Despland, Michel, 19, 20, 275–77; "On Not Solving Riddles Alone", 20–21
*deus absconditus*, 255
*dharma*, 217, 230, 231. See also *abhidharma*
Dharmakīrti, 247
dialectic, 2, 8, 74, 103, 108; negative, 97, 271, 278;

dialectic *(continued)*
Neoplatonic, 100,123; Platonic, 100, 104; -al, 3, 114, 176, 189, 264, 266
*Diamond Sūtra*, 239, 248, 250
didactic theology, 21
differance/*différance*, 5, 14, 88, 99, 132n, 200, 210, 214–15, 234, 240, 247, 258–59, 263, 264, 273, 275
Dionysius the Areopagite, 79–80, 83, 89–97, 100, 102, 109, 110–12, 116–18, 124, 129, 130, 132n, 136n, 140n, 199, 200, 211, 285, 297; *Divine Names*, 74, 77–78, 98, 109, 112, 137n, 138n, 211; *Ecclesiastical Hierarchy*, 92, 118; *Mystical Theology*, 80, 89, 91, 95, 112, 116–17, 131n, 137n; *Symbolic Theology*, 80; *Theological Sketches*, 80. *See also* Pseudo-Dionysius
Dionysus, 257, 258
Diotima, 154
disclosure, 27, 127, 260
divinity, 3, 11, 15, 76, 144;—beyond Being, 90
double bind, 26, 39, 63, 86, 308
*duḥkha* (dissatisfaction/frustration), 229, 238, 239, 245, 249. *See also* suffering
Duras, Marguerite, *The Seated Man in the Passage*, 64

Eckhart, Meister, 78, 83, 89, 100, 113–15, 120–21, 124, 128, 140n, 188–91, 199, 200, 202, 211, 255, 263, 268, 269–70, 287, 298, 312, 317; *Renouamini spiritu*, 120
Eco, Umberto, 277
economy, 80–81, 135n
Elohim, 50–51, 55, 56, 59, 64,170
emasculation, 42, 43, 46, 159. *See also* castration
Enlightenment, 60, 146. *See also* nirvāṇa
*envoi* (dispatch), 56–57, 58–59, 62, 63, 66, 289
*envois*, 38
Ephesus, 58
Epicureans, 146
epistemology, 218, 235
erasure, 125,127–29, 234, 261, 279
erotics, 109–10
*erôs*, 109
eschatological, 47, 49; discourse, 52, 242;—language, 158;—strategies, 52
eschatology, 49, 50, 218; Hegelian, 48, 242; Marxist, 48, 242; Nietzschean, 48, 242
*eskhaton*, 31
Europe, 316
European, 319
Evil, 106, 110, 188
Exodus, 207, 219

faith, 127, 130
Farley, Edward, 144
fiction, 18, 34, 80
figure, 80, 120
filiation, 294, 295, 320; double bind of, 39; double truth of, 313
Freud, Sigmund, 20, 43, 174, 176, 179; "The Infantile Genital Organization", 43; "Negation", 197n. *See also* *pre*–Freudian
Freudian, 9, 95,124,175–76

*gahakāraka* (builder of the house), 270
*gala*, 25–27, 41
Gans, Eric, 17,18; "Differences", 14, 15; *The End of Culture:*

*Toward a Generative Anthropology*, 15–17
*Gelassenheit* (living without a way), 268–69, 313, 316–17, 321
Genesis, 27, 148
Genet, Jean, 61
genitals, 27, 28, 43
genre, 28, 59, 61
geometry: mysticism of, 40
Girard, René, 14, 151
Glaucon, 103
God, 3, 4, 12, 18, 74, 76, 77–78, 86, 91–93, 95–98, 103, 106, 109–11, 113–22, 124, 126–28, 130, 140–41n;, 144, 146, 147, 148, 157, 158, 181, 182–84, 188, 191, 206–07, 209, 218–19, 238, 244, 255, 259, 269–70, 274, 278–79, 283–87, 289, 297, 302, 306–10, 313–14, 319–21; as without being, 77; death of, 48, 257, 266; desire of, 284–85, 318; lack of, in Buddhism, 229; names of, 315,—of revelation, 270; play of, 317; rhetoric of, 119; self of, 307; silence of, 211, 221–22, 274; unknowable, 300. *See also* Being; Non-God
god, 151–52, 257;—of negative theology, 258
goddess, 152–53
goddess, veiled, 46, 47. *See also* Isis
Godlessness, 295
Good/good, 101–2, 106, 109, 112–14, 187, 188, 306, 315
goodness, 288; hyperessential, 118
Gospels, 18
grammar, 65, 103, 213, 217–18, 259, 260; onto-theological, 79; politics of, 89
Grammarian, 21, 212. *See also* Bhartṛhari
grammatical, 73; -anthropomorphism, 79
Greek, 16, 17, 18, 26, 27, 28, 55, 68n, 71n, 89, 100, 107, 122, 149–50, 186–87, 190, 191, 194, 218–19, 221, 293, 305, 311; art, 16;—culture, 17; discovery of reason, 245;— inheritance, 275;—literature, 154;—ontotheology and metaphysics, 316
Guillermit, L., 36

Hadewijch, 255
Handelman, Susan, 274
Hart, Kevin, 279–80; *The Trespass of the Sign: Deconstuction, Theology, and Philosophy*, 11, 12
Hebrew Bible, 26, 217
Hebrew, 27, 28, 68n, 71n, 134n, 218;—prophets, 217
Hegel, Georg Wilhelm Friedrich, 40, 76, 100, 176, 186, 275; *Science of Logic*, 189.
Hegelian, 9, 263
Heidegger, Martin, 8, 9, 10, 49, 52, 64, 66, 106, 122–30, 132n, 149, 156–57, 172, 179, 188, 190–95, 244, 257–59, 68–69, 270–71, 284, 291, 299, 305–7, 309, 317, 320; *Einführung in die Metaphysik*, 123; *Hegel's Concept of Experience*, 139n; "Letter on Humanism", 130; *Nietzsche*, 139n; *Was heisst Denken?*, 123; *What is Metaphysics?;* 122; *Sein und Seit*, 124, 139n; *Zur Seinsfrage*, 125
Heideggerian, 174, 190, 262
Hellenic, 16;—Christian, 275. *See also* Greek

hermeneutic: seduction, 36; veils, 42
hermeneutics, 40, 42, 67, 97, 267–68, 274–75
Hierotheus, 138n
Hindu, 199, 228;—thought, 206, 211
Hinduism, 19, 271–72; negation in, 219
history, 19, 73, 99, 100, 118, 146, 159; (hi)story, 318, 321; end of, 48, 51;—of autobiography, 286;—of Christianity, 311;—of metaphysics, 52;—of philosophy, 143;—of theology, 144, 312
Hölderlin, Johann Christian Friedrich: *Patmos*, 49; *Wechsel der Töne*, 32, 49
Holy City, 83
Holy Spirit, 146
Homer, 154
Hua-yen, 235
human, 156;—consciousness, 14;—culture, 15;—happiness, 50
Hume, David, 247
Husserl, Edmund, 296
hyperbole: paradoxical, 305–6
*hyperbolism*, 101
*hyperekhon*, 102–3
hyperessential, 4;—Being, 120;—goodness, 118;—nothingness, 120;—Trinity, 116
hyperessentialism, 228
hyperessentiality, 3, 4, 5, 11, 12, 74, 77, 79, 80, 110, 111, 118, 132n, 189, 200–6, 248
*hyperousious*, 12

ignorance (*avidyā*), 204, 212, 213–14, 229–31, 266
imagination, 15, 19
India, 235, 245, 316
Indra's net, 235–37, 246, 247
ineffable, 84
intelligence, 152, 153
interpretations *(Auslegungen)*, 36
intuition: direct, 206–8, 209, 210, 214. *See also*, anubhava
irony, 154
Isis: veil of, 40, 41
Islam, 159
Islamic, 100, 122, 157, 191, 194, 195, 200, 262–63, 305

Jabès, Edmond, 208–9, 219, 222; *Book of Questions*, 274
Jacobi, Friedrich Heinrich, 39
Jerusalem, 83–84, 97, 118, 146
Jesus, 18, 55, 63, 118, 170
Jewish, 40, 122, 158, 191, 194, 195, 222, 263, 278, 305;—estrangement, 274;—thought, 100. *See also* Judaism; law, Mosaic
Johannine Apocalypse, 55. *See also* John's Apocalypse
John of Patmos, 49, 61, 67
John's Apocalypse, 26, 27, 31, 38, 50, 54, 57, 62–63, 68n, 170, 217
John's Gospel, 273
John, 49, 55, 56, 58, 115
Jones, John (commentary on Pseudo-Dionysius), 11, 12
Judaism, 157,159, 200, 206, 262
Judeo-Christian culture, 16
Jünger, Ernst, 125

Kant, Immanuel, 29, 30, 31, 32, 33, 34, 37, 38, 39, 40, 41, 42, 43, 44, 45, 46, 48, 51, 105, 140n, 146, 153, 235, 241–42; *Critique of Judgement*, 153; *Religion Within the Limits of Reason Alone*, 40; *The Conflict*

*of Faculties*, 35, 40, 45; *Von einem neuerdings erhobenen vornehmen Ton in der Philosophie*, 28, 36
Kantian, 156, 320;—meaning, 99,106; systematic, 34
*karma*, 213–14
*khora* (place, spacing, receptacle), 104–8, 117, 119–20, 123, 187–89, 195, 301, 314, 318, 321. *See also* place
Kierkegaard, Sören Aabye, 20, 154, 178
*King Lear*, 151
Kirke, 152, 276–77
koan, 228. *See also* Zen
Kofman and Norris, 156
Kofman, Sara, 150
Koran, 157
Köler, Christoph, 298
Kristeva, Julia, 159

Lacan, Jacques, 43, 93, 179, 262
Lacoue-Labarthe,Philippe, 9, 10, 11, 13, 18, 26, 50
language, 5, 6, 8, 17, 19, 21, 33, 49, 74, 79, 84, 99, 104, 148–50, 179–80, 184, 185–86, 207–19, 220, 233, 236, 239–41, 249–50, 259–60, 262, 264, 270, 273, 276, 278, 284, 294–96, 299–300, 303, 321; *(langue)* 26; apocalyptic structure of, 57;—as part of *māyā*, 208; Bhaṛtrhari's levels of, 220–21; double, 94; eschatological, 158;—games, 152; meta-, 158; negation of, 202–11; negative theology as, 304; phenomenal and noumenal dimension of, 21; predicative, 87, 90; referential transcendence of, 310; Śaṇkara's theory of, 209; therapeutic use of, 145, 213. *See also Śabdabrahman; speech; word(s)*
Latin, 36, 37, 55
law, 35, 37, 46, 47, 147; Mosaic, 228
Leavey, Jr., John, 170–71
Leibniz, Gottfried Wilhelm, 284, 295, 298
Lema, Reb, 206
Levinas, Emmanuel, 5, 62, 64, 90, 132n, 181–82, 184, 218–19, 222, 274, 275, 309
Leviticus, 28
Liddell, H.G. and R. Scott, 12
life-principle *(jīva)*, 230
linguistics, 52, 65
logic, 3, 65, 79, 83, 103, 113, 146, 186, 212, 260, 289, 295; Buddhist, 271; Nāgārjuna's, 264–65
logical, 73, 97
logocentric, 156, 227, 257, 263, 264, 269
logocentricism, 20,147,154, 238, 266–67, 278
logocentricity, 3, 228
*logos*, 20, 43, 45, 46, 51, 103–4, 154, 155, 156, 187, 207, 221–22, 273. *See also* reason
Longinus, Cassius: *On the Sublime*, 155
love, 257, 263, 277
Loy, David, 19, 20, 275; Nonduality, 264; "The Deconstruction of Buddhism", 21, 258, 263–65, 272
Luther, Martin, 127
Lyotard, Jean-François, 240

madhyamā (inner, mental language), 220–21
Mādhyamika, 21, 215, 221, 232, 234, 235, 263
Mahākāśyapa, 244
Mahāyāna, 232, 235. *See also* Buddhism; Hua-yen; Mādhyamika; Yogācāra; Zen

Marguerite of Porete, 255, 256
Marion, Jean-Luc, 3, 12, 90, 111, 131n, 132n, 135n, 137n, 140–41n, 200, 279, 305; *Dieu sans I 'être*, 133n
Marxism, 52
Marxist, 9
mathematics, 39
māyā (world, worldly experience), 208, 210–11, 212, 216, 220, 222, 271
Mechthild of Magdeburg, 255; "The Desert Has Twelve Things", 256
meditation, 16, 207–8, 214, 219–20, 235, 250, 266
messenger, 62–63
Messiah, 27, 56, 275
messianism, 60
metanarrative, 240
metaphor, 34, 42, 43, 44, 106, 284, 288, 295; castration as, 43;—of Indra's net, 235–37; pseudo-, 113
metaphoric Loftiness, 30
metaphysical, 10–12;—foundations, 258;—sublimation, 42
metaphysics, 11, 35, 43, 44, 48, 49, 52, 64, 141n, 148, 156, 234, 240–41, 244, 249, 265; empire of, 44; Greek tradition of, 218, 275, 316; history of, 52; ontotheological, 311; Platonic, 262; unconscious, 234, 240
Miśra, Maṇḍana, 206
MMK. See Nāgārjuna, *Mulamadhyamakakarikā*
mode, 33, 94; aesthetic, 47
modernity, 1, 2, 41, 45. *See also* postmodernism
mokṣa, 271. *See also* release
monologic, 20. *See also* nonmonologic
monologism, 148
moral law, 38, 47
morality: Judeo-Christian, 16
Mortley, Raoul, 18
Moses, 28, 91–92
mystagogues, 31–32, 33, 38, 41, 45, 46, 241–42
mystagogy, 42, 43
mystery, 33, 38, 93, 247, 268; sacred, 94
mystic, 263;—union, 80
mystical, 11, 12, 93, 94, 116, 263;—contemplation, 116;—Darkness, 91–92, 116;—illumination, 30, 40;—theology, 11, 12, 109, 124, 126, 128–29;—tradition, 74, 297
mysticism, 39, 124, 256, 279, 284, 311; apophatic, 287, 291; Christian, 305, 311;—of geometry, 40; Platonic, 42
*mystika theamata*, 79
myth of Er, *40. See also* Plato, *Republic*
myth, 80
*mythos*, 143

Nāgārjuna, 21, 206, 232–37, 239, 244, 247–49, 263–65, 268, 272; *Mulamadhyamakakarikā* (MMK), 232, 238–40, 246, 248–49, 264; *Vigrahavyāvartanī*, 232
Nancy, Jean-Luc, 26, 34
narrative, 8, 10; meta-, 240;—voice, 55
Nazism, 149
negation, 1, 2, 7,12, 90, 110, 122, 128, 175, 184, 214, 217, 256, 261, 263, 301; double movement of, 9; grammatical, 77;—in Hinduism, 219; logical, 77, 235;—of language, 206
negative theology, 2, 3, 4, 5, 6, 10, 11, 12, 20, 73–74, 75, 82–84, 88, 131, 132n,

145,147,149,154,172, 176–78, 188, 190, 194–95, 199, 211, 228, 248, 255–56, 258–61, 273, 278, 283–85, 288, 291–97, 299–300, 303, 305, 309–11, 314, 316, 321; as language, 304; Christian, 100,188,190, 200, 202; law of, 319; politics of, 319. *See also* atheology
negativity, 14, 18, 20, 77, 79, 101, 108, 113, 119, 122, 168, 221, 256; quasi-, 9
neologism, 9
Neoplatonic, 74, 100, 255, 306
Neoplatonism, 89, 176, 187, 312
*neti, neti* (not this, not that), 201–4, 209, 213–14, 219, 271
New Testament, 68–69n, 311;—theology, 305; "Revelation or Apocalypse of John", 217
Nicholas of Cusa, 100, 294
Nietzsche, Friedrich Wilhelm, 9, 16, 42, 48, 52, 149, 155, 240, 244, 245, 248, 257–58, 266; *Philosophenbuch*, 49; *The Gay Science*, 253n
nihilism, 3, 4, 77, 97, 125, 126, 205, 215, 244, 257
nihilist, 75
*nirguṇa*, 204–5, 208, 210, 212, 220. *See also* Brahman, formless
nirvāṇa, 19, 229, 232, 238, 240, 246–47, 249, 265, 266, 270
no-self, 19, 229. *See also* Self/self, *Ātman/ātman*
Noah, 27–28
non-being, 105, 110, 129, 187, 191, 244, 248. *See also* Nothing; nothingness
Non–God, 121
nonmonologic, 154. *See also,* monologic
nonphallogocentric, 154. *See also,* phallogocentric
Norris, Christopher, 157
Nothing, 127, 188, 256, 289. *See also* non-being
nothingness, 120, 238, 250, 256
Novalis, 299

obscurantism, 45, 65
*Odyssey*, 152–53
*Oedipus Rex*, 151–52. *See also* Sophocles
Oedipus, 48, 49–50, 150–52, 158, 243
onto-eschato-theology, 64
onto-theo-eschatology, 65
ontological cataphasis, 5
ontological: burden, 264;—grammar, 101
ontology, 65, 90, 103, 104, 105, 259, 295
ontotheological, 3, 79, 128, 192, 227; cataphatic, 3;—embarassments, 258;—grammar, 79;—trope, 236
ontotheology, 9, 49, 123, 148, 176, 232, 235, 238, 280; Greek, 315, 316; metaphysical, 130
oracle, 34, 36, 37
oracular voice, 36, 37
*Ort*, 126, 128, 175, 301–2. *See also* place
Osiris, 46

pagan, 114
Pali Canon, 229
Parmenides, 103
*parole*, 27, 83. *See also* word(s)
*parousia*, 51, 92, 96
Pascal, Blaise: *Pensées*, 312
*paśyantī* (unified silent idea), 220–21
Paul,Saint, 312, 320
pedagogy, 117

Penelope, 152
penis, 43
Persian, 40
phallogocentric, 20, 43
phallogocentricism, 147, 152, 276
phallus, 43, 46
*philia*, 291, 293, 316
philosopher(s), 41, 49, 90, 147, 149, 192, 240; as police, 35; Indian, 149; tone of a, 29
philosophical: discourse, 29, 30; progress, 235
philosophy, 15, 17, 29, 32, 35, 39, 42, 43, 44, 64, 145, 149, 156, 177, 227, 240, 250, 276, 310; Buddhist, 228, 243, 264; death/end of, 30–31, 33, 43, 44, 45, 48,157, 234; eschatological discourses in, 48; history of, 143; materialist, 105; tone in, 34; Western, 214, 218, 243, 245, 267
place, 64, 111, 117, 122–23, 126, 128, 129, 192, 301–02, 307, 314, 318. See also *Khora; Ort*
Plato, 9, 38–39, 42, 44, 45, 63, 89, 100, 103–6, 108–9, 120, 122–23, 143, 145, 150, 154, 158, 159, 176, 192, 193, 195, 214, 241, 245, 276, 312; *Lesser Hippias*, 150; *Phaedrus*, 143; *Republic*, 40, 41, 100–2, 187, 306; *Sophist*, 103; *Symposium*, 150, 154;—the academic, 39, 241; *Timaeus*, 100, 104–7, 120, 123, 149, 187
Platonic, 125, 193, 306;—argument, 119;—corpus, 143;—dialogues, 143, 147;—metaphysic, 106
Platonism, 20, 89, 105. *See also* Neoplatonism
*pli* (fold, envelope, letter, habit, message), 58–59, 67
Plotinian, 306
Plotinus, 309
poetry, 43, 44, 80, 97
Pope John Paul II, 316
positive theology, 12, 145, 147, 154, 188. *See also* affirmative theology; theology
postmodem nihilism, 77
postmodernism: Lyotard's definition of, 240
Potter, Karl, 205
*pratītya-samutpāda* (dependent origination), 229–32, 233, 247–48
*praxes*, 21
*praxis*, 19, 250; meditative, 21
prayer, 75, 91, 92, 94, 97, 98, 103, 108, 110–12, 116, 117, 121, 130–31, 158, 296, 315
pre-Freudian, 8. *See also* Freud, Sigmund; Freudian
predicate, 113
predicative language, 87, 90
priest, 36, 91
promise, 5–6, 84–85, 93, 97–98, 99, 107, 124, 148, 157, 179–80, 184, 196; Chinese, 235;—of Buddhism, 228
prophecy, 146, 151. *See also* Hebrew prophets; tone, prophetic
prophetism, 60
Protestant, 146
Pseudo-Dionysius, 11, 12, 18, 149, 155
*psyche*, 121, 146
Pythagoras, 39, 40

Rāmānuja, 203
Raschke, Carl, 258, 266–67
*ratio*, 43
reason, 20, 35–36, 42–43, 51, 103, 114, 245, 256–57, 263; castration of, 43; logocentric, 156; practical, 37; speculative, 37, See also *logos*

rebirth, 231
release *(mokṣa)*, 220
religion(s), 15, 127; end of, 48; Plato's philosophy of, 145
representation, 13, 14, 15, 18, 87, 125, 225n; secret, 17. See also *Vorstellung*
resurrection, 189
revelation, 18, 51, 52, 57, 58, 88, 90, 118, 123, 124, 127, 146, 153, 159, 206, 217, 270, 302, 311, 314, 315, 318
revolution, Copernican, 47
Ṛg Veda, 201
rhetoric, 2, 3, 20, 34, 52, 59, 74–75, 83, 97, 103, 105, 106, 119, 129, 130, 154, 260, 289, 295
rhetorical, 73, 88, 94,147;—trope, 6
rhythm, 33
Ricardou, Jean, 25–26
Roman Empire, 59
Rousseau, Jean-Jacques, 210, 214
Ruysbroeck, Jan van, 298

*Śabdabrahman* (Divine Word-Consciousness), 212–17, 221–22
*Śabdapūrvayoga* (yoga of the Word), 214
*saguṇa*, 204, 211. *See also* Brahman, formed
saṃsāra, 19, 21, 246, 265
Śaṇkara, 21, 201–12, 213–14, 220, 221, 222, 271–72; commentary on Brahman Sūtra, 201, 220
Sanskrit, 21, 229
Satan, 58
Saussure, Ferdinand de, 235
scapegoat, 151, 152
Schaerer, René: *La Question platonicienne, 143*
Schleiermacher, Friedrich Daniel Ernst, 42, 144
Schlosser: *Plato's Letters on the Syracuse Revolution, With an Introduction and Some Remarks*, 39, 42, 44
Schürmann, Reiner, 282n
science, 17, 32, 52,130
scientific wisdom, 32
Scripture, 96, 118, 157, 158, 159, 207, 274
secret, 7, 8, 13, 17–18, 33, 36, 86–91, 94–95, 175, 183–84, 228, 244, 260, 263, 302, 310, 321;—knowledge, 7;—manifestation, 119;—representation, 17; topitology of, 93
Self/self, 10, 17, 21, 65, 205, 208, 229, 231, 238, 249, 264, 265, 267, 269, 285; thinking, 15; true, 201;—as silence, 220; lack of, 230, 273;—of God, 307. See also Ātman/ātman; no self
selflessness, 264
Seneca: *Epistulae morales,146*
sexual prohibitions, 28
*shibboleth*, 93
signifer/signified, 235, 249, 250
signposting *(signalisation)*, 29
silence, 84, 90, 94, 116, 121, 209, 219–22, 260, 271, 321;—as *śūnya*, 216
Silesius, Angelus, 284, 298, 301, 304, 307, 310–13, 315, 316, 319–21; *Cherubinischer Wandersmann*, 144, 288–90, 294, 295, 309, 320–21
skilful means *(upaya)*, 19, 21
Socrates, 38, 154, 228
Socratic, 145–46, 150;—tradition, 20
Sophist(s), 89, 145
Sophocles, *Oedipus Rex*, 151–52, 154
soul, 191; theological, 18

speaking *(parole)*, 65, 289. See also *parole;* speech
speech, 84–86, 89, 91, 182, 184. See also *parole; vaikharī*
sphinx, 150–51
Stoics, 146
Stolberg, Count Leopold, 44
subject, 6, 10, 13, 18; (desiring) 19
subjectivity, 9, 10, 11
sublation *(Aufhebung)*, 2, 74
suffering, 230, 232, 245. See also *duḥkha*
*śūnyatā*—(emptiness, pregnant with possibilities), 19, 232–34, 238, 246, 248, 263–65; as compared with différance, 234
supplementarity, 12
Sureśvara, 204–5, 208
Suzuki, Daisetz T.: *Mysticism: Christian and Buddhist*, 269–70

Talmudists, 89
Taoism, 235
*tat tvam asi* (That thou art), 207–8, 213–14, 219, 271.
Tathatā, 269
Tauler, John, 298
Taylor, Mark C., 7, 19, 21, 148, 158, 262–63, 266–67, 288, 291, 292, 302; "nO nOt nO", 20
teleological, 215; non-, 236
teleology, 100, 149, 259
*telos*, 81, 259; ontological, 261
theologian(s), 94, 96, 109, 118, 149, 156, 192; Christian, 156–57,158
theological cataphasis, 5
theological soul, 18
theology, 35, 123, 128, 130, 172, 181, 193, 214, 235, 259, 276, 295, 308; apophatic, 3, 4, 103, 124, 158, 284, 321; didactic, 21; eschato-, 318; grammar of, 259; history of, 144, 312; New Testament, 305; rational, 40
theophany, 51
Thich Nhat Hanh, 237
Thomas, Saint, 102
time, 181, 190, 240; absence of, 177;—and space, 6
Timothy, 79, 90, 91, 112, 116–17, 129, 130, 297
tonal: change, 58;—difference, 32
tonality, 29, 48
tone, 29–31, 32, 33, 34, 35, 36, 38, 49, 51, 52, 53, 54, 57, 62, 147, 155, 159, 217, 245; as apocalyptic, 52–53, 57, 266; mutation of, 32; - in philosophy, 34; of a philosopher, 29; oracular, 318; overlordly, 36, 38; prophetic, 274
*tonos*, 32
topic *(propos, topos)*, 6, 31
*topos*, 7, 10, 11, 97. See also *atopos*
Tower of Babel, 317–18. *See also* Babel
trace, 5, 73, 87, 98–99, 107–8, 118, 121, 128–29, 159, 180, 215, 219, 221, 233, 237–38, 245, 250, 262–63, 273–74, 287, 300, 303–4; beginningless, 214; topology of, 261; undeterminable, 262
translation, 25, 26, 148, 157, 174–75, 182–83, 190, 229, 293; enigmas of, 25. *See also* untranslatable
translator, 170, 182
Trinity, 110, 111–12, 116, 120, 311
Trismegistus, pseudo-Hermes, 113
Trojan war, 154
tropology, 83

truth, 53, 114, 115, 156, 243, 245, 286–87, 310; model of, 153; as *satya, 205*
two-truths, 232, 239–46

Ulysses, 152–53, 276–77
unconscious order, 6, 7, 10
unconscious, 7, 14, 88
uncovered *(aperikalyptôs)*, 88
uncovering, 27–28
United States, 60
unthought, 8–9
untranslatable, 157, 174–75, 183
Upaniṣad(s), 201, 205, 220; Bṛhadāraṇyaka, 201, 203–4; Māṇḍūkya, 204–5. *See also* Vedānta
Upaniṣadic, 207, 229

*vaikharī* (spoken speech), 220–21
Veda(s), 201, 202, 211, 212, 213, 216, 217, 220, 273
Vedānta, 232, 235, 271–71. *See also* Advaita Vedānta; Upaniad(s)
Vernant, Jean Pierre, 151–52
*Verstimmung*, 37, 39, 52–53, 62. *See also* delerium
*via negativa*, 3, 18, 21, 108, 116, 188, 200–5, 209, 214, 293, 305, 313, 319
Vimalakīrti Sūtra, 264
Viśiṣṭādvaita Vedānta, 203
voice, 34, 36, 37, 38, 46, 49, 52, 63, 113, 308, 310, 320; middle, 10; moral, 38;—of reason, 36, 37; oracular, 36, 37
volitional tendencies (*saṃskārah*), 230
von Balthasar, Urs, 111,132n
*Vorstellung*, 13, 87, 125. *See also* representation
*Vākyapadīya*, 221. *See also* Bhartṛhari
Vṛṣabha, 214

Warburton, William, 36
West, 2, 3, 19; end of, 48, 51
Western, 48, 123, 158, 159, 214, 218, 238, 250, 263, 275;—philosophy, 242, 245, 261, 267
wisdom, 41, 43, 78, 113, 116, 149–50, 238, 287; scientific, 32
Witness *(sākṣin)*, 205
Wittgenstein, Ludwig, 74, 81; *Tractatus*, 81
women's spirituality, 255
word(s), 27, 111, 115–16, 125, 182, 257, 273, 301;—consciousness, 213, 221. See also *parole; Śabdabrahman*
wordless, 263

YHWH/Yahweh, 26, 27, 28, 219
Yoga, 235
Yogācāra, 234–35; *see also*, Mahāyāna
Yājñavalkya, 201

Zen, 21, 146, 228, 244. *See also* Buddhism; Mahāyāna
Zoroastrian, 40, 50